FOS
/15
S0-BIL-462

THE GOLD STANDARD

MCAT

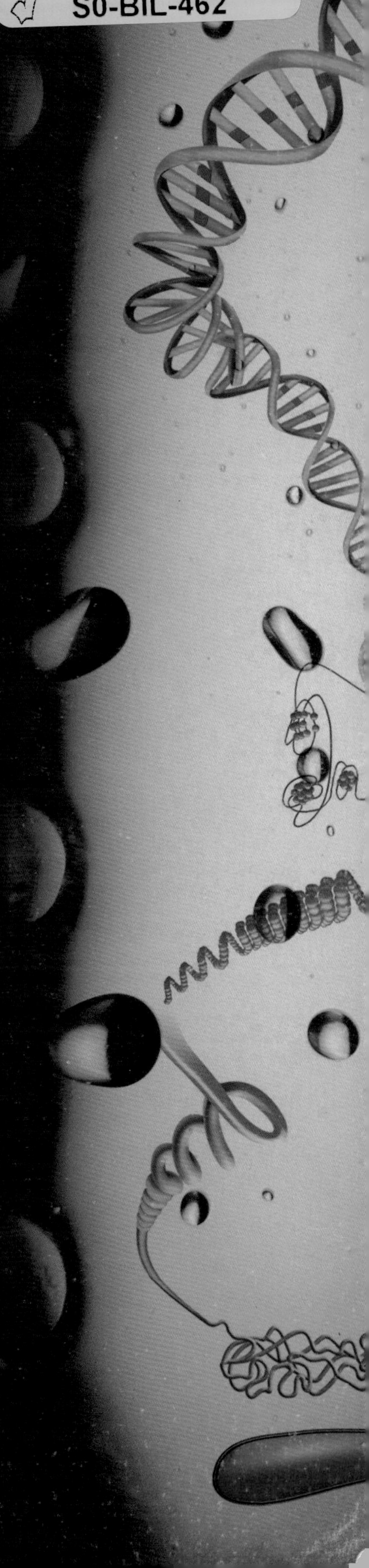

Editor and Author

Brett Ferdinand BSc MD-CM

Contributors

Lisa Ferdinand BA MA
Sean Pierre BSc MD
Kristin Finkenzeller BSc MD
Bamboo Dong BSc PhD

Illustrators

Daphne McCormack
Nanjing Design
- Ren Yi, Huang Bin
- Sun Chan, Li Xin

RuveneCo inc

Free Features Using Online Access Card*

(For the original owner of this textbook)

Additional Chapter Review Questions
2 Hours of Teaching Videos
Physics Equation List (cross-referenced)
Organic Chemistry Summary

*The online access card is found at the back of all new books. Be sure to register at www.MCAT-prep.com by clicking on Register in the top right corner of the website. Once you login, click on MCAT Textbook Owners in the right column and follow directions. Please Note: benefits are for 6 months from the date of online registration, for the original book owner only and are not transferable; unauthorized access and use outside the Terms of Use posted on MCAT-prep.com may result in account deletion; if you are not the original owner, you can purchase your virtual access card separately at MCAT-prep.com.

Visit The Gold Standard's Education Center at www.gold-standard.com.

Copyright (c) 2015 RuveneCo (Worldwide)

ISBN 978-1927338278

THE PUBLISHER AND THE AUTHORS MAKE NO REPRESENTATIONS OR WARRANTIES WITH RESPECT TO THE ACCURACY OR COMPLETENESS OF THE CONTENTS OF THIS WORK AND SPECIFICALLY DISCLAIM ALL WARRANTIES, INCLUDING WITHOUT LIMITATION WARRANTIES OF FITNESS FOR A PARTICULAR PURPOSE. NO WARRANTY MAY BE CREATED OR EXTENDED BY SALES OR PROMOTIONAL MATERIALS. THE ADVICE AND STRATEGIES CONTAINED HEREIN MAY NOT BE SUITABLE FOR EVERY SITUATION. THIS WORK IS SOLD WITH THE UNDERSTANDING THAT THE PUBLISHER IS NOT ENGAGED IN RENDERING LEGAL, ACCOUNTING, MEDICAL, DENTAL, CONSULTING, OR OTHER PROFESSIONAL SERVICES. IF PROFESSIONAL ASSISTANCE IS REQUIRED, THE SERVICES OF A COMPETENT PROFESSIONAL PERSON SHOULD BE SOUGHT. NEITHER THE PUBLISHER NOR THE AUTHORS SHALL BE LIABLE FOR DAMAGES ARISING HEREFROM. THE FACT THAT AN ORGANIZATION OR WEBSITE IS REFERRED TO IN THIS WORK AS A CITATION AND/OR A POTENTIAL SOURCE OF FURTHER INFORMATION DOES NOT MEAN THAT THE AUTHORS OR THE PUBLISHER ENDORSES THE INFORMATION THE ORGANIZATION OR WEBSITE MAY PROVIDE OR RECOMMENDATIONS IT MAY MAKE. READERS SHOULD BEWARE THAT INTERNET WEBSITES LISTED IN THIS WORK MAY HAVE CHANGED OR DISAPPEARED BETWEEN WHEN THIS WORK WAS WRITTEN AND WHEN IT IS READ.

All rights reserved. No part of this book may be reproduced, stored in a retrieval system, or transmitted in any form or by any means, electronic or mechanical, including photocopying, recording, or otherwise, without permission in writing from the publisher. Images in the public domain: Brandner, D. and Withers, G. (2013). The Cell: An Image Library, www.cellimagelibrary.org, CIL numbers 197, 214, 240, 9685, 21966, ASCB.

Address all inquiries, comments, or suggestions to the publisher. For Terms of Use go to: www.MCAT-prep.com

RuveneCo Publishing
334 Cornelia Street # 559
Plattsburgh, New York
12901, USA
learn@mcat-prep.com

MCAT is a registered trademark of the Association of American Medical Colleges (AAMC), which does not endorse this study guide or our methodology.

Printed in China.

PREFACE

With more than 20 years experience teaching MCAT through books, videos and courses, one of the lessons that I've learned is that a preface needs to be short for the message to be effective. My message: study efficiently, then practice and consolidate.

Though it is true that the new MCAT covers introductory level college Biochemistry (1 semester) and Biology (2 semesters), it does not mean that everything you may have studied at that level - or will study - is expected knowledge for the new MCAT. We are not trying to teach you Biochemistry and Biology. We are trying to teach you Biochemistry and Biology for the new MCAT. The AAMC publishes (print and online) the new exam syllabus listing all topics which are expected knowledge for the MCAT. Use the AAMC's syllabus as a guide to control your exposure to the specific content required for the MCAT while continuing to practice the content and reasoning used with relevant practice materials.

If you don't take the time to review the official syllabus for the new MCAT, then you will waste time trying to memorize irrelevant information. Don't trust rumours about the exam, or even 'well-known' publications, just stick to the official AAMC topic list. Instead of reviewing irrelevant content, do more practice questions, careful post-question analysis and create very brief notes which you revisit regularly. Learn the basics, work on developing your reasoning skills, then consolidate your achievements through notes and review.

Of all the material that you will study for the MCAT, no content is more relevant to the study and practice of medicine than the content in this 1 book. The reasoning skills that you will develop through the chapter review questions with solutions will hopefully also help for other sections of your exam. But most importantly, every time that you extend your study time a little more, in that quiet moment, remember that the most important reason that you are improving your science reasoning skills is so you can be a better doctor.

Let's begin.

– B.F., MD

Table of Contents

EXAM SUMMARY

Section	Topic	Questions	Time
Tutorial *(optional)*	-	-	10 minutes
1. Chemical and Physical Foundations of Biological Systems [Approx. ½ of this section is similar to the 'old' MCAT Physical Sciences]	• Biochemistry (25%) • Biology (5%) • General Chemistry (30%) • Organic Chemistry (15%) • Physics (25%)	59	95 minutes
Break *(optional)*	-	-	10 minutes
2. Critical Analysis and Reasoning Skills [Very similar to the 'old' MCAT Verbal Reasoning]	Non-sciences. All information necessary to answer the questions can be reasoned from the passages.	53	90 minutes
Mid-Exam/LUNCH Break *(optional)*	-	-	30 minutes
3. Biological and Biochemical Foundations of Living Systems [Most of this section is similar to the 'old' MCAT Biological Sciences]	• Biochemistry (25%) • Biology (65%) • General Chemistry (5%) • Organic Chemistry (5%)	59	95 minutes
Break *(optional)*	-	-	10 minutes
4. Psychological, Social, and Biological Foundations of Behavior [New section with no 'old' MCAT equivalent]	• Psychology (65%) • Sociology (30%) • Biology (5%)	59	95 minutes
Total Content Time	-	-	6 hours, 15 minutes
Total "Seated" Time (approx.)	-	-	7 hours, 30 minutes

Note: The total time does not include check-in time on arrival at the test center. Also note that in 2012, 65-67 and 60 questions were planned for the 95 and 90 minute new MCAT sections, which is proportional to the timing provided for the 'old' MCAT. Instead, the AAMC has allocated 59 and 53 questions. Because of this subtle change, the new MCAT has more working time per question than the 'old' MCAT. This means that overall, you will have more time to read passages, consider options, and make decisions about your answer choices. Also note that breakdown figures are approximations and subject to change. Consult AAMC.org for current information.

You will receive five scores for the MCAT: one for each of the four sections scored from a low of 118 to a high of 132, with a midpoint of 125; and one combined total score which will range from 472 to 528, with a midpoint of 500.

Common formula for acceptance:

GPA + MCAT score + Non-Academic Factors = Medical School Admissions

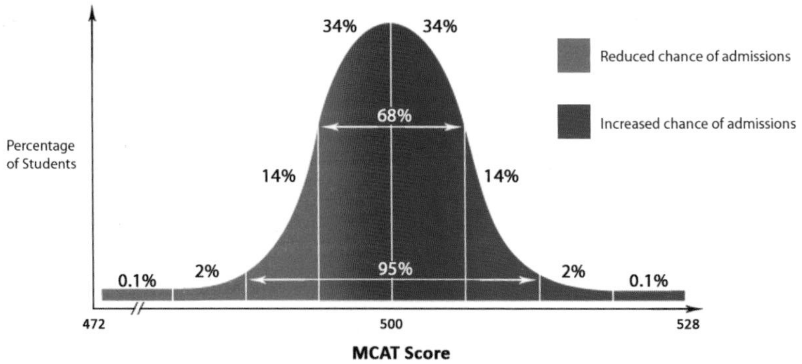

Overall new MCAT score distribution: the mean and range are confirmed; we are projecting the standard deviations and chance of admissions. Note that "non-academic factors" may include personal statements, references, medical school interviews, etc.

The MCAT is challenging, get organized.

mcat-prep.com/free-MCAT-study-schedule

MCAT Scores

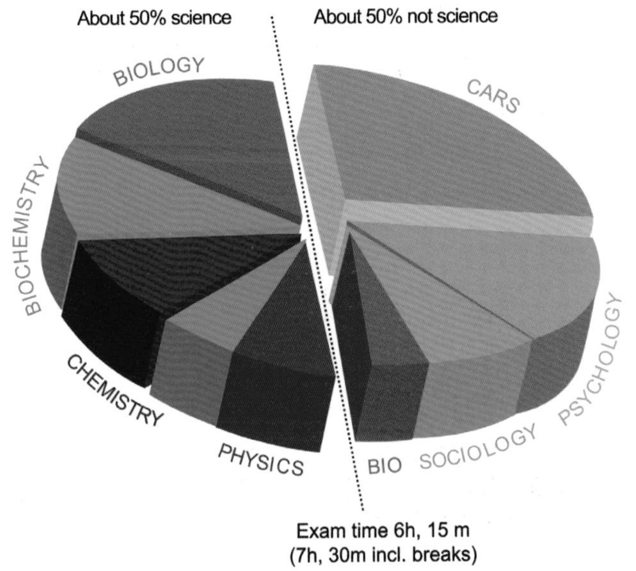

1. How to study:

1. Study the Gold Standard (GS) books and videos to learn; others: class notes, textbooks, Khan Academy, etc.
2. Do GS Chapter review practice questions and AAMC practice materials (only use non-full length materials and only targeted to the topics you are reviewing at that time)
3. Consolidate: create and review your ***brief***, personal summaries (= Gold Notes) daily

2. Once you have completed your studies:

1. Full-length practice test
2. Review mistakes, all solutions
3. Consolidate: review all your Gold Notes and create more
4. Repeat until you get beyond the score you need for your targeted medical school

3. Full-length practice tests:

1. AAMC practice exams
2. Gold Standard MCAT exams
3. Other sources if needed

Is there something in the Gold Standard that you did not understand? Don't get frustrated, get online: mcat-prep.com/forum

4. How much time do you need?

On average, 3-6 hours per day for 3-6 months; depending on life experiences, several weeks may be enough and 8 months could be insufficient.

To make the content easier to retain, you can also find aspects of the Gold Standard program in other formats such as:

THE GOLD STANDARD
MULTIMEDIA EDUCATION

Good luck with your studies!

Gold Standard Team

structure: into primary,
ary, tertiary and quaternary structures.
r structure is the seque
o acids as determi

onyl group
s are hexo
ns are trio
t chain fo

OXALOACETATE

CITRATE

Krebs
Cycle

MALATE

2H

ISOCITRATE

FUMARATE

2H

α-KETOGLUTARATE

SUCCINATE

NAD

2H

2H

cids, surfactants
saponification
micelles, liposomes, cholesterols
steroids, terpenes, terpenoids

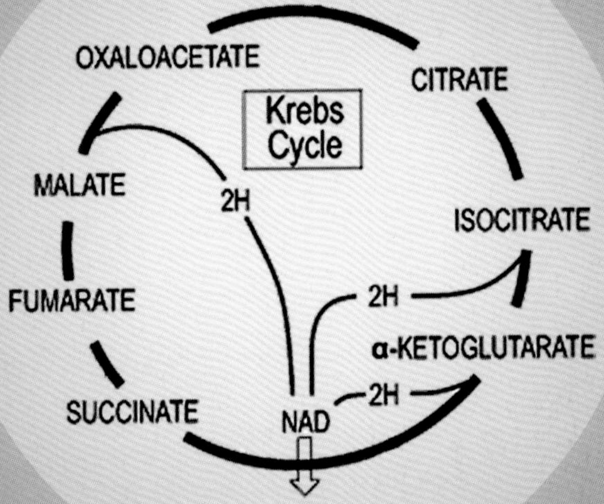

MCAT-Prep.com

BIOCHEMISTRY

BIOLOGICAL MOLECULES
Chapter 1

Memorize

* Basic stereochemistry and structure of building blocks
* Nomenclature and structures of common molecules
* Isoelectric point equation
* Define: amphoteric, zwitterions

Understand

* Effect of H, S, hydrophobic bonds
* Basic mechanisms of reactions
* Effect of pH, isoelectric point
* Protein structure
* Features: carbohydrates, lipids, steroids, nucleic acids, phosphorus

Clinical Correlation

Detecting abnormal molecules can help explain the clinical presentation of disease and, eventually, result in rational and effective treatments. Enzyme-linked immunosorbent assay (ELISA), which uses antibodies, is one of the most sensitive tests modern medicine uses to detect various biochemicals.

MCAT-Prep.com

Introduction

Biochemistry is the study of the chemical processes within and relating to living organisms. Just six elements —carbon, hydrogen, nitrogen, oxygen, calcium, and phosphorus—assemble into molecules and complexes representing 99% of the mass of the human body. Water represents 60% of that mass and though its role in biochemistry is vital as a solvent, its features (polarity, H-bonding) are reviewed in General Chemistry. The subject of biochemistry, the organic molecules, represent about one third of body mass and include amino acids and proteins, carbohydrates (glucose, disaccharides, polysaccharides), lipids (triglycerides, steroids) and nucleic acids (DNA, RNA).

Optional Gold Standard Resources

Free Forum

Online Videos

Flashcards

1.1 Amino Acids

Protein-building amino acids are molecules that contain a side chain (*R*), a carboxylic acid, and an amino group at the α carbon. Thus the general structure of α-amino acids is:

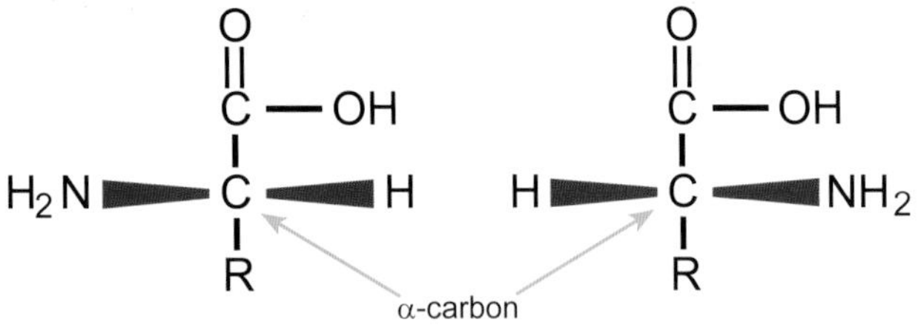

L - amino acid "left-handed" isomer   D - amino acid "right-handed" isomer

From your MCAT Organic Chemistry review, you should remember that the carbonyl carbon (C=O) is carbon-1 and the adjacent carbon (carbon-2) is the alpha position, carbon-3 is the beta position and carbon-4 is thus the gamma position.

Amino acids may be named systematically as substituted carboxylic acids, however, there are 20 important α-amino acids that are known by common names. These are naturally occurring and they form the building blocks of most proteins found in humans. The following are a few examples of α-amino acids:

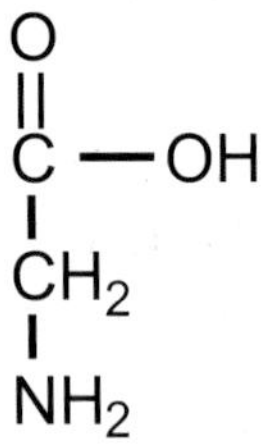

Glycine

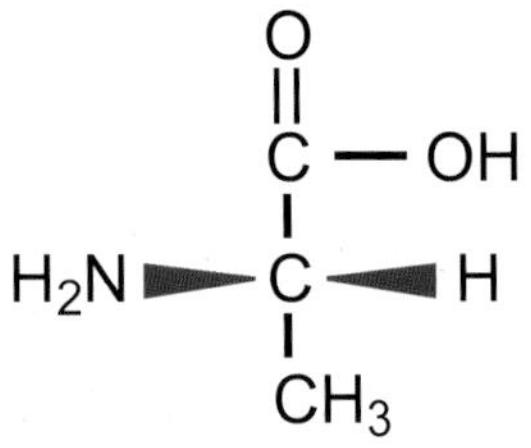

Alanine

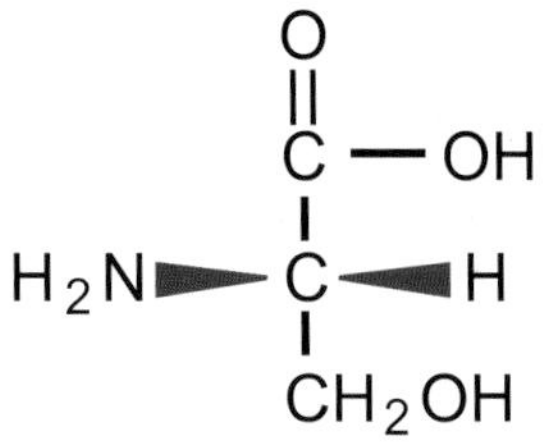

Serine

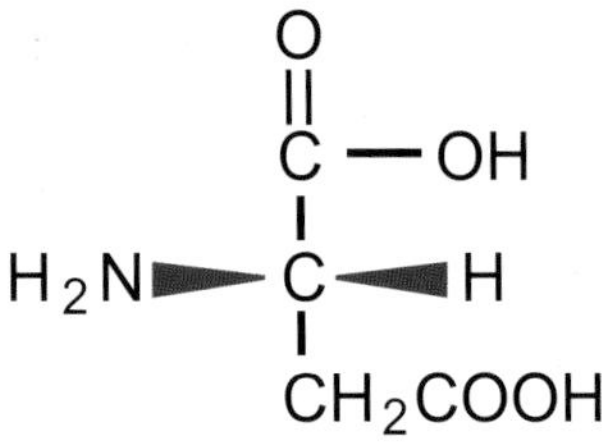

Aspartic acid

Note that the D/L system is commonly used for amino acid and carbohydrate chemistry. The reason is that naturally occurring amino acids have the same relative configuration, the L-configuration, while naturally occurring carbohydrates are nearly all D-configuration. However, the absolute configuration (i.e. R/S) depends on the priority assigned to the side group (*see* ORG 2.3.1 *for rules*).

In the preceding amino acids, the S-configuration prevails (*except glycine which cannot be assigned any configuration since it is not chiral*).

The following mnemonic is helpful for determining the D/L isomeric form of an amino acid: the "CORN" rule. The substituents **CO**OH, **R**, **N**H_2, and H are arranged around the chiral center. Starting with H away from the viewer, if these groups are arranged clockwise around the chiral carbon, then it is the D-form. If counter-clockwise, it is the L-form.

Also note that, except for glycine, the α-carbon of all amino acids are chiral indicating that there must be at least two different enantiomeric forms. Notice in the preceding illustrations that the alpha carbon in glycine is not bonded to 4 different substitutents since it is bonded to hydrogen twice; however, the alpha carbon in alanine, serine and aspartic acid has 4 different substituents in each case meaning that carbon is chiral. Notice that chirality of carbon hinges on its attachment to 4 different substituents (i.e. groups/ligands) and NOT necessarily 4 different atoms. A chiral carbon is sometimes referred to as a stereocenter or as a stereogenic or asymmetric carbon.

Many important amino acids can play critical non-protein roles within the body. For example, glutamate and gamma-aminobutyric acid ("GABA", a non-standard gamma-amino acid) are, respectively, the main excitatory and inhibitory neurotransmitters in the human brain (BIO 5.1).

Unless specified otherwise, the following sections will be exploring features of alpha amino acids.

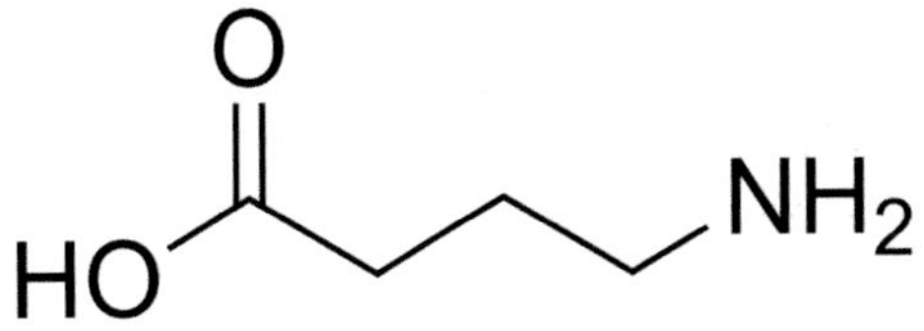

GABA: A gamma-amino acid.
Notice that the amino group is attached to the 3rd carbon from the carbonyl carbon (C=O).

1.1.1 Hydrophilic vs. Hydrophobic

Different types of amino acids tend to be found in different areas of the proteins that they make up. Amino acids which are ionic and/or polar are hydrophilic, and tend to be found on the exterior of proteins (i.e. *exposed to water*). These include aspartic acid and its amide, glutamic acid and its amide, lysine, arginine and histidine. Certain other polar amino acids are found on either the interior or exterior of proteins. These include serine, threonine, and tyrosine. Hydrophobic ('water-fearing") amino acids which may be found on the interior of proteins include methionine, leucine, tryptophan, valine and phenylalanine. Hydrophobic molecules tend to cluster in aqueous solutions (= *hydrophobic bonding*). Alanine is a nonpolar amino acid which is unusual because it is less hydrophobic than most nonpolar amino acids. This is because its nonpolar side chain is very short.

Glycine is the smallest amino acid, and the only one that is not optically active. It is often found at the 'corners' of proteins. Alanine is small and, although hydrophobic, is found on the surface of proteins.

1.1.2 Acidic vs. Basic

Amino acids have both acid and basic components (= *amphoteric*). The amino acids with the R group containing an amino ($-NH_2$) group, are basic. The two basic amino acids are lysine and arginine. Amino acids with an R group containing a carboxyl ($-COOH$) group are acidic. The two acidic amino acids are aspartic acid and glutamic acid. One amino acid, histidine, may act as either an acid or a base, depending upon the pH of the resident solution. This makes histidine a very good physiologic buffer. The rest of the amino acids are considered to be neutral.

The basic $-NH_2$ group in the amino acid is present as an ammonium ion, $-NH_3^+$. The acidic carboxyl $-COOH$ group is present as a carboxylate ion, $-COO^-$. As a result, amino acids are dipolar ions, or *zwitterions*. In an aqueous solution, there is an equilibrium present between the dipolar, the anionic, and the cationic forms of the amino acid:

Therefore the charge on the amino acid will vary with the pH of the solution, and with the isoelectric point. This point is the pH where a given amino acid will be neutral (i.e. have no net charge). This isoelectric point is the average of the two pK_a values of an amino acid (*depending on the dissociated group*):

$$\text{isoelectric point} = pI = (pK_{a1} + pK_{a2})/2$$

As this is a common MCAT question, let's further summarize for the average amino acid: When in a relatively acidic solution, the amino acid is fully protonated and exists as a cation, that is, it has two protons available for dissociation, one from the carboxyl group and one from the amino group. When in a relatively basic solution, the amino acid is fully deprotonated and exists as an anion, that is, it has two proton accepting groups, the carboxyl group and the amino group. At the isoelectric point, the amino acid exists as a neutral, dipolar zwitterion, which means that the carboxyl group is deprotonated while the amino group is protonated.

$$H_3\overset{+}{N} - CH - CO_2H \underset{H_3O^+}{\rightleftharpoons} H_3\overset{+}{N} - CH - CO_2^- \underset{H_3O^+}{\rightleftharpoons} H_2N - CH - CO_2^-$$

| Acidic | Neutral | Basic |

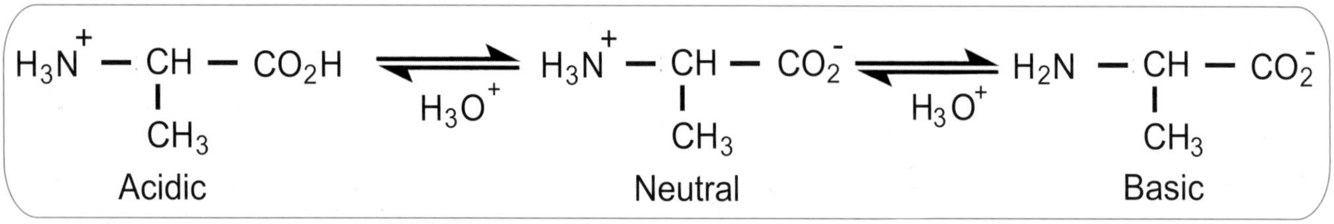

1.1.3 The 20 Alpha-Amino Acids

Approximately 500 amino acids are known - of these, only 22 are proteinogenic ("protein building") amino acids. Of these, 20 amino acids are known as "standard" and are found in human beings and other eukaryotes, and are encoded directly by the universal genetic code (BIO 3). The 2 exceptions are the "non-standard" pyrrolysine — found only in some methanogenic organisms but not humans — and selenocysteine which is present in humans and a wide range of other organisms.

Of the 20 standard amino acids, 9 are called "essential" for humans because they cannot be created from other compounds by the human body, and so must be taken in as food.

The following summarizes the categories of amino acids based on side chains, pK_a and charges at physiological pH:

1. Nonpolar amino acids: R groups are hydrophobic and thus decrease solubility. These amino acids are usually found within the interior of the protein molecule.

2. Polar amino acids: R groups are hydrophilic and thus increase the solubility. These amino acids are usually found on the protein's surface.

3. Acidic amino acids: R groups contain an additional carboxyl group. These amino acids have a negative charge at physiological pH.

4. Basic amino acids: R groups contain an additional amine group. These amino acids have a positive charge at physiological pH. Note that asparagine and glutamine have amide side chains and are thus not considered basic (see ORG 9.3).

Table IV.A.1.1: Basic Nomenclature for Biological Molecules. The exception to the monomer/polymer rule is lipids since lipid base units are not generally considered monomers.

Building block	Polymerizes to form...	Chemical bonds	Macromolecule
Monomers	Dimer, trimer, tetramer, oligomers, etc.	Covalent* bonds	Polymer
Amino acids	Dipeptide, tripeptide, tetra/oligopeptide, etc	Peptide bonds	Polypeptide, protein
Monosaccharides ('simple sugars'**)	Disaccharide, tri/tetra/oligosaccharide, etc.	Glycosidic bonds	Polysaccharide
Nucleotides	Nucleotide dimer, tri/tetra/oligomer, etc.	Phosphodiester bonds	Polynucleotides, nucleic acids

*There are exceptions. For example, in certain circumstances polypeptides are considered monomers and they may bond non-covalently to form dimers (i.e. higher orders of protein structure which will be discussed in following sections).

**Note that disaccharides are also sugars (i.e. sucrose is a glucose-fructose dimer known as 'table sugar'; lactose is a glucose-galactose dimer known as 'milk sugar').

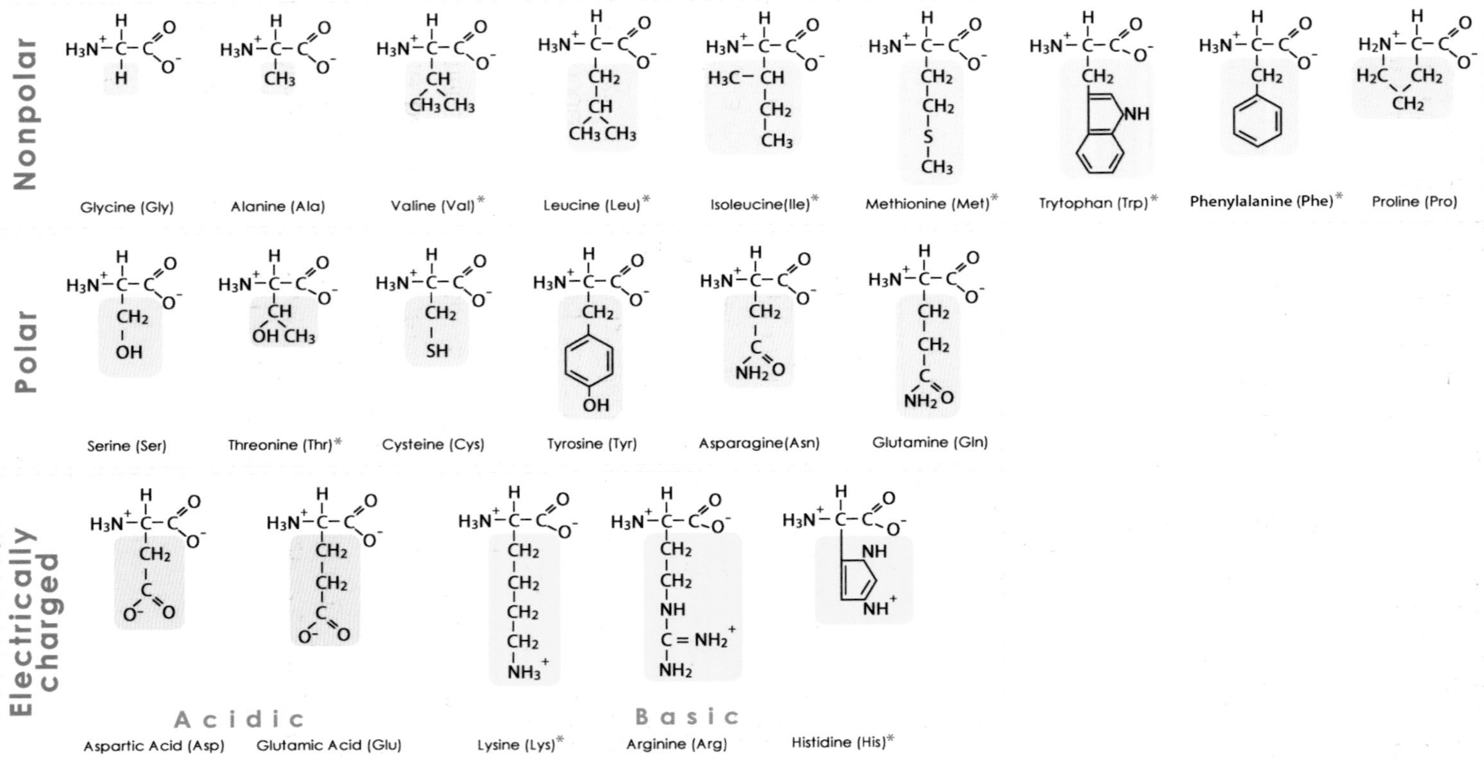

Figure IV.A.1.1: The 20 Standard Amino Acids. A red asterix * is used to indicate the 9 essential amino acids. Notice that if the acidic electrically charged amino acids are fully protonated, the overall charge would be +1 but if fully deprotonated, the overall charge would be -2. The opposite being true for basic amino acids: If fully protonated, the overall charge would be +2 but if fully deprotonated, the overall charge would be -1. These cases are different than for the average amino acid described at the end of section BCM 1.1.2.

1.2 Proteins

1.2.1 General Principles

An oligopeptide consists of between 2 and 20 amino acids joined together by amide *(peptide)* bonds. Oligopeptides include dipeptides (2 amino acids), tripeptides (3), tetrapeptides (4), pentapeptides (5), etc. Polypeptides - generally regarded to be between the size of oligopeptides and proteins - are polymers of up to 100 or even 1000 α-amino acids (depending on the molecule and the reference). Proteins are long chain polypeptides which often form higher order structures. These peptide bonds are derived from the amino group of one amino acid, and the acid group of another. When a peptide bond is formed, a molecule of water is released (*condensation = dehydration = water loss*). The bond can be broken by adding water (*hydrolysis = water lyses = water 'breaks apart' another molecule*).

Since proteins are polymers of amino acids, they also have isoelectric points. Classification as to the acidity or basicity of a protein depends on the numbers of acidic and basic amino acids it contains. If there is an excess of acidic amino acids, the isoelectric point will be at a pH of less than 7. At pH = 7, these proteins will have a net negative charge. Similarly, those with an excess of basic amino acids will have an isoelectric point at a pH of greater than 7. Therefore, at pH = 7, these proteins will have a net positive charge. Proteins can be separated according to their isoelectric point on a polyacrylamide gel (*electrophoresis*; BIO 15.7; ORG 13). We will be discussing protein synthesis in Biology Chapter 3.

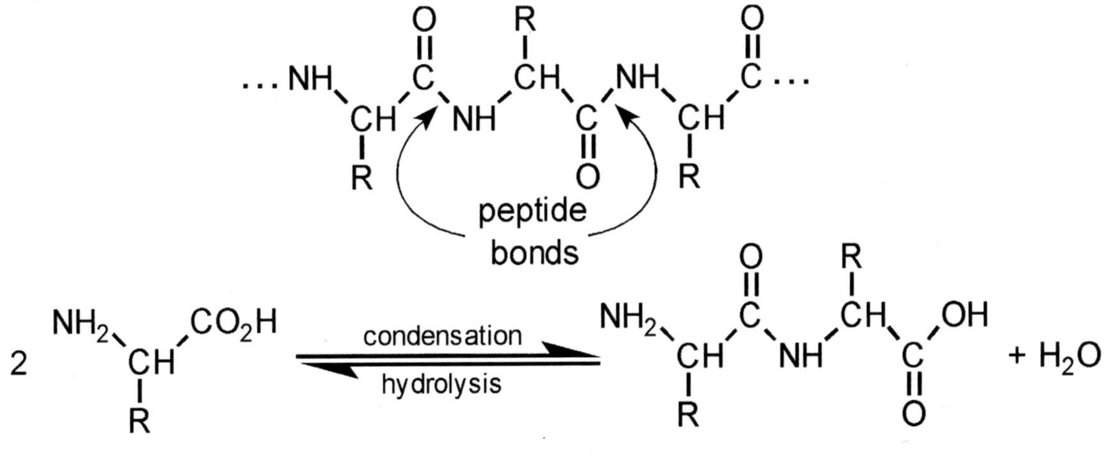

Figure IV.A.1.2: Condensation and hydrolysis. Note that the forward reaction shows 2 moles of amino acid producing a dipeptide and water. The dipeptide is composed of 2 amino acid 'residues' (i.e. what is left over once water is removed). By convention, the amino group (N-terminus) is on the left and the carboxyl group (C-terminus) on the right.

1.2.2 Protein Structure

Protein structure may be divided into primary, secondary, tertiary and quaternary structures. The <u>primary structure</u> is the sequence of amino acids as determined by the DNA and the location of covalent bonds (*including disulfide bonds*). This structure determines the higher order structures.

The primary structure is usually shown using 3-letter abbreviations for the amino acid residues as shown in Fig IV.A.1.1. By convention, the amino group (N-terminus) is on the left and the carboxyl group (C-terminus) on the right. For example, insulin (BIO 6.3.4) is composed of 51 amino acids in 2 chains. One chain has 30 amino acids, and the other has 21 amino acids with the following primary structure: GLY-ILE-VAL-GLU-GLN-CYS-CYS-THR-SER-ILE-CYS-SER-LEU-TYR-GLN-LEU-GLU-ASN-TYR-CYS-ASN.

The <u>secondary structure</u> is the orderly inter- or intramolecular *hydrogen bonding* of the protein chain. The resultant structure may be the more stable α-helix (e.g. keratin), or a β-pleated sheet (e.g. silk). Proline is an amino acid which cannot participate in the regular array of H-bonding in an α-helix. Proline disrupts the α-helix, thus it is usually found at the beginning or end of a molecule (i.e. hemoglobin).

The <u>tertiary structure</u> is the further folding of the protein molecule onto itself. This is the 3D shape (spatial organization) of an entire protein molecule. Protein folding is largely self-organising mainly based on the protein's primary structure. The tertiary struc-

ture is maintained by *noncovalent bonds* like hydrogen bonding, Van der Waals forces, hydrophobic bonding and electrostatic bonding (CHM 4.2). The resultant structure is a globular protein with a hydrophobic interior and hydrophilic exterior. Enzymes are classical examples of such a structure. In fact, enzyme activity often depends on tertiary structure.

The covalent bonding of cysteine (*disulfide bonds or bridge*) helps to stabilize the tertiary structure of proteins. Cysteine will form sulfur-sulfur covalent bonds with itself, producing *cystine*. For example, insulin is composed of 2 polypeptide chains, an A-chain and a B-chain (2 = a dimer), which are linked together by disulfide bonds.

$$2H_2N-CH-CO_2H \xrightarrow{-H_2}$$
$$CH_2SH$$
cysteine

$$H_2N-\underset{CH_2-S-S-CH_2}{\overset{CO_2H}{CH}} \quad \underset{}{\overset{CO_2H}{CH}}-NH_2$$
cystine

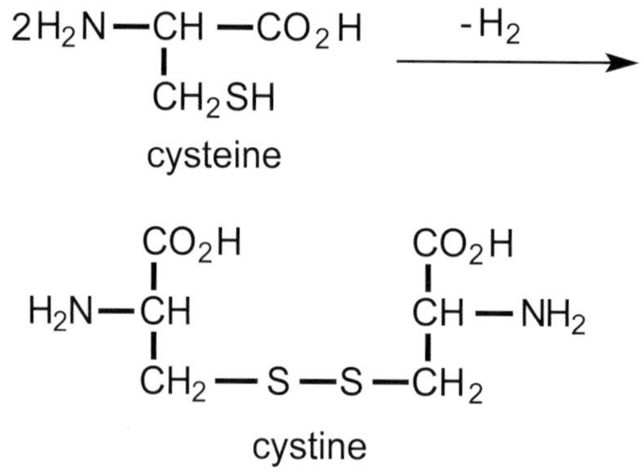

The <u>quaternary structure</u> is when there are two or more protein chains bonded together by noncovalent bonds. For example, hemoglobin (BIO 7.5.1) consists of four polypeptide subunits (*globin*) held together by hydrophobic bonds forming a globular almost tetrahedryl arrangement.

The secondary, tertiary, and quaternary structures of a protein may be destroyed in a number of ways (= *denaturation*). For example, heating (cooking) can break hydrogen bonds. Altering the pH can protonate or deprotonate the molecule and interrupt ionic interactions. Reducing agents can break disulfide bonds. Depending on the conditions, denaturation may be reversible.

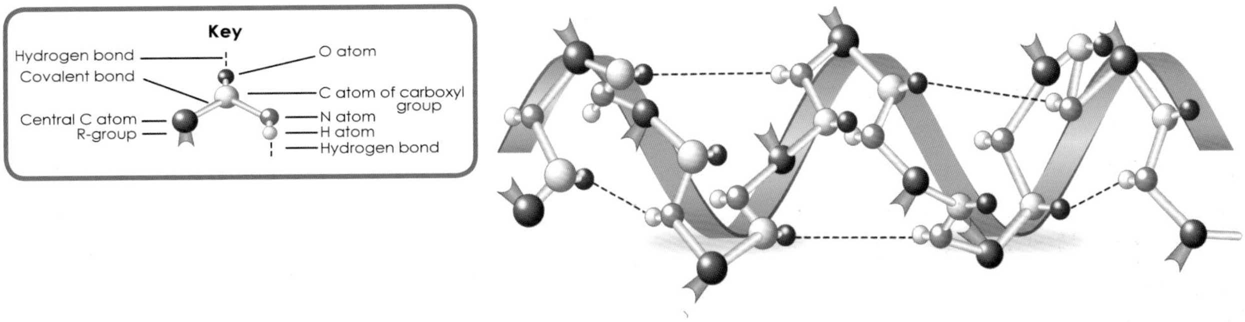

Figure IV.A.1.3: Secondary Structure: α-helix. This is a structure in which the peptide chain is coiled into a helical structure around a central axis. This helix is stabilized by hydrogen bonding between the N-H group and C=O group four residues away. A typical example with this secondary structure is keratin. Keratin is a fibrous, structural protein found in skin, hair and nails (BIO 13.2, 13.3.1) .

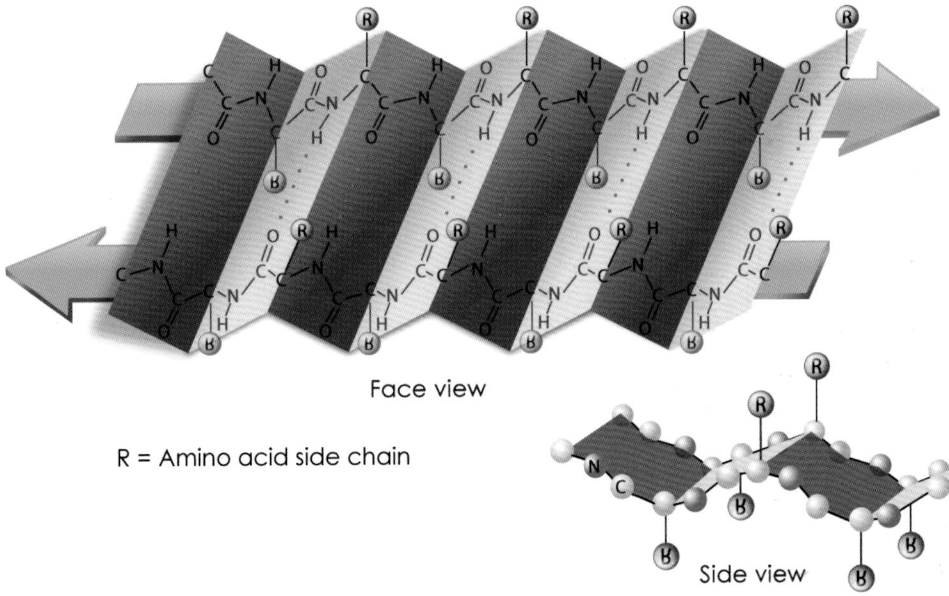

Figure IV.A.1.4: Secondary Structure: β-pleated sheet. Peptide chains lie alongside each other in a parallel manner. This structure is stabilized by hydrogen bonding between the N-H group on one peptide chain and C=O group on another. A typical example with this secondary structure is produced by some insect larvae: the protein fiber "silk" which is mostly composed of fibroin.

1.2.3 Protein Function and Detection

Over the chapters to come, we will be exploring many of the specific functions of proteins. Suffice to say for now that proteins are involved in virtually every process within cells. Proteins include the enzymes that catalyze biochemical reactions. Proteins also have both structural (cytoskeleton) and mechanical functions (actin and myosin). Other protein functions include cell signaling, immune responses, cell adhesion and the cell cycle. Proteins are a necessary component of our diets since we cannot synthesize all the amino acids we need and thus must obtain essential amino acids from food.

During the MCAT, it is likely that you will read passages that describe various methods in which proteins can be purified from other cellular components. These techniques include ultracentrifugation, precipitation, electrophoresis and chromatography (ORG 13). Protein structure and function are often studied using immunohistochemistry, site-directed mutagenesis, X-ray crystallography, nuclear magnetic resonance (NMR) and mass spectrometry (ORG 14).

1.3 Carbohydrates

1.3.1 Description and Nomenclature

In general, the names of most carbohydrates are recognizable by an -ose suffix. Carbohydrates are sugars and their derivatives. Formally they are 'carbon hydrates,' that is, they have the general formula $C_m(H_2O)_n$. Usually they are defined as polyhydroxy aldehydes and ketones, or substances that hydrolyze to yield polyhydroxy aldehydes and ketones. The basic units of carbohydrates are monosaccharides (sugars).

There are two ways to classify sugars. One way is to classify the molecule based on the type of carbonyl group it contains: one with an aldehyde carbonyl group is an *aldose*; one with a ketone carbonyl group is a *ketose*. The second method of classification depends on the number of carbons in the molecule: those with 6 carbons are hexoses, with 5 carbons are pentoses, with 4 carbons are tetroses, and with 3 carbons are trioses. Sugars may exist in either the ring form, as hemiacetals, or in the straight chain form, as polyhydroxy aldehydes. *Pyranoses* are 6 carbon sugars in the ring form; *furanoses* are 5 carbon sugars in the ring form.

In the ring form, there is the possibility of α or β *anomers*. Anomers occur when 2 cyclic forms of the molecule differ in conformation only at the hemiacetal carbon (carbon 1). Generally, pyranoses take the 'chair' conformation, as it is very stable, with all (usually) hydroxyl groups at the equatorial position. *Epimers* are diastereomers that differ in the configuration of

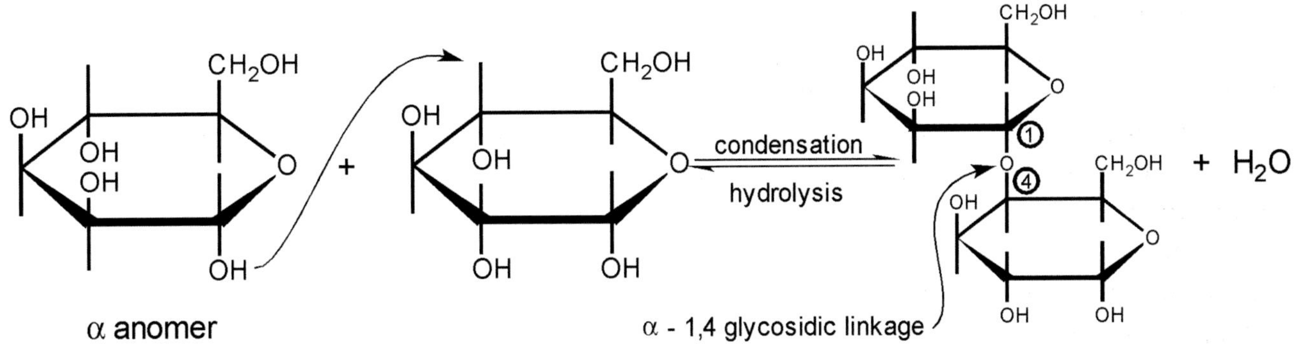

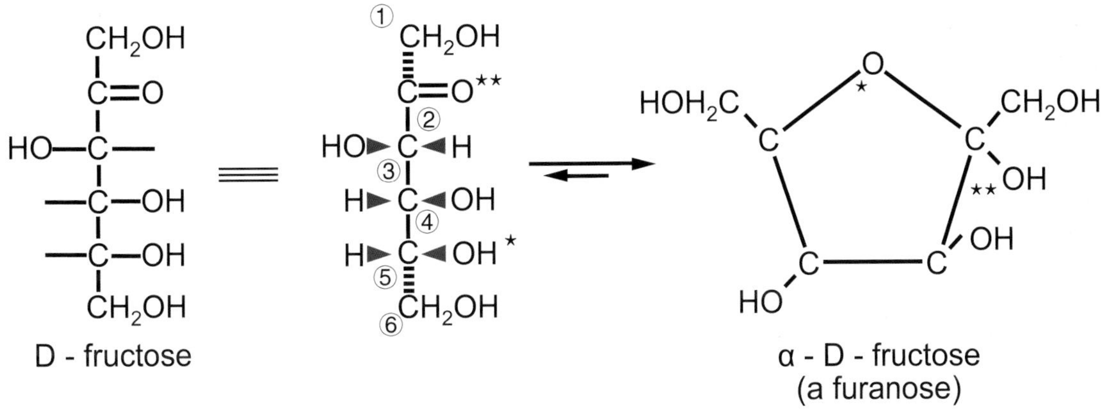

Figure IV.A.1.5 Part I: Names and configurations of common sugars. Notice that the asterix * and ** allow you to follow a specific oxygen atom. Following atoms through a reaction is a common MCAT-type question. An asterix, a prime symbol (') or a labelled isotope are examples of techniques that may be used to identify the atom that you must follow.

only one stereogenic center. For carbohydrates, epimers are 2 monosaccharides which differ in the conformation of one hydroxyl group.

To determine the number of possible optical isomers, one need only know the number of asymmetric carbons, normally 4 for hexoses and 3 for pentoses, designated as n. The number of optical isomers is then 2^n, where n is the number of asymmetric carbons (ORG 2.2.2).

Most but not all of the naturally occurring aldoses have the D-configuration. Thus they have the same *relative* configuration as D-glyceraldehyde. The configuration (D or L) is *only* assigned to the highest numbered chiral carbon. The *absolute* configuration can be determined for any chiral carbon. For example, using the rules from Section 2.3.1, it can be determined that the absolute configuration of D-glyceraldehyde is the R-configuration.

Most carbohydrates contain one or more chiral carbons. For this reason, they are optically active. The names and structures of some common sugars are shown in Figure IV.A.1.5.

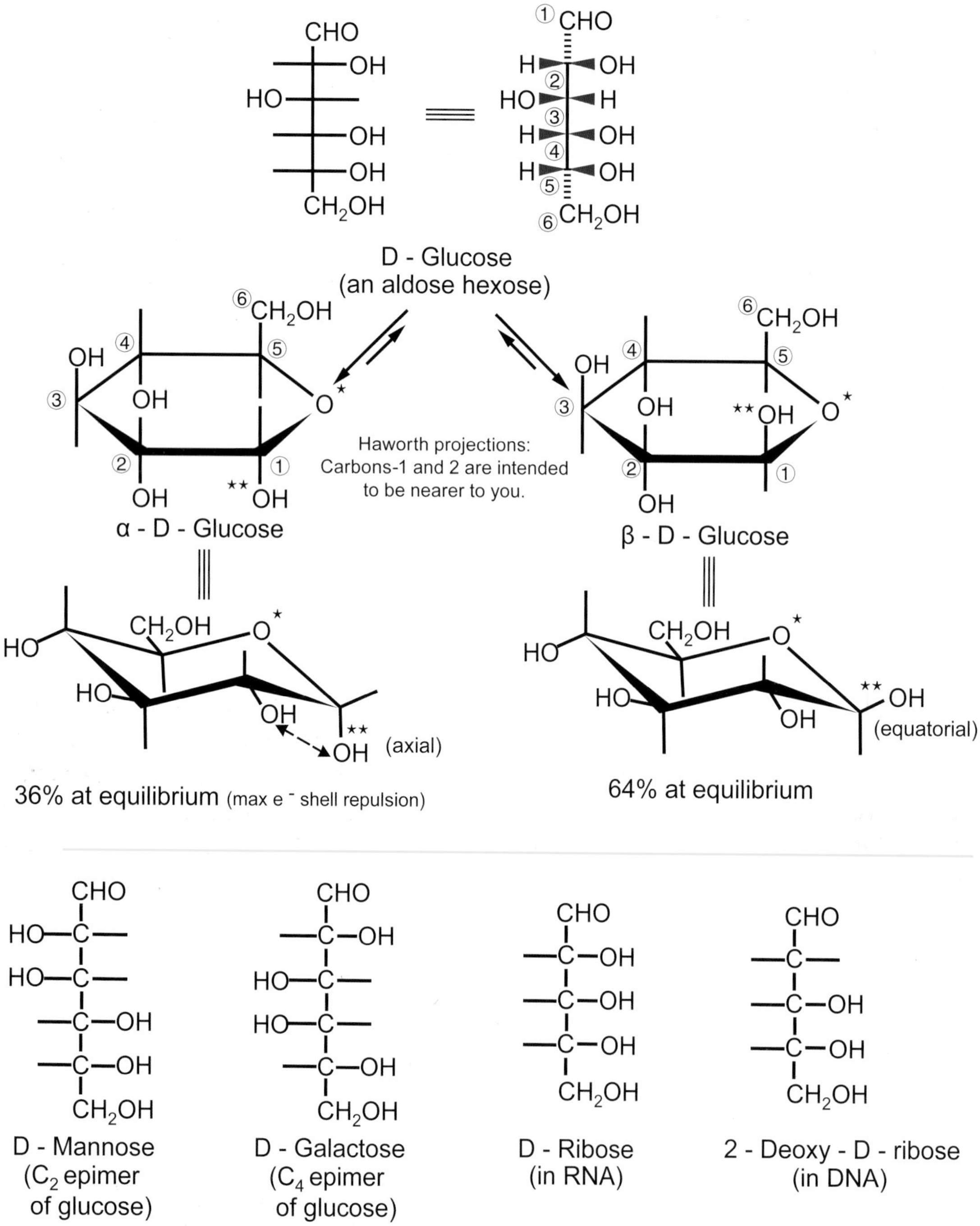

Figure IV.A.1.5 Part II: Names, structures and configurations of common sugars. Though not by convention, H belongs to the end of all empty bonds in the diagrams above. Note the following equivalent positions for substituents with glucose as an example: Right on Fischer = down on Hawthorne = alpha configuration = axial in the chair confirmation, and the opposite if on the left for a Fischer projection.

In the diagram that follows, you will notice a Fischer projection to the far left (see ORG 2.3.1). You will also find Fischer projections in the following pages since they are a common way to represent carbohydrates. Recall that the horizontal lines in a Fischer projection are projecting towards you.

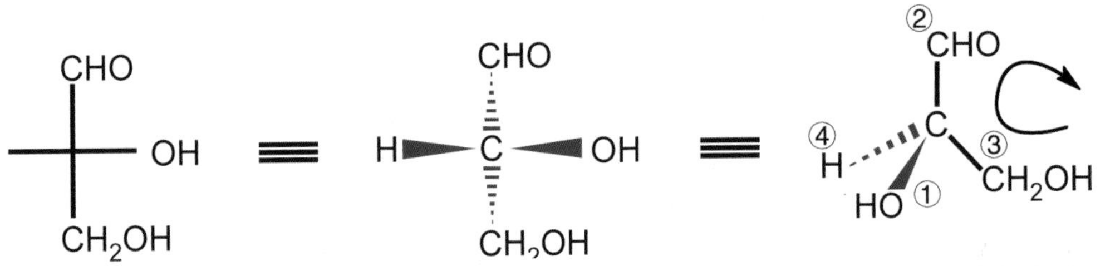

Fischer projection and 3-dimensional representation of D-glyceraldehyde, R-glyceraldehyde (*see* ORG 2.1, 2.2, 2.3 for rules).

1.3.2 Important Reactions of Carbohydrates

Hemiacetal Reaction

Monosaccharides can undergo an intramolecular nucleophilic addition reaction to form cyclic hemiacetals (see ORG 7.2.2). For example, the hydroxyl group on C4 of ribose attacks the aldehyde group on C1 forming a five-membered ring called furanose.

Diastereomers differing in configuration at this newly formed chiral carbon (= C1 where the straight chain monosaccharide converted into a furanose or pyranose) are known as anomers. This newly chiral carbon, which used to be a carbonyl carbon, is known as the

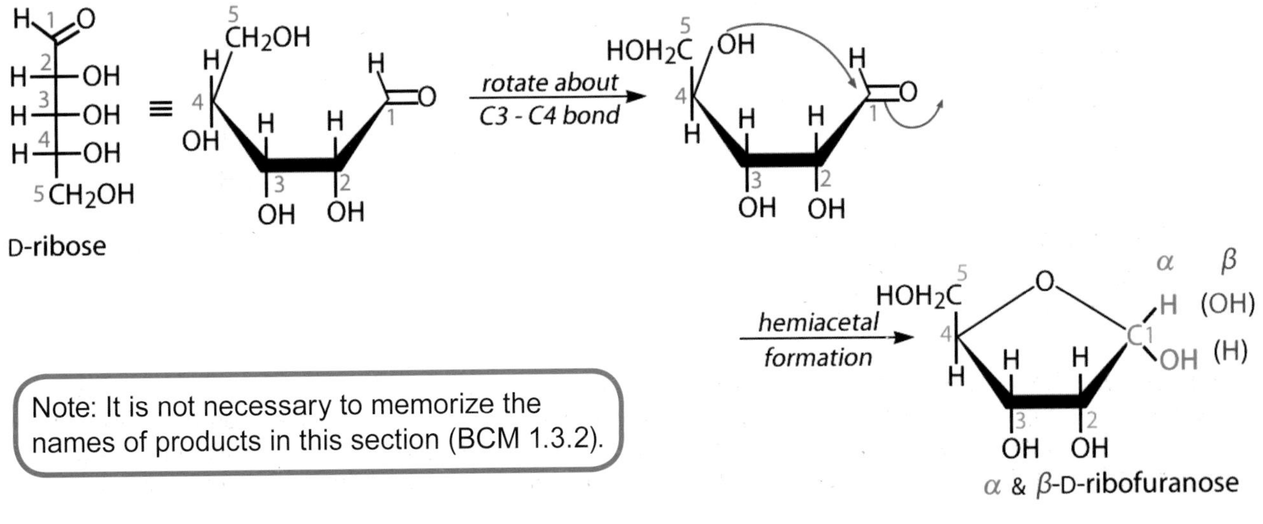

> Note: It is not necessary to memorize the names of products in this section (BCM 1.3.2).

anomeric center. When the OH group on C1 is *trans* to CH_2OH, it is called an α anomer. When the OH group on C1 is *cis* to CH_2OH, it is called a β anomer.

Mutarotation is the formation of both anomers into an equilibrium mixture when exposed to water.

Glycosidic Bonds

A disaccharide is a molecule made up of two monosaccharides, joined by a *glycosidic bond* between the hemiacetal carbon of one molecule, and the hydroxyl group of another. The glycosidic bond forms an α-1,4-glycosidic linkage if the reactant is an α anomer. A β-1,4-glycosidic linkage is formed if the reactant is a β anomer. When the bond is formed, one molecule of water is released (condensation). In order to break the bond, water must be added (hydrolysis):

- Sucrose (common sugar or table sugar) = glucose + fructose
- Lactose (milk sugar) = glucose + galactose
- Maltose (α-1,4 bond) = glucose + glucose
- Cellobiose (β-1,4 bond) = glucose + glucose

Ester Formation

Monosaccharides react with acid chloride or acid anhydride to form esters (see ORG 9.4, 9.4.1). All of the hydroxyl groups can be esterified.

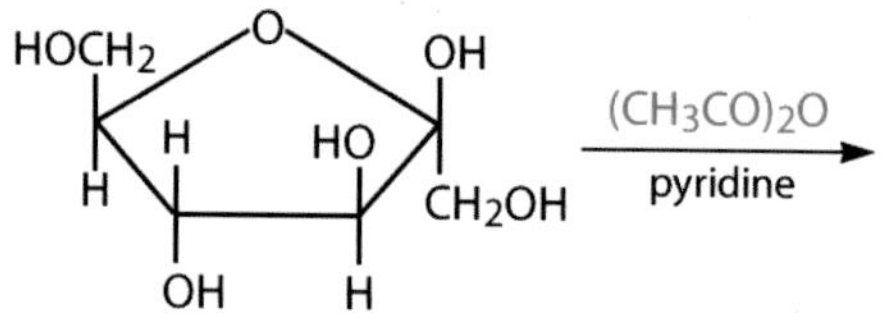

β-D-fructofuranose

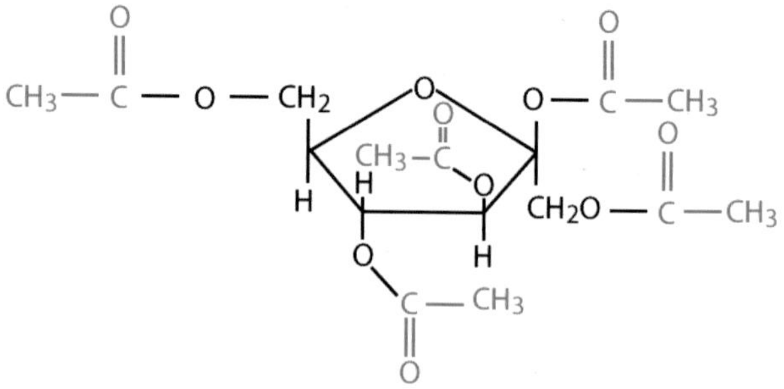
penta-*O*-*acetyl*-*β*-D-fructofuranoside

Ether Formation

Monosaccharides react with alkyl halide in the presence of silver oxide to form ethers. All of the hydroxyl groups are converted to -OR groups.

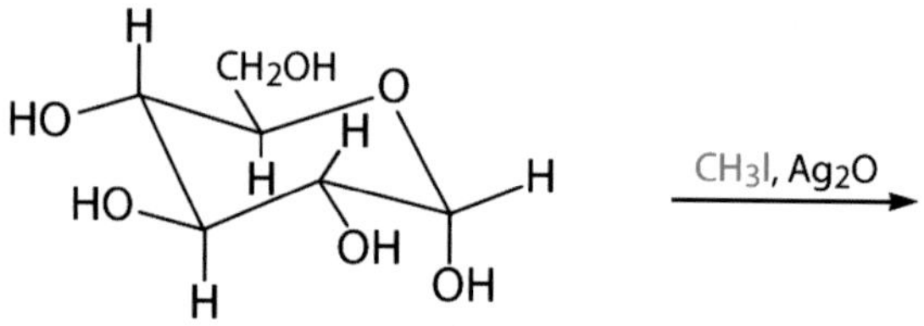

α-D-glucopyranose

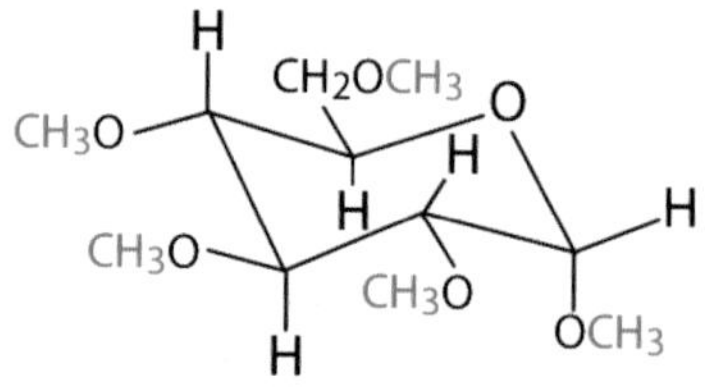
methyl 2, 3, 4, 6-tetra-*O*-methyl-α-D-glucopyranoside

Ether synthesis can also proceed using alcohols (see ORG 10.1):

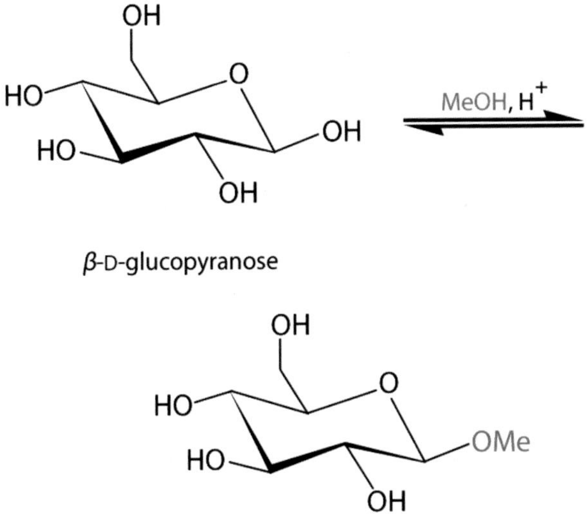

β-D-glucopyranose

methyl-β-D-glucopyranoside

Reduction Reaction

Open chain monosaccharides are present in equilibrium between the aldehyde/ketone and the hemiacetal form. Therefore, monosaccharides can be reduced by $NaBH_4$ to form polyalcohols (see ORG 6.2.2).

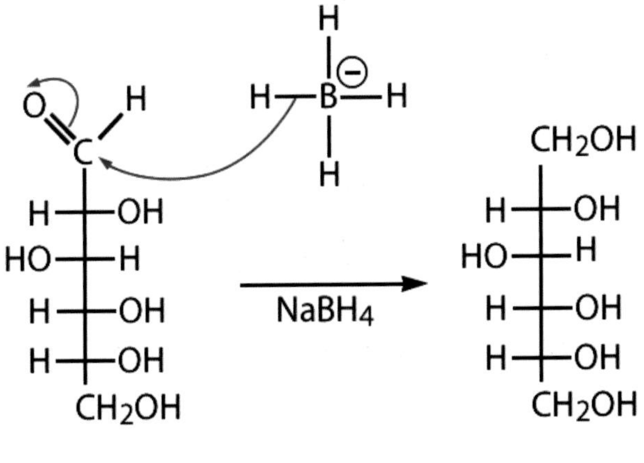

D-glucose

D-sorbitol

Oxidation Reaction

Again, the hemiacetal ring form is in equilibrium with the open chain aldehyde/ketone form. Aldoses can be oxidized by the Tollens' reagent $[Ag(NH_3)_2]^+$, Fehling's reagent ($Cu^{2+}/Na_2C_4H_4O_6$), and Benedict's reagent ($Cu^{2+}/Na_3C_6H_5O_7$) to yield carboxylic acids. If the Tollens' reagent is used, metallic silver is produced as a shiny mirror. If the Fehling's reagent or Benedict's reagent is used, cuprous oxide is produced as a reddish precipitate.

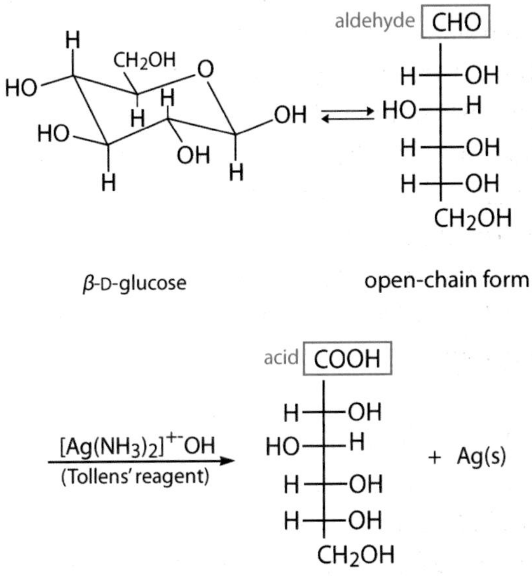

β-D-glucose

open-chain form

D-gluconic acid
(+ side products)

Redox (reduction/oxidation) and chain extending MCAT questions are usually easily solved by noticing that the stereochemistry of groups that are not directly involved in the reaction remain unchanged. For these substituents, the integrity of the Fischer projection is intact (in other words, whether the H or OH is on the left or right of the structure does not change).

When aldoses are treated with bromine water, the aldehyde is oxidized to a carboxylic acid group, resulting in a product known as an *aldonic acid*:

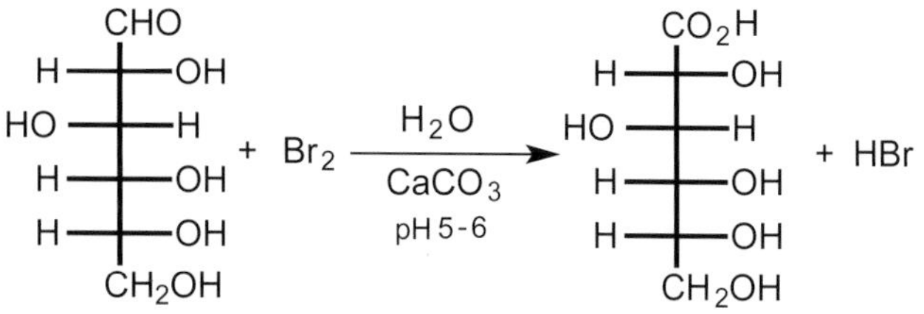

D - glucose
(an aldose)

D - Gluconic acid
(an aldonic acid)

Aldoses treated with dilute nitric acid will have both the primary alcohol and aldehyde groups oxidize to carboxylic acid groups, resulting in a product known as an *aldaric acid*:

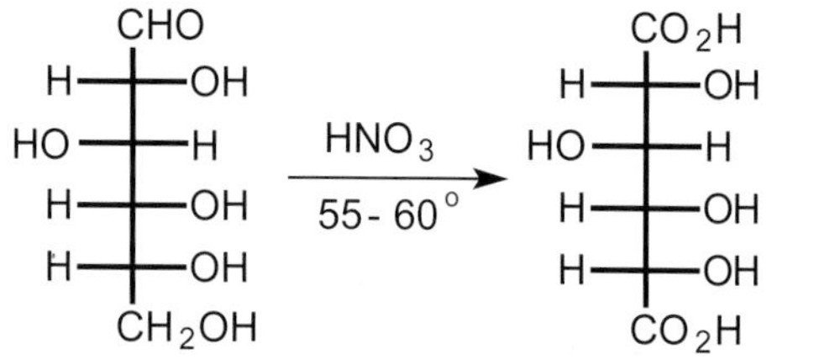

D - glucose
(an aldose)

D - Glucaric acid
(an aldaric acid)

Reducing Sugars/Non-reducing Sugars

All aldoses are reducing sugars because they contain an aldehyde carbonyl group. Some ketoses such as fructose are reducing sugars as well. They can be isomerized through keto-enol tautomerization (ORG 7.1) to an aldose, which can be oxidized normally. Glycosides are non-reducing sugars because the acetal group cannot be hydrolyzed to aldehydes. Thus they do not react with the Tollens' reagent.

1.3.3 Polysaccharides

Polymers of many monosaccharides are called polysaccharides. As in disaccharides, they are joined by glycosidic linkages. They may be straight chains, or branched chains. Some common polysaccharides are:

- Starch (plant energy storage)
- Cellulose (plant structural component)
- Glycocalyx (associated with the plasma membrane)
- Glycogen (animal energy storage in the form of glucose)
- Chitin (structural component found in shells or arthropods)

Carbohydrates are the most abundant organic constituents of plants. They are the source of chemical energy in living organisms, and, in plants, they are used in making the support structures. Cellulose consists of $\beta(1\rightarrow4)$ linked D-glucose. Starch and glycogen are mostly $\alpha(1\rightarrow4)$ glycosidic linkages of D-glucose.

1.4 Lipids

Lipids are a class of organic molecules containing many different types of substances, such as fatty acids, fats, waxes, triacyl glycerols, terpenes and steroids. The main biological functions of lipids include storing energy, signaling and acting as structural components of cell membranes.

Lipids are relatively water-insoluble or nonpolar. Lipids can be linear or ring in structure, and may or may not be aromatic. In general, the bulk of lipid structure is nonpolar or hydrophobic; however, often a part of their structure is polar or hydrophilic. This duality makes many lipids amphipathic (= amphiphilic) molecules (having both hydrophobic and hydrophilic portions).

Triacyl glycerols are oils and fats of either animal or plant origin. In general, fats are solid at room temperature, and oils are liquid at room temperature.

Triacyl glycerols are also commonly referred to as triglycerides (= triacylglycerides) and are, by definition, fatty acid triesters of the trihydroxy alcohol glycerol. {Note: "triacyl" refers to the presence of 3 acyl substituents (RCO-, ORG 9.1)}

> Glycerol + 3 Fatty acids = Triglyceride

The general structure of a triacyl glycerol is:

$$CH_2O-\overset{\overset{\textstyle O}{\|}}{C}-R$$

$$CHO-\overset{\overset{\textstyle O}{\|}}{C}-R'$$

$$CH_2O-\overset{\overset{\textstyle O}{\|}}{C}-R''$$

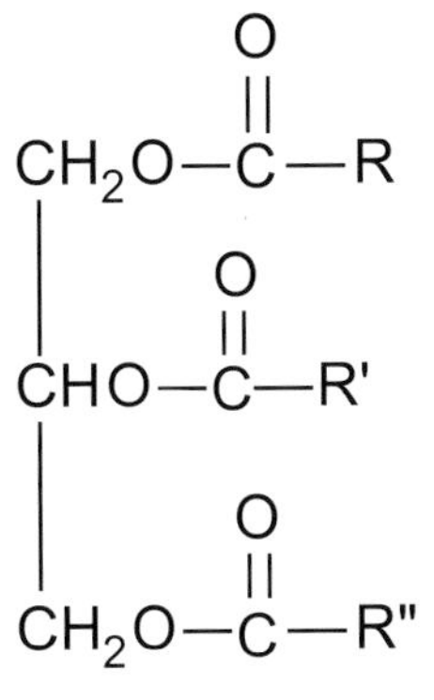

The R groups may be the same or different, and are usually long chain alkyl groups. Upon hydrolysis of a triacyl glycerol, the products are three fatty acids and glycerol. The fatty acids may be saturated (= no multiple bonds, i.e. *palmitic acid*) or unsaturated (= containing double or triple bonds, i.e. *oleic acid*). Unsaturated fatty acids are usually in the cis configuration. Saturated fatty acids have a higher melting point than unsaturated fatty acids. Some common fatty acids are:

$$CH_3(CH_2)_{14}COOH$$
palmitic acid

$$CH_3(CH_2)_{16}COOH$$
stearic acid

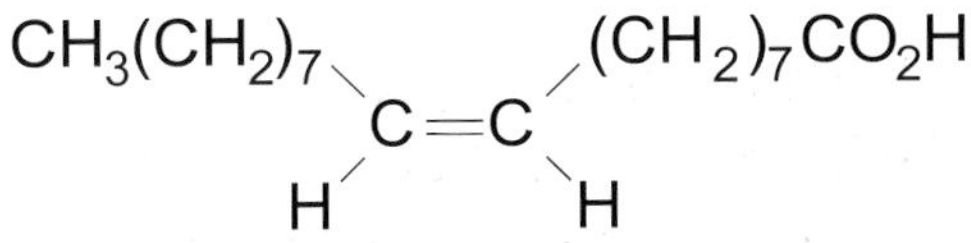

$$CH_3(CH_2)_7\underset{H}{\overset{}{C}}=\underset{H}{\overset{}{C}}(CH_2)_7CO_2H$$
oleic acid

> General formula for a saturated fatty acid =
> $C_nH_{2n+1}COOH = CH_3(CH_2)_nCOOH$

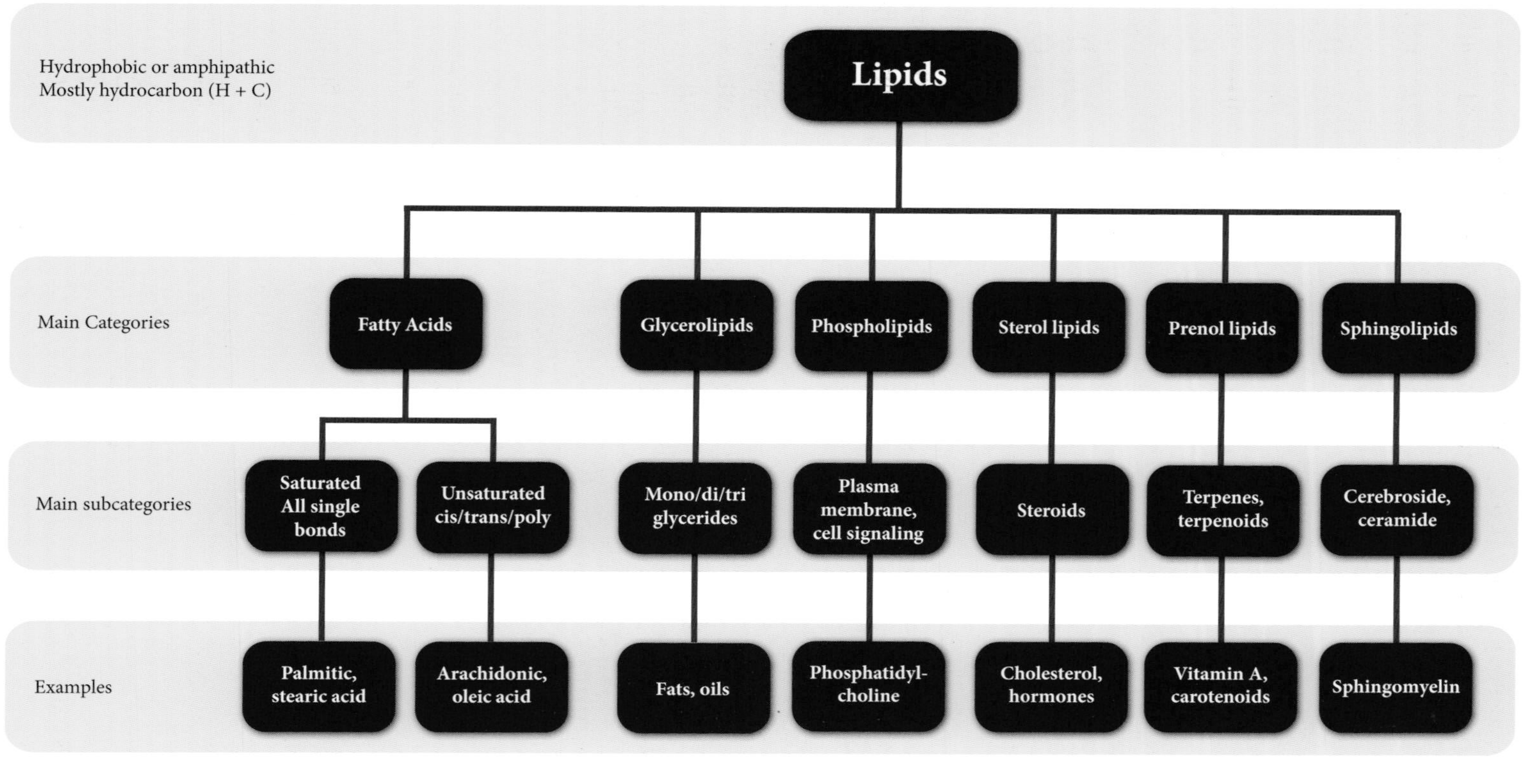

Figure A.1.6: Categories of lipids. Note that prostaglandins - hormone-like lipids - are derived from unsaturated fatty acids. Waxes, like oils and fats, are lipids. However, oils and fats are esters of glycerol whereas waxes may contain esters of carboxylic acids and long chain alcohols or combinations of long chain fatty acids and primary alcohols.

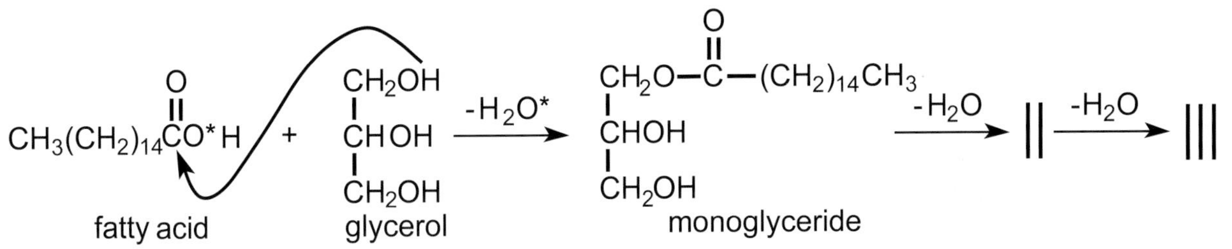

Biosynthesis of fats and oils. Fats and oils are a special class of esters (i.e. mono-, di-, and triglycerides). Fatty acids (= long chain carboxylic acids) may be added to the monoglyceride formed in the above reaction, forming diglycerides, and triglycerides.

"Essential" fatty acids are fatty acids that humans - and other animals - must ingest because the body requires them but cannot synthesize them. Only two are known in humans: alpha-linolenic acid and linoleic acid. Because they have multiple double bonds that begin near the methyl end, they are both known as polyunsaturated omega fatty acids (omega is the last letter of the Greek alphabet thus signifying the methyl end).

A wax is a simple ester of a fatty acid and a long-chain alcohol. In general, a wax, such as the wax in your ears, serves as a protective coating.

Soap is a mixture of salts of long chain fatty acids formed by the hydrolysis of fat. This process is called saponification. Soap possesses both a nonpolar hydrocarbon tail and a polar carboxylate head. When soaps are dispersed in aqueous solution, the long nonpolar tails are inside the sphere while the polar heads face outward. Recall that a sphere is the shape that minimizes surface tension (i.e. the smallest surface area relative to volume; CHM 4.2).

Soaps are surfactants (BIO 12.3). They are compounds that lower the surface tension of a liquid because of their amphipathic nature

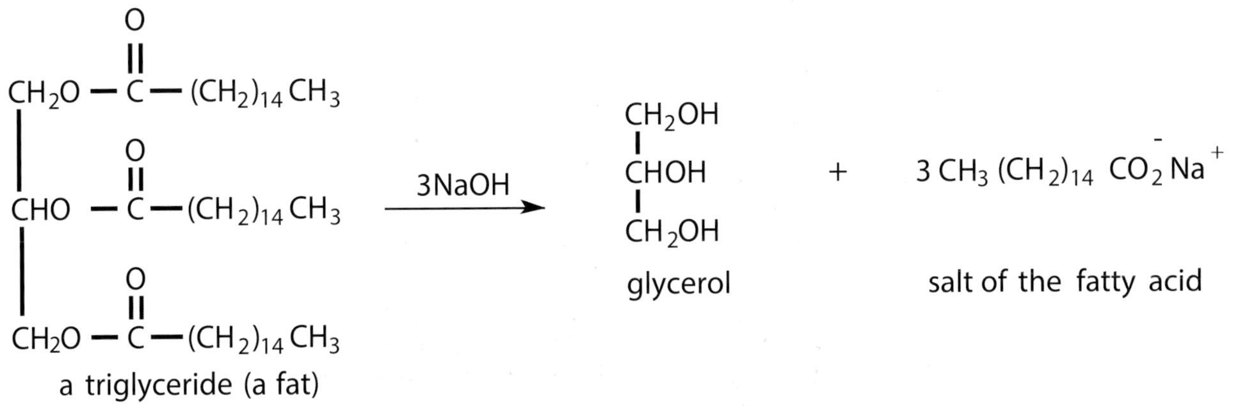

Saponification. Fats may be hydrolyzed by a base to the components glycerol and the salt of the fatty acids. The salts of long chain carboxylic acids are called soaps. Thus this process is called saponification.

(i.e. they contain both hydrophobic tails and hydrophilic heads; see BIO 1.1).

Of course, the cellular membrane is a lipid bilayer (Biology Chapter 1). The polar heads of the lipids align towards the aqueous environment, while the hydrophobic tails minimize their contact with water and tend to cluster together. Depending on the concentration of the lipid, this interaction may result in micelles (spherical), liposomes (spherical) or other lipid bilayers.

Micelles are closed lipid monolayers with a fatty acid core and polar surface. The main function of bile (BIO 9.4.1) is to facilitate the formation of micelles, which promotes the processing or emulsification of dietary fat and fat-soluble vitamins.

Liposomes are composed of a lipid bilayer separating an aqueous internal compartment from the bulk aqueous environment. Liposomes can be used as a vehicle for the administration of nutrients or pharmaceutical drugs.

The dual solubility nature of soap is why it removes oil or grease from skin or clothes. The soap forms a micelle that surrounds the nonpolar oil/grease in the nonpolar 'center' of the micelle. The polar end of the soap micelle is soluble in water, allowing the oil/grease to be removed during rinsing.

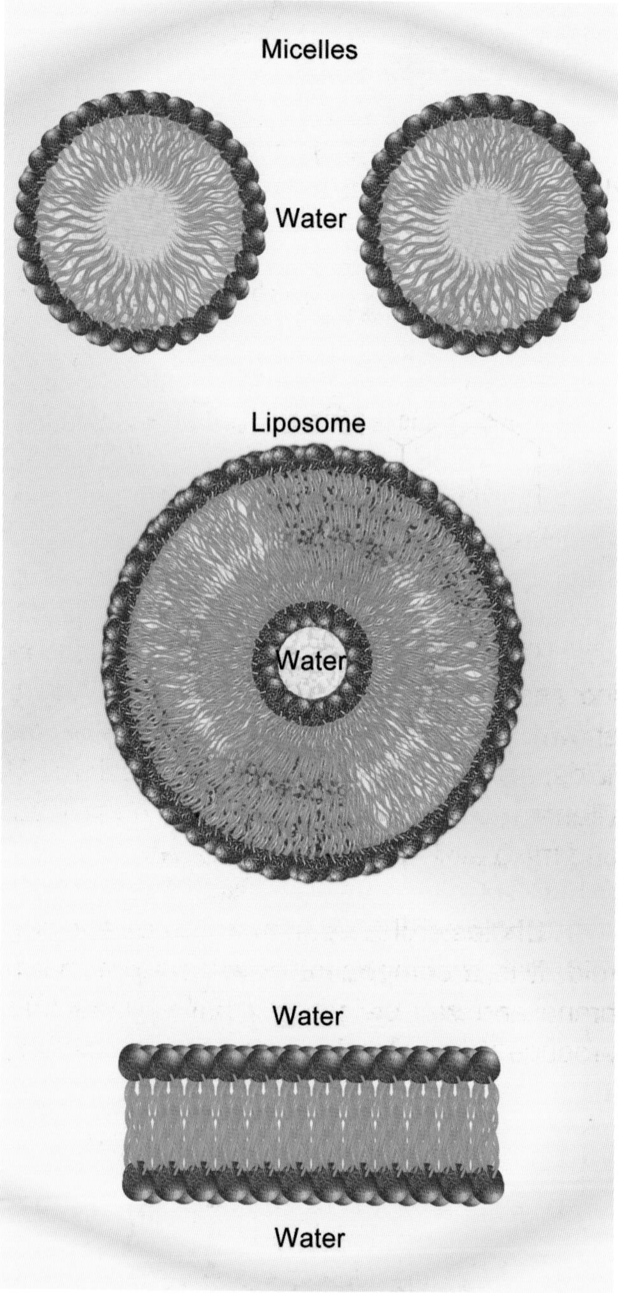

Figure IV.A.1.7. Amphipathic molecules arranged in micelles, a liposome and a bilipid layer.

1.4.1 Steroids

Steroids are a class of lipids which are derivatives of the basic ring structure:

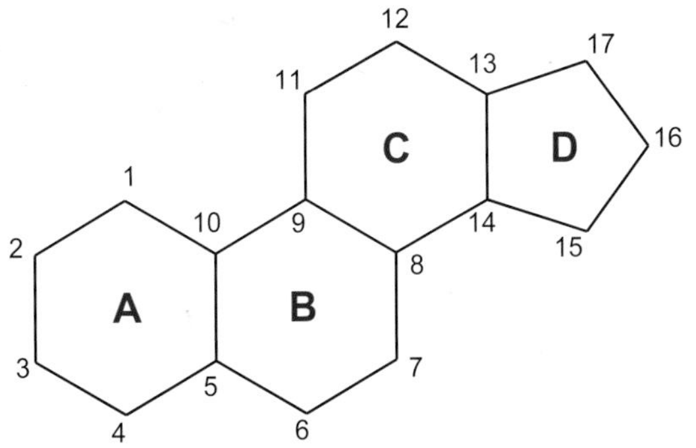

The IUPAC-recommended ring-lettering and the carbon atoms are numbered as shown. Many important substances are steroids, some examples include: cholesterol, D vitamins, bile acids, adrenocortical hormones, and male and female sex hormones.

Cholesterol is the most abundant steroid. It is a component of the plasma membrane and can serve as a building block to produce other steroids (including hormones) and related molecules. Cholesterol comes from the diet, but may be synthesized by the liver if necessary.

The rate limiting step in the production of steroids (= *steroidogenesis*) in humans is the conversion of cholesterol to pregnenolone, which is in the same family as progesterone. This occurs inside of mitochondria and serves as the precursor for all human steroids.

Since such a significant portion of a steroid contains hydrocarbons, which are hydrophobic, steroids can dissolve through the hydrophobic interior of a cell's plasma membrane (BIO 1.1, 6.3). Furthermore, steroid hormones contain polar side groups which allow the hormone to easily dissolve in water. Thus steroid hormones are well designed to be transported through the vascular space, to cross the plasma membranes of cells, and to have an effect either in the cell's cytosol or, as is usually the case, in the nucleus.

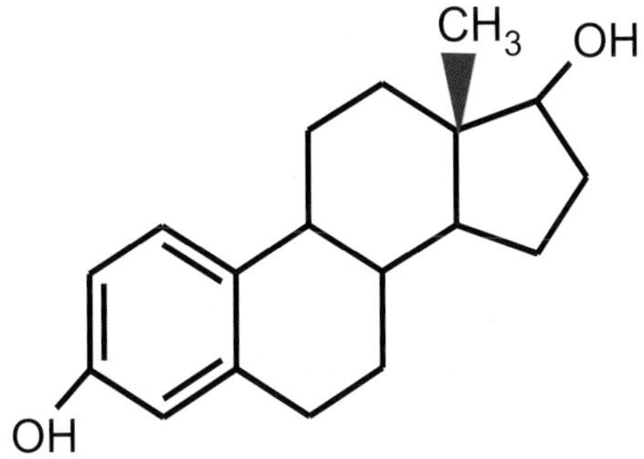

Estradiol
(an estrogen)

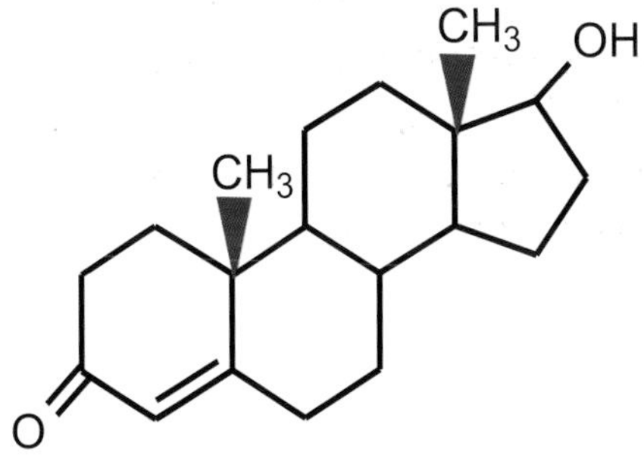

Testosterone
(an androgen)

1.4.2 Lipoproteins

Most biological molecules are proteins, followed by lipids. In fact, proteins and lipids by far dominate the biological molecules in the human body. Lipoproteins comprise unique biochemical assemblies (aggregates) containing both proteins and lipids, bound to the proteins, which allow lipids to move through hydrophilic intracellular and extracellular spaces. Many enzymes, structural proteins, transporters, antigens and toxins are lipoproteins.

Using electrophoresis and ultracentrifugation, lipoproteins can be classified according to size and density. Lipoproteins are larger and less dense when the fat to protein ratio is increased. Thus there are four major classes of plasma lipoproteins which enable lipids to be carried in the blood stream: (1) chylomicrons carry triglycerides from the intestines to the liver, to skeletal muscle, and to adipose tissue ("body fat"); (2) very low-density lipoproteins (VLDL) carry liver-synthesized triglycerides to adipose tissue; (3) low-density lipoproteins (LDL = "bad cholesterol") carry cholesterol from the liver to cells of the body; (4) and high-density lipoproteins (HDL = "good cholesterol") collect cholesterol from the body's tissues, and take it back to the liver.

1.5 Nucleic Acids

Deoxyribonucleic Acid (DNA) and ribonucleic acid (RNA) are essential components in constructing the proteins which act as the cytoskeleton, enzymes, membrane channels, antibodies, etc. It is the DNA which contains the genetic information of the cell.

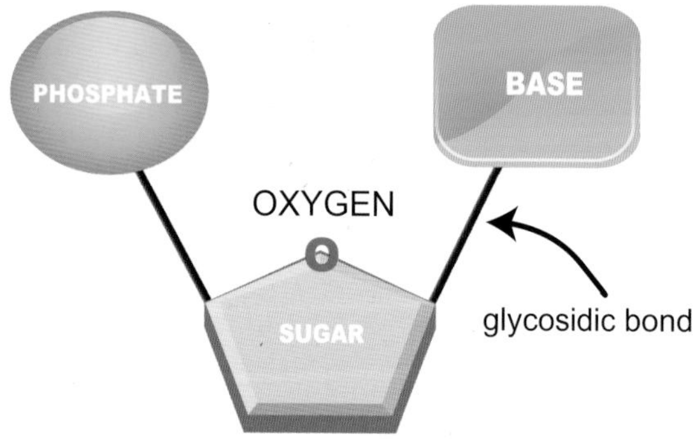

Figure IV.A.1.8: Key features of the building block for nucleic acids: a nucleotide (a monomer) which is also known as a nucleoside phosphate.

DNA and RNA are both important nucleic acids. Nucleotides are the subunits which attach in sequence or in other words polymerize via phosphodiester bonds to form nucleic acids. A nucleotide (also called a *nucleoside phosphate*) is composed of a five carbon sugar, a nitrogen base, and an inorganic phosphate. A glycosidic bond links the the base to the sugar.

The sugar in RNA is ribose but for DNA an oxygen atom is missing in the second position of the sugar thus it is 2-deoxyribose.

There are two categories of nitrogen bases: *purines* and *pyrimidines*. The purines have two rings and include adenine (A) and guanine (G). The pyrimidines contain one ring and include thymine (T), cytosine (C), and uracil (U).

Nitrogenous base	Ribonucleoside	Deoxyribonucleoside

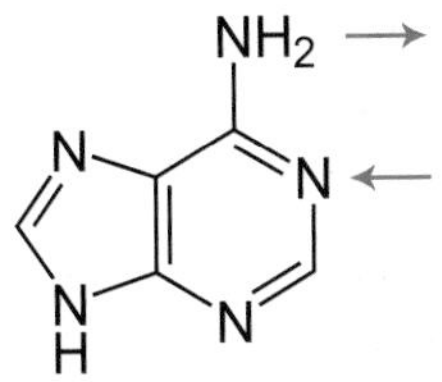

Adenine (A): Purine

- RNA, DNA
- Cofactors: nicotinamide adenine dinucleotide (NAD) and flavin adenine dinucleotide (FAD)

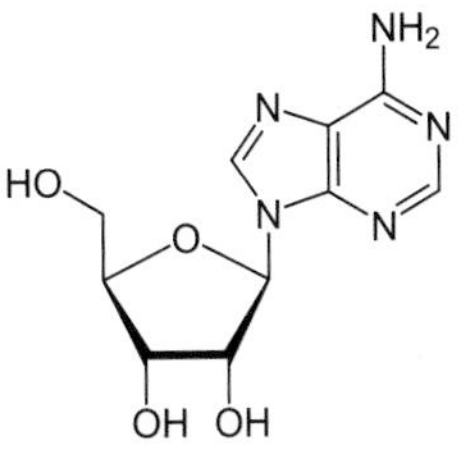

Adenosine

- RNA
- Energy: adenosine triphosphate (ATP), adenosine diphosphate (ADP)
- Signal transduction: cyclic adenosine monophosphate (cAMP)

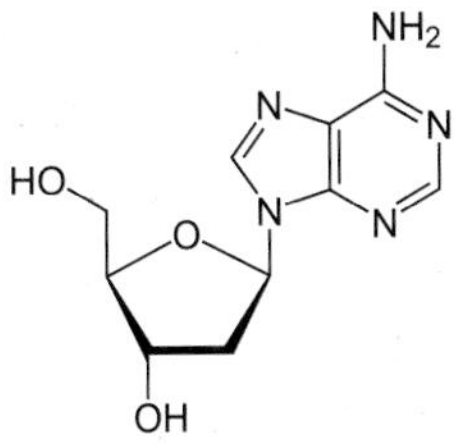

Deoxyadenosine (dA)

- DNA

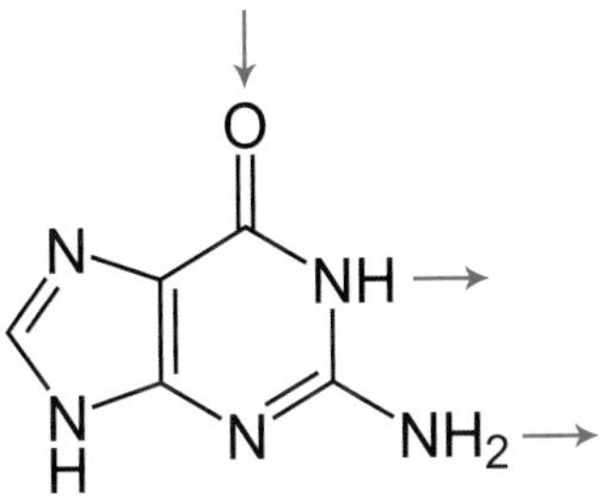

Guanine (G): Purine

- RNA, DNA

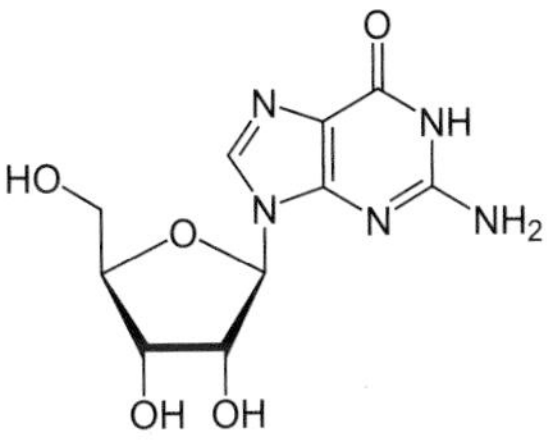

Guanosine

- RNA
- Analogous to adenosine: GTP, GDP, cGMP

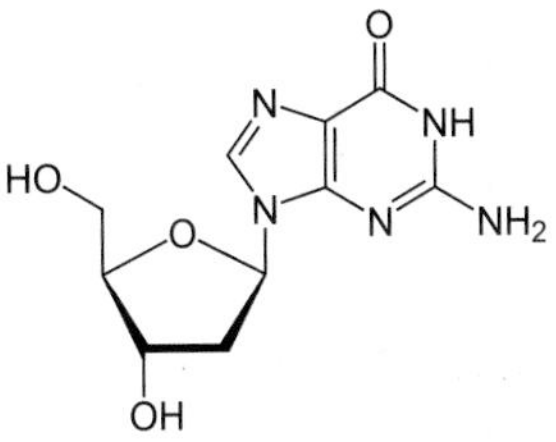

Deoxyguanosine (dG)

- DNA

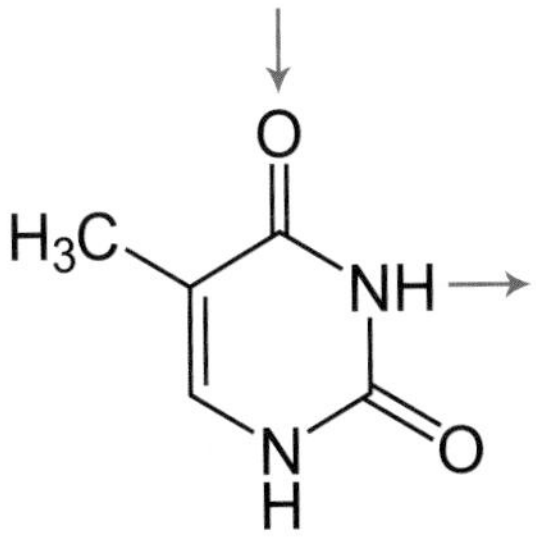

Thymine (T): Pyrimidine

- DNA

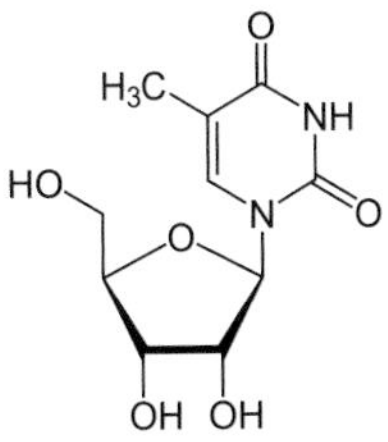

5-Methyluridine

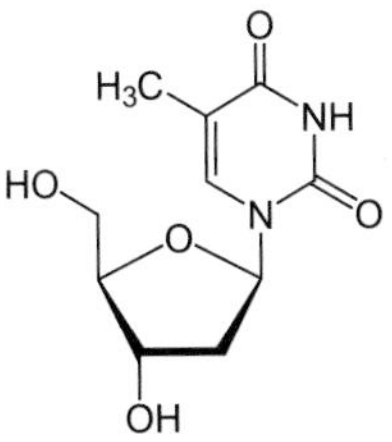

Thymidine (dT)

- DNA

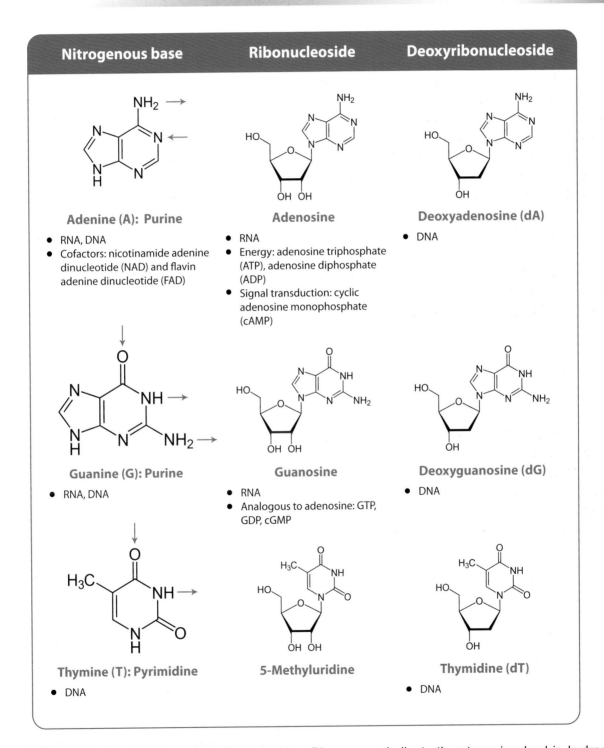

Figure IV.A.1.9, Part I: Summary of nucleosides. Blue arrows indicate the atoms involved in hydrogen bonding. For example, in cytosine, the amino group acts as the hydrogen bond donor and the C-2 carbonyl and the N-3 amine as the hydrogen-bond acceptor (*see* Part II). Guanine has the C-6 carbonyl group that acts as the hydrogen bond acceptor, while a group at N-1 and the amino group at C-2 act as the hydrogen bond donors.

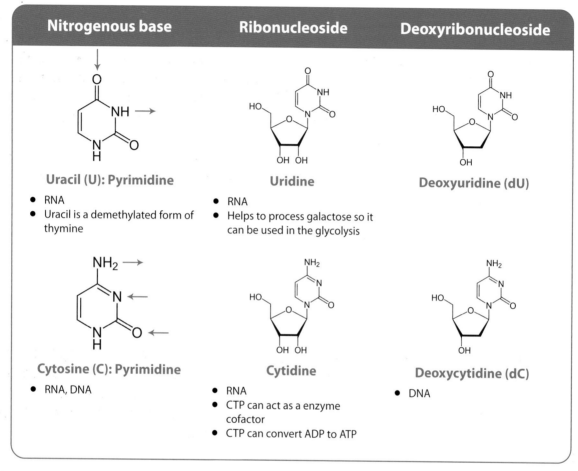

Nitrogenous base	Ribonucleoside	Deoxyribonucleoside
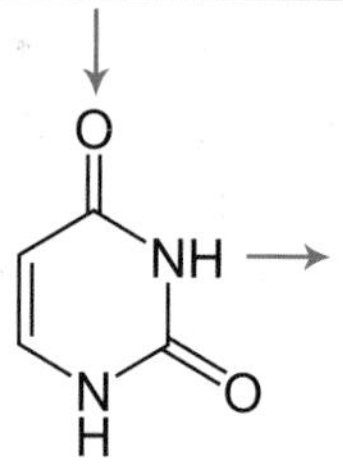	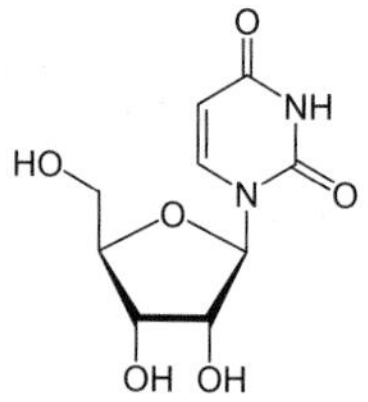	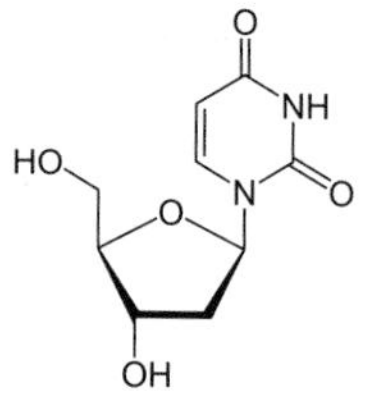
Uracil (U): Pyrimidine • RNA • Uracil is a demethylated form of thymine	**Uridine** • RNA • Helps to process galactose so it can be used in the glycolysis	**Deoxyuridine (dU)**
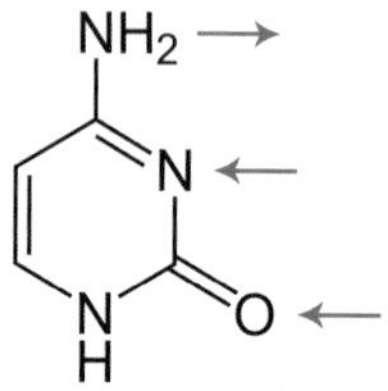	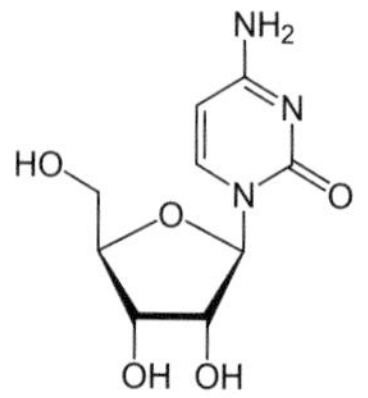	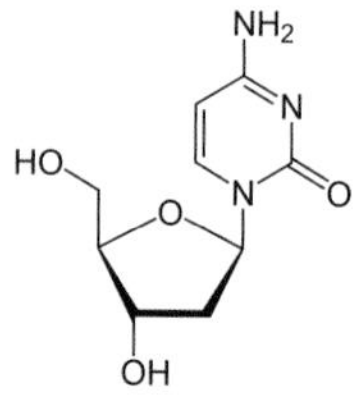
Cytosine (C): Pyrimidine • RNA, DNA	**Cytidine** • RNA • CTP can act as a enzyme cofactor • CTP can convert ADP to ATP	**Deoxycytidine (dC)** • DNA

Figure IV.A.1.9, Part II: Summary of nucleosides.

DNA contains the following four bases: adenine, guanine, thymine, and cytosine. RNA contains the same bases except uracil is substituted for thymine.

Watson and Crick's model of DNA has allowed us to get insight into what takes shape as the nucleotides polymerize to form this special nucleic acid. The result is a double *helical* or *stranded* structure.

The DNA double helix is composed of two complementary and anti-parallel DNA strands held together by hydrogen bonds between base pairing A-T and C-G {Mnemonic: **A**ll **T**igers and **C**ats **G**rowl}.

The facts from here to the end of this section are the source of many MCAT questions: DNA is made from deoxyribose while RNA is made from ribose. DNA is double stranded while RNA is single stranded. DNA contains thymine while RNA contains uracil.

The backbone of each helix is the 2-deoxyribose phosphates. The nitrogen bases project to the center of the double helix in order to hydrogen bond with each other (imagine the double helix as a winding staircase: each stair would represent a pair of bases binding to keep the shape of the double helix intact).

There is specificity in the binding of the bases: one purine binds one pyrimidine. In fact, adenine only binds thymine (through two hydrogen bonds) and guanine only binds cytosine (through three hydrogen bonds). The more the H-bonds (i.e. the more G-C), the more stable the helix will be.

We will be examining DNA replication and the cell cycle in Biology Chapter 1.

1.6 Phosphorous in Biological Molecules

Phosphorous is an essential component of various biological molecules including adenosine triphosphate (ATP), phospholipids in cell membranes (BIO 1.1), and the nucleic acids which form DNA (BIO 1.2.2). Phosphorus can also form phosphoric acid (key to making the phosphate buffer in plasma; BCM 2.10), and several phosphate esters.

A phospholipid is produced from three ester linkages to glycerol. Phosphoric acid is ester linked to the terminal hydroxyl group and two fatty acids are ester linked to the two remaining hydroxyl groups of glycerol (*see Biology Section 1.1 for a schematic view of a phospholipid*).

Among the following Biochemistry chapters, the production of ATP will be discussed. The components ADP and P_i (= *inorganic phosphate*) combine using the energy generated from a coupled reaction to produce ATP. We will be discussing the

$$HO-\overset{\overset{\displaystyle O}{\|}}{\underset{\underset{\displaystyle OH}{|}}{P}}-OH$$

phosphoric acid

$$RO-\overset{\overset{\displaystyle O}{\|}}{\underset{\underset{\displaystyle OH}{|}}{P}}-OH \qquad RO-\overset{\overset{\displaystyle O}{\|}}{\underset{\underset{\displaystyle OR'}{|}}{P}}-OH \qquad RO-\overset{\overset{\displaystyle O}{\|}}{\underset{\underset{\displaystyle OR'}{|}}{P}}-OR''$$

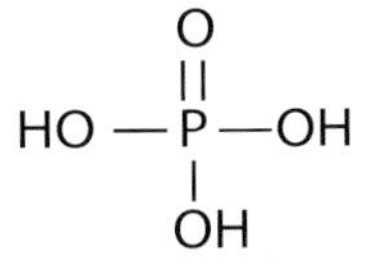

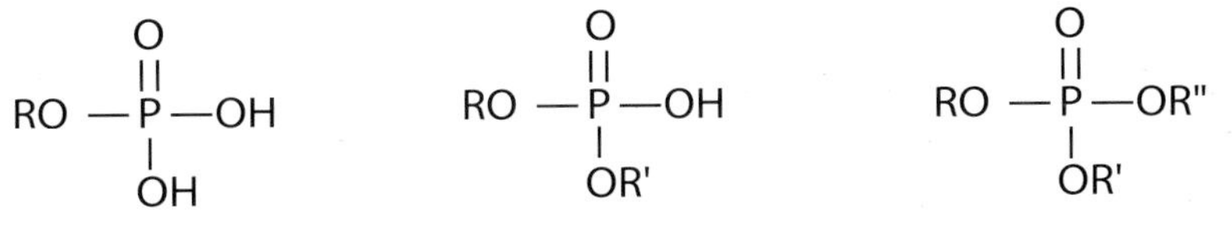

phosphate esters

bioenergetics of ATP in the next chapter. The linkage between the phosphate groups are via *anhydride bonds*:

$$\text{adenine} - \text{ribose} - O - \overset{\displaystyle O}{\underset{\displaystyle O^-}{\overset{\|}{P}}} - O - \overset{\displaystyle O}{\underset{\displaystyle O^-}{\overset{\|}{P}}} - OH$$

adenosine diphosphate

$$+ \quad HO - \overset{\displaystyle O}{\underset{\displaystyle O^-}{\overset{\|}{P}}} - O^- \xrightarrow{\text{energy}}$$

inorganic
phosphate

$$A - O - \overset{\displaystyle O}{\underset{\displaystyle O^-}{\overset{\|}{P}}} - O - \overset{\displaystyle O}{\underset{\displaystyle O^-}{\overset{\|}{P}}} - O - \overset{\displaystyle O}{\underset{\displaystyle O^-}{\overset{\|}{P}}} - O^- + H_2O$$

adenosine triphosphate

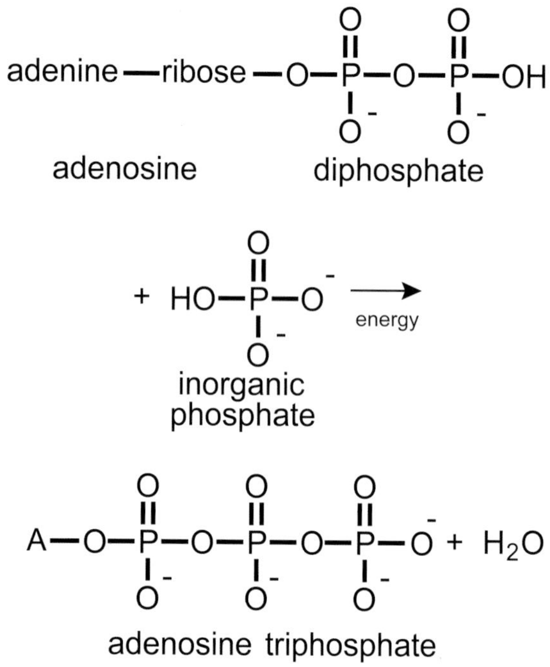

In DNA, the phosphate groups engage in two ester linkages creating phosphodiester bonds. It is the 5' phosphorylated position of one pentose ring which is linked to the 3' position of the next pentose ring (*see* BIO 1.2.2):

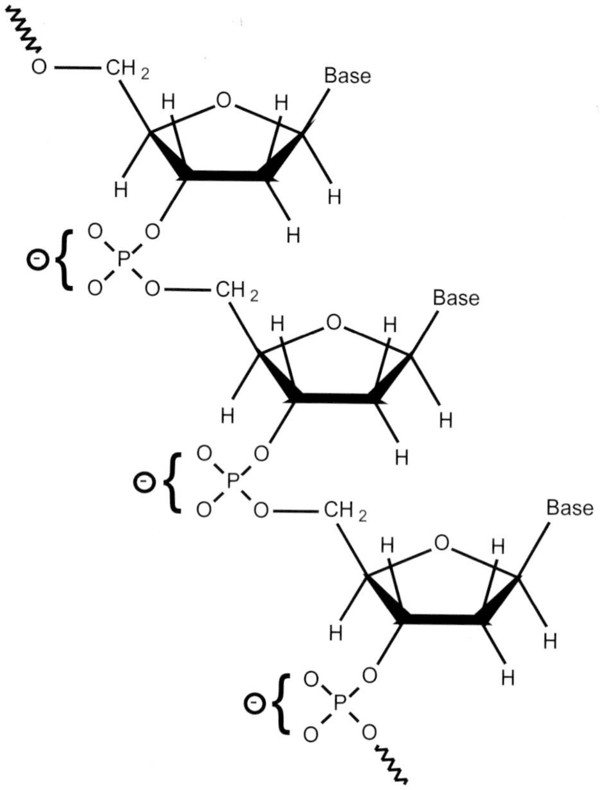

Nucleotides polymerizing to produce DNA and RNA is certainly a dominant theme but it should be remembered that nucleotides can bond to make other important molecules which we will also discuss later: NAD and the phosphorylated form, NADP. NAD (nicotinamide adenine dinucleotide) is formed when two nucleotides join through their phosphate groups (like ATP, this is an anhydride bond and NOT a phosphodiester bond which has the phosphate group between 2 carbons like in DNA/RNA).

One nucleotide in NAD contains an adenine base and the other nicotinamide. NAD famously exists in two forms, an oxidized and reduced form abbreviated as NAD^+ and NADH, respectively.

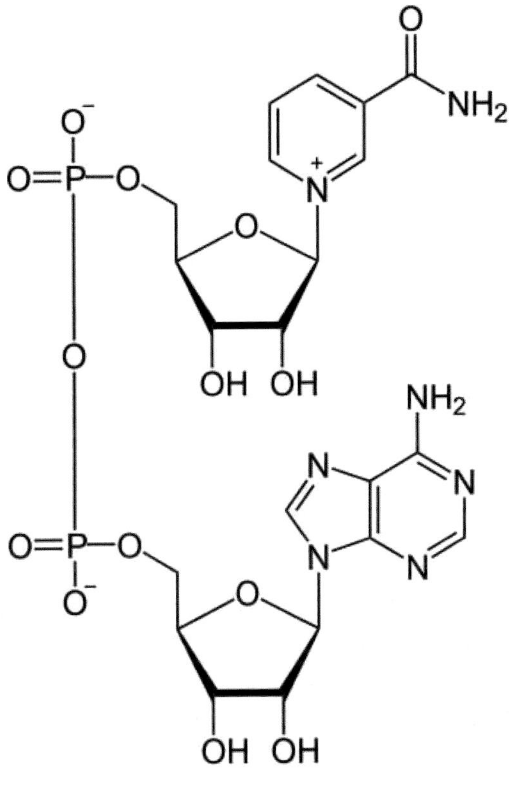

Nicotinamide adenine dinucleotide (NAD)

Recall from our introduction that just 6 elements combine to form 99% of the mass of the human body (C, H, O, N, P and Ca which is predominantly the inorganic portion of bone). A key point which is regularly tested is to ensure that you notice the importance of phosphate to nucleic acids, the uniqueness of sulfur in proteins, and the presence of nitrogen in protein and nucleic acids but not carbohydrates and lipids.

GOLD STANDARD WARM-UP EXERCISES

CHAPTER 1: Biological Molecules

1) The functional groups of the amino acids located in the interior of the enzyme phenylalanine hydroxylase are mostly likely:
   - A. basic.
   - B. acidic.
   - C. hydrophilic.
   - D. hydrophobic.

2) A student is synthesizing tripeptides using three different amino acids. How many distinct molecules can she create?
   - A. 3
   - B. 4
   - C. 6
   - D. 9

3) Which of the following best describes the primary structure of proteins?
   - A. The arrangement of different protein subunits in a multiprotein complex.
   - B. The order in which amino acids are linked together in a protein.
   - C. Regions of ordered structure within a protein.
   - D. The overall three dimensional shape of a protein.

4) It has been found that proinsulin, the precursor molecule to insulin, contains a portion that is held together by disulfide bonds. This information provides data most characteristic to what level of protein structure?
   - A. Primary structure
   - B. Secondary structure
   - C. Tertiary structure
   - D. Quaternary structure

5) Which of the following best identifies the following organic compound?

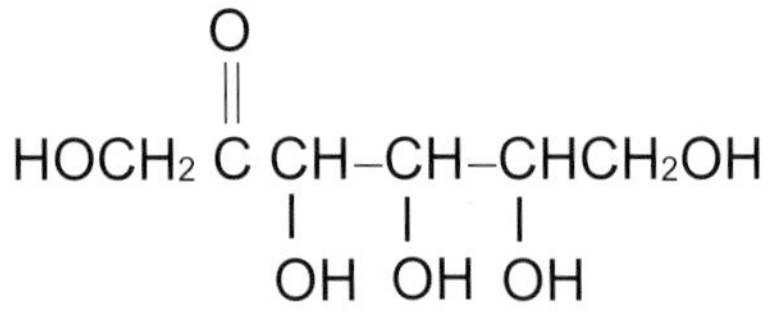

   - A. Aldehyde
   - B. Triacyl glyceride
   - C. Protein
   - D. Carbohydrate

6) Streptococcus mutans produces glucan, a sticky polymer of glucose that acts like a cement and binds the bacterial cells together and to the tooth surface. Glucan is formed only in the presence of the disaccharide sucrose (the type of sugar found in sweets), through a process catalyzed by an enzyme of the cocci. The enzyme links glucose molecules together to form glucan, while fructose molecules are fermented by the streptococci into lactic acid. Lactic acid can etch the surface of the teeth, enhancing microbial adherence.

   Given the preceding, the enzyme produced by Streptococcus mutans likely initially acts by:
   - A. catalyzing the formation of glycosidic bonds between glucose molecules.
   - B. splitting sucrose into fructose and glucose.
   - C. catalyzing the formation of glycosidic bonds between fructose molecules.
   - D. catalyzing the fermentation of fructose.

7) Fructose and glucose are:

A. isotopes.
B. monosaccharides.
C. six-carbon sugars.
D. both B and C.

8) Cholesterol, cortisone and cortisol are best identified as:

A. cholesterols.
B. corticosteroids.
C. bile acids.
D. steroids.

9) ATP is considered an "energy rich" compound because of what kind of bonds?

A. Phosphoanhydride
B. Phosphodiester
C. Phosphoglycosidic
D. Adenosine

10) Given a segment of a DNA double helix that is 100 nucleotide pairs long and contains 25 adenine bases, how many cytosine bases does it contain?

A. 25
B. 50
C. 75
D. 150

STOP

Reminder: Free additional chapter review questions are available online for the original owner of this textbook. Doing practice questions will help clarify concepts and ensure that you study in a targeted way. First, register at mcat-prep.com, then login and click on MCAT Textbook Owners in the right column so you can use your Online Access Code to have access to the Lessons section.

Your online access continues for 6 sequential months from your online registration.

GS ANSWER KEY

CHAPTER 1

		Cross-Reference			*Cross-Reference*
1.	D	BCM 1.1.1, 1.2.2	6.	B	BCM 1.3.2
2.	C	BCM 1.2.1, 1.2.2	7.	D	BCM 1.3.1, 1.3.2
3.	B	BCM 1.2.2	8.	D	BCM 1.4.1
4.	C	BCM 1.2.2	9.	A	BCM 1.6
5.	D	BCM 1.3.1, 1.3.2	10.	C	BCM 1.5, 1.6

* Explanations can be found at the back of the book.

ENZYMES, THERMODYNAMICS AND BUFFERS
Chapter 2

Memorize

* Equations: Equilibrium constant, Gibbs free energy
* Define: catabolism, anabolism, activation energy
* Define: metabolism, active/allosteric sites
* Basic types of enzymes
* Major buffer systems

Understand

* Competitive, non-competitive inhibition
* Potential energy graphs, saturation kinetics, dynamic equilibrium
* Le Chatelier's principle, Gibbs free energy and the sign conventions
* Enzyme kinetics, inhibition and activity
* Biological buffers and pH

Clinical Correlation

A heart attack results in dead cardiac (heart) cells which spill specific enzyme into the blood stream which are monitored to clarify a diagnosis. Many cancer cause tissue injury or destruction which can result in the elevation of specific enzymes which can suggest certain diagnoses.

MCAT-Prep.com

Introduction

Enzymes are highly selective biological catalysts, greatly accelerating both the rate and specificity of metabolic reactions, from food digestion to DNA synthesis. Since enzymes are selective for their substrates and speed up only a few reactions from among many, the set of enzymes made in a cell determines which metabolic pathways occur in that cell, tissue and organ.

Thermodynamics is the study of heat and energy, and how it relates to the matter in our universe. Thermodynamics can be used to determine if a reaction is spontaneous in the direction written. A buffer solution (more precisely, pH buffer or hydrogen ion buffer) is an aqueous solution of a mixture of a weak acid and its conjugate base, or vice versa. Life forms thrive in a relatively small pH range so buffers are used to maintain a relatively constant pH.

Optional Gold Standard Resources

Free Forum

Online Videos

Flashcards

2.1 Catalysis

A catalyst is a substance that speeds up a chemical reaction, but is not consumed by the reaction (the initial number of moles of this compound in the reaction mixture is equal to the number of moles of this compound once the reaction is completed). Catalysts work by providing an alternative mechanism for a reaction that involves a different transition state, one in which a lower activation energy occurs at the rate-determining step. Catalysts help lower the activation energy of a reaction and help the reaction to proceed.

Enzymes are the typical biological catalysts. They are protein molecules with very large molar masses containing one or more active sites (BCM 2.6 - 2.8). Enzymes are very specialized catalysts. They are generally specific and operate only on certain biological reactants called substrates. They also generally increase the rate of reactions by large factors. The general mechanism of operation of enzymes is as follows:

$$\text{Enzyme (E)} + \text{Substrate (S)} \rightarrow \text{ES (complex)}$$

$$\text{ES} \rightarrow \text{Product (P)} + \text{Enzyme (E)}$$

If we were to compare the energy profile of a reaction performed in the absence of an enzyme to that of the same reaction performed with the addition of an enzyme, we would obtain Figure III.A.2.1.

You may remember from your General Chemistry review (CHM 9.5) that activation

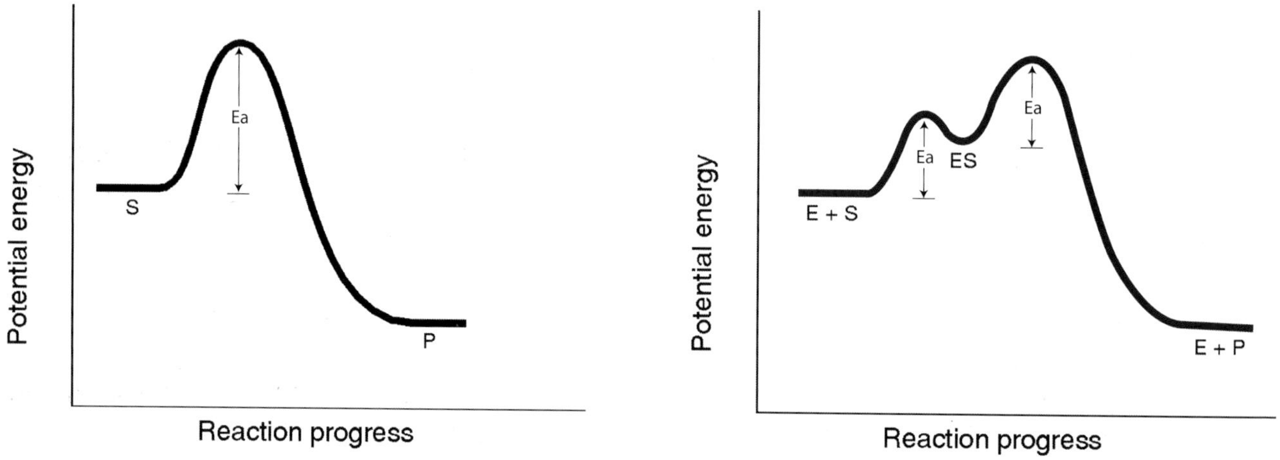

Figure III.A.2.1: Potential energy diagrams: without and with a catalyst. Since the product has lower energy than the reactant, energy must have been released indicating an exothermic reaction (negative change in enthalpy, ΔH). Had the diagram indicated product with a higher energy than the reactant, then that would indicate an endothermic reaction (positive ΔH).

energy (E_a) is the minimum energy required to activate atoms or molecules to a state in which they can undergo a chemical reaction. As you can see from the second diagram in Figure III.A.2.1, the reaction from the substrate to the product is facilitated by the presence of the enzyme because the reaction proceeds in two fast steps (low E_a's). Generally, catalysts (or enzymes) stabilize the transition state of a reaction by lowering the energy barrier between reactants and the transition state. Catalysts (or enzymes) do not change the energy difference between reactants and products. Therefore, catalysts do not alter the extent of a reaction or the chemical equilibrium itself. Generally, the rate of an enzyme-catalysed reaction is :

$$\text{rate} = k[ES]$$

The rate of formation of the product $\Delta[P]/\Delta t$ vs. the concentration of the substrate [*S*] yields a plot as in Figure III.A.2.2.

When the concentration of the substrate is large enough for the substrate to occupy all the available active sites on the enzyme, any further increase would have no effect on the rate of the reaction. This is called *saturation kinetics* (BIO 1.1.2).

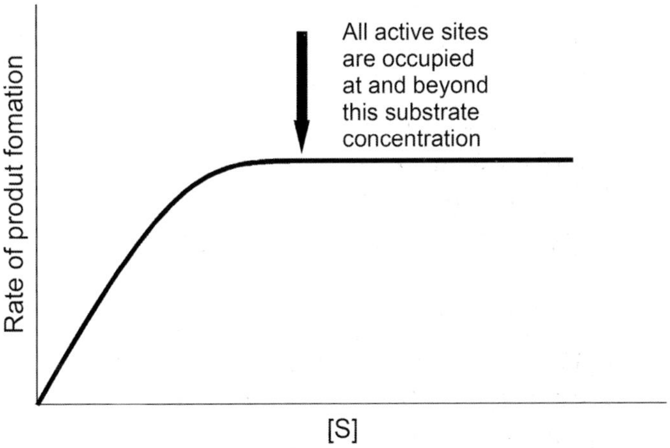

Figure III.A.2.2: Saturation kinetics.

2.2 Equilibrium in Reversible Biochemical Reactions

In most biochemical reactions once the product is formed, it reacts in such a way to yield back the initial reactants. Eventually, the system reaches a state where there are as many molecules of products being formed as there are molecules of reactants being generated through the reverse reaction. At equilibrium, the concentrations of reactants and products will not necessarily be equal, however, the concentrations remain the same. Hence, the relative concentrations of all components of the forward and reverse reactions become constant at equilibrium. This is called a state of "dynamic equilibrium". It is characterized by a constant K:

$$aA + bB \rightleftharpoons cC + dD$$

where a, b, c and d are the corresponding stoichiometric coefficients:

$$K = \frac{[C]^c\,[D]^d}{[A]^a\,[B]^b}$$

The equilibrium constant K (sometimes symbolized as K_{eq}) has a given value at a given temperature. If the temperature changes the value of K changes. At a given temperature, if we change the concentration of A, B, C or D, the system evolves in such a way as to re-establish the value of K. This is called the law of mass action. {Note: catalysts speed up the rate of reaction without affecting K_{eq}}

The following is an example of how an equilibrium constant K is calculated based on a chemical reaction at equilibrium. Remember that the equilibrium constant K can be directly calculated only when the equilibrium concentrations of reactants and products are known or obtained.

As an example, suppose that initially, 5 moles of reactant X are mixed with 12 moles of Y and both are added into an empty 1 liter container. Following their reaction, the system eventually reaches equilibrium with 4 moles of Z formed according to the following reaction:

$$X\ (g) + 2Y\ (g) \rightleftharpoons Z\ (g)$$

For this gaseous, homogeneous mixture (CHM 1.7), what is the value of the equilibrium constant K?

At equilibrium, 4 moles of Z are formed and therefore, 4 moles of X and 8 moles of Y are consumed based on the mole:mole ratio of the balanced equation. Since 5 moles X and 12 moles Y were initially available prior to equilibrium, at equilibrium following the reaction, there remains 1 mol X and 4 moles Y. Since all of the reaction takes place in a 1 L volume, the equilibrium concentrations are therefore, 1 mol/L for X, 4 mol/L for Y and Z, respectively.

Thus, the equilibrium constant can then be calculated as follows:

$$K = [Z]/[X][Y]^2 = [4]/[1][4]^2 = 0.25.$$

The K value is an indication of where the equilibrium point of a reaction actually lies, either far to the right or far to the left or somewhere in between. The following is a summary of the significance of the magnitude of an equilibrium constant K and its meaning:

1. If $K > 1$, this means that the forward reaction is favored and thus, the reaction favors product formation. If K is very large, the equilibrium mixture will then contain very little reactant compared to product.

2. If $K < 1$, the reverse reaction is favored and so the reaction does not proceed very far towards product formation and thus very little product is formed.

3. If $K = 1$, neither forward nor reverse directions are favored.

Note: Pure solids and pure liquids do not appear in the equilibrium constant. Thus in heterogeneous equilibria, since the liquid and solid phases are not sensitive to pressure, their "concentrations" remain constant throughout the reaction and so, mathematically, their values are denoted as 1.

Naturally, H_2O is one of the most common liquids dealt with in biochemical reactions. Remember to set its activity equal to 1 when it is a liquid but, if H_2O is written as a gas, then its concentration must be considered.

2.3 Le Chatelier's Principle

Le Chatelier's principle states that whenever a perturbation is applied to a system at equilibrium, the system evolves in such a way as to compensate for the applied perturbation. For instance, consider the following equilibrium:

$$N_2 + 3H_2 \rightleftharpoons 2NH_3$$

If we introduce some more hydrogen in the reaction mixture at equilibrium, i.e. if we increase the concentration of hydrogen, the system will evolve in the direction that will decrease the concentration of hydrogen (from left to right). If more ammonia is introduced, the equilibrium shifts from the right-hand side to the left-hand side, while the removal of ammonia from the reaction vessel would do the opposite (i.e. shifts equilibrium from the left-hand side to the right-hand side).

In a similar fashion, an increase in total pressure (decrease in volume) favors the direction which decreases the total number of compressible (i.e. gases) moles (from the left-hand side where there are 4 moles to the right-hand side where there are 2 moles). It can also be said that when there are different forms of a gaseous substance, an increase in total pressure (decrease in volume) favors the form with the greatest density, and a decrease in total pressure (increase in volume) favors the form with the lowest density.

Finally, if the temperature of a reaction mixture at equilibrium is increased, the equilibrium evolves in the direction of the endothermic (heat-absorbing) reaction. For example, we will soon be discussing two types of metabolic reactions which take place in cells: 'building up' (anabolism) and 'breaking down' (catabolism). Anabolic reactions use up energy (endergonic) while catabolic reactions give off energy (exergonic). In an anabolic reaction small molecules join to make larger ones. For example, the following condensation reactions that occur in cells are anabolic: 2 amino acids join together to make a dipeptide (BCM 1.2.1) and the process continues as large protein molecules are built up; 2 simple sugar molecules join together to make dissacharides (BCM 1.3.1) and the process continues as large polysaccharide molecules are built up; and thus we have the following endothermic reaction:

monomer + monomer + energy $\rightleftharpoons$ dimer + water

Not surprisingly, it takes energy to build up something. Considering Le Chatelier's principle, an increase in temperature would favor the forward reaction (condensation) over the backward reaction (hydrolysis). In other words, the condensation reaction resulting in the formation of the dimer increases with increasing temperature.

2.4 Thermodynamics of Biological Systems

Thermodynamics includes a collection of laws and principles describing the flow and interchange of heat, energy and matter in a system.

Thermodynamics, as an introductory level subject, has a different emphasis in Biochemistry than it does in Physics or General Chemistry (CHM 7.2, 8.8). A key strength, from a Biochemistry point of view, is that thermodynamics permits the determination as to whether a chemical process or reaction will occur spontaneously in the direction written. Thermodynamics does not tell us about reaction rates (i.e. kinetics; BCM 2.7).

First Law of Thermodynamics: The total amount of energy in an isolated system is conserved, though the form of energy may change.

Second Law of Thermodynamics: In all natural processes, the entropy of the universe increases.

Enthalpy: The heat content of a system (H). When a chemical reaction releases heat, it is exothermic and has a negative ΔH, and when it requires heat (BCM 2.3), it is endothermic and has a positive ΔH.

Gibbs Free Energy (G): The amount of energy capable of doing work during a reaction at constant temperature and pressure. When the system changes to possess less energy (free energy is released) then the free energy change (ΔG) is negative and the reaction is *exergonic* thus spontaneous. When the system changes to possess more energy (free energy is added) then the free energy change (ΔG) is positive and the reaction is *endergonic* thus not spontaneous. If ΔG is zero then the system is in a state of equilibrium meaning the reaction is spontaneous in both directions.

Entropy: Randomness or disorder of a system (S). When the products of a reaction are less complex and more disordered than the reactants, the reaction proceeds with a gain in entropy (positive ΔS). When the products have less disorder and more complexity than the reactants (i.e. the dimer formed from monomers), there is a reduction in entropy (negative ΔS).

Note that entropy differs from enthalpy in that the values of enthalpy that indicate favored reactions are negative and the values of entropy are positive. Together the terms enthalpy and entropy demonstrate that a system tends toward the highest entropy and the lowest enthalpy.

In biological systems, energy inputs from energy sources (i.e. exothermic chemical reactions) are "coupled" with reactions that are not entropically favored (i.e. have a Gibbs free energy above zero). Between two (or more) coupled reactions, the total entropy in the universe always increases. This coupling allows endergonic reactions, such as protein or DNA synthesis, to proceed without decreasing the total entropy of the universe. Thus biological systems do not violate the Second Law of Thermodynamics.

Enthalpy, Gibbs free energy and entropy are all state functions. In other words, they depend only on the nature of the reactants and products and are independent of the pathway by which the reaction occurs. Given the same pressure and temperature, the values of these state functions are additive. As an example, though an enzyme lowers the activation energy, it does not alter the energy of the reactants nor products and thus ΔG remains unchanged in the presence of an enzyme. Consider the following additional example and notice how the change in the standard free energy is additive and how certain molecules cancel.

First, a little background: free energy released from ATP hydrolysis can be used to drive unfavorable reactions (which we will examine further in BCM 2.5). The first step in glycolysis (BCM 3.3) is catalyzed by the enzyme hexokinase and uses ATP hydrolysis to drive the unfavorable reaction of glucose phosphorylation in a coupled reaction (ΔG^o values on the right):

$$\begin{array}{lr} \text{glucose + Pi} \rightleftharpoons \text{glucose-6-phosphate + } H_2O & 13.8 \text{ kJ/mol} \\ \text{ATP + } H_2O \rightleftharpoons \text{ADP + Pi} & -30.5 \text{ kJ/mol} \\ \hline \text{ATP + glucose} \rightleftharpoons \text{glucose-6-phosphate + ADP} & -16.7 \text{ kJ/mol} \end{array}$$

Note that the sum is done just like an application of Hess's Law (CHM 8.3): ΔG^o = 13.8 kJ/mol + -30.5 kJ/mol = -16.7 kJ/mol (negative value = spontaneous) and the inorganic phosphate Pi and water cancel from both sides of the summary equation.

Thus energy "stored" in the bonds of ATP is used to drive the synthesis of glucose-6-phosphate. Of course some energy will be "wasted" as heat which impacts body temperature.

2.4.1 Relationship between the Equilibrium Constant and the Change in the Gibbs Free Energy

In the "thermodynamics" section 2.4 we defined the Gibbs free energy. The *standard* Gibbs free energy ($G°$) is determined at 25 °C (298 K) and 1 atm. The change in the standard Gibbs free energy for a given reaction can be calculated from the change in the standard enthalpy and entropy of the reaction using:

$$\Delta G° = \Delta H - T\,\Delta S°$$

where T is the absolute temperature (i.e. temperature in degrees kelvin which means that the value of T can never be negative), and S is the entropy of the system (positive for increasing entropy/randomness, negative for decreasing entropy/randomness).

A common MCAT question tests your understanding of the following point: It is Gibbs free energy and not enthalpy that decides spontaneity. Many students think that if a reaction is exothermic (negative ΔH) then it must be spontaneous. This is incorrect and the equation shows us that a negative ΔH can result in a positive ΔG if ΔS is negative and if the temperature is high enough. Note that when it comes to thermodynamics, General Chemistry questions tend to focus on enthalpy but Biochemistry questions tend to focus on Gibbs free energy.

If this reaction happens to be the forward reaction of an equilibrium, the equilibrium constant associated with this equilibrium is simply given by:

$$\Delta G° = -R\,T\,ln\,K_{eq}$$

where R is the ideal gas constant (1.99 cal mol^{-1} K^{-1}) and ln is the natural logarithm (i.e. log to the base *e*).

Note that $\Delta G°$ = -RT(ln K_{eq}) = -2.303RT(log K_{eq})

- If K_{eq} = 1.0 (reaction at equilibrium; log(1) = 0) then ΔG is = 0.
- If K_{eq} is greater than 1, ΔG is negative (process is spontaneous)
- If K_{eq} is less than 1, ΔG is positive (recall that the log of a number below 1 is negative, and the negative of a negative is positive; thus the process is not spontaneous and will proceed in the reverse direction)

2.4.2 Gibbs Free Energy and the Solvation Layer

When a solute dissolves in a solvent, the solvent molecules in very close proximity form a *solvation layer* around the solute. When the solvent is water, which is naturally the norm in Biochemistry, the expressions 'hydration layer' or 'hydration shell' may be used.

Under typical cellular conditions, the enthalpy change for the solvation of nonpolar molecules is negative but the entropy change is also negative and quite large (i.e. unfavorable). Thus the net result (see first equation in BCM 2.4.1) is that Gibbs free energy is large and positive (i.e. not spontaneous, unfavorable). Not surprisingly, this is the basis for hydrophobic bonding (BCM 1.1.1) and the self-assembly of lipid molecules into bilayers and micelles (BCM 1.4), since in both cases, solvation in water is avoided.

Again consider cellular conditions but now there is a protein with polar amino acid residues: Water molecules in the solvation/ hydration layer do not have their random motion restricted in any way, entropy is positive, hydrogen bonding is fluid. Since enthalpy is negative, Gibbs free energy must be negative (spontaneous, favorable; recall: temperature in kelvin is always positive).

2.5 A Closer Look at ATP and Gibbs Free Energy

Why is ATP such a rich source of energy? It is not necessarily the molecule itself that is the source of the energy, but rather, the bonds between the phosphate groups of ATP. One molecule of ATP can be hydrolyzed into ADP + P_i, or AMP + PP_i, both of which release a large amount of energy ($\Delta G°$ = -31 and -45 kJ mol^{-1}, respectively). In comparison, the cleavage of the phosphoester in AMP only releases 13 kJ mol^{-1}, around three times less. Incidentally, those numbers only represent the energy released under standard, laboratory-controlled conditions; in actuality, the values are even higher (around 1.5-times higher). {Note: PP_i is known as *pyrophosphate* or *diphosphate*.}

Both ADP and AMP, as well as the inorganic phosphates, are much more stable than ATP. The negatively charged phosphate groups in ATP contribute to electrostatic repulsion, which is lessened after hydrolysis. While the products of ATP hydrolysis are likewise negatively charged, they are more solvated, which helps shield the charges.

To utilize the release of energy during hydrolysis, as alluded to in BCM 2.4, the process is frequently coupled to an endergonic process, one that has a positive $\Delta G°$ and does not occur spontaneously. Through the process called *phosphorylation*, a phosphate group is transferred from ATP to one of the reactants, which leads to a less stable intermediate. This then reacts with a second substrate to finish a reaction. With the addition of the ATP $\rightarrow$ ADP + P_i reaction, the overall reaction has a negative $\Delta G°$, and thus occurs spontaneously.

An example we can use is the synthesis of glutamine from glutamate and ammonia. Typically, this reaction has a standard Gibbs free energy change of approximately $\Delta G° = +14$ kJ mol^{-1}, which means under normal cellular conditions, it would never occur. In real life, though, this synthesis is driven by ATP. A phosphate group is transferred to glutamate, creating a less stable intermediate. Ammonia displaces the phosphate, completing the synthesis of glutamine. With $\Delta G° = -31$ kJ mol^{-1} for ATP $\rightarrow$ ADP + P_i, the net $\Delta G° = -17$ kJ mol^{-1}, which allows the reaction to proceed spontaneously.

Because of ATP's role as an energy-rich compound, it is present in much higher quantities than either ADP or AMP. Typically, the concentration of ATP in cells is between 2 – 10mM, while the concentration of ADP is under 1 mM, and the concentration of AMP only a small fraction of that. ATP can be regenerated readily through the addition of phosphate to ADP via catabolic pathways, and within the cell via other processes.

2.6 ATP Synthase

The importance of a proton concentration gradient cannot be understated. Without it, life as we know it would simply cease to be - at the very least, it would be drastically different than the biological systems we know of today. Whether energy is extracted from sugars and lipids, or sunlight (via photosynthesis), the end result is the same - a pH gradient across a membrane. For prokaryotes, this is established across the plasma membrane, while in eukaryotes, it is the inner mitochondrial membrane.

This proton gradient is what drives ATP synthase, a protein complex that synthesizes ATP from ADP + Pi (the latter being inorganic phosphate; *see* BCM 1.6, 2.4). Thus energy released from protons moving down their electrochemical gradient from the intermembrane space into the mitochondrial matrix drives the synthesis of ATP by the enzyme ATP synthase. The complex consists of two components (*fractions*), F_o and F_1, both of which have multiple subunits. F_o, which spans the membrane, is comprised

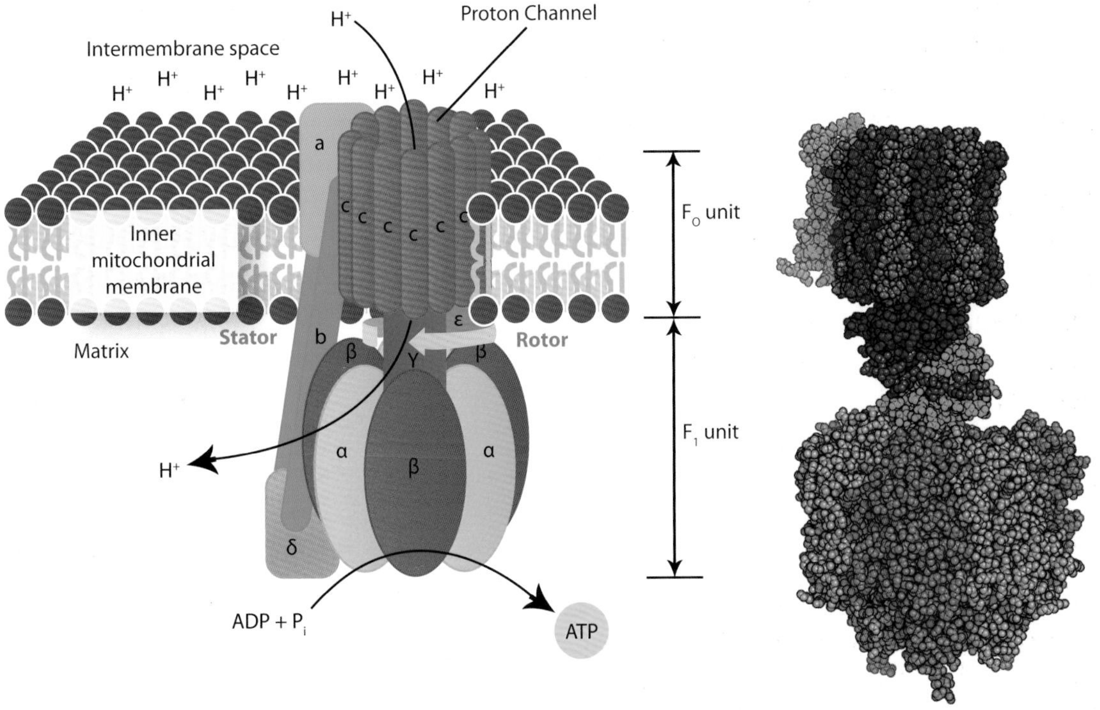

Figure III.A.2.3: Molecular model of ATP synthase (complex V). Do not focus on memorizing the names of subunits but rather consider the form and function of this protein enzyme machine catalyzing a vital process. Notice the rotor component (rotor stalk, like an axle) and the stator component (like an anchor, the stationary part). Since this process is related to osmosis, the diffusion of water across a membrane, it is called *chemiosmosis*. Thus ATP synthase is the enzyme that makes ATP by chemiosmosis. Compare our cartoon representation of ATP synthase to the molecular structure (without the stator component) on the right which was determined by X-ray crystallography (Alex.X - enWiki). X-ray crystallography uses diffraction to identify electron density and the mean positions of atoms in a crystal creating a three-dimensional picture.

of subunits $a_1b_2c_{10\text{-}14}$, with the subscripts denoting how many copies of each are present (the number of c subunits varies based on species; plants and animals have 14). F_1 is present on the inner surface of the membrane, and is comprised of subunits $\alpha_3\beta_3\gamma_1\delta_1\varepsilon_1$. {Note: The first 5 letters of the Greek alphabet are alpha - α, beta - β, gamma γ, delta - δ, epsilon - ε (cf: BCM 1.1).}

The component made up of the c, ε, and γ subunits function as a rotor that physically spins during ATP synthesis. For every rotation of a c subunit past a stationary point, one proton is translocated. The γ subunit likewise rotates, but only 120° at a time, which corresponds with conformational changes in the $\alpha_3\beta_3$ component, which contains three catalytic sites. Depending on which step of the process is occurring, each site is either open, at which point it can accept ADP + P_i or release new ATP; loose, which prevents the escape of ADP + P_i; or tight, when ATP is synthesized.

ATP synthase is essentially an ATP factory. Proton translocation rotates the c "gear," which rotates the γ shaft. And for every 120° rotation of the shaft, one molecule of ATP is synthesized from somewhere in the $\alpha_3\beta_3$ component. Typically, around three protons are translocated through the membrane in exchange for the synthesis of one molecule of ATP. Considering the high concentration of protons outside of the membrane versus the inside, this is a very efficient process; over 100 molecules of ATP can be generated every second.

2.7 Overview of Enzymes

Biochemical reactions are a necessary part of life, occuring in all organisms, and encompassing a wide variety of critical functions. All these biochemical reactions are collectively termed metabolism. In general, metabolism can be broadly divided into two main categories. They are:

(a) Catabolism which is the breakdown of macromolecules (larger molecules) such as glycogen to micromolecules (smaller molecules) such as glucose.

(b) Anabolism which is the building up of macromolecules such as protein using micromolecules such as amino acids. A good way to remember both is to break the terms down into their Greek roots - "cata" means "downward" (think catacombs), like the breaking *down* of macromolecules in catabolism, while "ana" means "upward." It's the same root words that give "cation" (a substance with fewer electrons than protons: +) and "anion" (a substance with more electrons than protons: -) their name.

As we all know, chemical reactions in general involve great energy exchanges when they occur. Similarly, most catabolic and anabolic reactions would involve massive amounts of energy if they were to occur *in vitro* (outside a living organism). However, all these reactions could be carried out *in vivo* (in a living organism) which is an environment of less free energy exchange, using molecules called enzymes.

What is an enzyme?

An enzyme is a protein catalyst. A protein is a large polypeptide made up of amino acid subunits. A catalyst is a substance that alters the rate of a chemical reaction without itself being permanently changed into another compound. A catalyst accelerates a reaction by decreasing the free energy of activation (see diagrams in BCM 2.1).

Six Basic Types of Enzymes

Class of Enzymes	*What They Catalyze*
Oxidoreductases	Redox Reactions
Transferases	The transfer of groups of atoms
Hydrolases	Hydrolysis
Lyases	Additions to a double bond, or the formation of a double bond
Isomerases	The isomerization of molecules
Ligases or synthetases	The joining of two molecules

Enzymes fall into two general categories:

(a) Simple proteins, which contain only amino acids like the digestive enzymes ribonuclease, trypsin and chymotrypsin.

(b) Complex proteins, which contain amino acids and a non-amino acid cofactor. Thus the complete enzyme is called a holoenzyme and is made up of a protein portion (apoenzyme) and a cofactor. Again, a helpful hint from Greek roots - "Apo" means "away from/separate," while "holo" means "whole."

Holoenzyme = Apoenzyme + Cofactor

A metal may serve as a cofactor. Zinc, for example, is a cofactor for the enzymes carbonic anhydrase and carboxypeptidase. An organic molecule such as pyridoxal phosphate or biotin may serve as a cofactor. Cofactors such as biotin, which are covalently linked to the enzyme, are called prosthetic groups or ligands.

In addition to their enormous catalytic power, which accelerates reaction rates, enzymes exhibit exquisite specificity in the types of reactions that each catalyzes, as well as specificity for the substrates upon which they act. Their specificity is linked to the concept of an active site. An *active site* is a cluster of amino acids within the tertiary (i.e. 3-dimensional) configuration of the enzyme where the actual catalytic event occurs. The active site is often similar to a pocket or groove with properties (chemical or structural) that accommodate the intended substrate with high specificity.

The suffix "-ase" is a dead giveaway that the molecule in question is an enzyme. It also gives a hint as to the function of the enzyme. For instance, lactase is responsible for breaking down lactose into glucose and galactose; ligases ligate two molecules

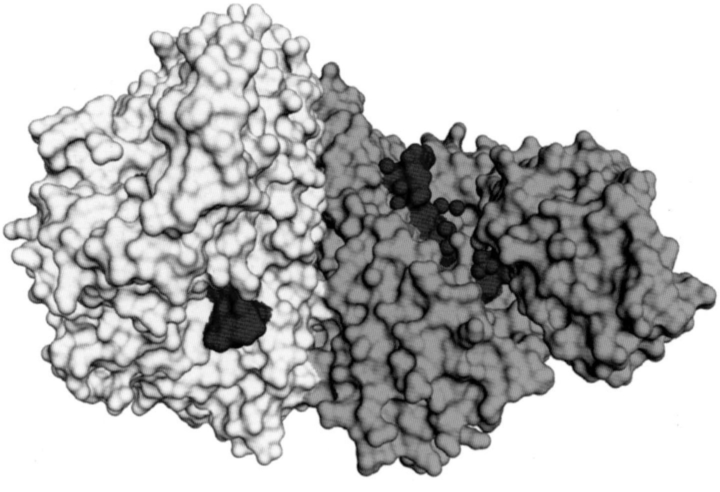

Figure III.A.2.4: Two molecules of human O-GlcNAc transferase, bound to their peptide substrates (dark blue), as determined my X-ray protein crystallography. The active site resembles a groove that selectively binds to its substrate with high specificity. (Protein Data Bank [pdb.org] code: 3PE4)

with covalent bonds; transferases transfer functional groups. Be careful, though - there are also many important enzymes that don't end with -ase, but as a general hint, it works.

Examples of such specificity are as follows: Phosphofructokinase catalyzes a reaction between ATP and fructose-6-phosphate. The enzyme does not catalyze a reaction between other nucleoside triphosphates. It is worth mentioning the specificity of trypsin and chymotrypsin, though both of them are proteolytic (i.e. they degrade or hydrolyse proteins). Trypsin catalyzes the hydrolysis of peptides and proteins only on the carboxyl side of polypeptidic lysine and arginine. Chymotrypsin catalyzes the hydrolysis of peptides and proteins on the carboxyl side of polypeptidic amino acids phenylalanine, tyrosine and tryptophan.

The degree of specificity described in the previous examples originally led to the **Lock and Key Model** which has been generally replaced by the **Induced Fit Hypothesis**. While the former suggests that the spatial structure of the active site of an enzyme fits exactly that of the substrate, the latter is more widely accepted and describes a greater flexibility at the active site and a conformational change in the enzyme to strengthen binding to the substrate.

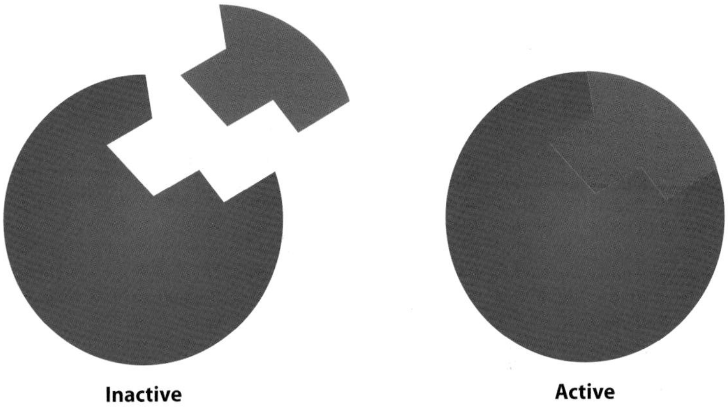

Figure III.A.2.5: Lock and Key model. On the left, the enzyme (blue) is rigid, with a pocket that is highly specific to a particular key, the substrate (red). On the right, when the key enters the lock, the enzyme becomes active.

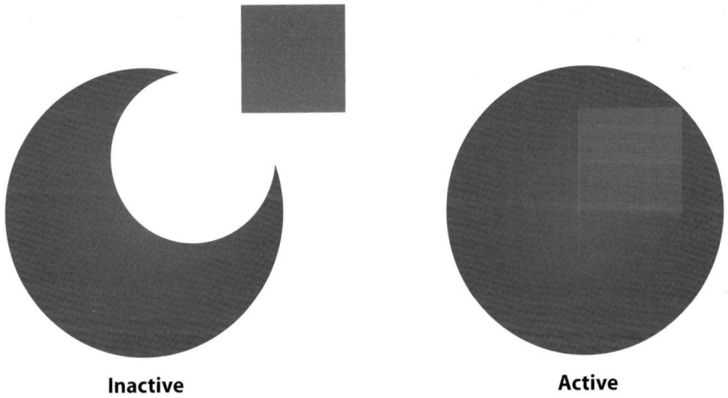

Figure III.A.2.6: Induced fit model. On the left, the active site of the enzyme (blue) is more flexible, but still specific to its substrate (red). On the right, upon binding, the substrate induces a conformational change, allowing the enzyme to change from an inactive form to an active form.

2.8 Enzyme Kinetics and Inhibition

There is an increase in *reaction velocity* (= reaction rate) with an increase in the concentration of substrate. At increasingly higher substrate concentrations, the increase in activity is progressively smaller. From this, it could be inferred that enzymes exhibit saturation kinetics (note: be sure you are comfortable with this concept and the graph - BCM 2.1, 2.9; BIO 1.1.2 - because it is the source of standard MCAT questions). The mechanism of the preceding lies largely with the saturation of the enzyme's active sites. As substrate concentration increases, more and more enzymes are converted to the substrate- bound enzyme complex until all the enzyme active sites are bound to substrate. After this point, further increase in substrate concentration will not increase reaction rate.

Enzyme inhibitors are classified as: competitive inhibitor, noncompetitive inhibitor and irreversible inhibitor. In competitive inhibition, the inhibitor and the substrate are analogues that compete for binding to the active site, forming an unreactive enzyme-inhibitor complex. However, at higher substrate concentration, the inhibition can be reversed. In noncompetitive inhibition, the inhibitor can bind to the enzyme at a site different from the active site where the substrate binds to, thus forming either an unreactive enzyme-inhibitor complex or enzyme-substrate-inhibitor complex. However, a higher substrate concentration does not reverse the inhibition. In irreversible inhibition, the inhibitor binds permanently to the enzyme and inactivates it (e.g. heavy metals, aspirin, organophosphates). The effects caused by irreversible inhibitors are only overcome by synthesis of new enzyme.

2.9 Regulation of Enzyme Activity

The activity of enzymes in the cell is subject to a variety of regulatory mechanisms. The amount of enzyme can be altered by increasing or decreasing its synthesis or degradation. Enzyme induction refers to an enhancement of its synthesis. Repression refers to a decrease in its biosynthesis.

Enzyme activity can also be altered by covalent modification. Phosphorylation of specific serine residues by protein kinases increases or decreases catalytic activity depending upon the enzyme. Proteolytic cleavage of proenzymes or *zymogens* (e.g., chymotrypsinogen, trypsinogen, protease and clotting factors) converts an inactive form to an active form (e.g., chymotrypsin, trypsin, etc.).

Enzyme activity can be greatly influenced by its environment (esp. pH and temperature). For example, most enzymes exhibit optimal activity at a pH in the range 6.5 to 7.5. However, pepsin (an enzyme found in the stomach) has an optimum pH of ~ 2.0. Thus it cannot function adequately at a higher pH (i.e. in the small intestine). Likewise, enzymes function at an optimal temperature. When the temperature is lowered, kinetic energy decreases and thus the rate of reaction decreases. If the temperature is raised too much then the enzyme may become denatured and thus non-functional.

Enzyme activity can also be modified by an *allosteric* mechanism which involves binding to a site other than the active site.

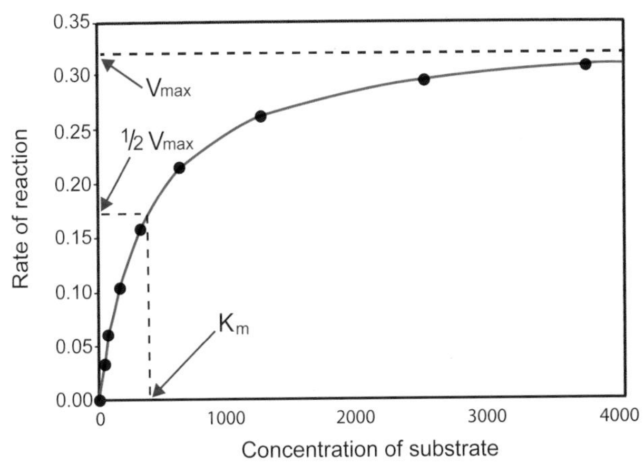

Michaelis-Menten Kinetics: Enzymes with single-substrate mechanisms usually follow the Michaelis-Menten model, in which the plot of velocity vs. substrate concentration [S] produces a rectangular hyperbola. Initially, the reaction rate [V] increases as substrate concentration [S] increases over a range of substrate concentration. However, as [S] gets higher, the enzyme becomes saturated with substrate and eventually the reaction rate [V] reaches maximum velocity V_{max} when the enzyme is fully saturated with substrate. Compare the diagram above with the curve of carrier-mediated transport (i.e. showing saturation kinetics) for solutes crossing the plasma membrane in BIO 1.1.2. The K_m is the substrate concentration at which an enzyme-catalyzed reaction occurs at half its maximal velocity, $V_{max}/2$. K_m is called the Michaelis constant. Each enzyme has a unique K_m value.

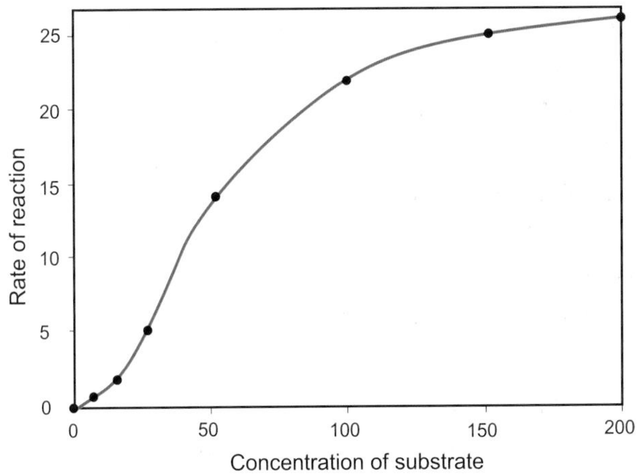

Non-Michaelis-Menten Kinetics: Some enzymes with multiple-substrate mechanisms exhibit the non-Michaelis-Menten model, in which the plot of velocity vs. substrate concentration [S] produces a sigmoid curve. This characterizes cooperative binding of substrate to the active site, which means that the binding of one substrate to one subunit affects the binding of subsequent substrate molecules to other subunits. This behavior is most common in multimeric enzymes with several active sites. Positive cooperativity occurs when binding of the first substrate increases the affinity of the other active sites for the following substrates. Negative cooperativity occurs when binding of the first substrate decreases the affinity of the other active site for the following substrates.

Fig. IV. A.2.7 Enzyme Kinetic Curve Plot.

Isocitrate dehydrogenase is an enzyme in the Krebs Tricarboxylic Acid Cycle, which is activated by ADP. ADP is not a substrate or substrate analogue. It is postulated to bind to a site *distinct* from the active site called the *allosteric site.* Positive effectors stabilize the more active form of enzyme and enhance enzyme activity, while negative effectors stabilize the less active form of enzyme and inhibit enzyme activity.

Some enzymes fail to behave by simple saturation kinetics. In such cases a phenomenon called positive cooperativity is explained, in which binding of one substrate or ligand shifts the enzyme from the less active form to the more active form, and makes it easier for the second substrate to bind. Instead of a hyperbolic curve of velocity vs. substrate concentration [S] that many enzymes follow, sigmoid curve of velocity vs. [S] characterizes cooperativity (i.e. see the Enzyme Kinetic Curve Plot in this section as well as hemoglobin and myoglobin, BIO 7.5.1).

2.10 Biological pH Buffers

A pH buffer is like a molecular sponge for protons. They are molecules which have the ability to minimize changes in pH when an acid - or base - is added to it.

Plasma pH is normally maintained at 7.4. A pH less than 7.35 is acidosis, whereas a pH of greater than 7.45 is alkalosis. Either condition can be a result of either respiratory or metabolic changes.

It is expected for the MCAT that you have an understanding of the chemistry of buffers including pH, pK_a, titration and the Henderson-Hasselbalch Equation (GS MCAT General Chemistry Chapter 6). These fundamental concepts will not be reviewed here.

It should be noted that the major buffer system in extracellular fluids (BIO 7.6) is the CO_2-bicarbonate buffer system mediated by the enzyme carbonic anhydrase (BIO 12.4.1). This is responsible for about 75% of extracellular buffering. Protein and phosphate buffers dominate the intracellular space. Other buffer systems, though important, have a lesser impact and include ammonia (urine), calcium carbonate (bone), hemoglobin (red blood cells), and many others.

The amino acid histidine is a very good physiologic buffer (mentioned in BCM 1.1.2). Among the reasons is that its pK_a of 6.5 is not far from plasma pH and when protonated, it is resonance stabilized. Histidine is one of the building blocks of carbonic anhydrase, hemoglobin and many other proteins.

Major Buffer Systems of the Human Body

Bicarbonate buffer	$CO_2 + H_2O \rightleftharpoons H_2CO_3 \rightleftharpoons H^+ + HCO_3^-$	In blood plasma, interstitial fluids
Hemoglobin	$Hb\text{-}H \rightleftharpoons Hb^- + H^+$	Interior of red blood cells
Phosphate buffer	$H_2PO_4^- \rightleftharpoons H^+ + HPO_4^{2-}$	Most important in urine but also intracellular fluid
Protein	$Pr\text{–}H \rightleftharpoons Pr^- + H^+$	Most important in intracellular fluid with a relatively minor effect in blood

2.10.1 Acidosis and Alkalosis

Although buffers in the body fluids help resist changes in pH, the respiratory system and the kidneys regulate the pH of the body fluids. Malfunctions of either the respiratory system or renal system can result in acidosis or alkalosis which may be beyond the capacity of the buffers to repair without the intervention of one of these organ systems.

Respiratory acidosis occurs with an increase in concentration (= partial pressure) of carbon dioxide (i.e. impaired breathing or ventilation as seen in COPD, chronic obstructive pulmonary disease which includes chronic bronchitis and emphysema). The result is a lowered ratio of bicarbonate to pCO_2 resulting in a decrease in pH (acidosis; see BIO 12.4.1). The acidosis is reversed gradually when kidneys increase the rate at which they secrete hydrogen ions into the filtrate and increase the absorption of bicarbonate.

Metabolic acidosis can result from the loss of bicarbonate ions (i.e. severe diarrhea) or the accumulation of metabolic acids (i.e. lactic acid, keto acids). This can lead to severe metabolic complications warranting intravenous bicarbonate therapy. The reduced pH stimulates the respiratory center which causes hyperventilation. During hyperventilation, carbon dioxide is eliminated at a greater rate.

Respiratory alkalosis occurs during hyperventilation, when excessive carbon dioxide is eliminated from the system (which lowers pCO_2), the pH of the blood increases, resulting in alkalosis. This can be seen in conditions such as hysteria, stroke and hepatic (liver) failure. The kidneys help to compensate for respiratory alkalosis by decreasing the rate of hydrogen ions secretion into the urine and the rate of bicarbonate ion reabsorption.

Metabolic alkalosis generally results when bicarbonate levels are higher in the blood. This can be observed, for example, after sustained vomiting of acidic gastric juices. Kidneys compensate for alkalosis by increasing the excretion of bicarbonate ions. The increased pH inhibits respiration. Reduced respiration allows carbon dioxide to accumulate in the body fluids.

GOLD STANDARD WARM-UP EXERCISES

CHAPTER 2: Enzymes, Thermodynamics, and Buffers

1) Which of the following must be true for a reaction to occur spontaneously?
   A. ΔG must be negative
   B. ΔH must be negative
   C. ΔS must be positive
   D. More than one of the above

2) A biochemical reaction at constant temperature and pressure in a cellular environment is at equilibrium when the absolute temperature is equal to which of the following?
   A. 0
   B. $-(\Delta H)(\Delta S)$
   C. $-RT \log K_{eq}$
   D. $\Delta H/\Delta S$

3) When glucose monomers are joined together by glycosidic linkages to form a glycogen polymer, the changes in free energy, total energy, and entropy are as follows:
   A. $+\Delta G, -\Delta H, -\Delta S$
   B. $-\Delta G, +\Delta H, +\Delta S$
   C $+\Delta G, +\Delta H, -\Delta S$
   D. $+\Delta G, +\Delta H, +\Delta S$

4) Oxidation of fats and carbohydrates within a cell would be an example of:
   A. biosynthesis.
   B. catabolism.
   C. anabolism.
   D. positive co-operativity.

5) If individuals with PKU disease lack the protein phenylalanine hydroxylase, what would best explain their being able to metabolize small amounts of phenylalanine?
   A. Non-specificenzymes cleave phenylalanine.
   B. Phenylalanine catalyzes reactions in theliver.
   C. Phenylalanine is broken down mechanically in the formation of chyme in the stomach.
   D. Phenylalanine is defecated from the body.

6) Phenylalanine hydroxylase most likely:
   A. cleaves a $-OCH_3$ group from phenylalanine.
   B. adds a $-OCH_3$ group to phenylalanine.
   C. cleaves a $-OH_2$ group from phenylalanine.
   D. adds a -OH group to phenylalanine.

7) Prostaglandins are complex lipid molecules, some of which mediate the sensation of pain. Aspirin, a common pain reliever, likely works by:
   A. acting like a non-competitive reversible inhibitor and binding to the active site on the prostaglandin molecule.
   B. acting like a competitive inhibitor and binding to a site other than the active site on the prostaglandin molecule.
   C. acting like an allosteric inhibitor of the prostaglandin molecule.
   D. inhibiting the synthesis of the prostaglandin molecule.

8) The three most important buffer systems in body fluids include the bicarbonate buffer system, the phosphate buffer system, and which of the following?

A. Hemoglobin
B. Protein
C. Sodium benzoate
D. Calcium carbonate

9) What is the most effective intracellular inorganic buffer?

A. Phosphate
B. Protein
C. Hemoglobin
D. Bicarbonate

10) What is the normal pH of blood?

A. 7.3-7.4
B. 7.25-7.35
C. 7-8
D. 7.35-7.45

For the following 3 questions, you can answer as "open book" practice questions. Since the MCAT would more likely ask these 3 questions in the context that they were preceded by an explanatory passage, you can consider the content in section 2.10 and 2.10.1.

11) Diabetic ketoacidosis is an example of which of the following imbalances?

A. Respiratory acidosis
B. Respiratory alkalosis
C. Metabolic acidosis
D. Metabolic alkalosis

12) All of the following can be seen as a consequence of vomiting EXCEPT one. Which one is the EXCEPTION?

A. Metabolic alkalosis
B. Dehydration
C. Metabolic acidosis
D. Respiratory alkalosis

13) Normal pCO_2 is 40 mmHg with the normal range being 35-45 mmHg. If a patient's pH is 7.3 and pCO_2 is 50 mmHg, the patient must have:

A. respiratory acidosis.
B. respiratory alkalosis.
C. metabolic acidosis.
D. metabolic alkalosis.

GS ANSWER KEY

CHAPTER 2

		Cross-Reference			Cross-Reference
1.	A	BCM 2.4, 2.5	8.	B	BCM 2.10, 2.11
2.	D	BCM 2.4	9.	A	BCM 2.10, 2.11
3.	C	BCM 1.1.3, 1.3.2, 1.3.3, 2.3	10.	D	BCM 2.10, 2.11
4.	B	BCM 2.7, 2.9	11.	A	BCM 2.10, 2.11
5.	A	BCM 2.7, 2.9	12	B	BCM 2.10, 2.11; BIO 9.4.2
6.	D	BIO 3.0, 1.2.1, BCM 2.7	13.	A	BCM 2.10, 2.11; BIO 12.4.1
7.	D	BCM 1.4, 2.7, 3.1			

* Explanations can be found at the back of the book.

APPENDIX

CHAPTER 2: Enzymes, Thermodynamics, and Buffers

Practice MCAT Passage: The Symmetry Model (MWC Model)

Several models have been developed for relating changes in dissociation constants to changes in the tertiary and quaternary structures of oligomeric proteins. One model suggests that the protein's subunits can exist in either of two distinct conformations, R and T. At equilibrium, there are few R conformation molecules: 10 000 T to 1 R and it is an important feature of the enzyme that this ratio does not change. The substrate is assumed to bind more tightly to the R form than to the T form, which means that binding of the substrate favors the transition from the T conformation to R.

The conformational transitions of the individual subunits are assumed to be tightly linked, so that if one subunit flips from T to R the others must do the same. The binding of the first molecule of substrate thus promotes the binding of the second and if substrate is added continuously, all of the enzyme will be in the R form and act on the substrate. Because the concerted transition of all of the subunits from T to R or back, preserves the overall symmetry of the protein, this model is called the symmetry model (= the concerted model or MWC model, an acronym for Monod-Wyman-Changeux). The model further predicts that allosteric activating enzymes make the R conformation even more reactive with the substrate while allosteric inhibitors react with the T conformation so that most of the enzyme is held back in the T shape.

14) What assumption is made about the T and R conformations and the substrate?

A. In the absence of any substrate, the T conformation predominates.
B. In the absence of any substrate, the R conformation predominates.
C. In the absence of any substrate, the T and R conformations are in equilibrium.
D. In the absence of any substrate, the enzyme exists in another conformation, S.

15) The substrate binds more tightly to R because:

A. T has a higher affinity for the substrate than R.
B. R has a higher affinity for the substrate than T.
C. there are 10 000 times more T conformation molecules than R conformation molecules.
D. the value of the equilibrium constant does not change.

16) The symmetry model would NOT account for an enzyme:

A. with many different biologically active conformations.
B. which engages in positive cooperativity.
C. with a complex metal cofactor.
D. which is a catalyst for anabolic reactions.

17) Allosteric enzymes differ from other enzymes in that they:

A. are not denatured at high temperatures.
B. are regulated by compounds which are not their substrates and which do not bind to their active sites.
C. they operate at an optimum pH of about 2.0.
D. they are not specific to just one substrate.

18) The symmetry model describes a form of cooperative binding. Most enzymes do not engage in cooperative binding. The predicted shape of a graph representing the addition of substrate to most enzymes over a period of time would be expected to be:

A. a hyperbola.
B. a straight line with a positive slope.
C. a straight line with a negative slope.
D. sigmoidal.

19) The relationship between T and R is best described as which of the following?

A. Different molecules
B. Structural isomers
C. Stereoisomers
D. Functional group isomers

20) For the next question, consider the following diagram.

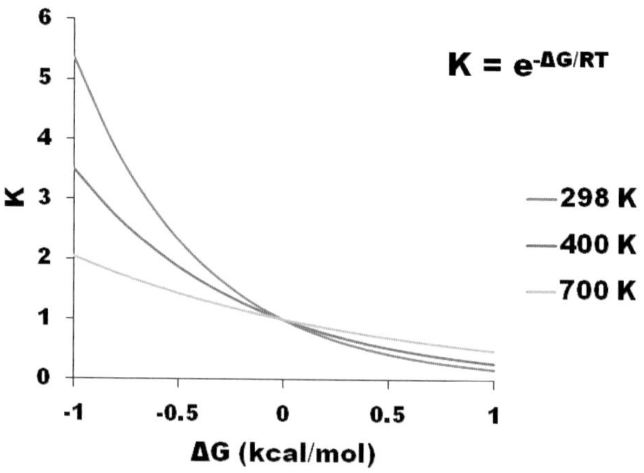

Figure 1: Equilibrium distribution of two conformers at different temperatures given the free energy of their interconversion. (Mr.Holmium)

All of the following statements are consistent with Figure 1 EXCEPT:

A. The products must have less free energy than the reactants in the exergonic reactions at the various temperatures.
B. The equation for the equilibrium constant K used to construct the graph is derived from $\Delta G = -RT \ln K_{eq}$.
C. The 3 different temperature curves intersect at a point where the reaction is at equilibrium.
D. Higher temperatures favor relatively more of the more stable conformer.

ANSWER KEY

ADVANCED TOPICS - CHAPTER 2

		Cross-Reference
14.	A	P1
15.	B	BCM 2.7, 2.8, 2.9
16.	A	BCM 2.7, 2.8, 2.9, BIO 7.5.1
17.	B	BCM 2.7,2.8, 2.9
18.	A	BCM 2.7,2.8, 2.9
19.	C	ORG 2.1, 2.2, 2.3
20.	D	Deduce; BCM 2.2-2.5

P = paragraph; *S* = sentence; *E* = equation; *T* = table; *F* = figure

GOLD NO[illegible]ES

CELLULAR METABOLISM
Chapter 3

Memorize

* Substrates/products, especially: Acetyl CoA, pyruvate
* Enzymes: kinase, phosphatase
* Basic steps

Understand

* Krebs cycle, electron transport chain: main features
* Oxidative phosphorylation, substrates and products, general features
* Metabolism: carbohydrates (glucose), fats and proteins

Clinical Correlation

"Inborn errors of metabolism" are genetic disorders in which the body cannot properly turn food into energy. The majority are due to defects of single genes that code for enzymes that help convert some molecules (substrates) into others (products). Based on the study of these disorders the "one gene-one enzyme" hypothesis developed over a century ago.

MCAT-Prep.com

Introduction

Cells require energy to grow, reproduce, maintain structure, respond to the environment, etc. Biochemical reactions and other energy producing processes that occur in cells, including cellular metabolism, are regulated in part by enzymes.

Optional Gold Standard Resources

Free Forum

Online videos

Flashcards

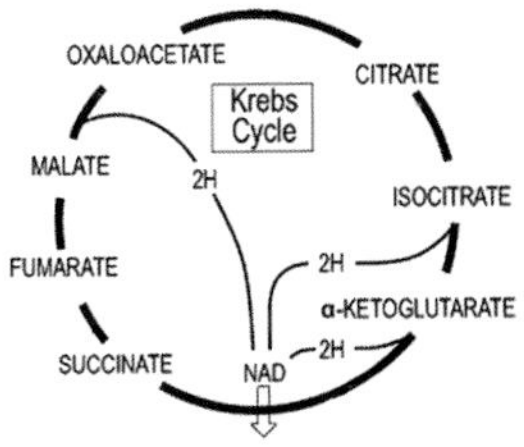

Special Guest

3.1 Bioenergetics

Biological species must transform energy into readily available sources in order to survive. ATP (adenosine triphosphate) is the body's most important short-term energy storage molecule. It can be produced by the breakdown or oxidation of protein, lipids (i.e. fat) or carbohydrates (esp. glucose). If the body is no longer ingesting sources of energy, it can access its own stores; glucose is stored in the liver as glycogen, lipids are stored throughout the body as fat, and ultimately, muscle can be catabolized to release protein (esp. amino acids).

We will be examining four key processes that can lead to the production of ATP: glycolysis, Krebs Citric Acid Cycle, the electron transport chain (ETC), and oxidative phosphorylation. Figure IV.A.4.1 is a schematic summary.

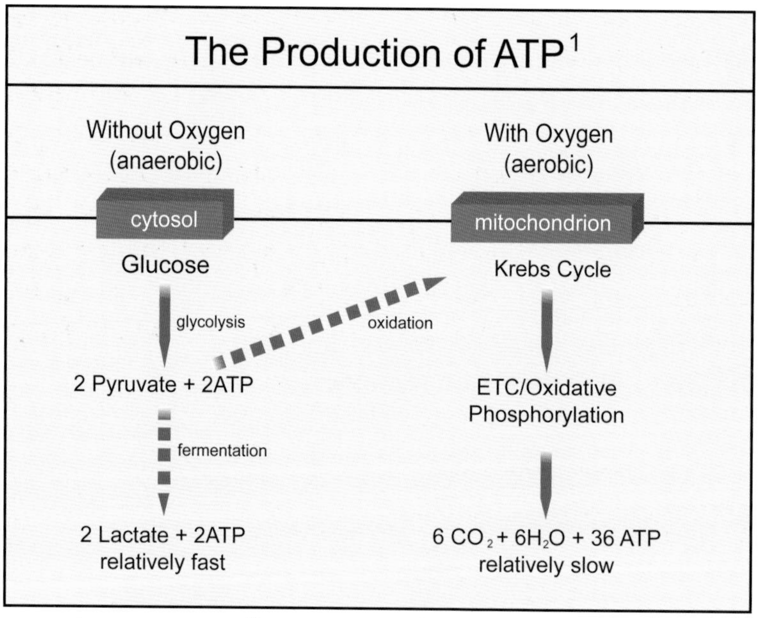

[1]from 1 molecule of glucose

Figure IV.A.3.1: Summary of ATP production.
Evolving research suggests that the actual yield per molecule glucose of aerobic respiration is somewhat less than 36 ATP.

3.2 Glycolysis: A Negative Perspective

An interesting way to summarize the main events of glycolysis is to follow the fate of the phosphate group which contains a negative charge (BCM 1.6). Note that *kinases* and *phosphatases* are enzymes that can add or subtract phosphate groups, respectively.

The first event in glycolysis is the phosphorylation of glucose, in which a phosphoryl group is transferred from the ATP to glucose. This results in the glucose becoming negatively charged, which prevents it from leaking out of the cell. Then glucose-6-phosphate becomes its isomer (= *same* molecular formula, *different* structure; ORG 2.1) fructose-6-phosphate which is further phosphorylated to fructose-1,6-diphosphate. Imagine that this six carbon sugar (*fructose*) now contains two large negatively charged ligands which repel each other! The six carbon sugar (*hexose*) sensibly breaks into two three-carbon compounds (*triose phosphates*).

A triose phosphate is ultimately converted to 1,3-diphosphoglycerate which is clearly an unstable compound (i.e. *two negative phosphate groups*). Thus it transfers a high energy phosphate group onto ADP to produce ATP. When ATP is produced from a substrate (i.e. 1,3-diphosphoglycerate), the reaction is called *substrate level phosphorylation*.

A closer look at ATP and glycolysis: from one molecule of glucose, 2 molecules of pyruvate are obtained. During the glycolytic reaction, 2 ATP are used (one used in the phosphorylation of glucose to glucose 6-phosphate and one used in the phosphorylation of fructose 6-phosphate to fructose 1,6-bisphosphate) and 4 ATP are generated (two in the conversion of 1,3-bisphophoglycerate to 3-phosphoglycerate and two in the conversion of phosphoenolpyruvate to pyruvate).

3.3 Glycolysis: Step by Step

The initial steps in the catabolism or *lysis* of D-glucose constitute the Embden - Meyerhof glyco*lytic* pathway. This pathway can occur in the absence of oxygen (anaerobic). The enzymes for glycolysis are present in all human cells and are located in the cytosol. The overall reaction can be depicted as follows (ADP: adenosine diphosphate, NAD: nicotinamide adenine dinucleotide, P_i: inorganic phosphate):

$$\text{Glucose} + 2\text{ADP} + 2\ \text{NAD}^+ + 2\text{P}_i \longrightarrow 2\text{Pyruvate} + 2\text{ATP} + 2\text{NADH} + 2\text{H}^+$$

Note that the preceding is the *net* reaction. The first stage (hexose stage) of glycolysis consumes two molecules of ATP, converting them into ADP. In the second stage (triose stage), four molecules of ATP are formed for each molecule of glucose metabolized. Thus, with two ATP consumed and four ATP produced, the net ATP production per glucose metabolized is two. The first step in glycolysis involves the phosphorylation of glucose by ATP. The enzyme that catalyzes this irreversible reaction is either hexokinase or glucokinase. Phosphohexose isomerase then catalyzes the conversion of glucose-6-phosphate to fructose-6-phosphate. Phosphofructokinase (PFK) catalyzes the second phosphorylation. It is an irreversible reaction. This reaction also utilizes 1 ATP. This step, which produces fructose-1,6-diphosphate, is said to be the rate limiting or pacemaker step in glycolysis. Aldolase then catalyzes the cleavage of fructose-1,6-diphosphate to glyceraldehyde-3-phosphate and dihydroxyacetone phosphate (= 2 triose phosphates). Triose phosphate isomerase catalyzes the interconversion of the two preceding compounds. Glyceraldehyde-3-phosphate dehydrogenase mediates a reaction between the designated triose, NAD^+ and P_i to yield 1,3-diphosphoglycerate.

Next, phosphoglycerate kinase catalyzes the reaction of the latter, an energy rich compound, with ADP to yield ATP and phosphoglycerate. This reaction generates 2 ATP per glucose molecule. Phosphoglycerate mutase catalyzes the transfer of the phosphoryl group to carbon two to yield 2-phosphoglycerate. Enolase catalyzes a dehydration reaction to yield phosphoenolpyruvate and water. The enzyme enolase is inhibited by fluoride at high, nonphysiological concentrations. This is why blood samples that are drawn for estimation of glucose are added to fluoride to inhibit glycolysis. Phosphoenolpyruvate is then acted upon by pyruvate kinase to yield pyruvate which is a three carbon compound and 2 ATP.

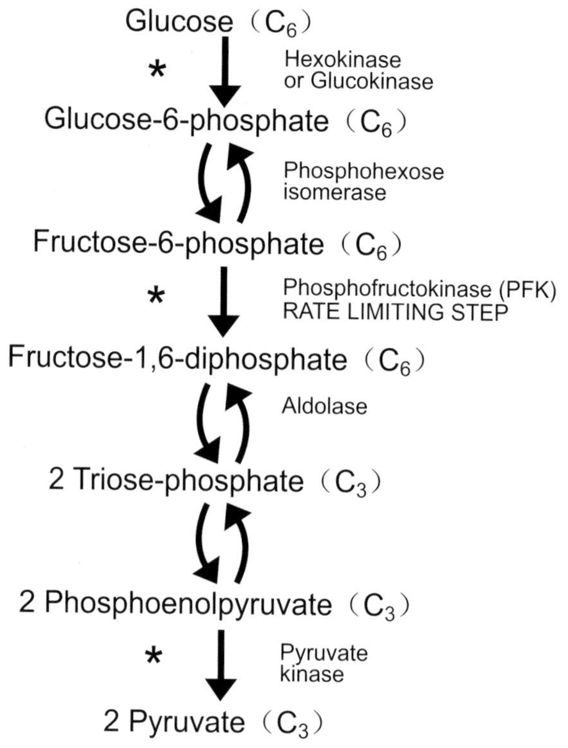

The symbol in brackets represents the number of carbons in each compound. The asterix represents steps which are functionally irreversible under physiologic conditions. PFK is involved in the rate limiting step which is activated by ADP and inhibited by ATP.

Figure IV.A.3.2: Summary of glycolysis.

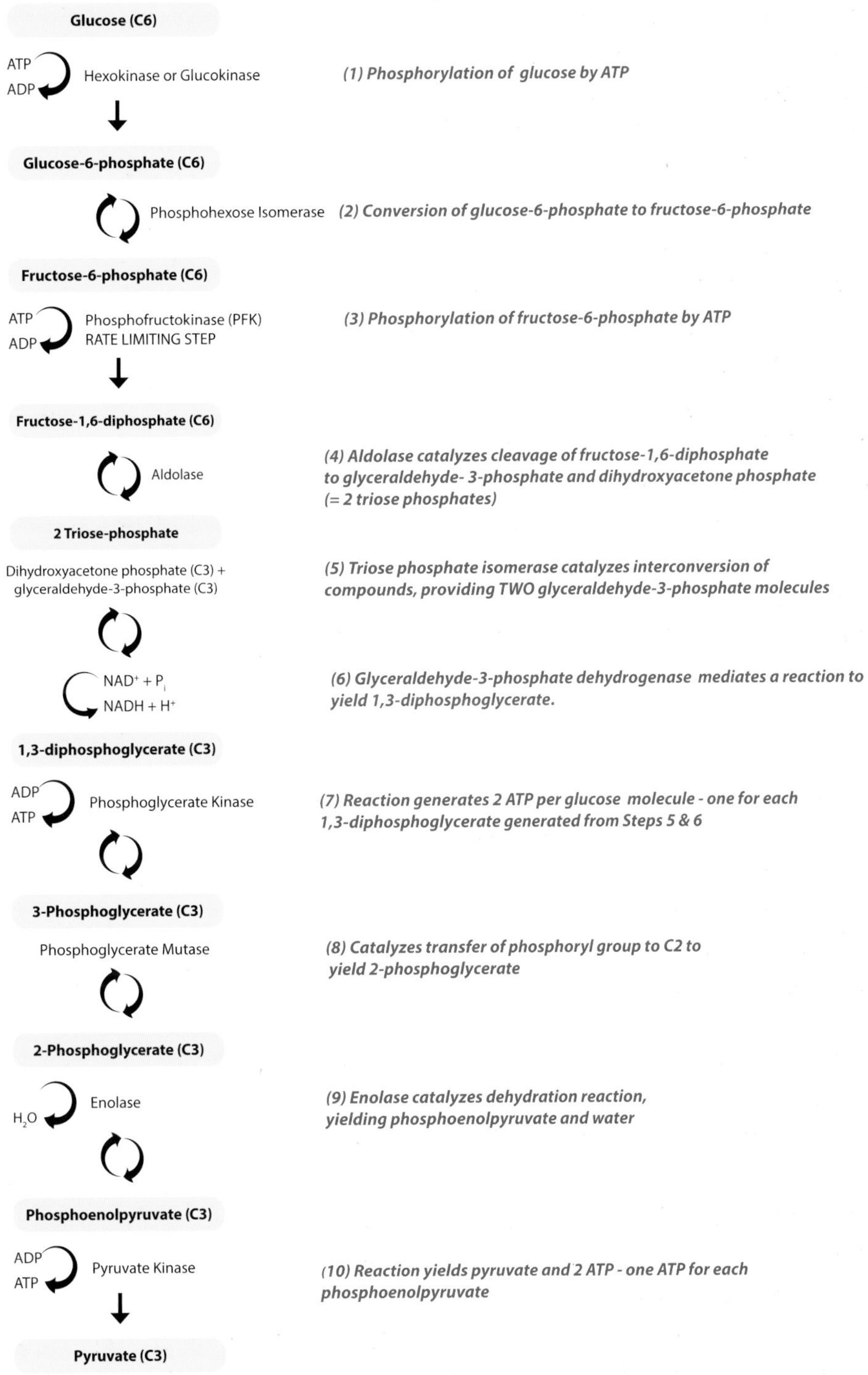

Figure IV.A.3.3: More detailed summary of glycolysis.

NADH produced in glycolysis must regenerate NAD^+ so that glycolysis can continue. Under **aerobic** conditions (i.e. in the presence of oxygen) pyruvate is converted to Acetyl CoA which will enter the Krebs Cycle followed by oxidative phosphorylation producing a total of 38 ATP per molecule of glucose (i.e. 2 pyruvate). Electrons from NADH are transferred to the electron transfer chain located on the inside of the inner mitochondrial membrane and thus NADH produced during glycolysis in the cytosol is converted back to NAD^+.

Under **anaerobic conditions**, pyruvate is quickly reduced by NADH to lactic acid using the enzyme lactate dehydrogenase and NAD^+ is regenerated. A net of only 2 ATP is produced per molecule of glucose (this process is called *fermentation*).

Oxygen Debt: After running a 100m dash, you may find yourself gasping for air even if you have completely ceased activity. This is because during the race you could not get an adequate amount of oxygen to your muscles and your muscles needed energy quickly; thus the anaerobic pathway was used. The lactic acid which built up during the race will require you to *pay back* a certain amount of oxygen in order to oxidize lactate to pyruvate and continue along the more energy-efficient aerobic pathway.

3.4 Krebs Citric Acid Cycle

Aerobic conditions: for further breakdown of pyruvate to occur, it has to enter the mitochondria where a series of reactions will cleave the molecule to water and carbon dioxide. All these reactions (which were discovered by Hans. A. Krebs) are collectively known as the Tricarboxylic Acid Cycle (TCA) or Krebs Citric Acid Cycle. Not only carbohydrates, but also lipids and proteins use the TCA for channelling their metabolic pathways. This is why the TCA is often called the final common pathway of metabolism.

The glycolysis of glucose (C_6) produces 2 pyruvate (C_3), which in turn produces 2 CO_2 and 2 acetyl CoA (C_2). Pyruvate is oxidized to acetyl CoA and CO_2 by the pyruvate dehydrogenase complex (PDC). The PDC is a complex of 3 enzymes located in the mitochondria of eukaryotic cells (and of course, in the cytosol of prokaryotes). This step is also known as the *link reaction* or *transition step* since it links glycolysis and the TCA cycle.

The catabolism of both glucose and fatty acids yield acetyl CoA. Metabolism of amino acids yields acetyl CoA or actual intermediates of the TCA Cycle. The Citric Acid Cycle provides a pathway for the oxidation of acetyl CoA. The pathway includes eight discrete steps. Seven of the enzyme activities are found in the mitochondrial matrix; the eighth (succinate dehydrogenase) is associated with the Electron Transport Chain (ETC) within the inner mitochondrial membrane.

The following includes key points to remember about the TCA Cycle: i) glucose → 2 acetyl CoA → 2 turns around the TCA Cycle; ii) 2 CO_2 per turn is generated as a waste product, which will eventually be blown off in the lungs; iii) one GTP (guanosine triphosphate) per turn is produced by substrate level phosphorylation; one GTP is equivalent to one ATP (*GTP + ADP → GDP + ATP*); iv) *reducing equivalents* are hydrogens which are carried by NAD^+ (→ NADH + H^+) three times per turn and FAD (→ $FADH_2$) once per turn; v) for each molecule of glucose, 2 pyruvates are produced and oxidized to acetyl CoA in the "fed" state (as opposed to the "fasting" state). The acetyl CoA then enters the TCA cycle, yielding 3 NADH, 1 $FADH_2$, and 1 GTP per acetyl CoA. These reducing equivalents will eventually be oxidized to produce ATP (*oxidative phosphorylation*) and eventually produce H_2O as a waste product (the last step in the ETC); vi) the hydrogens (*H*) which are reducing equivalents are not protons (*H^+*) - quite the contrary! Often the reducing equivalents are simply called electrons.

3.5 Oxidative Phosphorylation

The term oxidative phosphorylation refers to reactions associated with oxygen consumption and the phosphorylation of ADP to yield ATP. The synthesis of ATP is coupled to the flow of electrons from NADH and $FADH_2$ to O_2 in the electron transport chain. Oxidative phosphorylation is associated with an Electron Transport Chain, or Respiratory Chain which is found in the inner mitochondrial membrane of eukaryotes. A similar process occurs within the plasma membrane of prokaryotes such as *E.coli*.

The importance of oxidative phosphorylation is that it accounts for the reoxidation of reducing equivalents generated in the reactions of the Krebs Cycle as well as in glycolysis. This process accounts for the preponderance of ATP production in humans. The electron flow from NADH and $FADH_2$ to oxygen by a series of carrier molecules located in the inner mitochondrial membrane (IMM) provides energy to pump hydrogens from the mitochondrial matrix to the intermembrane space against the proton electrochemical gradient. The proton motive force then drives the movement of hydrogen back into the matrix thus providing the energy for ATP synthesis by ATP synthase (BCM 2.6). A schematic summary is in Figure IV.A.4.4.

The term *chemiosmosis* refers to the movement of protons across the IMM (a selectively permeable membrane) down their

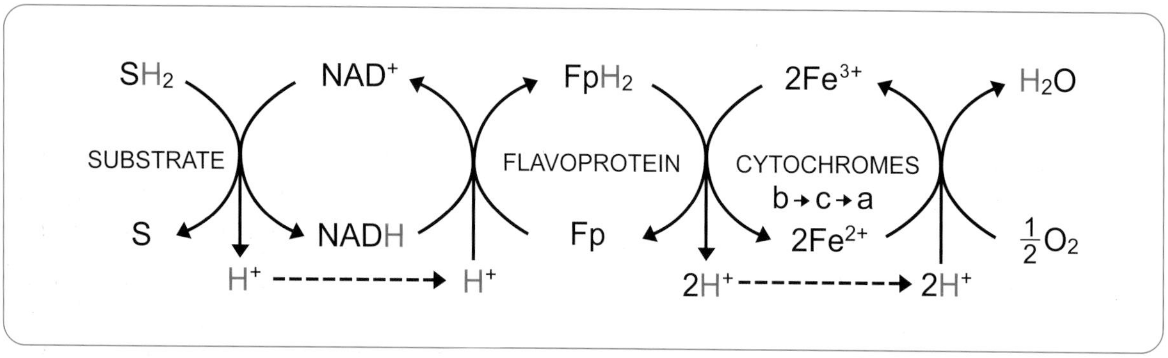

Figure IV.A.35: Transport of reducing equivalents through the respiratory chain. Examples of substrates (S) which provide reductants are isocitrate, malate, etc. Cytochromes contain iron (Fe).

electrochemical gradient using the kinetic energy to phosphorylate ADP making ATP. The generation of ATP by chemiosmosis occurs in chloroplasts and mitochondria as well as in some bacteria. ATP synthase is the enzyme that makes ATP by chemiosmosis (BCM 2.6).

3.6 Electron Transport Chain (ETC)

The electron transport chain is as large and complex as it is vital to life – it plays a large role in generating a proton electrochemical gradient, necessary for ATP synthesis. It's comprised of four complexes, each made up of several protein subunits and cofactors.

The following are the components of the ETC: iron – sulphur proteins, cytochromes c, b, a and coenzyme Q or *ubiquinone*. The respiratory chain proceeds from NAD specific dehydrogenases through flavoprotein, ubiquinone, then cytochromes and ultimately molecular oxygen. Reducing equivalents can enter the chain at two locations. Electrons from NADH are transferred to NADH dehydrogenase. In reactions involving iron - sulphur proteins, electrons are transferred to coenzyme Q; protons are translocated from the mitochondrial matrix to the exterior of the inner membrane during this process. This creates a proton gradient, which is coupled to the production of ATP by ATP synthase.

Electrons entering from succinate dehydrogenase ($FADH_2$) are donated directly to coenzyme Q. Electrons are transported from reduced coenzyme Q to cytochrome b and then cytochrome c. Electrons are then carried by cytochrome c to cytochrome a. Cytochrome a is also known as *cytochrome oxidase*. It catalyzes the reaction of electrons and protons with molecular oxygen to produce water. Cyanide and carbon monoxide are powerful inhibitors of cytochrome oxidase.

3.7 Summary of Energy Production

Note the following: i) 1 NADH produces 3 ATP molecules while 1 $FADH_2$ produces only 2 ATP; ii) there is a cost of 2 ATP to get the two molecules of NADH generated in the cytoplasm (see point number 2. in the table below) to enter the mitochondrion, thus the *net yield for eukaryotes is 36 ATP.*

The efficiency of ATP production is far from 100%. Energy is lost from the system primarily in the form of heat. Under standard conditions, less than 40% of the energy generated from the complete oxidation of glucose is converted to the production of ATP. For some perspective, the first piston steam engine, developed around 1710, was slightly over one half percent (0.5%) efficient. Today's gasoline internal combustion engine has an efficiency rating of about 25-35%, and increasing.

More recent research suggests that further inefficiencies during respiration may reduce the net theoretical yield into the 30-32 ATP range (per molecule glucose).

Process of reaction	ATP yield
1. Glycolysis (Glucose → 2 Pyruvate)	2
2. Glycolysis (2NADH from glyceraldehyde-3-phosphate dehydrogenase)	6
3. Pyruvate dehydrogenase (2NADH)	6
4. Isocitrate dehydrogenase (2NADH)	6
5. Alpha-ketoglutarate dehydrogenase (2NADH)	6
6. Succinate thiokinase (2GTP)	2
7. Succinate dehydrogenase ($2FADH_2$)	4
8. Malate dehydrogenase (2NADH)	6
TOTAL	38 ATP yield per hexose.

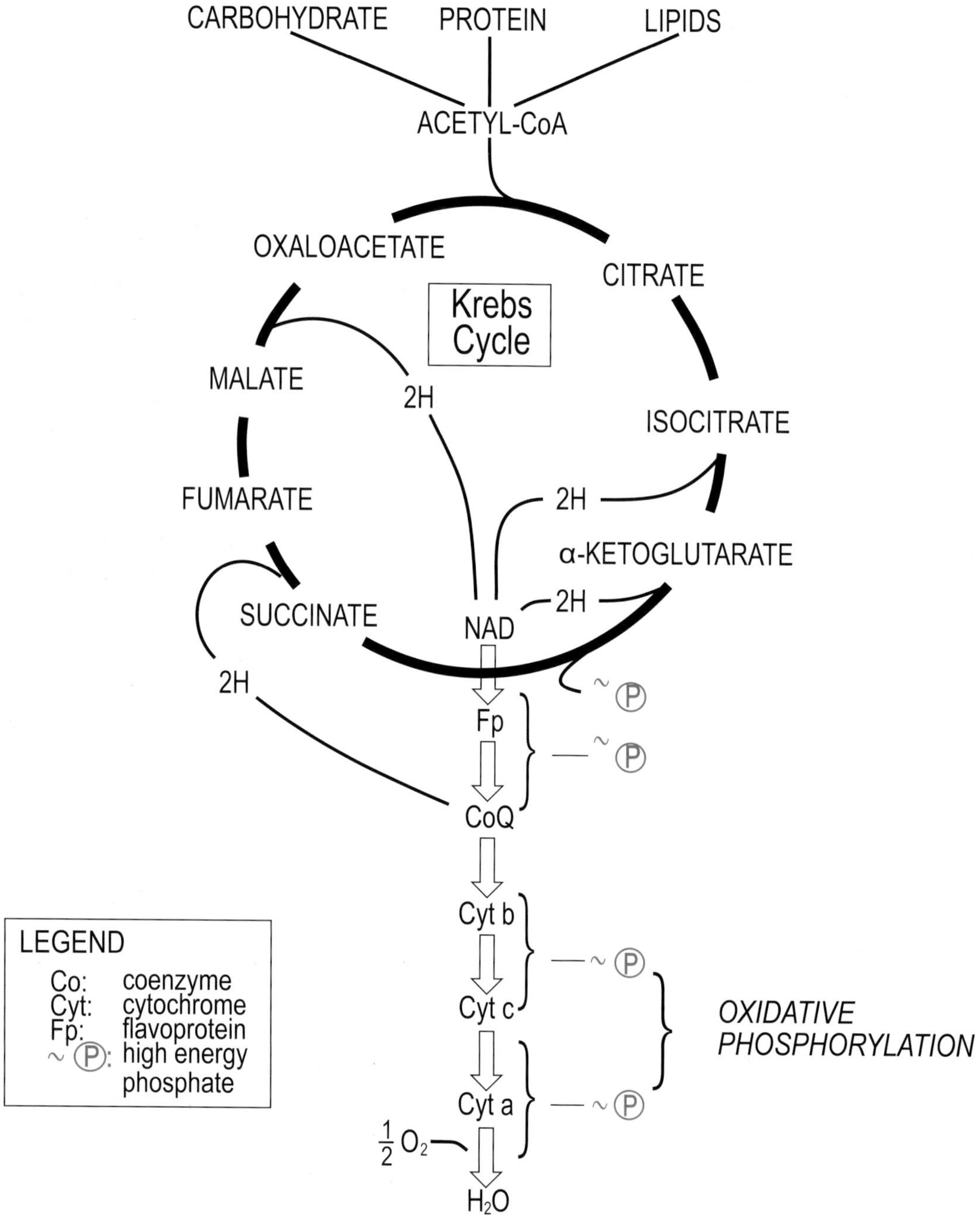

Figure IV.A.3.5: Summary of the Krebs Cycle and the Electron Transport Chain.
Note: Acetyl CoA can be the product of carbohydrate, protein, or lipid metabolism. Thick black arrows represent the Krebs Cycle while white arrows represent the Electron Transport Chain. High energy phosphate groups are transferred from ADP to produce ATP. Ultimately, oxygen accepts electrons and hydrogen from Cyt a to produce water.

GOLD STANDARD WARM-UP EXERCISES

CHAPTER 3: Cellular Metabolism

1) What controls the steps in the respiration of glucose?

A. Enzymes
B. Rate of photosynthesis
C. Amount of water present
D. Absence of NAD

2) Which of the following is NOT a product of glycolysis?

A. A net 2 ATP
B. Carbon dioxide
C. Pyruvate
D. Reducing equivalents

3) Most body heat, under normal conditions, is produced by:

A. the reduction of foods.
B. the oxidation of foods.
C. the breakdown of skeletal muscle.
D. the release of thyroid stimulating hormone.

4) What is the role of electron transfer in ATP synthesis?

A. Pump protons to create an electrochemical potential
B. Create a pH gradient
C. Create a concentration gradient
D. Create a chemical gradient

5) Why do you think the inner mitochondrial membrane (IMM) is impermeable to protons?

A. Because the IMM is positively charged.
B. Because the IMM is negatively charged.
C. Because the IMM is polar.
D. Because the IMM is highly selective due to its complex structure generating a gradient.

6) The highest amount of ATP per molecule of glucose would be generated as a result of:

A. glycolysis.
B. the Krebs cycle.
C. the hydrolysis of glycogen.
D. the transamination of amino acids.

7) Which of the following reactions is catalyzed by a protein kinase?

A. The hydrolysis of phosphate groups in protein substrates
B. The hydrolysis of phosphate groups in ATP and GTP
C. The phosphorylation of alcohol groups in protein substrates
D. The phosphorylation of alcohol groups in carbohydrates

For more chapter review practice questions, go to your mcat-prep.com account and click on Lessons in the top menu.

GS ANSWER KEY

CHAPTER 3

		Cross-Reference			*Cross-Reference*
1.	A	BCM 3.2, BIO 1.2.2	5.	D	BCM 3.4-3.7
2.	B	BCM 3.2, 3.3	6.	B	BCM 3.4-3.7
3.	B	BCM 3.1-3.7; BIO 6.3.3	7.	C	BCM 2.7, 3.2, 3.3
4.	A	BCM 3.4-3.7			

* Explanations can be found at the back of the book.

METABOLISM II
Chapter 4

Memorize	Understand	Clinical Correlation
* Substrates/products * Basic steps	* Gluconeogenesis, Pentose phosphate pathway * Regulation of glycolysis and gluconeogenesis * Metabolism of glycogen, fatty acids, protein * Fatty acid oxidation, ketone bodies * Regulation of metabolism	A type I diabetic under biological stress (infection, heart attack, no insulin) will increase fatty acid metabolism into ketones (by liver cells) to supply energy to peripheral cells. The heart and brain can use ketones for energy. High levels of ketones produce a smell of acetone in the breath.

MCAT-Prep.com

Introduction

Bioenergetics, at its very simplest, is exactly what the word implies—it is the energetics, or energy changes, in biological systems. Everything in life requires energy, whether it's the creation of energy, or the storage of energy. While different organisms utilize the various metabolic pathways differently—plants store energy as starches, for instance, while animals store energy as fat—there are plenty of similarities. Humans may not look anything like the primitive bacteria *H. salinarum*, but just like we use the Electron Transport Chain and various ion pumps to generate a proton gradient which can be used by ATP synthase to create ATP, *H. salinarum* generates its proton gradient using a combination of light-activated ion pumps like bacteriorhodopsin. In this chapter, we'll focus on the storage of energy, as well as the utilization of stored energy.

Optional Gold Standard Resources

Free Forum

Video: Online or DVD

Flashcards

4.1 Gluconeogenesis

Gluconeogenesis is the conceptual opposite of glycolysis – rather than breaking down glucose, it synthesizes it, even conserving some of the reversible steps seen in the glycolysis pathway. Even though both glycolysis and gluconeogenesis share some similar steps, the pathways are not identical, and both have irreversible steps that are unique to each.

All life forms have a gluconeogenesis pathway, including those that typically consume glucose as an energy source. In mammals, this process takes place mostly in the liver, kidneys, and small intestine. Glucose is largely used by the brain and muscle cells, the latter of which may break down glucose into lactate and pyruvate.

Just as pyruvate is the end product of glycolysis, it is likewise the starting point of gluconeogenesis. Two molecules of pyruvate are required to synthesize one molecule of glucose, along with 4 ATP, 2 GTP, and 2 NADH. The pathway can be summarized using the following net equation:

$$\text{2 Pyruvate} + \text{4 ATP} + \text{2 GTP} + \text{2 NADH} + 6\ H_2O + 2\ H^+ \rightarrow \text{Glucose} + \text{4 ADP} + \text{2 GDP} + 2\ NAD^+ + 6\ P_i$$

As with glycolysis, there are two distinct stages of gluconeogenesis – a three-carbon triose stage, and a six-carbon hexose stage – hence the starting requirement of two pyruvate molecules.

A key step in gluconeogenesis is the conversion of pyruvate to oxaloacetate via carboxylation, which is catalyzed by the enzyme pyruvate carboxylase. The reaction consumes one molecule of ATP, generating one molecule of ADP and an inorganic phosphate in the process. Notably, while oxaloacetate can continue down the gluconeogenesis pathway, a sizable portion of the oxaloacetate that is made from pyruvate is actually not used for this purpose; it is an important intermediate in the citric acid cycle, and is often replenished by this carboxylation of pyruvate.

In the gluconeogenesis pathway, however, oxaloacetate is converted to phosphoenolpyruvate through decarboxylation and phosphorylation, which is catalyzed by phosphoenolpyruvate carboxykinase (PEPCK). This step requires the consumption of GTP in animals (bacteria, fungi, and plants use ATP). It is sometimes considered a rate-limiting step (= RDS, rate-determining step) due to the length of time required for oxaloacetate to travel between the mitochondria and cytoplasm. However, some sources point to the conversion of fructose-1,6-biphosphate to fructose-6-phosphate as being the only rate-limiting step. Interestingly, there are many species of bacteria that can skip this two-step process from pyruvate to phosphoenolpyru-

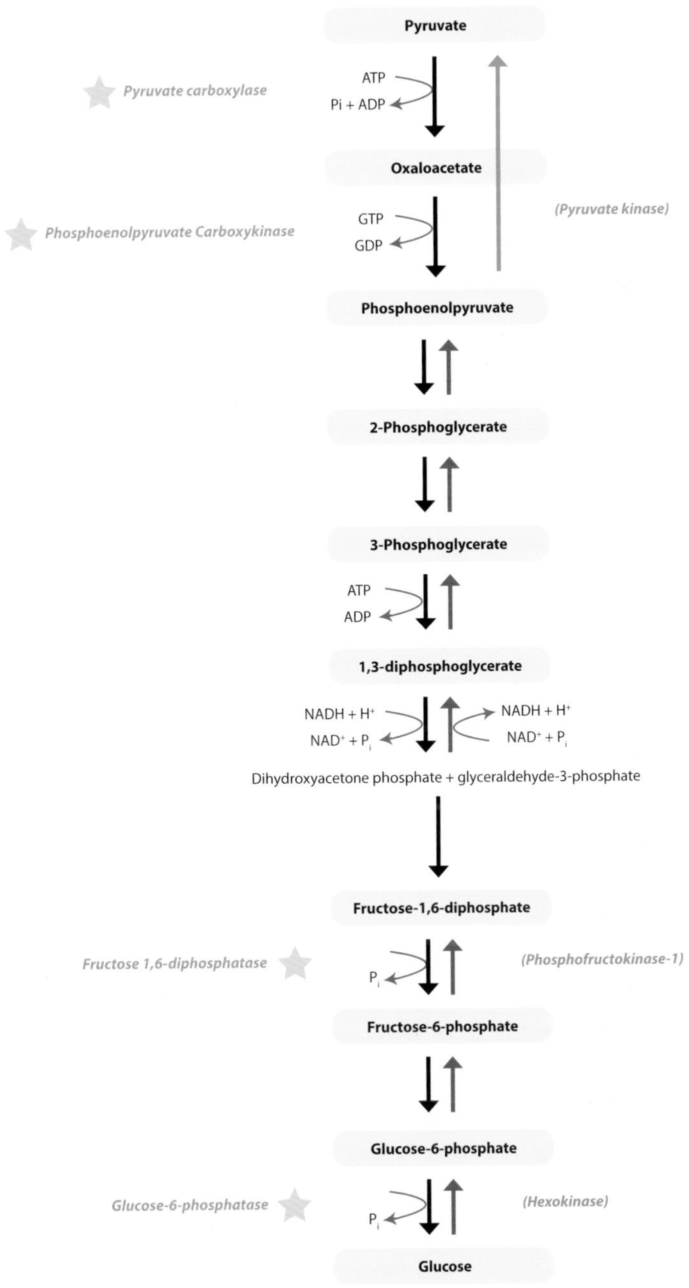

Figure IV.A.4.1: Comparison of Gluconeogenesis and Glycolysis. From the top, down, the steps represent gluconeogenesis. Note that pathway is very similar to that of glycolysis (right side of the pathway; from the bottom to the top); the gluconeogenesis steps that consume ATP are the same steps in glycolysis that generate it. Similarly, the steps in gluconeogenesis that generate inorganic phosphate are the same ones in glycolysis that consume ATP. While all of the steps in this pathway are shown with double-arrows, signifying that the reaction is the same in the opposite direction, note that in glycolysis, some of the steps are irreversible. Stars designate the steps in gluconeogenesis that are irreversible; they are catalyzed by different enzymes in the reverse direction.

vate and synthesize the latter directly from pyruvate in an ATP-consuming reaction catalyzed by phosphoenolpyruvate synthase.

As Figure IV.A.4.1 shows, there are four steps in the gluconeogenesis pathway that are metabolically irreversible. The first two involve the conversion of pyruvate to oxaloacetate and phosphoenolpyruvate. The second two involve the conversion of fructose-1,6-diphosphate to fructose 6-phosphate, which is catalyzed by fructose-1,6-diphosphatase; and the conversion of glucose-6-phosphate to glucose, a reaction catalyzed by glucose-6-phosphatase.

Besides pyruvate, gluconeogenesis can generate glucose from other non-carbohydrate carbon substrates such as lactate, glycerol, and certain amino acids. The degradation of glycogen (glycogenolysis; BCM 4.6) and gluconeogenesis are the two main mechanisms humans and many other animals use to keep blood glucose levels from dropping too low (hypoglycemia).

4.2 Pentose Phosphate Pathway

Each nucleic acid (BCM 1.5) has a sugar component, and it turns out that glucose also plays a role in creating these building blocks. It all starts in the pentose phosphate pathway. The pathway does not make DNA and RNA directly, but it does synthesize three different pentose phosphates: ribulose 5-phosphate, xylulose 5-phosphate, and ribose 5-phosphate, the latter of which is required for the synthesis of DNA and RNA. In addition to these three end products, the pathway also produces two molecules of NADPH in its first oxidative stage, an important reducing agent in many biosynthetic reactions. Note that although the pathway does involve the oxidation of glucose, its primary role is anabolic rather than catabolic.

The pathway begins with glucose-6-phosphate, which is not only the second-to-last product in the gluconeogenesis pathway, but also a substrate for various other carbohydrate synthesis pathways including glycogen, which we'll discuss later, and plant carbohydrates like starch and sucrose, which is interesting to know, but not necessary for the MCAT.

The part of the pathway between the glucose-6-phosphate and the ribulose-5-phosphate is known as the oxidative stage, due to the oxidation of two compounds - glucose-6-phosphate and 6-phosphogluconate. A significant amount of regulation goes into this first stage, depending on the needs of the cells. If a large quantity of NADPH and nucleotides need to be synthesized, the pentose phosphate pathway will be truncated, and all of the ribulose-5-phosphate will be converted to ribose-5-phosphate, a reaction catalyzed by ribose-5-phosphate isomerase. The ribose-5-phosphate is used for the synthesis of nucleotides, while NADPH is used

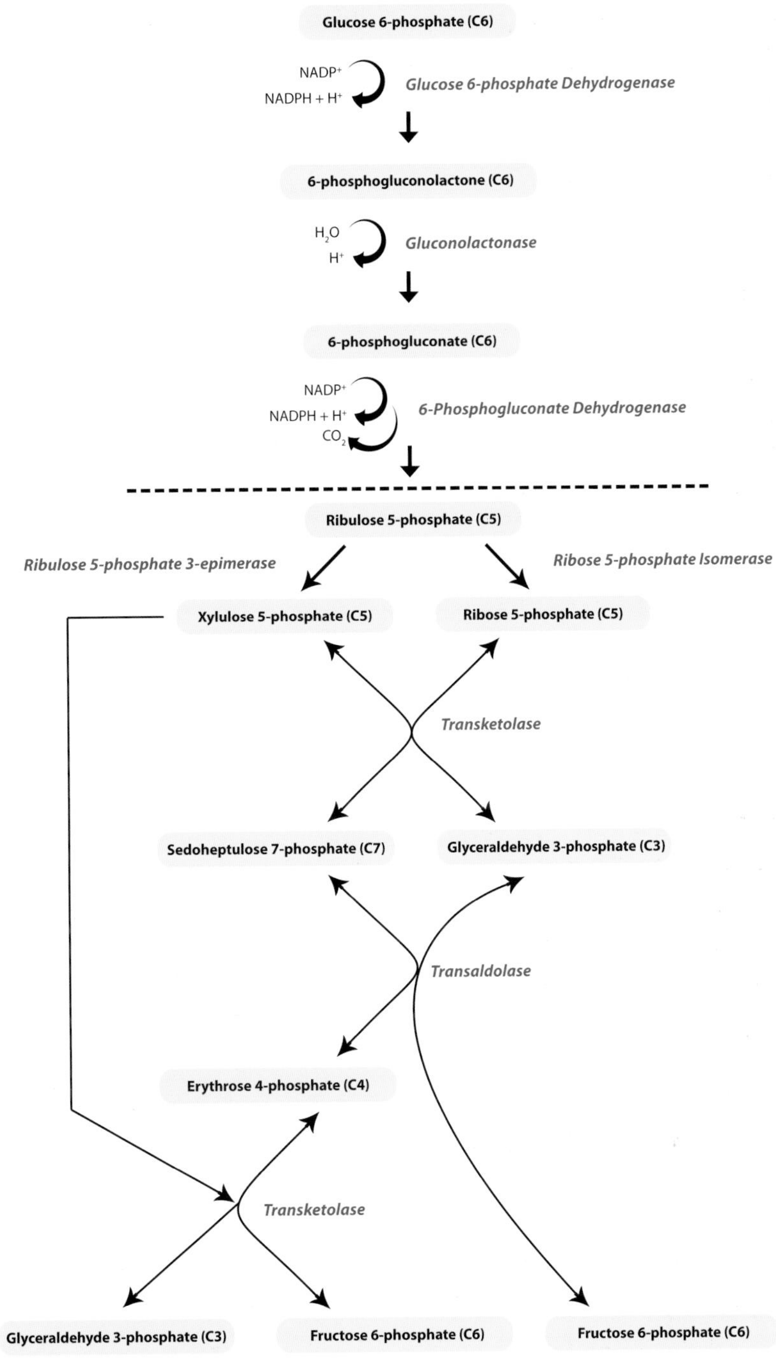

Figure IV.A.4.2: Pentose phosphate pathway. The steps above the dashed line are part of the oxidative state. Note the intermediate product ribulose 5-phosphate. If the cell finds it necessary to generate large amounts of NADPH and nucleotides, all of the intermediate will be converted to ribose 5-phosphate, which is required for DNA and RNA synthesis. Otherwise, the pathway will continue.

as a reducing agent to reduce ribonucleotides to deoxyribonucleotides.

If the pathway is allowed to continue, however, then the pentose phosphates that are generated along the way are converted into glyceraldehyde-3-phosphate and fructose-6-phosphate, both intermediates in the glycolysis and gluconeogenesis pathways. In many cases, both compounds can be recycled back into the production of glucose-6-phosphate.

4.3 Regulation of Glycolysis and Gluconeogenesis

Both glycolysis and gluconeogenesis are tightly regulated at a cellular level, and there are several factors that can tip the metabolic scales in favor of either pathway. One important term to learn is *substrate cycle*, so called because one substrate can be cycled between two different reactions. In glycolysis and gluconeogenesis, there are two – one between fructose-6-phosphate and fructose-1,6-diphosphate (in glycolysis, the reaction is catalyzed by phosphofructokinase-1; in gluconeogenesis, fructose-1,6-diphosphatase), and one between pyruvate and phosphoenolpyruvate (in glycolysis, pyruvate kinase; in gluconeogenesis, pyruvate carboxylase and phosphoenolpyruvate carboxykinase).

When trying to understand substrate cycles and their role in regulation, consider this – suppose both glycolysis and gluconeogenesis were occurring simultaneously, which is possible, although not usually the case. While pyruvate is steadily being converted to phosphoenolpyruvate (which consumes one ATP and generates one ADP and phosphate), in the opposite direction, phosphoenolpyruvate is being converted to pyruvate (and creating an ATP in the meantime). This means that either pathway could be regulated by simply altering the availability of the catalyst. If one used a pyruvate kinase inhibitor, one would discover that not only would glycolysis slow down, but gluconeogenesis would be stimulated, due to a sudden increase in the availability of phosphoenolpyruvate.

In addition to the concentration or availability of enzyme catalysts, other proteins and molecules can also regulate the substrate cycles. Certain hormones can stimulate gluconeogenesis, such as glucagon, which functions for the sole purpose of increasing the level of glucose in the bloodstream (BIO 6.3.4). It does so by activating protein kinase A, which stimulates gluconeogenesis by phosphorylating (and thus inactivating) phosphofructokinase-2, which causes a decrease in fructose-2,6-diphosphate. This disables the activation of phosphofructokinase-1. As one might surmise, this decreases the rate of glycolysis, and increases the rate of gluconeogenesis.

As much of this chapter focuses on bioenergetics, it's important to also focus on the regulation of glycolysis, which is important for animals, and especially mammals. Thinking back to glycolysis, you may remember that while the pathway consumes two molecules of ATP, it also generates four molecules of ATP, generating a net of two ATP. Thus, when more ATP is needed in cells, it makes sense that glycolysis would be activated.

Like any pathway, the abundance of one intermediate compound or substrate has a profound response on the availability of others. Think of a metabolic pathway as an efficient assembly line – if there are more wheels than there are bicycles, then production of wheels will halt until the production of bicycles can catch up. While this is an overly simplistic analogy of feedback mechanisms, it helps illustrate the delicate balance of materials and cellular demand that rule metabolic regulation.

If there is too much glucose-6-phosphate, for instance, then hexokinase is inhibited – or else glycolysis would proceed unchecked. Likewise, phosphofructose kinase-1 (PFK-1) is inhibited by an excess of ATP. Otherwise, glycolysis would proceed through this irreversible step (converting fructose 6-phosphate into fructose 1,6-diphosphate), adding to the already abundant supply of ATP. As ATP is consumed, however, it leads to an abundance of AMP, an allosteric regulator of PFK-1 that instigates the conformational changes needed to once again activate the enzyme. In a sense, PFK-1 is like a knob on a faucet, regulating the rate of glycolysis in accordance with the cell's energy needs. As a side note, PFK-1 is regulated by a multitude of molecules, including, but not limited to, ATP, AMP and fructose 2,6-disphosphate.

4.4 Net Molecular and Energetic Results of Respiration Processes

The entire respiration process is a well-oiled machine, and one that works efficiently to provide organisms with the energy they need to survive and function. Overall, the respiration process is the culmination of three metabolic stages: glycolysis, the Krebs Citric Acid Cycle, and the Electron Transport Chain and oxidative phosphorylation. The first two – glycolysis and the Krebs Citric Acid Cycle – break down glucose and other materials, with the former working in the cytosol, and the latter working in the mitochondrial matrix.

During those two processes, NADH is produced as a by-product of redox reactions, consuming NAD^+ and releasing NADH. The ETC then uses the electrons generated from the processes, transferring them down the chain until they are combined with hydrogen and oxygen to form water. This flow of electrons is coupled to the synthesis of ATP in oxidative phosphorylation, recouping any released energy through the phosphorylation of ADP to ATP.

In total, this respiration process generates 38 molecules of ATP for every molecule of glucose, eventually exchanging it for the CO_2 and H_2O that are released during respiration. We have discussed the issue of inefficiencies in the process in BCM 3.7.

4.5 Metabolism of Glycogen

Once glucose is made, it must be stored somewhere. In plants, glucose is largely stored as starch, but in animals, as well as bacteria, protists, and fungi, it's stored as glycogen. In vertebrates, glycogen is largely stored in muscle and liver cells. A quick overview of energy needs reveals why – muscles require a large amount of ATP, while the liver plays an important part in regulating the body's blood sugar levels by juggling both glycolysis and gluconeogenesis.

In order to discuss the metabolism of glycogen, however, we need to first look at how it is synthesized. It starts with glucose-6-phosphate, the second-to-last product in gluconeogenesis, which is converted to glucose-1-phosphate with catalytic help from phosphoglucomutase. This is then converted to UDP-glucose in a reaction that uses one molecule of UTP and releases one molecule of pyrophosphate (PPi). The third step involves the enzyme glycogen synthase, which adds a glucose residue from UDP-glucose onto the non-reducing end of glycogen. Over time, glucose units are added one by one onto a polysaccharide chain. When glucose is needed, polysaccharide phosphorylases (such as glycogen phosphorylase in non-plant organisms) catalyze the removal of one glucose molecule, resulting in α-D-glucose-1-phosphate. This product is quickly converted to glucose-6-phosphate, which is then ready for glycolysis. Incidentally, glycolysis using glucose-6-phosphate released from glycogen is more energetically efficient than using free glucose – no ATP is required by glycogen phosphorylase during the reaction, providing a net yield of three ATP for the glycolysis pathway, versus two.

Like with everything else seen so far, glycogen metabolism is also tightly regulated. Glycogen phosphorylase has four major sites of interest – a catalytic site, a glycogen binding site, a phosphorylation site, and for activation and inhibition purposes, an allosteric binding site. The enzyme is activated by AMP, but allosterically inhibited by ATP, as well as glucose-6-phosphate.

Glycogen metabolism is largely controlled in mammals by hormones such as insulin, glucagon (mentioned earlier), and epinephrine, also known as adrenaline (BIO 6.3). When blood glucose levels increase, insulin is released, signaling the organism that it is in a "fed" state and needs to start storing glucose. As a result, glycogen synthesis is stimulated. In contrast, glucagon is secreted in response to low blood glucose levels. Rather than stimulating glycogen synthesis, it actually stimulates glycogen degradation until baseline blood glucose levels are reached.

Suppose an animal is in danger, though, and is met with a "fight-or-flight" situation where it needs a sudden burst of energy (BIO 6.1.4). This is where epinephrine comes in. It is released by the adrenal glands in response to signals that turn on the "fight-or-flight" response, and in turn, stimulates glycogen degradation, providing valuable glucose-6-phosphate in times of need. This allows muscle cells to speed up glycolysis.

4.6 Regulation of Metabolism

By now, you may have realized the important role that glucose plays in all organisms, both in the breakdown of it, its synthesis, as well as its storage. If a body is a vehicle, then glucose is the primary fuel source. And, like with any valuable fuel source, its consumption needs to be regulated.

Earlier we discussed (BCM 2.7, 2.8, 2.9) the modification of enzyme activity through allosteric mechanisms, but **allosteric regulation** itself plays a critical role in the control of metabolism. Allosteric regulation is a fairly straightforward concept – allosteric activators can help stabilize an enzyme in its "active" form by binding to its allosteric site and allowing substrates access to the active site, while allosteric inhibitors stabilize the "inactive" form. This allows enzymes to be turned "on" and "off" in accordance to external stimuli, such as an abundance of blood glucose or ATP, or perhaps a lack thereof. As an example, some catabolic enzymes have allosteric sites that can bind either ATP or AMP – when a cell has an excess of ATP, it will bind to the allosteric site and inhibit the enzyme. When ATP runs low, AMP accumulates and binds to the allosteric site, re-activating the enzyme. This type of regulation is called **feedback inhibition** because an end product provides "feedback" to inhibit an enzyme along the pathway. It's a cell's own auto-shutoff valve, preventing it from wasting valuable resources.

Enzymes with multiple protein subunits can also be regulated via a method called **cooperativity**. The binding of one substrate can cause a conformational change that causes all of the other subunits to also take on their active form. In essence, it forces the subunits to "cooperate," readying the enzyme to accept even more substrates.

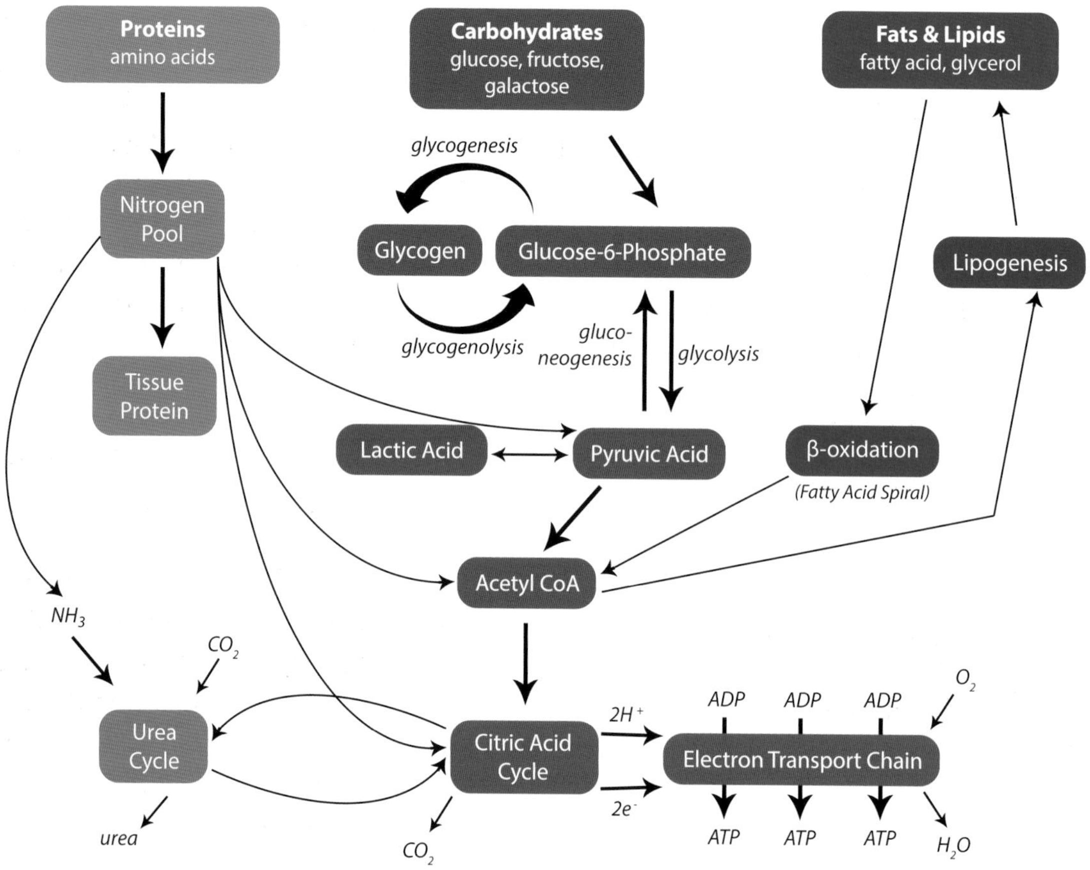

Figure IV.A.4.3: Summary of metabolism.

4.7 Metabolism of Fatty Acids and Proteins

Aside from glycogen, energy is also stored in the body as triacylglycerols. While glucose is terrific for the short bursts of energy necessary to chase after prey or run away from a predator, lipids are good for long-term energy needs, like running a marathon, hibernating, or migrating long distances.

Digestion of fats generally takes place in the small intestine (BIO 9.5). Bile salts, such as taurocholate and glycocholate, cover particles of fat, aiding in the absorption of fats by transporting them in micelles (BCM 1.4). Once inside the intestinal cells, fatty acids are broken down into fatty acyl CoA molecules, which can then be combined with glycerol or monoacylglycerol to form triacylglycerol (BCM 1.4).

The synthesis of triacylglycerols is initiated with the formation of phosphatidate, a compound that is created from a reaction that transfers acyl groups from fatty acyl CoA molecules to glycerol-3-phosphate, and catalyzed by two acyltransferases - glycerol-3-phosphate acyltransferase and 1-acylglycerol-3-phosphate acyltransferase. Phosphatidate is the precursor for several lipid products, including triacylglycerol and also phosphatidylcholine, phosphatidylserines, and phosphatidylethanolamine, which are present in the lipid bilayers of biological membranes - the latter makes up almost 70% of the inner membrane of *E. coli* cells. In the case of triacylglycerol synthesis, phosphatidate is dephosphorylated in a reaction catalyzed by phosphatidate phosphatase, the product of which can be acylated with the help of diacylglycerol acyltransferase to create triacylglycerol.

In order for triacylglycerols to be stored for later, they must first be transported to adipose tissue, which requires concerted communication between various cells and tissues. Because lipids are not water soluble, they combine with phospholipids and amphipathic proteins, along with cholesterol, to form lipoproteins (literally, spheres containing lipids and protein; BCM 1.4.2). The triacylglycerols are packed into the lipoprotein's hydrophobic core, while the hydrophilic surface contains the amphipathic molecules.

When the triacylglycerols eventually make their way to adipose tissue, they are hydrolyzed into their original components - fatty acids and glycerol, which can be absorbed by adipocytes, or fat cells. The reaction is catalyzed by lipoprotein lipase, an enzyme that binds to the extracellular surface of endothelial cells in adipose tissue. Once the fatty acids make their way into the fat cells, they once again combine with glycerol to form triacylglycerol.

4.7.1 Fatty Acid Oxidation

Fatty acid oxidation: The four-step process includes oxidation, hydration, oxidation again, and thiolysis. For saturated fats, the first step involves the oxidation of fatty acyl CoA, which forms a double bond between the C-2 and C-3 carbons of the acyl group. This is catalyzed by acyl-CoA dehydrogenase, an enzyme with different isozymes that are specific for different fatty acid chain lengths. The hydration step converts the product from the previous reaction into L-3-hydroxyacyl CoA. The next oxidation step consumes one molecule of NAD^+, converting the previous product into 3-ketoacyl CoA, and generates NADH along the way. The last step is thiolysis, which releases the acetyl CoA molecule, cleaving it from the now-shorter fatty acyl CoA. The β-oxidation cycle repeats until all units are converted into acetyl CoA, generating a large quantity of ATP.

In eukaryotes, this process takes place in the mitochondria, as well as organelles called peroxisomes (BIO 1.2.1). The name provides a hint for a small difference in the pathway - instead of acyl-CoA dehydrogenase, the first oxidation step is catalyzed by acyl-CoA oxidase, which releases H_2O_2, hydrogen peroxide.

Fatty acid synthesis actually follows a similar path, only in reverse. The four steps are instead condensation, reduction, dehydration, and reduction, methodically adding two-carbon units to the end of a growing fatty acid chain via a three-carbon substrate, malonyl CoA.

The oxidation of unsaturated fats is similar, but requires an additional two enzymes to contend with the double bonds. After the first oxidation step in β-oxidation, there is a trans-double bond (denoted as *trans*-Δ) between the C-2 and C-3 carbons (denoted as *trans*-Δ^2) of the acyl group. With unsaturated fats, the first step produces a cis-3,4 double bond, which needs to be rectified before the oxidation cycle can continue. The cycle stalls again at a later junction, which requires a second enzyme to catalyze a separate reaction. Further details are beyond the scope of this exam.

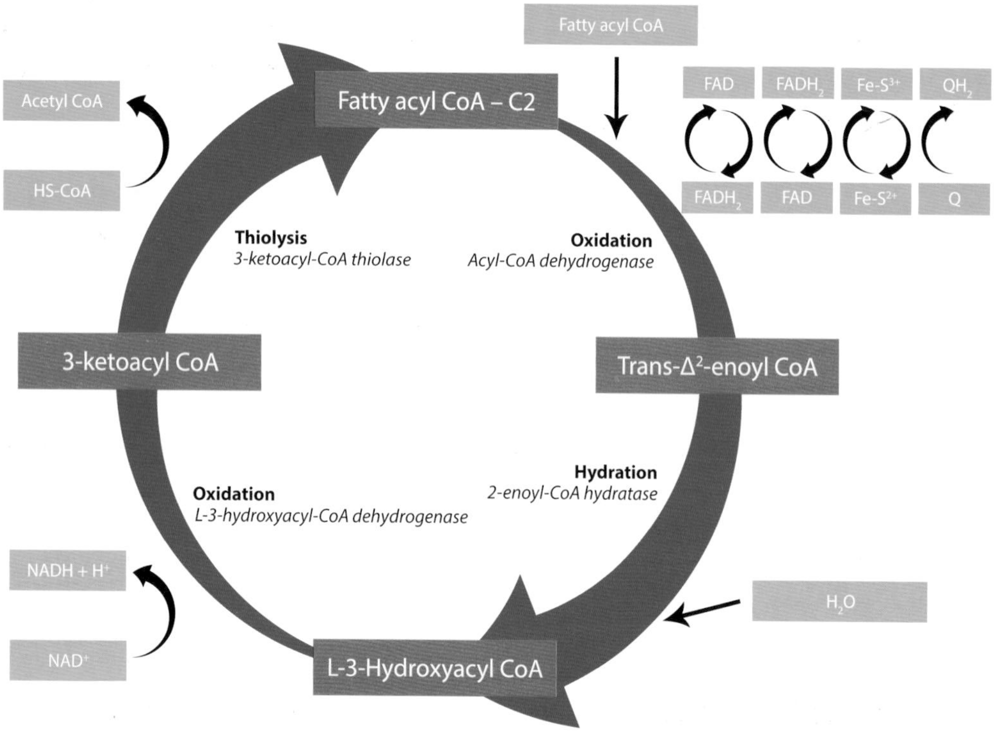

Figure IV.A.4.4: Mitochondrial β-oxidation spiral. Each round results in a fatty acyl CoA molecule that is two carbons shorter than it was previously. Note that every subsequent cyclic reaction after the first oxidation step that converts an FAD to $FADH_2$, and so on, is catalyzed by a different enzyme. The *trans*-Δ^2 in the intermediate above means that the double bond is between C-2 and C-3, and in the trans configuration.

4.7.2 Ketone Bodies

Although most of the acetyl CoA generated from fatty acid oxidation is used up in the Citric Acid Cycle, there are times in which it exists in abundance, such as times of increased gluconeogenesis, which uses up all of the available oxaloacetate. In these instances, the excess acetyl CoA is used to form **ketone bodies**.

The three endogenous (= *made within the organism*) ketone bodies are acetone, acetoacetic acid, and beta-hydroxybutyric acid (the latter is the only of the 3 which is chiral: note that C-3 is its stereocenter thus there are 2 enantiomers; BCM 1.1; ORG 2.2.2, 2.3). These compounds are synthesized in the liver and have the advantage of being water-soluble, which means they can be easily transported in blood plasma. Ketone bodies are predominantly produced in large quantities during periods of starvation, which is marked by a decrease in glycolysis.

Two of the three ketone bodies are used as a source of energy in the heart and brain while the third (acetone) is a degradation breakdown product of acetoacetic acid. As mentioned in the introductory page for this chapter, high levels of ketones produce a smell of acetone in the breath (acetone is the active ingredient in nail polish remover and paint thinner).

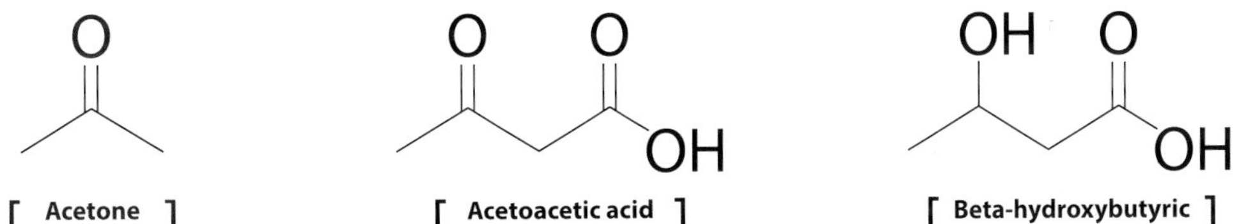

[**Acetone** (propanone)] [**Acetoacetic acid** (3-oxobutanoic acid)] [**Beta-hydroxybutyric** (3-hydroxybutanoic acid)]

4.8 Hormonal Regulation of Metabolism

Many of the same hormones that regulate the synthesis, breakdown, and storage of glucose - insulin, glucagon, epinephrine - also affect the synthesis, breakdown, and storage of lipids.

While insulin signifies an increase in blood glucose levels, it also signifies the availability of carbohydrates to be used as energy sources and also as precursors for fatty acid synthesis. Likewise, when the secretion of glucagon signals that there is not enough glucose in the bloodstream to be used as energy, it tells the body that fatty acids can be used as fuel instead. As for epinephrine, it is released when insulin concentrations are low, which tells the body that glucose reserves are being depleted. Epinephrine binds to receptors on fat cells, activating an enzyme that catalyzes the activation of hormone-sensitive lipases. These lipases catalyze a reaction that hydrolyzes triacylglycerols into their fatty acid and monoacylglycerol components, the latter of which can be converted into glycerol via a reaction catalyzed by monoacylglycerol lipase.

GOLD STANDARD WARM-UP EXERCISES

CHAPTER 4: Metabolism II

1) Which of the following is true regarding the conversion of oxaloacetate to phosphoenolpyruvate in gluconeogenesis?

   A. It is catalyzed by phosphofructokinase-1.
   B. It requires NADPH.
   C. The reverse reaction is one of the steps in glycolysis.
   D. It is slower than the conversion from pyruvate to oxaloacetate.

2) As citrate builds up in the cell, it inhibits the activities of phosphofructokinase-1. What effect will this have on a cell's glucose metabolism?

   A. Fatty acid synthesis will be inhibited.
   B. Gluconeogenesis will be inhibited.
   C. Glycolysis will be stimulated.
   D. Gluconeogenesis will be stimulated.

3) What citric acid cycle product is necessary for gluconeogenesis from pyruvate?

   A. NADPH
   B. NADH
   C NAD^+
   D. Acetyl CoA

4) The majority of the ATP produced from the oxidation of a saturated fatty acid is generated from what metabolic process?

   A. Oxidative phosphorylation
   B. Glycolysis
   C. Citric Acid Cycle
   D. Urea Cycle

5) Ketone bodies are likely to be found in the:

   A. liver.
   B. small intestines.
   C. heart.
   D. muscle.

6) An over-abundance of AMP causes all of the following EXCEPT:

   A. the activation of glycogen phosphorylase.
   B. increase in the rate of glycolysis.
   C. inhibition of insulin production.
   D. the activation of phosphofructose kinase-1.

GS ANSWER KEY

CHAPTER 4

		Cross-Reference			Cross-Reference
1.	D	BCM 4.1	4.	C	BCM 3.5, 3.6, 4.7, 4.7.1
2.	D	BCM 4.1, 4.3, 4.7	5.	A	BCM 4.7.2
3.	B	BCM 3.4, 4.1	6.	C	BCM 3.3, 4.1, 4.3, 4.5

* Explanations can be found at the back of the book.

APPENDIX

CHAPTER 4: Metabolism II

Practice MCAT Passage: Glycogen Storage Disease (GSD)

Glycogen storage disease type V, also known as GSD-V or McArdle disease, is an autosomal recessive disease that results in the deficiency of myophosphorylase, an isoform of glycogen phosphorylase found in muscle cells. Patients with GSD-V experience severe muscle cramps after strenuous exercise and exercise intolerance.

Physicians may order two histology stains of the patient's muscle tissue in order to aid in the diagnosis (see Figure 1): (A) A Periodic acid-Schiff (PAS) stain uses periodic acid to detect polysaccharides in tissues. The reaction of the acid with sugar creates a pair of aldehydes, which then react with a reagent to give a purple color; (B) A phosphorylase stain identifies the presence of the enzyme using a dark blue color indicator.

Despite initial pain during exercise, many patients with GSD-V have been able to increase their exercise tolerance by engaging in moderate periods of aerobic exercise. Muscle pain and fatigue subsides after a few minutes, a response that researchers call the "second wind" phenomenon.

Patients who experienced "second wind" typically experienced lowered heart rate and a reported decrease in exercise effort after 7-10 minutes. A similar effect was seen in the same patients after an intravenous infusion of glucose.

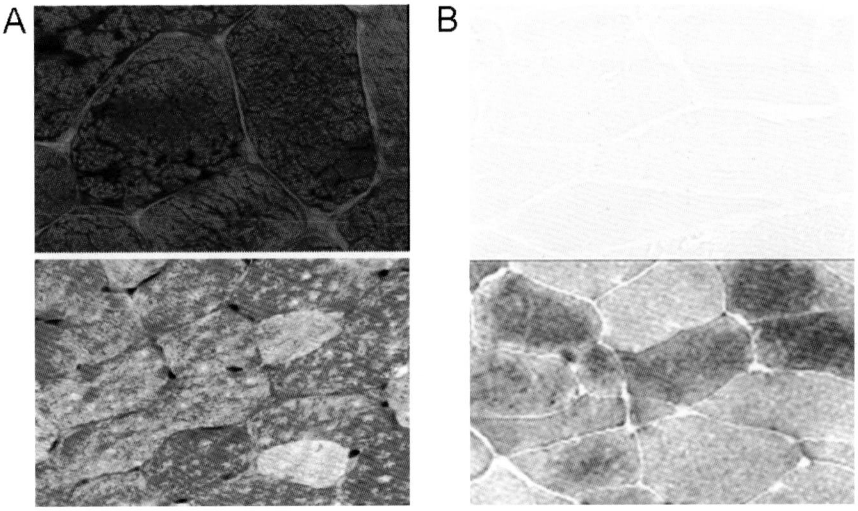

Figure 1. Comparative histochemistry of GSD-V and healthy individual. A) PAS stain of muscle tissue shows an accumulation of glycogen in the GSD-V individual (top) compared to the control (bottom). B) Phosphorylase stain of muscle tissue reveals an absence of phosphorylase in the GSD-V individual (top).

	Heart rate [BPM] (minutes after exercise)					
	Initial (0)	Initial (7)	SW (14)	SW (21)	Glucose (28)	Glucose (35)
Subject A	70	175	125	175	150	175
Subject B	75	170	90	165	100	170

Figure 2. Measured heart rates in two GSD-V patients during sustained exercise. Two subjects were asked to ride stationary bicycles at a steady rate over the course of 40 minutes. The subjects' heart rates were measured continuously, with high and low values coinciding with 7-minute intervals. Glucose was injected intravenously after 21 minutes. SW = Second Wind.

Adapted from Bhavaraju-Sanka R, Howard J. Jr, Chahin N (2014). SOJ Neurol 1(1), 1-3. and Haller RG, Vissing J. Arch Neurol. 2002;59(9):1395-1402.

7) Biopsies of the patients showed glycogen accumulation in muscle cells (Figure 1A), but not in the liver. What is the most likely explanation for this observation?

A. Glycogen is not stored in the liver.
B. Liver cells use a different isomer of glycogen phosphorylase.
C. Glycogen is transported out of the liver via carrier-mediated transport.
D. Muscles do not require ATP.

8) Muscle biopsies offer valuable data that can aid physicians in the diagnosis. However, they can be painful and invasive. A less invasive test uses a blood pressure cuff placed on the upper arm, which blocks blood flow to the arm. The patient affected by GSD-V is then asked to perform a strenuous arm exercise, such as squeezing a rubber ball. After some time, blood is drawn, and its chemical contents are compared to pre-exercise blood samples. One would expect to see:

A. a decrease in calcium.
B. an increase in lactate.
C. an increase in glucose.
D. no increase in lactate.

9) For a patient affected by GSD-V, which one of these scenarios describes the concentrations of metabolism products in muscle cells after exercise?

A. Increased concentrations of ADP, but decreased concentrations of P_i.
B. Increased concentrations of ATP, but decreased concentrations of P_i.
C. Decreased concentrations of ATP, and increased concentrations of P_i.
D. Decreased concentrations of ADP, and increased concentrations of P_i.

10) The "second wind" phenomena experienced by GSD-V patients is most likely due to a(n):

A. activation of phosphofructosekinase-1.
B. decrease in venous lactic acid.
C. metabolic switching to oxidative phosphorylation.
D. increase in insulin.

ANSWER KEY

Advanced Topics - Chapter 4

		Cross-Reference
7.	B	BCM 3.1, 4.5, 4.6
8.	D	BCM 3.3, 4.5
9.	C	BCM 3.3, 4.5
10.	C	BCM 3.3, 4.7, 4.7.1, 4.8

P = paragraph; *S* = sentence; *E* = equation; *T* = table; *F* = figure

CHAPTER REVIEW SOLUTIONS

Question 1 D

See: BCM 1.1.1, 1.2.2

Hydrophobic portions (R-groups) of the enzyme are on the interior of an enzyme because the external portion of the molecule is in an aqueous medium and the internal portion protects the hydrophobic R groups.

Question 2 C

See: BCM 1.2.1, 1.2.2

This question is essentially a mathematics problem. It is asking how many different ways a certain number of things can be ordered (permutations). There are three different amino acids and they can be arranged in 3! different ways to create six different molecules:

$$n! = 3! = 3 \times 2 \times 1 = 6.$$

If you did not know the math, you can use your note board and do it the long way: ABC, ACB, BAC, BCA, CAB, CBA. Recall that the tripeptides A-B-C and C-B-A are different since one end has an amino group and the other has a carboxylic acid group.

Question 3 B

See: BCM 1.2.2

Primary structure of a protein is defied as the order or sequence of the amino acids in the protein. Secondary structure indicates regions of ordered structure, and tertiary structure is the overall structure of the protein. Quaternary structure refers to the structure of a multiprotein complex.

Question 4 C

See: BCM 1.2.2

Technically, disulfide bonds influence all levels of protein structure but it most characteristic of one level in particular. Disulfide bonds are sulfur-sulfur covalent bonds that help to stabilize the tertiary structure of proteins. Primary structures involve the amino acid sequence with the amino acids held together by amide bonds. Secondary structures involve the conformation of the polypeptide backbone through hydrogen bonds. Tertiary structures pertain to the 3 dimensional folding of one polypeptide chain involving both covalent (sulfur bridges) and non-covalent bonds, whereas quaternary structures involve the 3 dimensional folding of more than one polypeptide.

Question 5 D

See: BCM 1.3.1, 1.3.2

Carbohydrates are polyhydroxy ketones or polyhydroxy aldehydes.

Question 6 B

See: BCM 1.3.2

We are told that glucan is formed only in the presence of sucrose, which is a disaccharide made up of fructose and glucose. The enzyme acts on glucose molecules to form glucan and fructose molecules to form lactic acid. However, the question asks how the enzyme acts initially. To get the glucose and fructose which the enzyme will ultimately change, the enzyme fist needs to split its starting product, sucrose, into those constituent sugars.

Question 7 D

See: BCM 1.3.1, 1.3.2

The six-carbon monosaccharides fructose + glucose form the disaccharide sucrose.

Question 8 D

See: BCM 1.4.1

All these compounds have the basic structure of steroids. It is important to understand that the dietary fat cholesterol is a steroid but all steroids are not cholesterols. "Steroidogenesis" is the process by which steroids are generated from cholesterol and transformed into other steroids.

Question 9 A

See: BCM 1.6

Adenosine triphosphate (ATP) has energy stored in its bonds which is released when ATP breaks down into ADP and Pi (= *inorganic phosphate*). The linkage which breaks between the phosphate groups are *anhydride bonds*. In DNA, the phosphate groups engage in two ester linkages creating phosphodiester bonds.

Question 10 C

See: BCM 1.5, 1.6

Since there are 100 nucleotide pairs, there must be a total of 200 nucleotides. Because of base pairing (A to T, G to C), if there are 25 adenine there must also be 25 thymine. This leaves 200 – 50 = 150 nucleotides to be divided evenly between guanine and cytosine.

Question 1 A

See: BCM 2.4, 2.5

The definition of biochemical spontaneity requires that Gibbs free energy be negative. However, as seen by $\Delta G = \Delta H - T\Delta S$, ΔG can be negative if ΔH is positive as long as ΔS is a high enough positive number (which makes $T\Delta S$ negative enough to overpower the positive ΔH). On the other hand, if ΔS is negative (which makes the $T\Delta S$ positive), Gibbs free energy can still be negative as long as ΔH is negative enough. The key point is that the question stem is seeking what "must" be true and only one characteristic must be true for spontaneity: $-\Delta G$.

Question 2 D

See: BCM 2.4

We are given that the temperature and pressure are constant.
Since $\Delta G = \Delta H - T\Delta S$ and $\Delta G = 0$ at equilibrium, we get:
$0 = \Delta H - T\Delta S$, thus $T\Delta S = \Delta H$ and finally:
$T = \Delta H/\Delta S$

Question 3 C

See: BCM 1.1.3, 1.3.2, 1.3.3, 2.3

Building a molecule (anabolic) requires energy (endothermic; BCM 2.3) thus $+\Delta H$. Going from more than 1 molecule (monomers) to just one molecule (dimer or polymer) is more ordered, less entropy thus $-\Delta S$. Keeping in mind that the temperature T in kelvin is always positive, we get $\Delta G = \Delta H - T\Delta S = (+) - (+)(-) = (+) + (+) = (+)$

We cannot be surprised that Gibbs free energy is positive which suggests that building complex molecules is not a spontaneous reaction. Of course we know these reactions can occur as long as they are coupled with a favorable reaction (i.e. the hydrolysis of ATP).

Question 4 B

See: BCM 2.7, 2.9

Catabolism is the breakdown of macromolecules into smaller molecules.

Question 5 A

See: BCM 2.7, 2.9

Proteins can undergo cleavage by non-specific enzymes. The cleaved products are then used as metabolites by the body.

Question 6 D

See: BIO 3.0, 1.2.1, BCM 2.7

OH is a hydroxyl group and an enzyme named hydroxylase would be expected to affect the hydroxyl group.

Question 7 D

See: BCM 1.4, 2.7, 3.1

Aspirin inhibits the synthesis of prostaglandins. This answer is best reached through elimination. Answer choices *A.*, *B.* and *C.* can be discounted because they describe various types of inhibition of the prostaglandin molecule by aspirin, however, prostaglandins are not enzymes and consequently, are unaffected by inhibitors (*Note:* the question states that prostaglandins are lipids but enzymes are proteins).

Question 8 B

See: BCM 2.10, 2.11

The bicarbonate system dominates the extracellular space and the phosphate and, particularly, the protein buffer system (because of the molecular structure of contributing amino acids) dominate the intracellular space as buffers.

Question 9 A

See: BCM 2.10, 2.11

Hemoglobin and proteins are organic. Bicarbonate is the most effective extracellular buffer. Phosphate is the most effective intracellular inorganic buffer.

Question 10 D

See: BCM 2.10, 2.11

Plasma pH is normally maintained at 7.4. A pH less than 7.35 is acidosis, whereas a pH of greater than 7.45 is alkalosis.

Question 11 A

See: BCM 2.10, 2.11

On the Surface: If there is an acidosis OR alkalosis that is NOT because of the respiratory system then we know that it must be metabolic and not respiratory. Thus only one answer is possible: metabolic acidosis.

Going Deeper: Keto acids contain a ketone group (= keto) and a carboxylic acid group (= acid). Keto acids are involved in the Krebs cycle and glycolysis (pyruvic acid, oxaloacetic acid).

When ingested carbohydrate levels are low, stored fats and proteins become the primary source of ATP production. Fats can be used to form ketone bodies. Amino acids can be deaminated to produce alpha keto acids and ketone bodies.

Diabetic ketoacidosis (DKA) is potentially life-threatening and results from a shortage of insulin; since the body can't bring the glucose into cells for use, the body switches to burning fatty acids and producing acidic ketone bodies that can cause symptoms and complications.

Question 12 B

See: BCM 2.10, 2.11; BIO 9.4.2

On the Surface: "Respiratory" means that the origin of the problem is the lungs (hyperventilation vs. hypoventilation) which is not consistent with the act of vomiting, thus D must be the exception.

Going Deeper: Vomiting results in loss of fluids (dehydration, B) and the loss of gastric acid (BIO 9.3) leaving the body relatively basic (metabolic alkalosis, A). However, prolonged vomiting may lead to the vomiting of intestinal contents including bile and pancreatic juice (which is high in bicarbonate to neutralize acid from the stomach; BIO 9.4.2). This could lead to metabolic alkalosis (A). It would be very rare to have a question this challenging on the MCAT.

Question 13 A

See: BCM 2.10, 2.11; BIO 12.4.1

Acidosis is a pH of < 7.35 so only answers A and C are possible; "respiratory" means that the source of the problem is ventilation (breathing). Hypoventilation reduces the lungs ability to 'blow off' carbon dioxide so CO_2 accumulates in the blood which increases hydrogen ion concentration (pH decreases = acidosis; see BIO 12.4.1). So the answer must be A, respiratory acidosis.

Question 14 A

See: PI

Information concerning the relative amounts of T and R conformations present before substrate is added is given in the passage.

Question 15 B

See: BCM 2.7, 2.8, 2.9

If a molecule has a high affinity for something, it is likely to be associated with it maximally. The substrate binds more tightly to the R conformation even though the R conformation is present in small amounts because R has a higher affinity for the substrate than T.

Question 16 A

See: BCM 2.7, 2.8, 2.9, BIO 7.5.1

The graph described would have time along the horizontal axis and the amount of substrate-enzyme complex (amount of substrate added to enzyme) along the vertical axis. The amount of substrate-enzyme complex would increase steadily as more substrate is added until a point at which all enzymes are involved in a substrate-enzyme complex, and any more substrate added will have no effect. The graph would show a steadily increasing line of positive slope which reaches a point at which it levels off into a horizontal line. This curve is called a hyperbola. A sigmoidal shape would be expected in cooperative binding (i.e. the symmetry model as described in the passage or hemoglobin; see diagrams in BCM 4.3 and BIO 7.5.1).

Question 17 B

See: BCM 2.7,2.8, 2.9

The symmetry model describes an instance of something which may be described as positive cooperativity (P2). The model does not exclude the enzyme from having cofactors, and places no restriction on what the enzyme's function will be. However, the symmetry model does not account for the existence of any other conformations than the two described (P2).

Question 18 A

See: BCM 2.7,2.8, 2.9

You must be familiar with how enzyme function is regulated to answer this question. An allosteric enzyme has a site other than the one for the substrate at which a molecule (not the substrate) that directs the function of the enzyme can bind.

Question 19 C

See: ORG 2.1, 2.2, 2.3

If you have not yet done your Organic Chemistry review then no problem! Otherwise, recognize that the new MCAT can ask any type of question in any of the science sections. Also, a 'conformation' is a stereoisomer.

Structural (ORG 2.1) isomers have a difference in the order and/or kinds of bonds (i.e. the connectivity is different). Stereoisomers have the same connectivity (the enzyme/protein is the same, the order of the amino acids - the primary structure - is the same). However, the 3 dimensional shape creates 2 different conformers: stereoisomerism.

"Different molecules" may imply that the molecular formula is different but isomers share the same molecular formula and "stereoisomer" is a far more accurate, precise answer (recall in the question stem "best described").

Functional group isomers are a subcategory of structural isomers which means the connectivity is altered which is definitely not the case here (that would require chemical reactions resulting in a change in bonding creating different molecules as opposed to a shape/conformational change).

Question 20 D

See: Deduce; BCM 2.2-2.5

Conformational isomers exist in a dynamic equilibrium, where the relative free energies of isomers determines the population of each isomer and the energy barrier of rotation determines the rate of interconversion between isomers. Incidentally, the enzyme subunits described in the passage exist in one of two conformations which stands for 'tensed' (T) or 'relaxed' (R), and as described relaxed subunits bind substrate more readily than those in the tense state.

Answer choice A: The graphs shows that for exergonic reactions ($\Delta G < 0$), the equilibrium constant K is always greater than 1 (meaning that the forward reaction is favored which implies that the products are more stable).

Answer choice B: divide both sides by -RT then raise both sides to the power of e. Remember from your rules of logarithms than e to the power of ln x = x. Also recall that ln is log to the base e.

Answer choice C: From the graph, at a free energy difference of 0 kcal/mol (= equilibrium), this also gives an equilibrium constant of 1 (also consistent with BCM 2.2-2.5).

Answer choice D: A negative difference in free energy means that a conformer interconverts to a thermodynamically more stable conformation, thus the equilibrium constant will always be greater than 1. However, notice that K decreases with increasing temperature meaning that there is more, relatively, of the less stable conformer (in other words, energy from the higher temperature is able to over ride the energy barrier to conversion to the less stable conformer). Thus answer choice D is incorrect.

Going a bit further: notice that a positive difference in free energy means the conformer already is the more stable one, so the interconversion is an unfavorable equilibrium ($K < 1$). Even for highly unfavorable changes (large positive ΔG), the equilibrium constant between two conformers can be increased by increasing temperature, meaning the amount of the less stable conformer present at equilibrium does increase slightly (see graph).

Question 1 A
See: BCM 3.2, BIO 1.2.2

DNA is only able to control the activities of a cell through the expression of proteins which includes enzymes.

Question 2 B
See: BCM 3.2, 3.3

Glycolysis is the process by which glucose is broken down into two molecules of pyruvate. At this point the lysis of glucose (glyco-lysis) is finished. The following step of converting the pyruvate molecules into acetyl-CoA is not a part of glycolysis.

Question 3 B
See: BCM 3.1-3.7; BIO 6.3.3

Mammals oxidize food (answer choice *B*), but NOT reduction (answer choice *A*). Clearly mammals do not break down muscle under normal circumstances to maintain heat (answer choice *C*). Though TSH (thyroid stimulating hormone from the anterior pituitary) increases metabolism indirectly through the activity of hormones from the thyroid gland, it is secreted, like other homeostatic hormones, when higher metabolism is required. In other words, it is not secreted to be the main source of normal baseline body heat. Oxidation of foods creates ATP but the process is not 100% efficient. Most of the waste goes to the creation of heat energy.

Question 4 A
See: BCM 3.4-3.7

The function of the electron transport chain is to produce a transmembrane proton electrochemical gradient as a result of the redox reactions. If protons flow back through the membrane, they enable mechanical work, such as rotating bacterial flagella. ATP synthase converts this mechanical into chemical energy by producing ATP. A small amount of ATP is available from substrate-level phosphorylation, for example, in glycolysis. In most organisms the majority of ATP is generated in electron transport chains, while only some obtain ATP by fermentation.

Question 5 D
See: BCM 3.4-3.7

Because the phospholipid bilayer is impermeable to ions, protons are able to cross the membrane only through a protein channel. This restriction allows the energy in the electrochemical gradient to be harnessed and converted to ATP as a result of the action of a complex involved in oxidative phosphorylation, ATP synthase.

If the inner mitochondrial membrane was permeable to the diffusion of ions, the electrochemical gradient would be destroyed.

Question 6 B
See: BCM 3.4-3.7

In animal cells, one mole of glucose initially produces a total of *8* ATPs [2 net ATP directly 2 NADH (recall that 1 NADH => 3 ATPs during oxidative phosphorylation)]. In turn, the conversion of pyruvate to Acetyl-CoA produces *6* ATP (via 2 NADH) and finally the Krebs cycle produces the remaining *24* ATPs [2 GTP 2 FADH (recall that 1 FADH => 2 ATPs during oxidative phosphorylation) 6 NADH], <u>for a total of *38* ATPs per mole of glucose</u> (net = 36 ATP; the actual number is less due to inefficiencies in the system). Therefore, the Krebs cycle produces the most ATP (indirectly). The hydrolysis of glycogen (a polymer of glucose-phosphate) produces mainly glucose-phosphate monomers and the (leftover) glycogen polymer. Transamination consists of interconversions involving keto acids and amino acids; this reaction does not involve the net production of ATP.

Question 7 C
See: BCM 2.7, 3.2, 3.3

Protein kinase enzymes are responsible for catalyzing phosphorylations of alcohol or phenol groups on protein substrates (OH to phosphate). The hydrolysis of phosphates is catalyzed by phosphorylases and not by kinases. Carbohydrates contain alcohol functional groups, but they are clearly not proteins and thus do not act as substrates for protein kinases.

CHAPTER REVIEW SOLUTIONS CHAPTER 4

Question 1 D
See: BCM 4.1

As one of the rate-limiting steps, it is necessarily slower than the first reaction in gluconeogenesis, which is the conversion from pyruvate to oxaloacetate. The other answers are incorrect because the step is catalyzed by phosphoenolpyruvate carboxykinase (PEPCK), and consumes ATP or GTP. The step is unique to gluconeogenesis.

Question 2 D
See: BCM 4.1, 4.3, 4.7

This is a good example of substrate cycle regulation. Phosphofructokinase-1 is the enzyme that catalyzes the conversion of fructose-6-phophate into fructose-1,6-bisphosphate in glycolysis. When it is inhibited, less fructose-6-phosphate is converted to fructose-1,6-biphosphate. Instead, more is available for gluconeogenesis, where it is converted to glucose-6-phosphate. As for wrong answer A, fatty acid synthesis is actually activated by citrate, which breaks down into acetyl-CoA and oxaloacetate, the former of which is a necessary building block of fatty acids.

Question 3 B
See: BCM 3.4, 4.1

NADH is a direct by-product of the Citric Acid Cycle, and is used as a reducing agent in gluconeogenesis. Incidentally, gluconeogenesis also requires GTP, another by-product of the Citric Acid Cycle.

Question 4 C

See: BCM 3.5, 3.6, 4.7, 4.7.1

For an even-numbered saturated fatty acid, n rounds of β-oxidation will generate n molecules of QH2 (ubiquinol), n molecules of NADH, and n+1 molecules of acetyl CoA. While QH2 and NADH can both generate ATP through oxidative phosphorylation and the electron transport chain, roughly 3x more ATP is generated by oxidation of acetyl-CoA by the citric acid cycle.

Question 5 A

See: BCM 4.7.2

While it's true that ketone bodies are used as energy sources in the heart and muscle, and other organs that require a consistent supply of energy, they are produced by the liver from fatty acids during fasting conditions. Because they are water-soluble, they can be readily transported to parts of the body where they are needed.

Question 6 C

See: BCM 3.3, 4.1, 4.3, 4.5

An excess of AMP triggers the allosteric activation of phosphofructose kinase-1 and the activation of glycogen phosphorylase, both of which lead to an increase in the rate of glycolysis. However, it does not inhibit insulin production. In fact, the opposite happens. When AMP is abundant, it means that energy levels in the cell are low. Thus, glycolysis is kickstarted, and once blood glucose levels are sufficient, insulin is produced to signify a "fed" state. Incidentally, the release of insulin works to suppress AMP, telling cells to slow glycolysis, and instead switch to storing glucose in the form of glycogen.

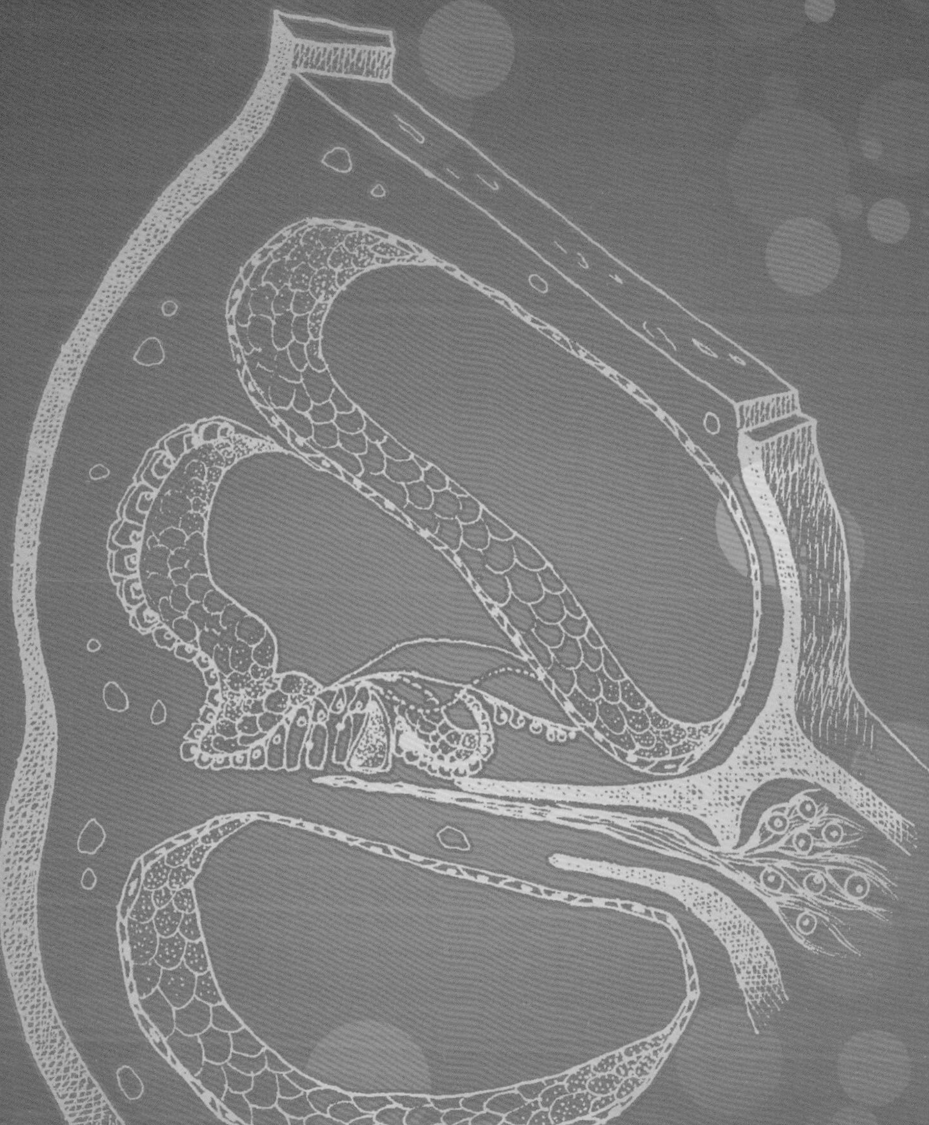

MCAT-Prep.com

BIOLOGY

GENERALIZED EUKARYOTIC CELL
Chapter 1

Memorize

* Structure/function: cell/components
* Components and function: cytoskeleton
* DNA structure and function
* Transmission of genetic information
* Mitosis, events of the cell cycle
* Cell junctions

Understand

* Membrane transport
* Hyper/hypotonic solutions
* Saturation kinetics: graphs
* Unique features of eukaryotes
* Transmission of genetic information
* Mitosis, basic microscopy, Cell Theory
* Not required: Plant cells, chloroplasts, etc.

Clinical Correlation

Understanding the impact of medications and surgery on a cell is vital. The ability of stem cells to self-renew means that, in our lifetime, a new branch of medicine may change our approach to the treatment of disease.

MCAT-Prep.com

Introduction

Cells are the basic organizational unit of living organisms. They are contained by a plasma membrane and/or cell wall. Eukaryotic cells (*eu* = true; *karyote* refers to nucleus) are cells with a true nucleus found in all multicellular and nonbacterial unicellular organisms including animal, fungal and plant cells. The nucleus contains genetic information, DNA, which can divide into 2 cells by mitosis.

Optional Gold Standard Resources

Free Online Q&A + Forum

Online Videos

Flashcards

Special Guest

1.1 Plasma Membrane: Structure and Functions

The plasma membrane is a semipermeable barrier that defines the outer perimeter of the cell. It is composed of lipids (fats) and protein. The membrane is dynamic, selective, active, and fluid. It contains phospholipids which are <u>amphipathic</u> molecules. They are amphipathic because their tail end contains fatty acids which are insoluble in water (*hydrophobic)*, the opposite end contains a charged phosphate head which is soluble in water (*hydrophilic*). The plasma membrane contains two layers or "leaflets" of phospholipids thus it is called a bilipid layer. Unlike eukaryotic membranes, prokaryotic membranes do not contain steroids such as cholesterol.

The <u>Fluid Mosaic Model</u> tells us that the hydrophilic heads project to the outside and the hydrophobic tails project towards the inside of the membrane. Further, these phospholipids are <u>fluid</u> - thus they move freely from place to place in the membrane. Fluidity of the membrane increases with increased temperature and with decreased saturation of fatty acyl tails. Fluidity of the membrane decreases with decreased temperature, increased saturation of fatty acyl tails and increase in the membrane's cholesterol content. The structures of these and other biological molecules were discussed in Biochemistry Chapter 1 of this book.

Glycolipids are limited to the extracellular aspect of the membrane or outer leaflet. The carbohydrate portion (= *glyco*) of glycolipids extends from the outer leaflet into the extracellular space and forms part of the glycocalyx. "Glycocalyx" is the sugar coat on the outer surface of the outer leaflet of plasma membrane. It consists of oligosaccharides (= *glycans*) linked

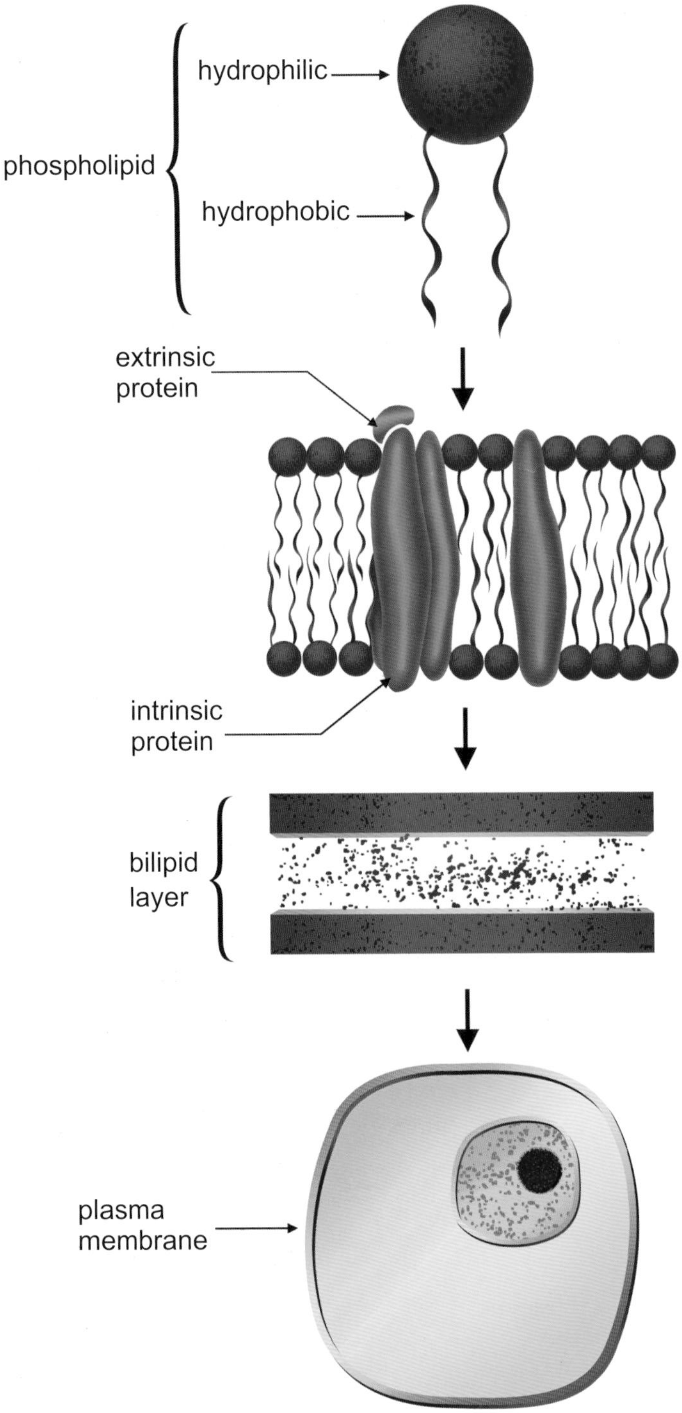

Figure IV.A.1.1: Structure of the plasma membrane. Note that: hydro = water, phobic = fearing, philic = loving

to protein or lipids of the plasma membrane. The glycocalyx aids in attachment of some cells, facilitates cell recognition, helps bind antigen and antigen-presenting cells to the cell surface. Distributed throughout the membrane is a mosaic of proteins with limited mobility.

Proteins can be found associated with the outside of the membrane (extrinsic or peripheral) or may be found spanning the membrane (intrinsic or integral). Integral proteins are dissolved in the lipid bilayer. Transmembrane proteins contain hydrophilic and hydrophobic amino acids and cross the entire plasma membrane. Most transmembrane proteins are glycoproteins. They usually function as membrane receptors and transport proteins.

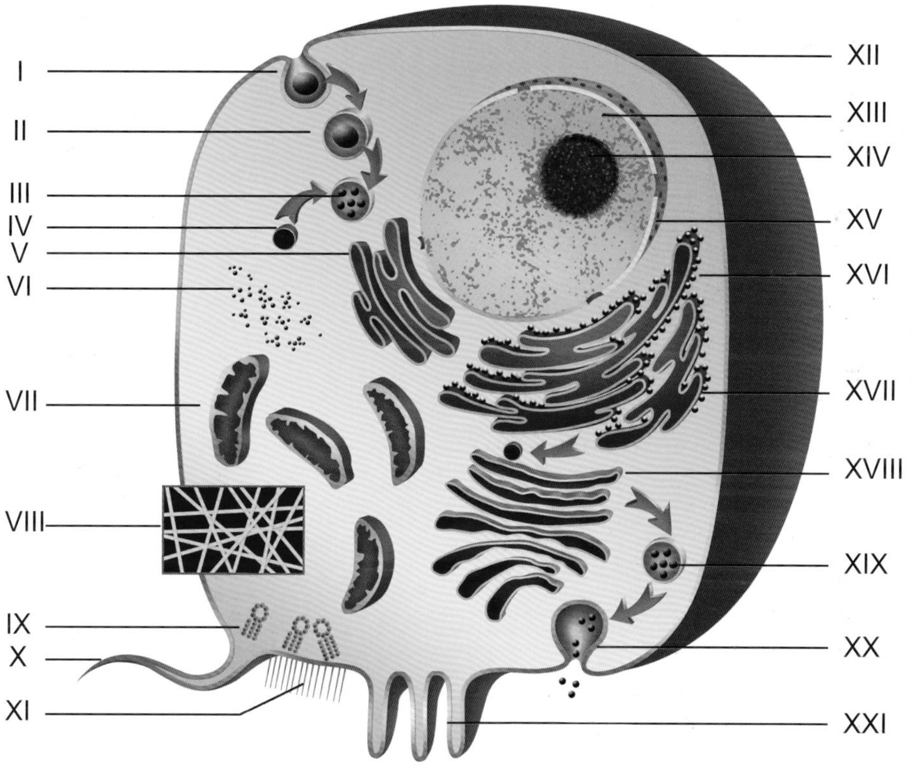

Figure IV.A.1.2: The generalized eukaryotic cell

I endocytosis
II endocytotic vesicle
III secondary lysosome
IV primary lysosome
V smooth endoplasmic reticulum
VI free ribosomes
VII mitochondrion
VIII cytoskeleton (further magnified)
IX basal body (magnified)
X flagellum
XI cilia
XII plasma membrane
XIII nucleus
XIV nucleolus
XV nuclear envelope
XVI cytosol
XVII rough endoplasmic reticulum
XVIII Golgi apparatus
XIX exocytotic vesicle
XX exocytosis
XXI microvillus

Peripheral proteins do not extend into the lipid bilayer but can temporarily adhere to either side of the plasma membrane. They bond to phospholipid groups or integral proteins of the membrane via noncovalent interactions. Common functions include regulatory protein subunits of ion channels or transmembrane receptors, associations with the cytoskeleton and extracellular matrix, and as part of the intracellular second messenger system.

The plasma membrane is semipermeable. In other words, it is permeable to small uncharged substances which can freely diffuse across the membrane (i.e. O_2, CO_2, urea). The eukaryotic plasma membrane does not have pores, as pores would destroy the barrier function. On the other hand, it is relatively impermeable to charged or large substances which may require transport proteins to cross the membrane (i.e. ions, amino acids, sugars) or cannot cross the membrane at all (i.e. protein hormones, intracellular enzymes). Substances which can cross the membrane may do so by simple diffusion, carrier-mediated transport, or by endo/exocytosis.

1.1.1 Simple Diffusion

Simple diffusion is the spontaneous spreading of a substance going from an area of higher concentration to an area of lower concentration (i.e. a concentration gradient exists). Gradients can be of a chemical or electrical nature. A chemical gradient arises as a result of an unequal distribution of molecules and is often called a concentration gradient. In a chemical (or concentration) gradient, there is a higher concentration of molecules in one area than there is in another area, and molecules tend to diffuse from areas of high concentration to areas of lower concentration.

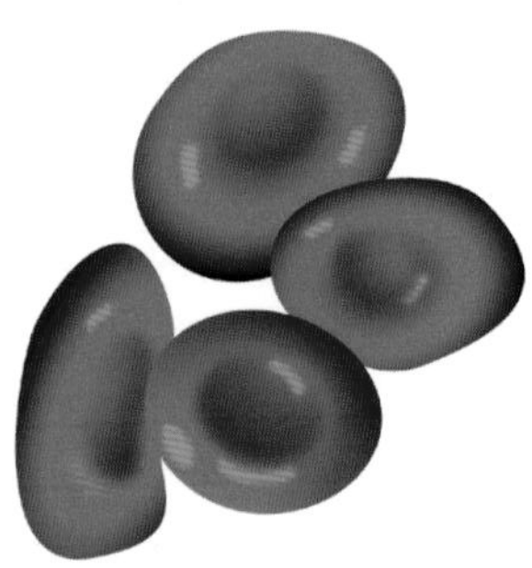

Figure IV.A.1.2.1a: Isotonic Solution.
The fluid bathing the cell (i.e. red blood cell or RBC in this case; see BIO 7.5) contains the same concentration of solute as the cell's inside or cytoplasm. When a cell is placed in an isotonic solution, the water diffuses into and out of the cell at the same rate.

An electrical gradient arises as a result of an unequal distribution of charge. In an electrical gradient, there is a higher concentration of charged molecules in one area than in another (this is independent of the concentration of all molecules in the area). Molecules tend to move from areas of higher concentration of charge to areas of lower concentration of charge.

Figure IV.A.1.2.1b: Hypertonic Solution. Here the fluid bathing the RBC contains a high concentration of solute relative to the cell's cytoplasm. When a cell is placed in a hypertonic solution, overall (= net), water diffuses out of the cell, causing the cell to shrivel (crenation).

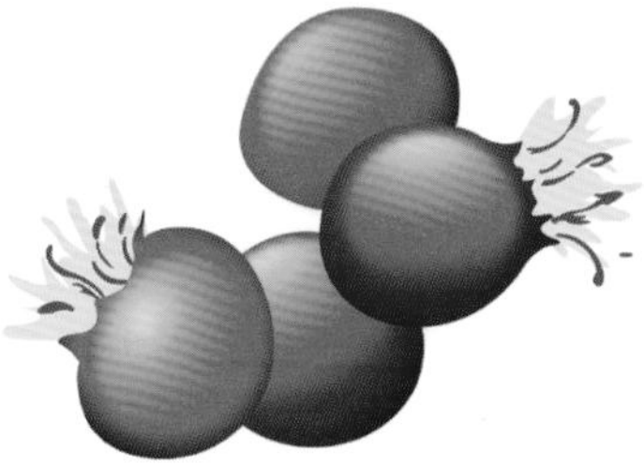

Figure IV.A.1.2.1c: Hypotonic Solution. Here the surrounding fluid has a low concentration of solute relative to the cell's cytoplasm. When a cell is placed in a hypotonic solution, overall (= net), water diffuses into the cell, causing the cell to swell and possibly rupture (lyse).

Osmosis (BIO 7.5.2; CHM 5.1.3) is the diffusion of water across a semipermeable membrane moving from an area of higher water concentration (i.e. lower solute concentration = hypotonic) to an area of lower water concentration (i.e. higher solute concentration = hypertonic). The hydrostatic pressure needed to oppose the movement of water is called the osmotic pressure. Thus, an isotonic solution (i.e. the concentration of solute on both sides of the membrane is equal), would have an osmotic pressure of zero.

{Memory guide: notice that the "O" in hyp-O-tonic looks like a swollen cell. The O is also a circle which makes you think of the word "around." So IF the environment is hypOtonic AROUND the cell, then fluid rushes in and the cell swells like the letter O}.

1.1.2 Carrier-mediated Transport

Amino acids, sugars and other solutes need to reversibly bind to proteins (carriers) in the membrane in order to get across. Because there are a limited amount of carriers, if the concentration of solute is too high, the carriers would be saturated, thus the rate of crossing the membrane would level off (= *saturation kinetics*).

The two carrier-mediated transport systems are:

(i) facilitated transport where the carrier helps a solute diffuse across a membrane it could not otherwise penetrate. Facilitated diffusion occurs via ion channels or carrier proteins and transport molecules down a concentration or electrochemical gradient. Ions and large molecules are therefore able to cross the membrane that would otherwise be impermeable to them.

ii) active transport where energy (i.e. ATP) is used to transport solutes against their

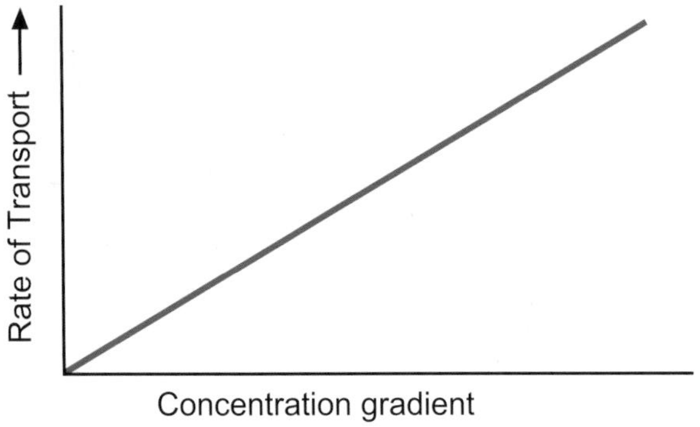

Simple Diffusion: the greater the concentration gradient, the greater the rate of transport across the plasma membrane.

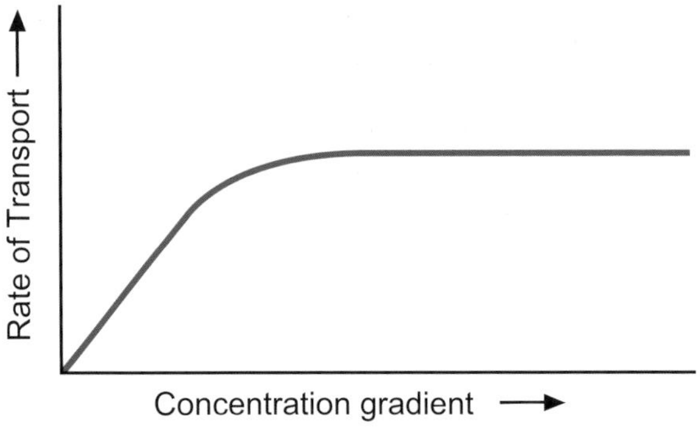

Carrier-mediated Transport: increasing the concentration gradient increases the rate of transport up to a maximum rate, at which point all membrane carriers are saturated. Compare with Fig. IV.A.4.1 in BIO 4.3.

Figure IV.A.1.3: Simple diffusion versus Carrier-mediated transport: Frequent MCAT questions.

concentration gradients. The Na^+–K^+ exchange pump uses ATP to actively pump Na^+ to where its concentration is highest (outside the cell) and K^+ is brought within the cell where its concentration is highest (see Neural Cells and Tissues, BIO 5.1.1).

1.1.3 Endo/Exocytosis

Endocytosis is the process by which the cell membrane actually invaginates, pinches off and is released intracellularly (endocytotic vesicle). If a solid particle was ingested by the cell (i.e. a bacterium), it is called phagocytosis. If fluid was ingested, it is pinocytosis.

The receptor-mediated endocytosis of ligands (e.g. low density lipoprotein, transferrin, growth factors, antibodies, etc.) are mediated by clathrin-coated vesicles (CCVs). CCVs are found in virtually all cells and form areas in the plasma membrane termed clathrin-coated pits. Caveolae are the most common reported non-clathrin-coated plasma membrane buds, which exist on the surface of many, but not all cell types. They consist of the cholesterol-binding protein caveolin with a bilayer enriched in cholesterol and glycolipids.

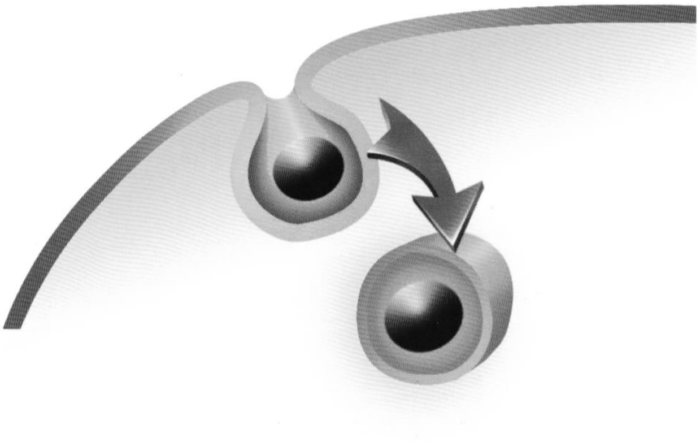

Figure IV.A.1.4: Endocytosis.

Exocytosis is, essentially, the reverse process. The cell directs an intracellular vesicle to fuse with the plasma membrane thus releasing its contents to the exterior (i.e. neurotransmitters, pancreatic enzymes, cell membrane proteins/lipids, etc.).

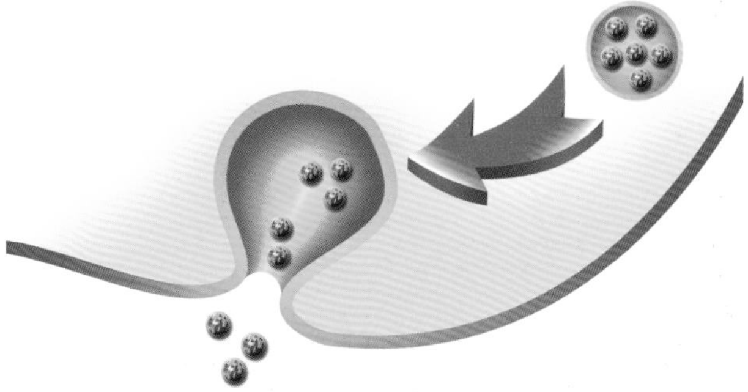

Figure IV.A.1.5: Exocytosis.

The transient vesicle fusion with the cell membrane forms a structure shaped like a pore (= *porosome*). Thus porosomes are cup-shaped structures where vesicles dock in the process of fusion and secretion. Porosomes contain many different types of protein including chloride and calcium channels, actin, and SNARE proteins that mediate the docking and fusion of vesicles with the cell membrane. The primary role of SNARE proteins is to mediate vesicle fusion through full fusion exocytosis or open and close exocytosis. The former is where the vesicle collapses fully into the plasma membrane; in the latter, the vesicle docks transiently with the membrane (= "kiss-and-run") and is recycled (i.e. in the synaptic terminal; BIO 1.5.1, 5.1).

1.2 The Interior of a Eukaryotic Cell

Cytoplasm is the interior of the cell. It refers to all cell components enclosed by the cell's membrane which includes the cytosol, the cytoskeleton, and the membrane bound organelles. Transport within the cytoplasm occurs by *cyclosis* (circular motion of cytoplasm around the cell).

Cytosol is the solution which bathes the organelles and contains numerous solutes like amino acids, sugars, proteins, etc.

Cytoskeleton extends throughout the entire cell and has particular importance in shape and intracellular transportation. The cytoskeleton also makes extracellular complexes with other proteins forming a matrix so that cells can "stick" together. This is called cellular adhesion.

The components of the cytoskeleton in increasing order of size are: microfilaments, intermediate filaments, and microtubules. Microfilaments are important for cell movement and contraction (through the actions of actin and myosin; *see* Contractile Cells and Tissues, BIO 5.2). Microfilaments, also known as actin filaments, are composed of actin monomers (G actin) linked into a double helix. They display *polarity* (= having distinct and opposite poles), with polymerization and depolymerization occuring preferentially at the barbed end [also called the plus (+) end which is where ATP is bound to G actin; BIO 5.2]. Microfilaments squeeze the membrane together in phagocytosis and cytokinesis. They are also important for muscle contraction and microvilli movement.

Intermediate filaments and microtubules extend along axons and dendrites of neurons acting like railroad tracks, so organelles or protein particles can shuttle to or from the cell body. Microtubules also form:

(i) the core of cilia and flagella (see the 9 doublet + 2 structure in BIO 1.5);
(ii) the mitotic spindles which we shall soon discuss; and
(iii) centrioles.

A flagellum is an organelle of locomotion found in sperm and bacteria. Eukaryotic flagella are made from microtubule configurations while prokaryotic flagella are thin strands of a single protein called flagellin. Thus, eukaryotic flagella move in a whip-like motion while prokaryotic flagella rotate. Cilia are hair-like vibrating organelles which can be used to move particles along the surface of the cell (e.g., in the fallopian tubes cilia can help the egg move toward the uterus). Microtubules are composed of tubulin subunits. They display polarity, with polymerization and depolymerization occuring preferentially at the plus end where GTP is bound to the tubulin subunit. Microtubules are involved in flagella and cilia construction, and the spindle apparatus. Centrioles are cylinder-shaped complexes of microtubules associated with the mitotic spindle (MTOC, see later). At the base of flagella and cilia, two centrioles can be found at right angles to each other: this is called a basal body.

Microvilli are regularly arranged finger-like projections with a core of cytoplasm (see BIO 9.5). They are commonly found in the small intestine where they help to increase the absorptive and digestive surfaces (= brush border).

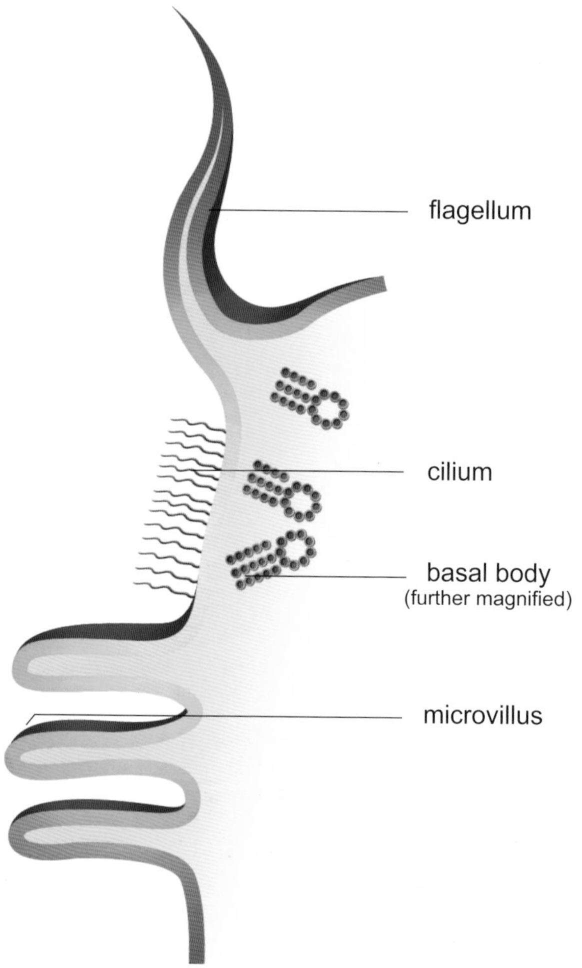

Figure IV.A.1.6: Cytoskeletal elements and the plasma membrane. The core of cilia and flagella is composed of 9 doublet or pairs of microtubules with another *doublet* in the center (= *axoneme*; see BIO 1.5).

1.2.1 Membrane Bound Organelles

Mitochondrion: The Power House

Mitochondria produce energy (i.e. ATP) for the cell through aerobic respiration (BCM 3.4). It is a double membraned organelle whose inner membrane has shelf-like folds which are called cristae. The matrix, the fluid within the inner membrane, contains the enzymes for the Krebs cycle and circular DNA. The latter is the only cellular DNA found outside of the nucleus with the exception of chloroplasts (note: plant biology is not part of the syllabus for the new MCAT). There are numerous mitochondria in muscle cells. Mitochondria synthesize ATP via the Krebs cycle via oxidation of glucose, amino acids or fatty acids (BCM 3.4, 3.5, 3.6).

Mitochondria have their own DNA and ribosomes and replicate independently from eukaryotic cells. However, most proteins used in mitochondria are coded by nuclear DNA, not mitochondrial DNA (BIO 15.7).

Figure IV.A.1.7: Mitochondria.

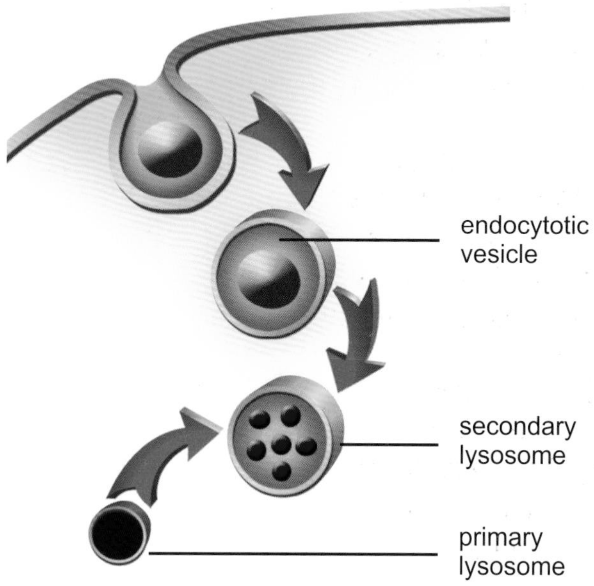

Figure IV.A.1.8: Heterolysis.

Lysosomes: Suicide Sacs

In a diseased cell, lysosomes may release their powerful acid hydrolases to digest away the cell (autolysis). In normal cells, a primary (normal) lysosome can fuse with an endocytotic vesicle to form a secondary lysosome where the phagocytosed particle (i.e. a bacterium) can be digested. This is called heterolysis. There are numerous lysosomes in phagocytic cells of the immune system (i.e. macrophages, neutrophils).

Endoplasmic Reticulum: Synthesis Center

The endoplasmic reticulum (ER) is an interconnected membraned system resembling flattened sacs and extends from the cell membrane to the nuclear membrane.

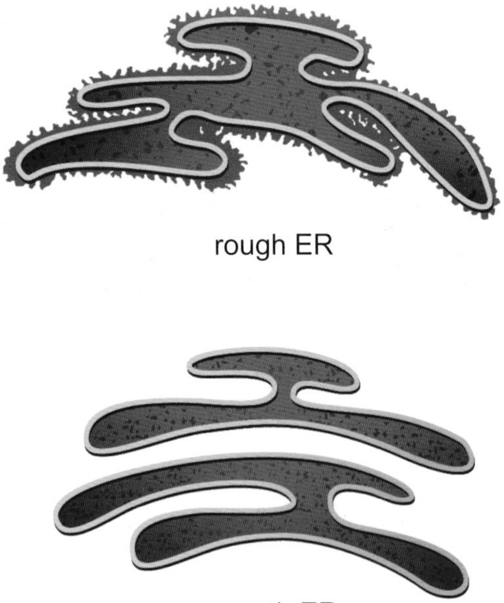

Figure IV.A.1.9: The endoplasmic reticulum.

There are two kinds: (i) dotted with ribosomes on its surface which is called rough ER and (ii) without ribosomes which is smooth ER.

Ribosomes are composed of ribosomal RNA (rRNA) and numerous proteins. They may exist freely in the cytosol or bound to the rough ER or outer nuclear membrane. The ribosome is the site where mRNA is translated into protein BIO 3).

Rough ER (rER) is important in protein synthesis and is abundant in cells synthesizing secretory proteins. It is associated with the synthesis of secretory protein, plasma membrane protein, and lysosomal protein. Smooth ER is abundant in cells synthesizing steroids, triglycerides and cholesterol (i.e. testes, ovaries, and sebaceous glands; BIO 13.3). It is associated with the synthesis and transport of lipids such as steroid hormone and detoxification of a variety of chemicals (important among liver cells; BIO 9.4.1). It is also common in muscle cells (*sarcoplasmic reticulum*; BIO 5.2) causing muscle contraction and relaxation. Smooth ER has a central role in plasma membrane biosynthesis since it is a key factor in phospholipid and fatty acid synthesis and metabolism.

Golgi Apparatus: The Export Department

The Golgi apparatus forms a stack of smooth membranous sacs or *cisternae* that function in protein modification, such as the addition of polysaccharides (i.e. glycosylation). The Golgi also packages secretory proteins in membrane bound vesicles which can be exocytosed.

The Golgi apparatus has a distinct polarity with one end being the "cis" face and the other being "trans". The cis face lies close to a separate vesicular-tubular cluster (VTC) also referred to as the ER-Golgi intermediate compartment (ERGIC) which is an organelle. The ERGIC mediates trafficking between the ER

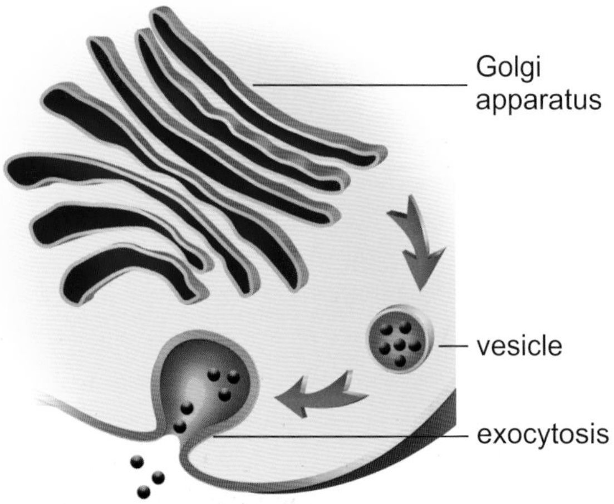

Figure IV.A.1.10: Golgi apparatus.

and Golgi complex, facilitating the sorting of 'cargo'. The medial (middle) compartment of the Golgi lies between the cis and trans faces. The trans face is oriented towards vacuoles and secretory granules. The trans Golgi network separates from the trans face and sorts proteins for their final destination.

An abundant amount of rER and Golgi is found in cells which produce and secrete protein. For example, *B-cells* of the immune system which secrete antibodies, *acinar cells* in the pancreas which secrete digestive enzymes into the intestines, and *goblet cells* of the intestine which secrete mucus into the lumen.

Peroxisomes (Microbodies)

Peroxisomes are membrane bound organelles that contain enzymes whose functions include oxidative deamination of amino acids, oxidation of long chain fatty acids and synthesis of cholesterol.

The name "*perox*isome" comes from the fact that it is an organelle with enzymes that can transfer hydrogen from various substrates to oxygen, producing and then degrading hydrogen *perox*ide (H_2O_2).

The Nucleus

The nucleus is surrounded by a double membrane called the nuclear envelope. Throughout the membrane are nuclear pores which selectively allow the transportation of large particles to and from the nucleus. The nucleus is responsible for protein synthesis in the cytoplasm via ribosomal RNA (rRNA), messenger RNA (mRNA), and transfer RNA (tRNA).

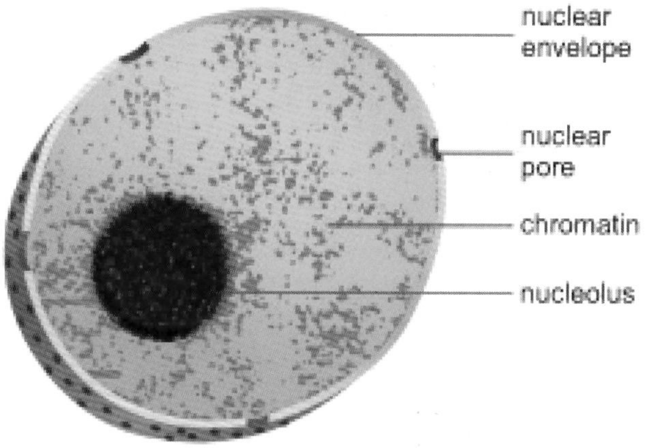

Figure IV.A.1.11: The nucleus.

DNA can be found within the nucleus as chromatin (DNA complexed to proteins like *histones*) or as chromosomes which are more clearly visible in a light microscope. The nucleolus is not membrane bound. It contains mostly ribosomal RNA and protein as well as the DNA necessary to synthesize ribosomal RNA.

The nucleolus is associated with the synthesis of ribosomal RNA (rRNA) and its assembly into ribosome precursors.

Chromosomes are basically extensively folded chromatin maintained by histone proteins. Each chromosome is composed of DNA and associated proteins, forming a *nucleosome*, the basic structural unit of chromatin. Chromatin exists as heterochromatin and euchromatin. Heterochromatin is a transcriptionally inactive form of chromatin while euchromatin is a transcriptionally active form of chromatin. Chromatin is responsible for RNA synthesis.

1.2.2 DNA: The Cell's Architect

We have reviewed nucleic acids in Biochemistry Chapter 1 (BCM 1.5, 1.6). We discussed the fact that deoxyribonucleic acid (DNA) and ribonucleic acid (RNA) are essential components in constructing the proteins which act as the cytoskeleton, enzymes, membrane channels, antibodies, etc. It is the DNA which contains the genetic information of the cell.

Our focus in this section is to explore DNA replication.

Watson and Crick's model of DNA has allowed us to get insight into what takes shape as the nucleotides polymerize to form this special nucleic acid. The result is a double *helical* or *stranded* structure.

The *replication* (duplication) of DNA is semi-conservative: each strand of the double helix can serve as a template to generate a complementary strand. Thus for each double helix there is one parent strand (*old*) and one daughter strand (*new*). The latter is synthesized using one nucleotide at a time, enzymes including DNA polymerase, and the parent strand as a template. The preceding is termed "DNA Synthesis" and occurs in the S stage of interphase during the cell cycle (BIO 1.3).

Each nucleotide has a hydroxyl or phosphate group at the 3rd and 5th carbons designated the 3′ and 5′ positions (see BCM 1.3.2, 1.5). Phosphodiester bonds can be formed between a free 3′ hydroxyl group and a free 5′ phosphate group. Thus the DNA strand has *polarity* since one end of the molecule will have a free 3′ hydroxyl while the other terminal nucleotide will have a free 5′ phosphate group.

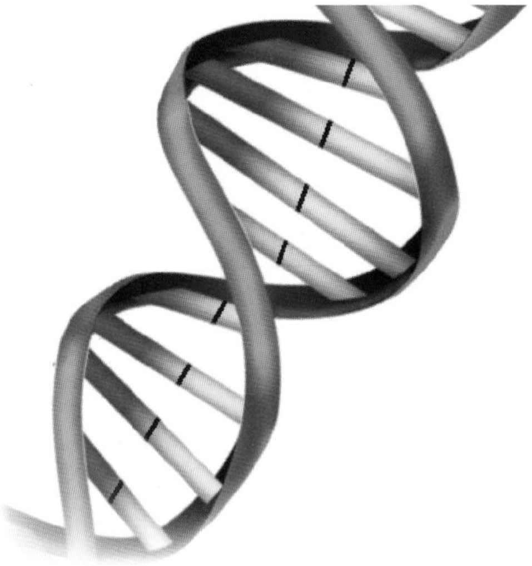

Polymerization of the two strands occurs in opposite directions (= *antiparallel*). In other words, one strand runs in the 5′ - 3′ direction, while its partner runs in the 3′ - 5′ direction.

DNA replication is semi-discontinuous. DNA polymerase can only synthesize DNA in the 5′ to 3′ direction. As a result of the anti-parallel nature of DNA, the 5′ - 3′ strand is replicated continuously (the *leading strand*), while the 3′ - 5′ strand is replicated discontinuously (the *lagging strand*) in the reverse direction. The short, newly synthesized DNA fragments that are formed on the lagging strand are called *Okazaki fragments*. DNA synthesis begins at a specific site called the replication origin (*replicon*) and proceeds in both directions. Eukaryotic chromosomes contain multiple origins while prokaryotic chromosomes contain a single origin. The parental strand is always read in the 3′ - 5′ direction and the daughter strand is always synthesized in the 5′ - 3′ direction. Due to the Y-shaped region of the replicon, it can be described as a 'replication fork'.

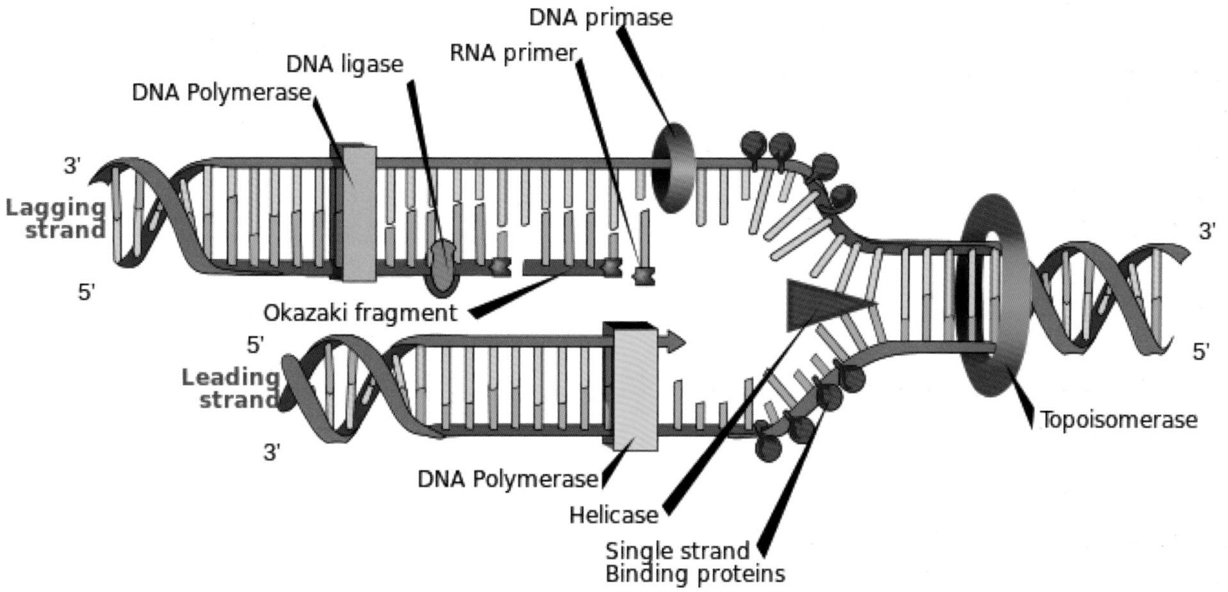

Figure IV.A.1.12: DNA synthesis, the replication fork and the main actors. (Ruiz)

DNA Polymerases (Pol): A family of enzymes that carry out all forms of DNA replication by extending existing DNA. A short fragment of RNA, called a 'primer', must be created and paired with the template DNA strand to begin synthesis by DNA Pol.

DNA Polymerase III: Synthesizes nucleotides onto the leading end in the classic 5' to 3' direction.

DNA Polymerase I: Synthesizes nucleotides onto primers on the lagging strand, forming Okazaki fragments.

DNA Ligase: "Glues" together Okazaki fragments, an area that DNA Pol I is unable to synthesize.

DNA Primase: Polymerizes nucleotide triphosphates in a 5' to 3' direction; also synthesizes RNA primers to act as a template for future Okazaki fragments to build on to.

Helicase: Uses the hydrolysis of ATP to unwind or "unzip" the DNA helix at the replication fork to allow the resulting single strands to be copied.

Single Strand Binding Proteins: Responsible for holding the replication fork of DNA open while polymerases read the templates and prepare for synthesis.

Topoisomerase: Introduces a single-strand nick in the DNA, enabling it to swivel and thus relieve the accumulated winding strain generated during unwinding of the double helix.

Nuclease: Excises (cuts out) unwanted or defective segments of nucleotides in a DNA sequence.

Telomerase: Adds a specific sequence of DNA to the telomeres of chromosomes after they divide, giving the chromosomes stability over time. Note: telomere shortening is associated with aging.

Only a basic understanding of recombinant DNA techniques, restriction enzymes, denaturation, reannealing, hybridization, DNA repair mechanisms, etc., is required for the new MCAT. These topics will be discussed here, and in BIO 2.2.1, and mostly in Chapter 4, Biotechnology. The following is an overview regarding DNA repair.

Because of environmental factors including chemicals and UV radiation, any one of the trillions of cells in our bodies may undergo as many as 1 million individual molecular "injuries" per day. Structural damage to DNA may result and could have many effects such as inducing mutation. Thus our DNA repair system is constantly active as it responds to damage in DNA structure.

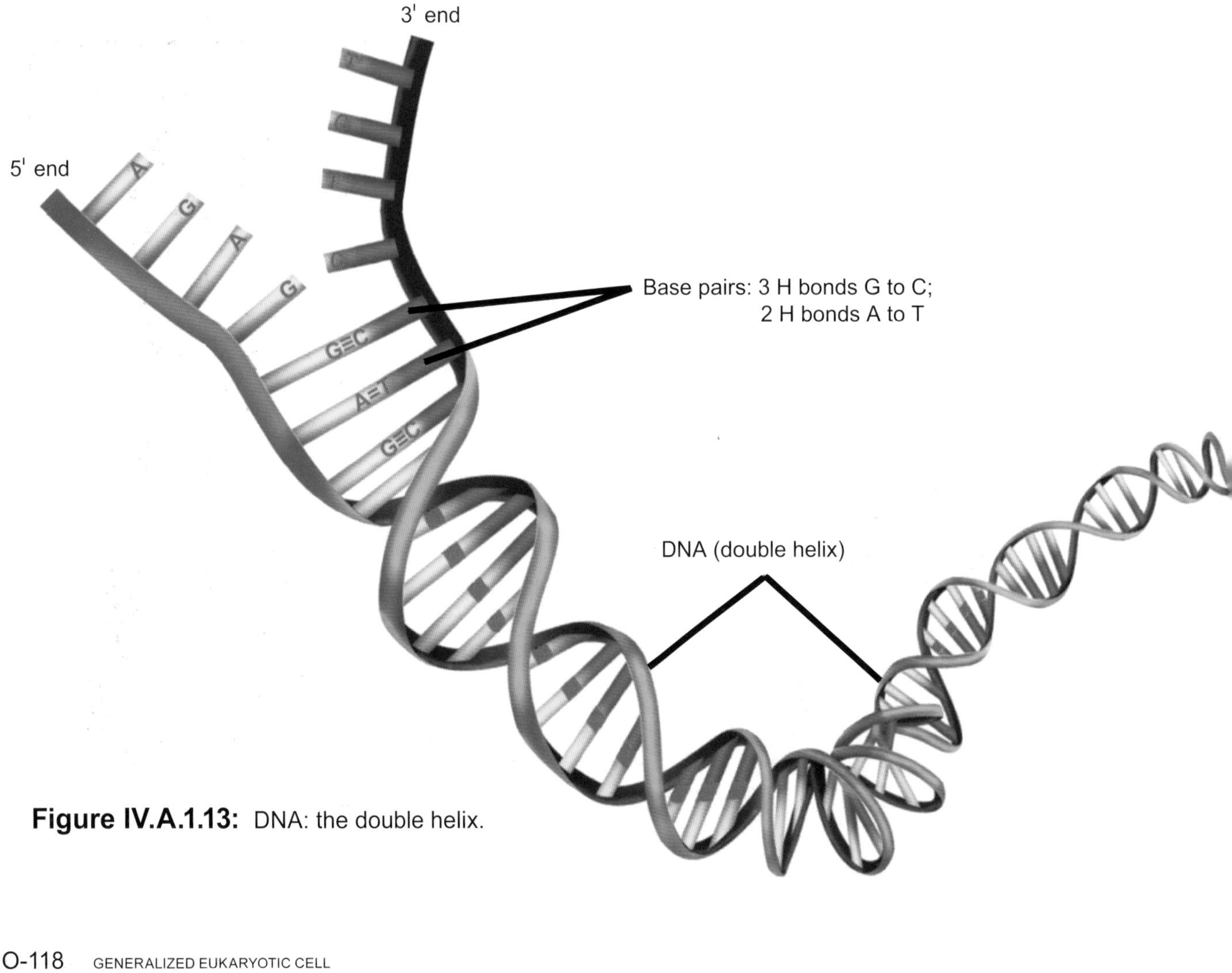

Figure IV.A.1.13: DNA: the double helix.

A cell that has accumulated a large amount of DNA damage, or one that no longer effectively repairs damage to its DNA, can: (1) become permanently dormant; (2) exhibit unregulated cell division which could lead to cancer; (3) succumb to cell suicide, also known as *apoptosis* or programmed cell death.

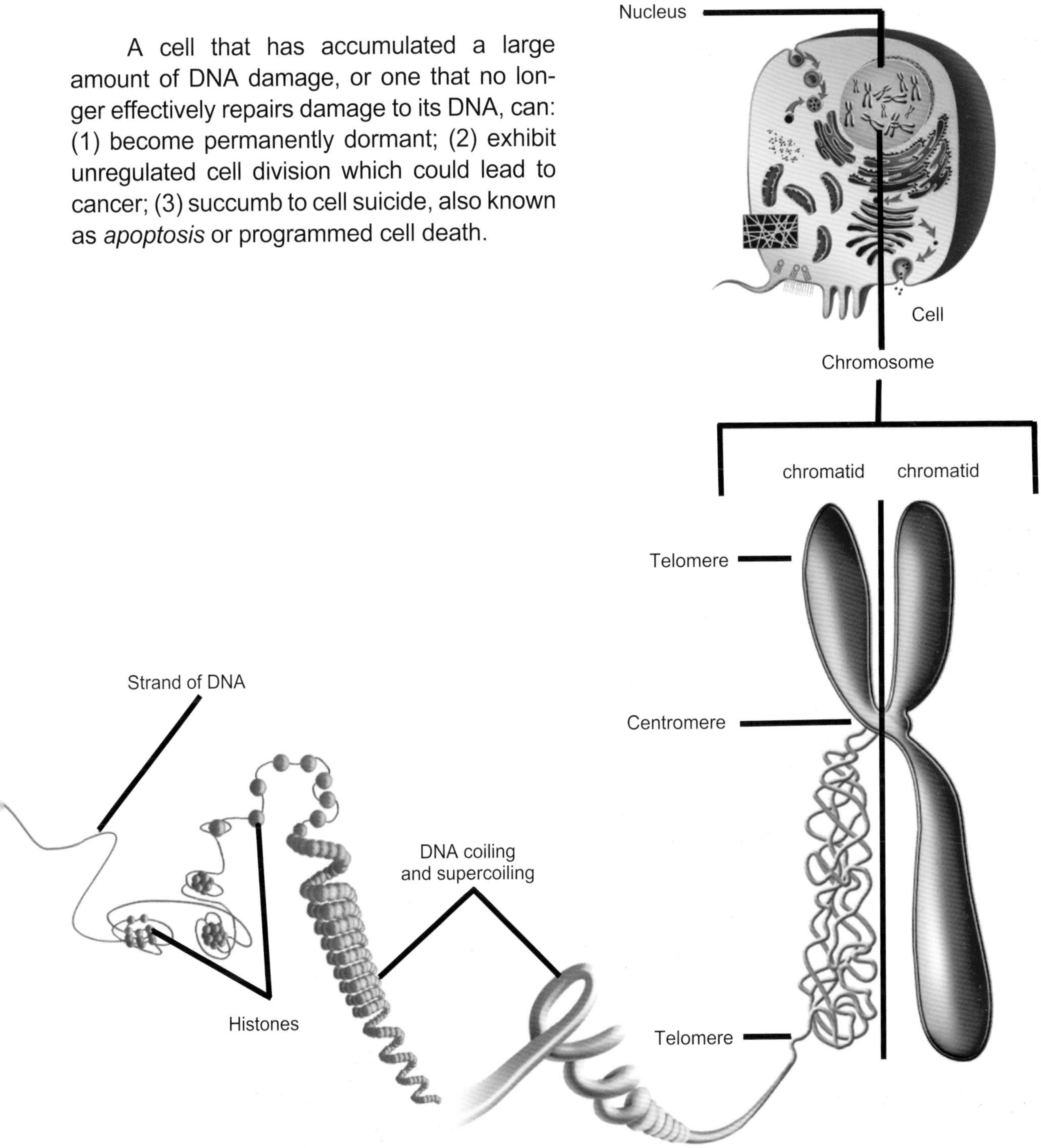

1.3 The Cell Cycle

The cell cycle is a period of approximately 18 - 22 hours during which the cell can synthesize new DNA and partition the DNA equally; thus the cell can divide. Mitosis involves nuclear division (*karyokinesis*) which is usually followed by cell division (*cytokinesis*). Mitosis and cytokinesis together define the mitotic (M) phase of the cell cycle - the division of the mother cell into two daughter cells, genetically identical to each other and to their parent cell. The cell cycle is divided into a number of phases: interphase (G_1, S, G_2) and mitosis (prophase, metaphase, anaphase and telophase).

The cell cycle is temporarily suspended in resting cells. These cells stay in the G_0 state but may reenter the cell cycle and start to divide again. The cell cycle is permanently suspended in non-dividing differentiated cells such as cardiac muscle cells. Cancer cells usually cannot enter G_0 and therefore begin to divide uncontrollably.

Interphase occupies about 90% of the cell cycle. During interphase, the cell prepares for DNA synthesis (G_1), synthesizes or replicates DNA (S) resulting in duplication of chromosomes, and ultimately begins preparing for mitosis (G_2). During interphase, the DNA is not folded and the individual chromosomes are not visible. Also, centrioles grow to maturity, RNA and protein for mitosis are synthesized. Mitosis begins with prophase.

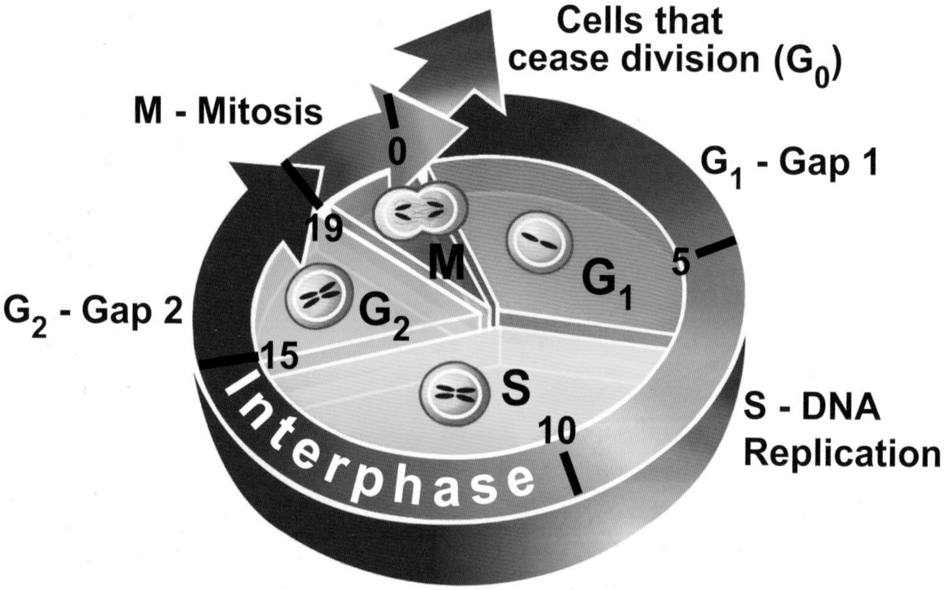

Figure IV.A.1.14: The cell cycle.
The numbers represent time in hours. Note how mitosis (M) represents the shortest period of the cycle.

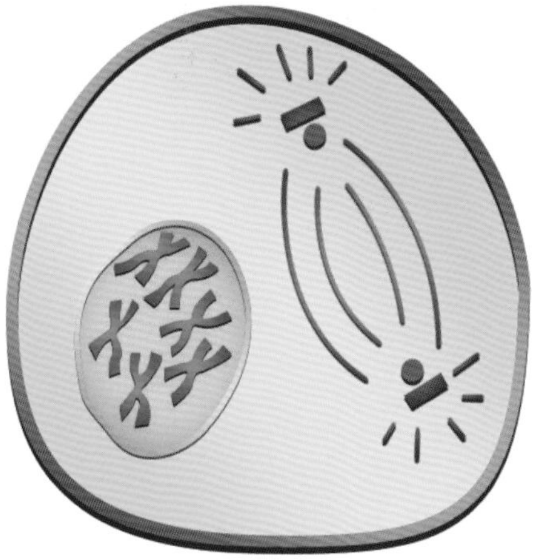

Figure IV.A.1.15: Prophase.

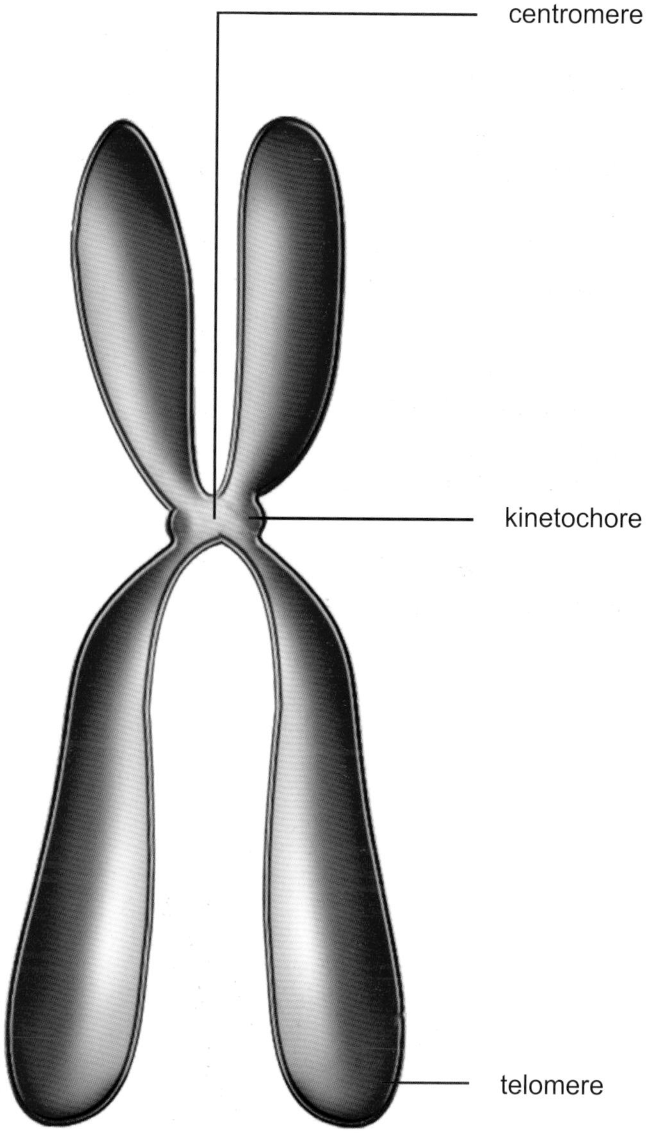

Figure IV.A.1.16: Chromosome Anatomy. Each chromosome has two arms separated by the centromere, labeled p (the shorter, named for 'petit' meaning 'small') and q (the longer of the two). The telomeres contain repetitive nucleotide sequences which protect the end of the chromosome. Over time, due to each cell division, the telomeres become shorter.

Prophase: pairs of centrioles migrate away from each other while microtubules appear in between forming a spindle. Other microtubules emanating from the centrioles give a radiating star-like appearance; thus they are called asters. Therefore, centrioles form the core of the Microtubule Organizing Centers (MTOC). The MTOC is a structure found in eukaryotic cells from which microtubules emerge and are associated with the protein tubulin.

Simultaneously, the diffuse nuclear chromatin condenses into the visible chromosomes which consist of two sister chromatids - each being identical copies of each other. Each chromatid consists of a complete double stranded DNA helix. The area of constriction where the two chromatids are attached is the *centromere*. Kinetochores develop at the centromere region and function as MTOC. Just as centromere refers to the center, *telomere* refers to the ends of the chromosome (note: as cells divide and we age, telomeres progressively shorten). Ultimately, the nuclear envelope disappears at the end of prophase.

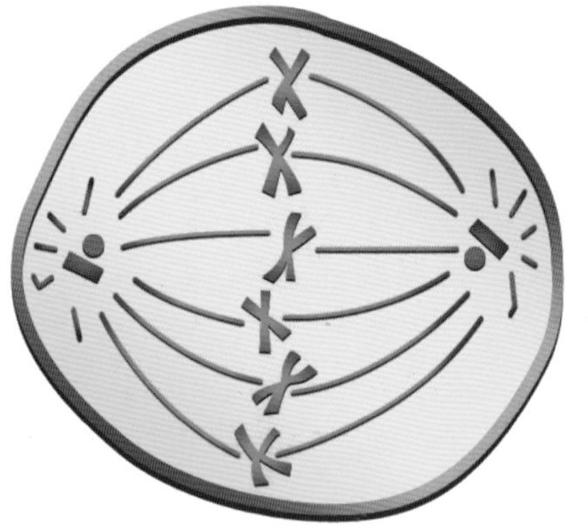

Figure IV.A.1.17: Metaphase.

Figure IV.A.1.19: Telophase.

Metaphase: centromeres line up along the equatorial plate. At or near the centromeres are the *kinetochores* which are proteins that face the spindle poles (asters). Microtubules, from the spindle, attach to the kinetochores of each chromosome.

Anaphase: sister chromatids are pulled apart such that each migrates to opposite poles being guided by spindle microtubules. At the end of anaphase, a cleavage furrow forms around the cell due to contraction of actin filaments called the contractile ring.

Telophase: new membranes form around the daughter nuclei; nucleoli reappear; the chromosomes uncoil and become less distinct (decondense). At the end of telophase, the cleavage furrow becomes deepened, facilitating the division of cytoplasm into two new daughter cells - each with a nucleus and organelles.

Finally, *cytokinesis* (cell separation) occurs. The cell cycle continues with the next interphase. {Mnemonic for the sequence of phases: P. MATI}

Figure IV.A.1.18: Anaphase.

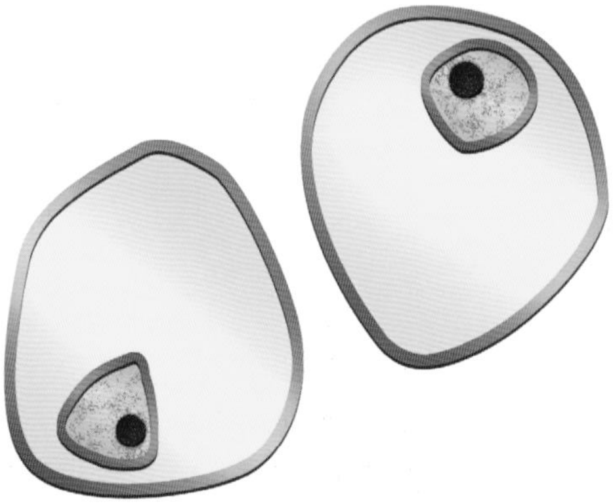

Figure IV.A.1.20: Interphase.

1.4 Cell Junctions

Multicellular organisms (i.e. animals) have cell junctions or intercellular bridges. They are especially abundant in epithelial tissues and serve as points of contact between cells and/or the extracellular matrix (BIO 4.3, 4.4). The multiprotein complex that comprise cell junctions can also build up the barrier around epithelial cells (*paracellular*) and control paracellular transport.

The molecules responsible for creating cell junctions include various ***c***ell ***a***dhesion ***m***olecules (CAMs). CAMs help cells stick to each other and to their surroundings. There are four main types: selectins, cadherins, integrins, and the immunoglobulin superfamily.

1.4.1 Types of Cell Junctions

There are three major types of cell junctions in vertebrates:

1. **Anchoring junctions**: (note: "adherens" means "to adhere to"): (i) Adherens junctions, AKA "belt desmosome" because they can appear as bands encircling the cell (= zonula adherens); they link to the actin cytoskeleton; (ii) desmosomes, AKA macula (= "spot") adherens analogous to spot welding. Desmosomes include cell adhesion proteins like cadherins which can bind intermediate filaments and provide mechanical support and stability; and (iii) hemidesmosomes ("hemi" = "half"), whereas desmosomes link two cells together, hemidesmosomes attach one cell to the extracellular matrix (usually anchoring the 'bottom' or basal aspect of the epithelial cell or keratinocyte to the basement membrane; see Fig. IV.A.1.21 and BIO 5.3).
2. **Communicating junctions**: Gap junctions which are narrow tunnels which allow the free passage of small molecules and ions. One gap junction channel is composed of two connexons (or hemichannels) which connect across the intercellular space.
3. **Occluding junctions**: Tight junctions, AKA zonula occludens, as suggested by the name, are a junctional complex that join together forming a virtually impermeable barrier to fluid. These associate with different peripheral membrane proteins located on the intracellular side of the plasma membrane which anchor the strands to the actin component of the cytoskeleton. Thus, tight junctions join together the cytoskeletons of adjacent cells. Often tight junctions form narrow belts that circumferentially surround the upper part of the lateral (i.e. "side") surfaces of adjacent epithelial cells.

Invertebrates have several other types of specific junctions; for example, the septate junction which is analogous to the tight junction in vertebrates.

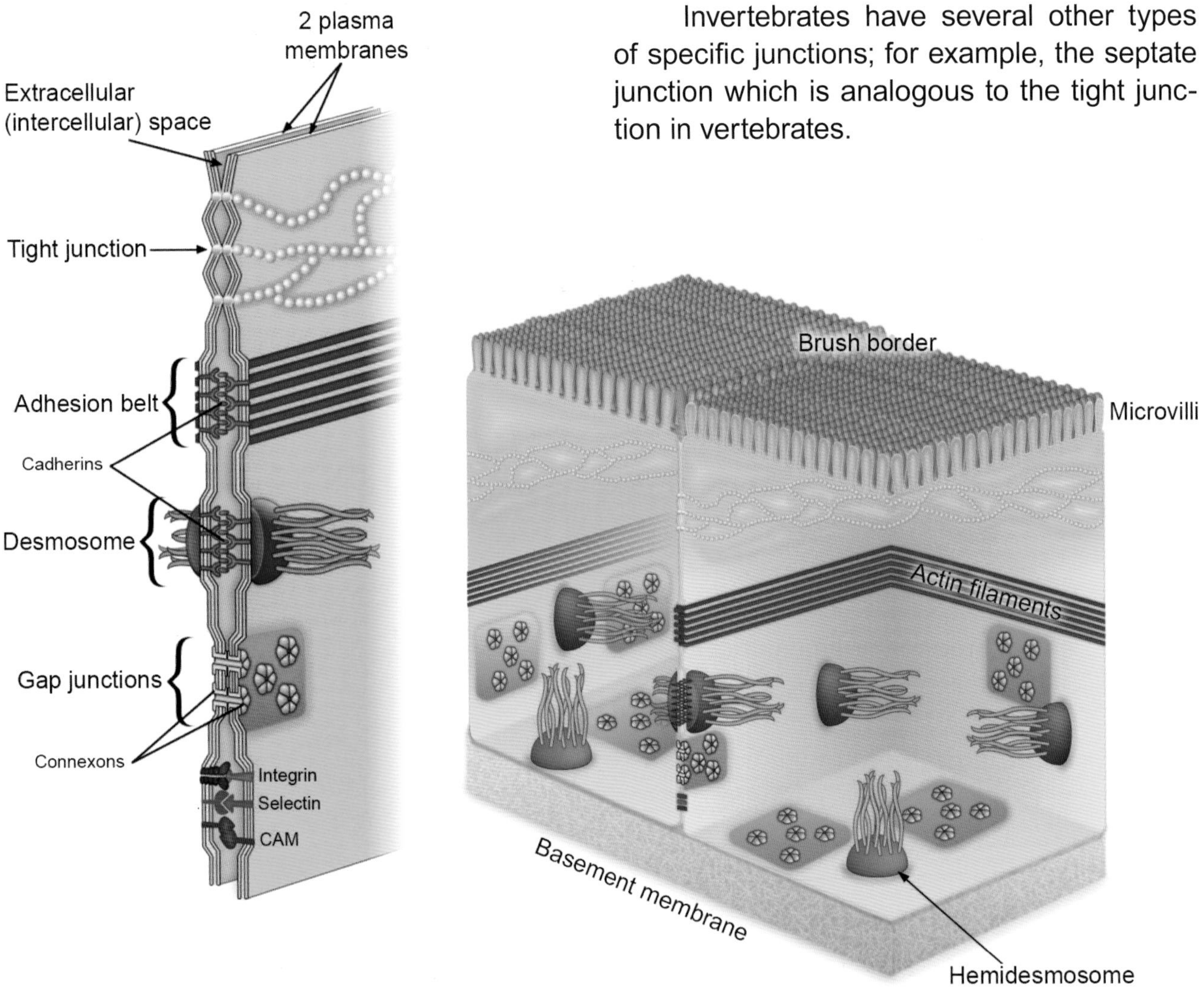

Figure IV.A.1.21: Various cell junctions in epithelia with microvilli at the surface (brush border, BIO 9.5).

1.5 Cell Theory and Microscopy

The story of "cell theory" begins in the 17th century with the instrument used to produce magnified images of objects too small to be seen by the naked eye: the microscope. The discovery of the microscope is largely attributed to Robert Hooke who coined the word "cell". After much debate and more than a century after Hooke's death, cell theory was formulated based on the following tenets:

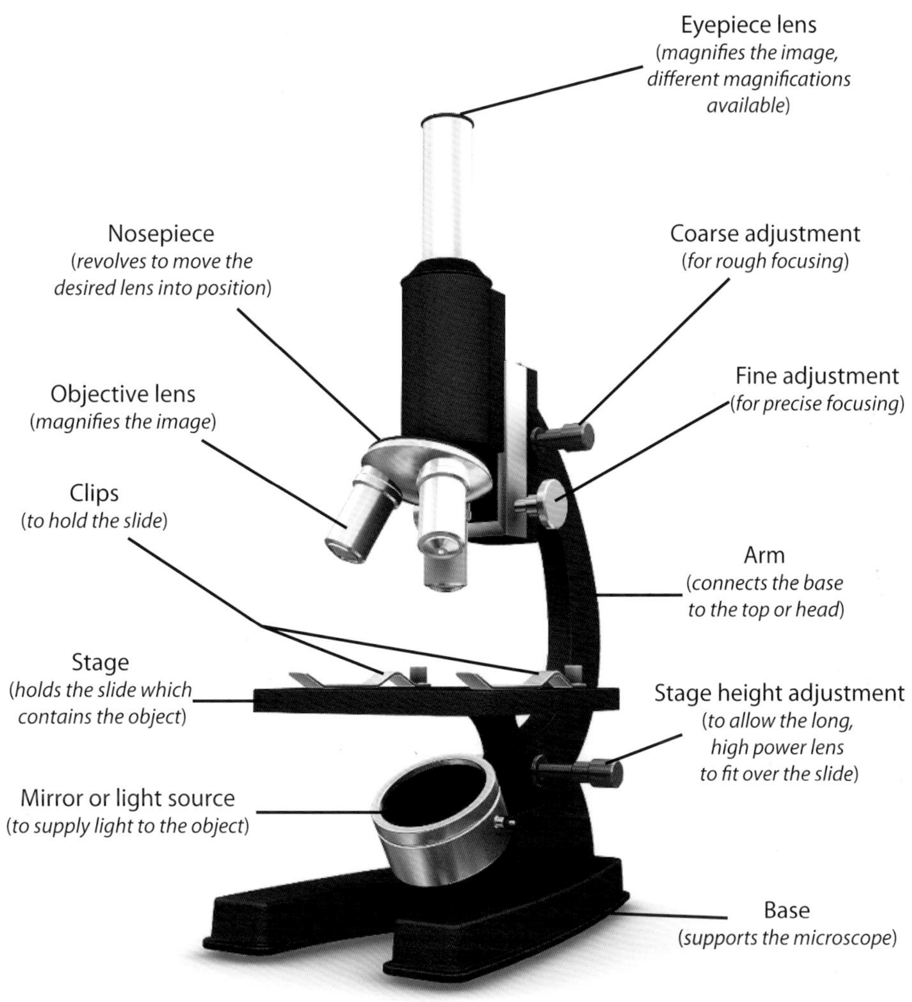

Figure IV.A.1.21: Compound light microscope. Typical magnification for the eyepiece is 10x and for the objective: 10x, 40x or 100x.

1. All living organisms are composed of one or more cells.
2. The cell is the most basic unit of life.
3. All cells arise from pre-existing, living cells.

Microscopy is an invaluable tool to understand and explore the functional unit of life - the cell. Let us compare the basic principles of two popular methods of microscopy utilized by the vast majority of molecular biology research scientists: (1) the optical or light microscope; and (2) the electron microscope (the transmission electron microscope or TEM and the scanning electron microscope or SEM).

Light microscopy involves the use of an external or internal light source. The light first

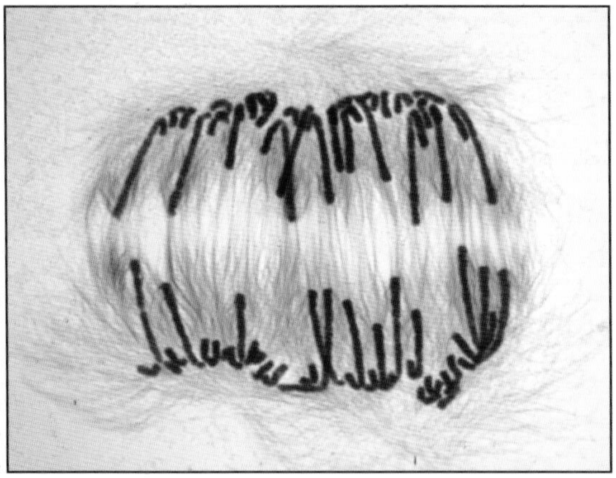

(Bajer, CIL: 197)

Figure IV.A.1.22: Light microscope image of a cell from an African lily. Staining shows microtubules in red and chromosomes in blue during late anaphase (BIO 1.3).

passes through the *iris* which controls the amount of light reaching the specimen. The light then passes through a *condenser* which is a lens that focuses the light beam through the specimen before it ultimately meets the *objective lens* which magnifies the image depending on your chosen magnification factor. Two terms you should be familiar with are *magnification* (how much bigger the image appears) and *resolution* (the ability to distinguish between two points on an image).

Magnification (PHY 11.3, 11.5) is the ratio between the apparent size of an object (or its size in an image) and its true size, and thus it is a dimensionless number usually followed by the letter "x". A compound microscope uses multiple lenses to collect light from the sample or specimen (this lens is the objective with a magnification of up to 100x), and then a separate set of lenses to focus the light into the eye or camera (the eyepiece, magnification up to 10x). So the total magnification can be 100 x 10 = 1000 times the size of the specimen (1000x makes a 100 nanometer object visible).

Light microscopes enjoy their popularity thanks to their relative low cost and ease of use. A very important feature is that they can be used to view live specimens. Their shortfall is that the magnification is limited.

Common Units of Length in Biology

- m = meter(s)
- cm = centimeter(s) (1 cm = 10^{-2} m)
- mm = millimeter(s) (1 mm = 10^{-3} m)
- µm = micrometer(s) (1 µm = 10^{-6} m)
  NOT micron or µ
- nm = nanometer(s) (1 nm = 10^{-9} m)
- Å = angstrom(s) (1 Å = 10^{-10} m)
- pm = picometer(s) (1 pm = 10^{-12} m)

The term "micron" is no longer in technical use.

Electron microscopy is less commonly used due to its high price and associated scarcity. It also cannot observe live organisms as a vacuum is required and the specimen is flooded with electrons. All images being produced are in black and white though color is sometimes added to the raw images. Its primary advantage lies in the fact that it is possible to achieve a magnification up to 10,000,000x and it is the obvious choice when a high level of detail is required using an extremely small specimen. In fact, an object as tiny as a small fraction of a nanometer becomes visible with an incredible 50 picometer resolution. TEM shows the interior of the cell while SEM shows the surface of the specimen.

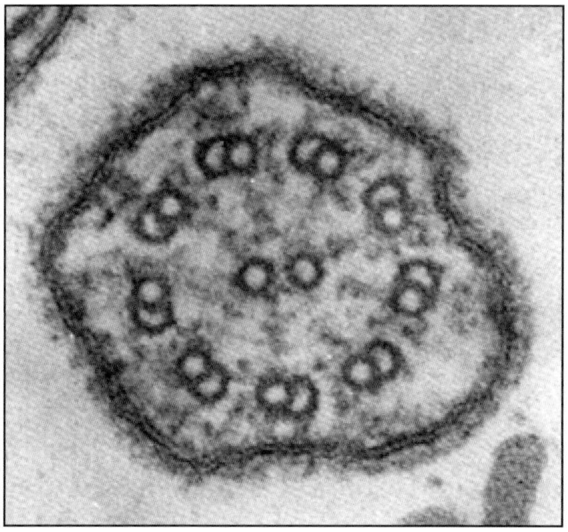

Figure IV.A.1.23: TEM of the cross section of a cilium (BIO 1.2) showing an axoneme consisting of 9 doublet and 2 central microtubules (= 9x2 + 2). Each doublet is composed of 2 subfibers: a complete A subfiber with dynein and an attached B subfiber. Eukaryotic flagella are also 9x2 + 2.

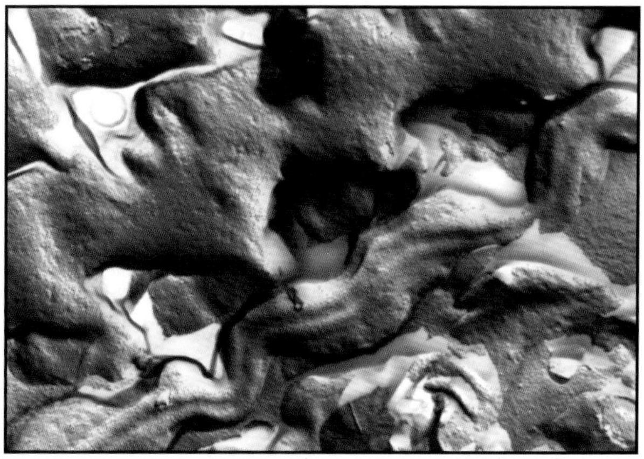

Figure IV.A.1.24: TEM freeze fracture of the plasma membrane which is cleaved between the acyl tails of membrane phospholipids (BIO 1.1; BCM 1.4), leaving a monolayer on each half of the specimen. The "E" face is the inner face of the outer lipid monolayer. The complementary surface is the "P" face (the inner surface of the inner leaflet of the bilayer shown above). The 2 large ribbons are intrinsic proteins.

1.5.1 Fluorescent Microscopy and Immunofluorescence

Lastly, you should be familiar with fluorescent microscopy which is commonly used to identify cellular components (organelles, cytoskeleton, etc.) and microbes with a high degree of specificity and color. The fluorescent microscope makes use of a special filter that only permits certain radiation wavelengths that matches the fluorescing material being analyzed. It is an optical microscope and very similar to the light microscope except that a highly intensive light source is used to excite a fluorescent species in the sample of interest.

Immunofluorescence is a technique that uses the specificity of the antibody-antigen interaction (BIO 8.2) to target fluorescent dyes to specific molecules in a cell. Immunofluorescence can be used on tissue sections, cultured cell lines or individual cells. This can be called *immunostaining*, or specifically, *immunohistochemistry* where the location of the antibodies can be seen using fluorophores (= a fluorescent chemical that can re-emit light upon light excitation; PHY 12.5, 12.6).

There are two classes of immunofluorescence: direct (= primary) and indirect (= secondary).

Direct immunofluorescence uses a single antibody linked to a fluorophore. The antibody binds to the target molecule (antigen), and the fluorophore attached to the antibody can be detected with a microscope. This technique is cheaper, faster but less sensitive than indirect immunofluorescence.

Indirect immunofluorescence uses two antibodies: (1) the unlabeled first, or primary, antibody binds the antigen; and (2) the secondary antibody, which carries the fluorophore and recognizes the primary antibody and binds to it.

Photobleaching is the photochemical destruction of a dye or a fluorophore. Thus the fluorescent molecules are sometimes destroyed by the light exposure necessary to stimulate them into fluorescing. On the other hand, photobleaching can be fine tuned to improve the signal-to-noise ratio (like seeing the tree from the forest). Photobleaching can also be used to study the motion of molecules (i.e. FRAP).

Immunofluorescence samples can be seen through a simple fluorescent microscope (*epifluorescence*) or through the more complex *confocal* microscope.

A confocal microscope is a state-of-the-art fluorescent microscope which uses a laser as the light source. The confocal microscope is used in FRAP, ***f***luorescence ***r***ecovery ***a***fter ***p***hotobleaching, which is an optical technique used to "view" the movement of proteins or molecules. FRAP is capable of quantifying the 2D diffusion of a thin film of molecules containing fluorescently labeled probes, or to examine single cells. FRAP has had many uses including: studies of cell membrane diffusion and protein binding; determining if axonal transport is retrograde or anterograde, meaning towards or away from the neuron's cell body (soma), respectively.

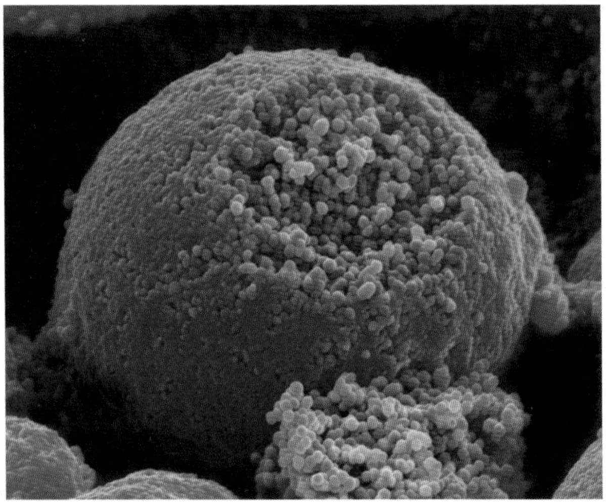

(Carvalho, CIL: 214)

Figure IV.A.1.25: SEM colorized image of a neuron's presynaptic terminal (BIO 5.1) that has been broken open to reveal the synaptic vesicles (orange and blue) beneath the cell membrane.

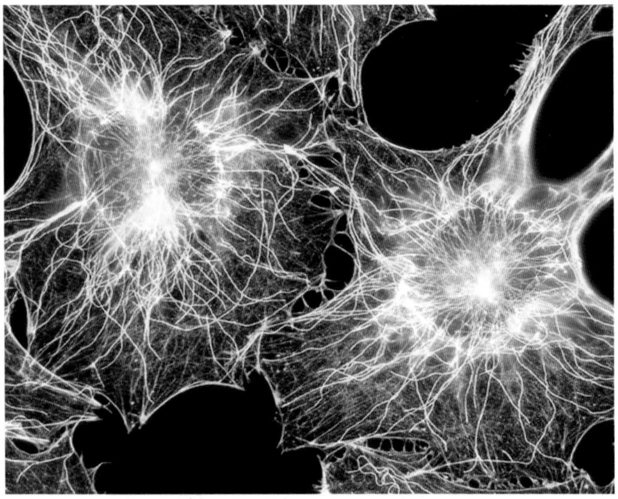

(Wittmann, CIL: 240)

Figure IV.A.1.26: Fluorescence microscopy of two interphase cells with immunofluorescence labeling of actin filaments (purple), microtubules (yellow), and nuclei (green).

GOLD STANDARD WARM-UP EXERCISES

CHAPTER 1: Generalized Eukaryotic Cell

1) Proteins in the plasma membrane can diffuse laterally, however, the specific orientations maintained by integral membrane proteins with respect to the bilayer suggest that rotation of these molecules through the plane of the bilayer very rarely occurs. The most likely reason for this is:

A. the carbohydrate attachments to many of the proteins makes rotation impossible.
B. rotation of these proteins would affect their ability to channel specific ions and molecules.
C. rotation of these proteins would affect the permeability of the plasma membrane.
D. since most integral proteins have some hydrophilic surface area, a transverse rotation would be energetically unfavorable.

2) Some peripheral proteins are bound to the membrane due to interactions with the integral membrane proteins. These interactions are likely:

A. hydrophobic in nature.
B. electrostatic in nature.
C. covalent in nature.
D. due to Van Der Waal's bonds.

3) Proteins are frequently adorned by straight/chain or branched oligosaccharides, in which case they are called glycoproteins. This type of modification can serve a variety of functions including to provide the protein with surface characteristics that facilitate its recognition. In which of the following cellular components would the greatest proportion of glycoproteins be expected?

A. Lysosomes
B. Microfilaments
C. Mitochondria
D. Phospholipid bilayer

4) Oligosaccharide modification most likely occurs in the:

A. smooth endoplasmic reticulum.
B. Golgi apparatus.
C. lysosomes.
D. cytosol.

5) Sweat is less concentrated than blood plasma and is secreted by the activity of sweat glands under the control of pseudomotor neurons. The transport of electrolytes in sweat from blood plasma to the sweat glands is best accounted for by which of the following processes?

A. Osmosis
B. Simple diffusion
C. Active transport
D. All of the above

6) Microfilaments and microtubules would have an important locomotive function in all but which of the following organelles?

A. Flagella
B. Endocytotic vesicles
C. Lysosomes
D. None of the above

7) All of the following are closely associated with microtubules EXCEPT:

A. flagella.
B. cilia.
C. villi.
D. centrioles.

8) Fas/APO-1 is a transmembrane receptor which, when stimulated, may activate intracellular mechanisms leading to cell death. Fas/APO-1 is likely:

A. a phospholipid.
B. a complex carbohydrate.
C. synthesized in the nucleus.
D. synthesized by rough endoplasmic reticulum.

9) The ATP-dependent dopamine transporter can be found at the presynaptic terminal of nerve cells. By which of the following mechanisms would the dopamine transporter most likely work?

A. Simple diffusion
B. Facilitated transport
C. Passive co-transport
D. Active transport

10) An effect of UV radiation on DNA is the formation of harmful covalent bonds among bases. For example, adjacent thymines form thymine dimers. Which of the following is most likely true of the bonds which create the dimers?

A. They consist of two carbon-carbon bonds between purines.
B. They consist of two carbon-carbon bonds between pyrimidines.
C. They consist of one carbon-carbon bond and one oxygen-sulfur bond between pyrimidines.
D. They consist of one carbon-carbon bond and one nitrogen-sulfur bond between pyrimidines.

11) Which of the following statements could be held LEAST accountable for DNA maintaining its helical structure?

A. Unwinding the helix would separate the base pairs enough for water molecules to enter between the bases, making the structure unstable.
B. The helix is stabilized by hydrogen bonds between bases.
C. The sugar phosphate backbone is held in place by hydrophilic interactions with the solvent.
D. C-G pairs have 3 hydrogen bonds between them but A-T pairs only have 2.

12) Apo-X is a drug which blocks prophase from occurring. When Apo-X is added to a tissue culture, in which phase of the cell cycle would most cells be arrested?

A. Mitosis
B. G_1
C. G_2
D. Synthesis

13) Evidence that DNA replication occurs in a bidirectional manner would be that shortly after initiation:

A. each gene in the E. coli genome would be represented only once.
B. each gene in the E. coli genome would be represented twice.
C. DNA duplication would begin on both sides of the origin of replication.
D. gene frequencies should be very high for regions symmetrically disposed about the origin.

14) If E. coli was allowed to replicate in the presence of ^{3}H-thymidine, during the second round of replication, what would an autoradiograph, which detects irradiation, show proving that the replication was semi-conservative?

A. A uniformly unlabeled structure
B. A uniformly labeled structure
C. One branch of the growing replication eye would be half as strongly labeled as the remainder of the chromosome
D. One branch of the growing replication eye would be twice as strongly labeled as the remainder of the chromosome

15) Colchicine is a plant alkaloid that inhibits normal mitosis by delaying the formation of daughter cells by inhibiting chromatid segregation. The advantage of colchicine treatment in this experiment is that in tissue so treated many cells become arrested in the state where the sister chromatids are paired. Colchicine might act by:

A. disrupting mitotic spindle formation.
B. inhibiting DNA synthesis.
C. inhibiting the replication of chromosomes.
D. preventing the degeneration of the nuclear envelope.

16) The Sanger method for sequencing DNA uses newly synthesized DNA that is randomly terminated. The method employs chain-terminating dideoxynucleotide triphosphates (ddXTPs) to produce a continuous series of fragments during catalyzed reactions. The ddXTPs act as terminators because while they can add to a growing chain during polymerization, they cannot be added onto because they must lack a:

A. hydroxyl group on their phosphoric acid component.
B. hydroxyl group on C1 of their ribose component.
C. hydroxyl group on C3 of their ribose component.
D. hydroxyl group on C5 of their ribose component.

17) When DNA is being sequenced, the appropriate enzymes are added to make a complementary copy of a primed single-stranded DNA fragment. Which of the following enzymes would have to be included in the Sanger method in order for it to work?

A. DNA gyrase
B. DNA polymerase
C. Reverse transcriptase
D. DNA helicase

18) The least likely of the following radioactive deoxynucleoside triphosphates to be used to label DNA fragments is:

A. dATP
B. dGTP
C. dUTP
D. dCTP

19) E. coli bacteriophages were added to E. coli cells in a medium containing inorganic ^{32}P-labelled phosphate and ^{35}S-labelled inorganic sulfate. After infection of the cells had occurred, examination of the progeny would show that:

A. the phosphorus had been incorporated into both the DNA and the protein components of the bacteriophages
B. the sulfur became incorporated into both the DNA and protein components of the bacteriophages.
C. the phosphorus became incorporated into the DNA component of the phages and the sulfur into their protein component.
D. the sulfur became incorporated into the DNA component of the phages and the phosforus into their protein component.

20) If increasing the concentration gradient across the plasma membrane increases the rate of transport until a maximum rate is reached, this would be convincing evidence for:

A. simple diffusion.
B. carrier-mediated transport.
C. osmosis.
D. the Fluid Mosaic model.

21. Receptor-mediated endocytosis is usually associated with:

A. clathrin.
B. selectin.
C. integrin.
D. tubulin.

22. In desmosomes, cadherins link to what aspect of an adjacent cell?

A. Intermediate filaments
B. Connexons
C. Actin
D. Integrins

23. Which of the following surrounds the cell like a belt and prevents the passage of substances between the cells?

A. Hemidesmosome
B. Tight junction
C. Desmosome
D. Gap junction

24. If the ocular of a light microscope is 10x and the objective is set at 40x, then what is the total magnification of the microscope?

A. 400x
B. 50x
C. 40x
D. 10x

25. A microscope used to visualize specific fluorophore-labeled proteins in a living cell is the:

A. compound light microscope.
B. transmission electron microscope (TEM).
C. scanning electron microscope (SEM).
D. confocal microscope.

GS ANSWER KEY

CHAPTER 1

		Cross-Reference			*Cross-Reference*
1.	D	BIO 1.1, ORG 12.1.1	14.	D	BIO 1.2.2
2.	B	BIO 1.1, ORG 12.1-12.2.2, CHM 4.2	15.	A	BIO 1.2, 1.3
3.	D	BIO 1.1	16.	C	BIO 1.2.2, ORG 12.5
4.	B	BIO 1.2.1	17.	B	BIO 1.2.2
5.	B	BIO 1.1.1	18.	C	BIO 1.2.2
6.	D	BIO 1.2, 1.2.1, 7.5F	19.	C	BIO 1.2.2, ORG 12.2.2
7.	C	BIO 1.2	20.	B	BIO 1.2.2
8.	D	BIO 1.1, 1.2.1	21.	A	BIO 1.1.3
9.	D	BIO 1.2.2	22.	A	BIO 1.4.1
10.	B	BIO 1.2.2, ORG 12.2.2	23.	B	BIO 1.4.1
11.	A	BIO 1.2.2	24.	A	BIO 1.5
12.	C	BIO 1.3	25.	D	BIO 1.5, 1.5.1
13.	C	BIO 1.2.2, 3.0			

*** Explanations can be found at the back of the book.**

Go online to MCAT-prep.com/forum to join the discussion about our GS chapter review questions.

MICROBIOLOGY
Chapter 2

Memorize

* Structures, functions, life cycles
* Generalized viral life cycle
* Basic categories of bacteria
* Equation for bacterial doubling
* Differences, similtarities

Understand

* Eukaryotes vs. Prokaryotes
* General aspects of life cycles
* Gen. aspects of genetics/reproduction
* Calculation of exponential growth
* Basics: operons and vectors
* Scientific method

Clinical Correlation

In the past, microbiologists relied on cell cultures, staining and microscopy. Now microbiologists also use extraction or detection of nucleic acids (i.e. DNA or RNA sequences). On the positive side of microorganisms, they can be used to make antibiotics, enzymes, vitamins, vaccines, etc.

MCAT-Prep.com

Introduction

Microbiology is the study of microscopic organisms including viruses, bacteria and fungi. It is important to be able to focus on the differences and similarities between these microorganisms and the generalized eukaryotic cell you have just studied. Their differences and similarities form the basis of perennial MCAT questions.

Optional Gold Standard Resources

Free Online Q&A + Forum

Online Videos

Flashcards

Special Guest

2.1 Viruses

Unlike cells, viruses are too small to be seen directly with a light microscope. Viruses infect all types of organisms, from animals and plants to bacteria and archaea (BIO 2.2). Only a very basic and general understanding of viruses is required for the MCAT.

Viruses are obligate intracellular parasites; in other words, in order to replicate their genetic material and thus multiply, they must gain access to the inside of a cell. Replication of a virus takes place when the virus takes control of the host cell's synthetic machinery. Viruses are often considered non-living for several reasons:

(i) they do not grow by increasing in size

(ii) they cannot carry out independent metabolism

(iii) they do not respond to external stimuli

(iv) they have no cellular structure.

The genetic material for viruses may be either DNA or RNA, never both. Viruses do not have organelles or ribosomes. The nucleic acid core is encapsulated by a protein coat (capsid) which together forms the head region in some viruses. The tail region helps to anchor the virus to a cell. An extracellular viral particle is called a *virion*.

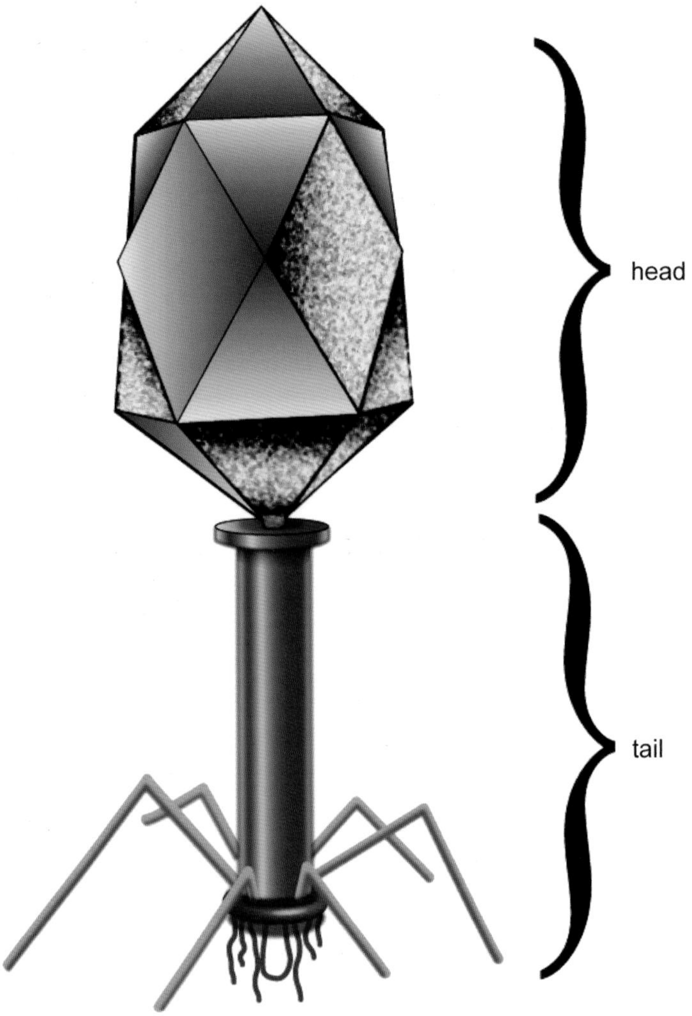

Figure IV.A.2.1: A virus.

Viruses are much smaller than prokaryotic cells (i.e. bacteria) which, in turn, are much smaller than eukaryotes (i.e. animal cells, fungi). A virus which infects bacteria is called a bacteriophage or simply a phage.

The life cycle of viruses has many variants; the following represents the main themes for MCAT purposes. A virus attaches to a specific receptor on a cell. Some viruses may now enter the cell; others, as in the diagram, will simply inject their nucleic acid. Either way, viral molecules induce the metabolic machinery of the host cell to produce more viruses.

The new viral particles may now exit the cell by lysing (bursting). This is also a feature of many bacteria. The preceding is deemed lytic or virulent. Some virus lie latent for long periods of time without lysing the host and its genome becomes incorporated by genetic recombination into the host's chromosome. Therefore, whenever the host replicates, the viral genome is also replicated. These are called lysogenic or temperate viruses. Eventually, at some point, the virus may become activated and lyse the host cell.

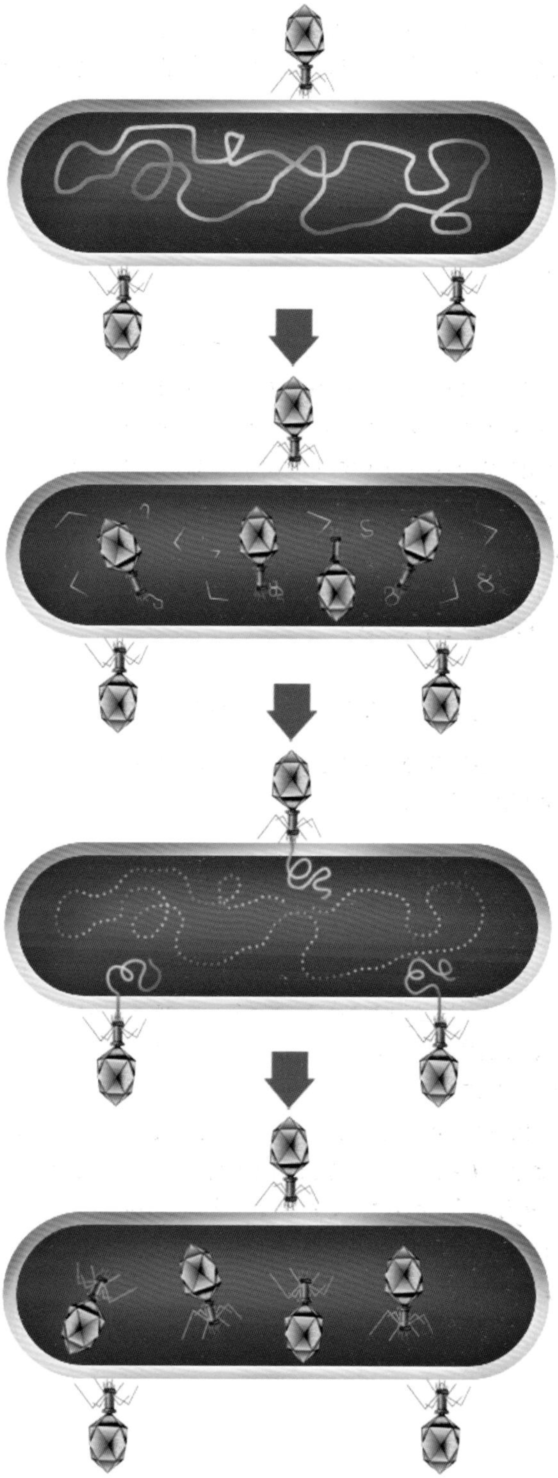
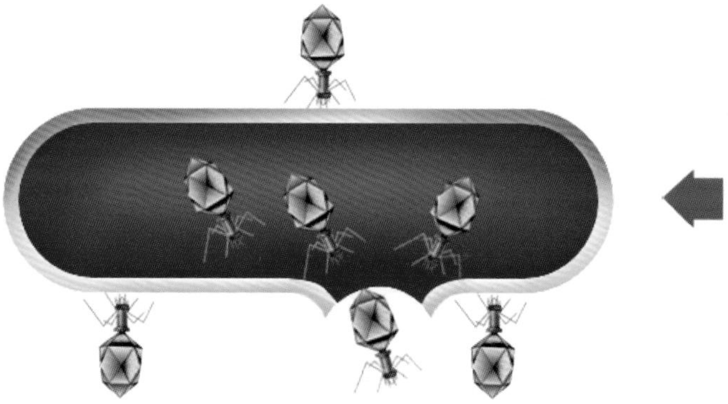

Figure IV.A.2.2: Lytic viral life cycle in a rod shaped bacterium (bacilli).

2.1.1 Retroviruses

A retrovirus uses RNA as its genetic material. It is called a retrovirus because of an enzyme (reverse transcriptase) that gives these viruses the unique ability of transcribing RNA (their RNA) into DNA (see Biology Chapter 3 for the central dogma regarding protein synthesis). The retroviral DNA can then integrate into the chromosomal DNA of the host cell to be expressed there. The human immunodeficiency virus (HIV), the cause of AIDS, is a retrovirus.

Retroviruses are used, in genetics, to deliver DNA to a cell (= a vector); in medicine, they are used for gene therapy.

2.2 Prokaryotes

Prokaryotes (= pre-nucleus) are organisms without a membrane bound nucleus which includes 2 types of organisms: bacteria (= Eubacteria) and archaea (= bacteria-like organisms that live in extreme environments). For the purposes of the MCAT, we will focus on bacteria. They are haploid and have a long circular strand of DNA in a region called the nucleoid.

The nucleoid is a region in a bacterium that contains DNA but is not surrounded by a nuclear membrane. Because bacterial DNA is not surrounded by a nuclear membrane, transcription and translation can occur at the same time, that is, protein synthesis can begin while mRNA is being produced. Bacteria also have smaller circular DNA called plasmid, which is extra chromosomal genetic element that can replicate independently of the bacterial chromosome and helps to confer resistance to antibiotics.

Bacteria do not have mitochondria, Golgi apparatus, lysosomes, nor endoplasmic reticulum. Instead, metabolic processes can

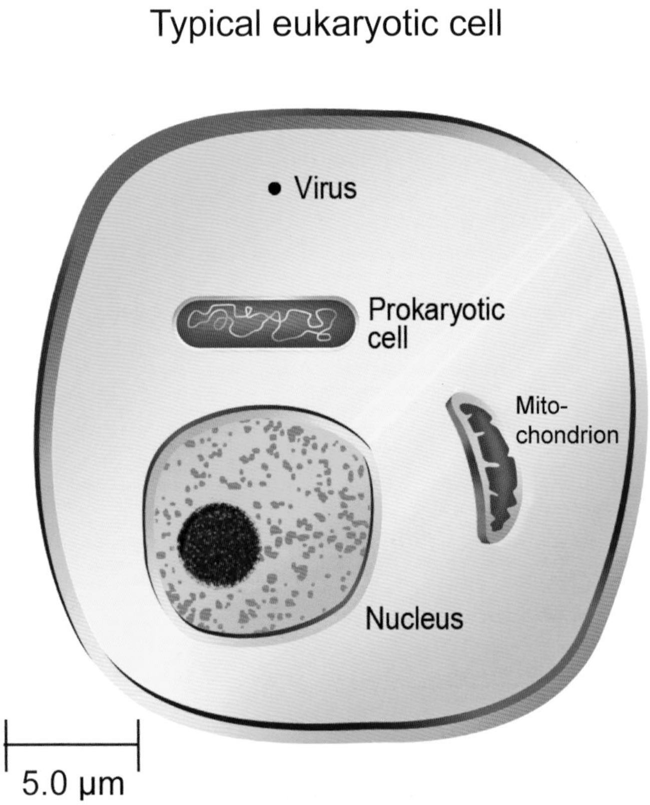

Figure IV.A.2.3
Comparing the size of a typical eukaryote, prokaryote and virus. Note that both the prokaryote and mitochondrion are similar in size and both contain circular DNA suggesting an evolutionary link.

be carried out in the cytoplasm or associated with bacterial membranes. Bacteria have ribosomes (smaller than eukaryotes), plasma membrane, and a cell wall. The cell wall, made of peptidoglycans, helps to prevent the hypertonic bacterium from bursting. Some bacteria have a slimy polysaccharide mucoid-like capsule on the outer surface for protection.

Bacteria can achieve movement with their flagella. Bacterial flagella are helical filaments, each with a rotary motor at its base which can turn clockwise or counterclockwise.

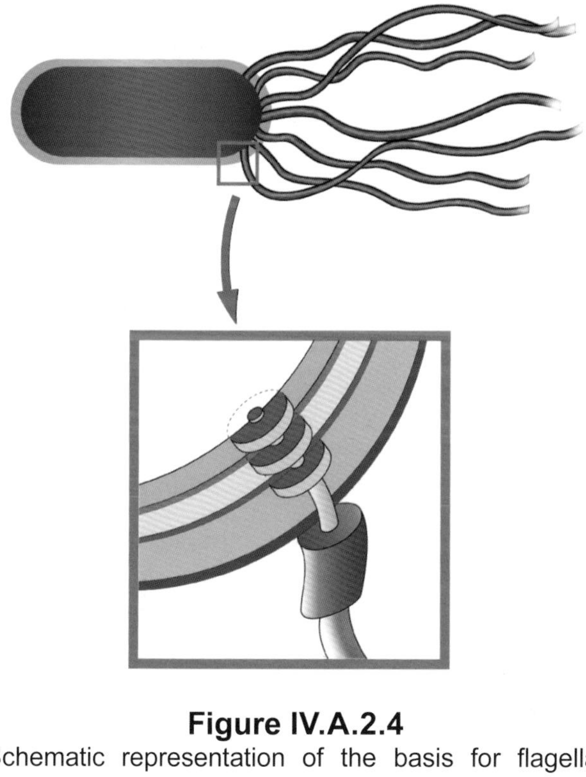

Figure IV.A.2.4
Schematic representation of the basis for flagellar propulsion. The flagellum, similar to a flexible hook, is anchored to the membrane and cell wall by a series of protein rings forming a motor. Powered by the flow of protons, the motor can rotate the flagellum more than 100 revolutions per second. Compare with ATP Synthase (BCM 2.6).

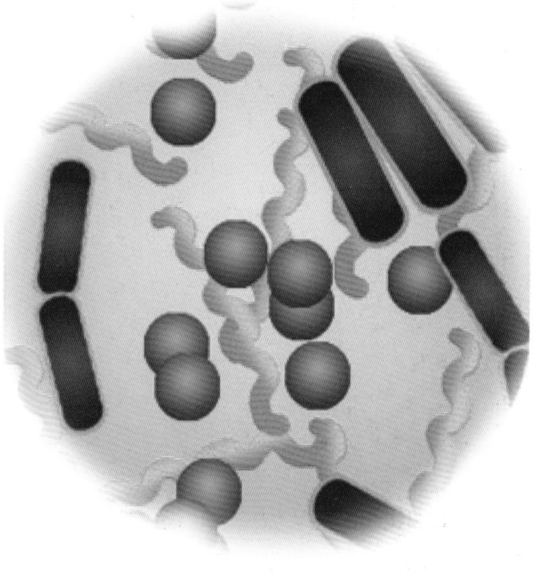

Figure IV.A.2.5
Schematic representation of bacteria colored for the purpose of identification: cocci (spherical, green), bacilli (cylindrical, purple) and spirilli (helical, orange).

The form and rotary engine of flagella are maintained by proteins (i.e. flagellin) which interact with the plasma membrane and the basal body (BIO 1.2). Power is generated by a proton motive force similar to the proton pump in metabolism (BCM 2.6, 3.5).

Bacteria also have short, hairlike filaments called pili (also called fimbriae) arising from the bacterial cell wall. These pili are much shorter than flagella. Common pili can serve as adherence factors which promote binding of bacteria to host cells. Sex pili, encoded by a self-transmissible plasmid, are involved in transferring of DNA from one bacterium to another via conjugation.

Bacteria are partially classified according to their shapes: <u>cocci</u> which are spheri-

Prokaryotic Cells	Eukaryotic Cells
Small cells (1-10 μm)	Larger cells (10-100 μm)
Always unicellular	Often multicellular
No nuclei or any membrane-bound organelles, such as mitochondria	Always have nuclei and other membrane-bound organelles
DNA is circular, without proteins	DNA is linear and associated with proteins to form chromatin
Ribosomes are small (70S)	Ribosomes are large (80S)
No cytoskeleton	Always has a cytoskeleton
Motility by rigid rotating flagellum made of flagellin)	Motility by flexible waving cilia or flagellae (made of tubulin)
Cell division is by binary fission	Cell division is by mitosis or meiosis
Reproduction is always asexual	Reproduction is asexual or sexual
Great variety of metabolic pathways	Common metabolic pathways

Table IV.A.2.1: Summary of the differences between prokaryotic and eukaryotic cells.

cal or sometimes elliptical; bacilli which are rod shaped or cylindrical (Fig. IV.A.2.2 in BIO 2.1 showed phages attacking a bacillus bacterium); spirilli which are helical or spiral. They are also classified according to whether or not their cell wall reacts to a special dye called a Gram stain; thus they are gram-positive if they retain the stain and gram-negative if they do not.

Most bacteria engage in a form of asexual reproduction called binary fission. Two identical DNA molecules migrate to opposite ends of a cell as a transverse wall forms, dividing the cell in two. The cells can now separate and enlarge to the original size. Under ideal conditions, a bacterium can undergo fission every 10-20 minutes producing over 10^{30} progeny in a day and a half. If resources are unlimited, exponential growth would be expected. The doubling time of bacterial populations can be calculated as follows:

$$b = B \times 2^n$$

where b is the number of bacteria at the end of the time interval, B is the number of bacteria at the beginning of the time interval and n is the number of generations. Thus if we start with 2 bacteria and follow for 3 generations then we get:

$$b = B \times 2^n = 2 \times 2^3 = 2 \times 8 = 16$$

bacteria after 3 generations.

{Note: bacterial doubling time is a relatively popular question type.}

Bacteria do not produce gametes nor zygotes, nor do they undergo meiosis; however, four forms of genetic recombination do occur: transduction, transformation, conjugation and transposon insertion.

In transduction, fragments of bacterial chromosome accidentally become packaged into virus during a viral infection. These viruses may then infect another bacterium. A piece of bacterial DNA that the virus is accidentally carrying will be injected and incorporated into the host chromosome if there is homology between the newly injected piece of DNA and the recipient bacterial genome.

In transformation, a foreign chromosome fragment (plasmid) is released from one bacterium during cell lysis and enters into another bacterium. The DNA can then become incorporated into the recipient's genome if there is homology between the newly incorporated genome and the recipient one.

In conjugation, DNA is transferred directly by cell-to-cell contact formed by a conjugation bridge called the sex pilus. For conjugation to occur, one bacterium must have the sex factor called F plasmid. Bacteria that carry F plasmids are called F^+ cells. During conjugation, a F^+ cell replicates its F factor and will pass its F plasmid to an F^- cell, converting it to an F^+ cell. This type of exchange is the major mechanism for transfer of antibiotic resistance.

In transposon insertion, mobile genetic elements called transposons move from one position to another in a bacterial chromosome or between different molecules of DNA without having DNA homology.

Most bacteria cannot synthesize their own food and thus depend on other organisms for it; such a bacterium is heterotrophic. Most heterotrophic bacteria obtain their food from dead organic matter; this is called saprophytic. Some bacteria are autotrophic meaning they can synthesize organic compounds from simple inorganic substances. Thus some are photosynthetic producing carbohydrate and releasing oxygen, while others are chemoautotrophic obtaining energy via chemical reactions including the oxidation of iron, sulfur, nitrogen, or hydrogen gas.

Bacteria can be either aerobic or anaerobic. The former refers to metabolism in the presence of oxygen and the latter in the absence of oxygen (i.e. fermentation).

Based on variations in the oxygen requirement, bacteria are divided into four types:

1) Obligate aerobes: require oxygen for growth

2) Facultative anaerobes: are aerobic; however, can grow in the absence of oxygen by undergoing fermentation
3) Aerotolerant anaerobes: use fermentation for energy; however, can tolerate low amounts of oxygen
4) Obligate anaerobes: are anaerobic, can be damaged by oxygen

Symbiosis generally refers to close and often long term interactions between different biological species. Bacteria have various symbiotic relationships with, for example, humans. These include mutualism (both benefit: GI tract bacteria, BIO 9.5), parasitism (parasite benefits over the host: tuberculosis, appendicitis) and commensalism (one benefits and the other is not significantly harmed or benefited: some skin bacteria).

2.2.1 Operons

E. coli is a gram-negative, rod-shaped intestinal bacterium with DNA sequences called *operons* that direct biosynthetic pathways. Operons are composed of:

1. A repressor which can bind to an operator and prevent gene expression by blocking RNA polymerase. However, in the presence of an inducer, a repressor will be bound to the inducer instead, forming an inducer-repressor complex. This complex cannot bind to an operator and thus gene expression is permitted.
2. A promoter which is a sequence of DNA where RNA polymerase attaches to begin transcription.
3. Operators which can block the action of RNA polymerase if there is a repressor present.
4. A regulator which codes for the synthesis of a repressor that can bind to the operator and block gene transcription.
5. Structural genes that code for several related enzymes that are responsible for production of a specific end product.

The *lac operon* controls the breakdown of lactose and is the simplest way of illustrating how gene regulation in bacteria works. In the lac operon system there is an active repressor that binds to the operator. In this scenario RNA polymerase is unable to transcribe the structural genes necessary to control the uptake and subsequent breakdown of lactose. When the repressor is inactivated (in the presence of lactose) the RNA polymerase is now able to transcribe the genes that code for the required enzymes. These enzymes are said to be *inducible* as it is the lactose that is required to turn on the operon.

Lac Operon

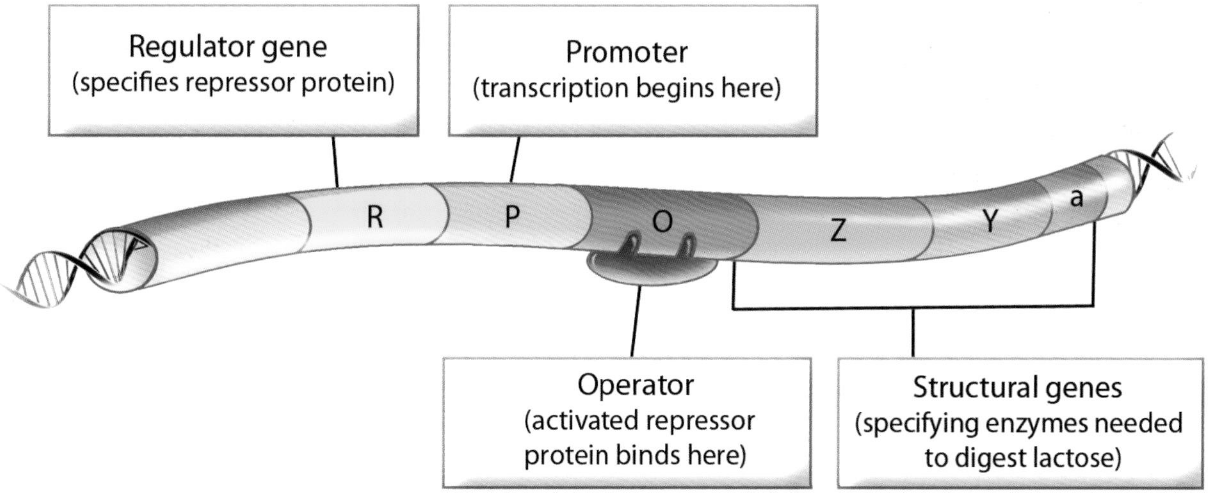

2.3 Fungi

Fungi are eukaryotic (= true nucleus) organisms which absorb their food through their chitinous cell walls. They may either be unicellular (i.e. yeast) or filamentous (i.e. mushrooms, molds) with individual filaments called hyphae which collectively form a mycelium. Fungal cell membranes contain ergosterol rather than cholesterol found in cell membranes of other eukaryotes.

Fungi often reproduce asexually. In molds, spores can be produced and then liberated from outside of a sporangium; or, as in yeast, a simple asexual budding process may be used. Sexual reproduction can involve the fusion of opposite mating types to produce asci (singular: ascus), basidia (singular: basidium), or zygotes. All of the three preceding diploid structures must undergo meiosis to produce haploid spores. If resources are unlimited, exponential growth would be expected.

Fungi are relatively important for humans as a source of disease and a decomposer of both food and dead organic matter. On the lighter side, they also serve as food (mushrooms, truffles), for alcohol and food production (cheese molds, bread yeast) and they have given us the breakthrough antibiotic, penicillin (from penicillium molds).

2.4 Vectors

A vector can be a person, animal or microorganism that carries and transmits an infectious organism (i.e. bacteria, viruses, etc.) into another living organism. Examples: the mosquito is a vector for malaria; bats are vectors for rabies and a SARS-like virus.

2.5 The Scientific Method

The scientific method could be used in conjunction with any MCAT subject experiment but microbiology is most common.

The point of the experiment is to test your ability to read scientific material, understand what is being tested, and determine if the hypothesis has been proved, refuted or neither. When a hypothesis survives rigorous testing, it graduates to a *theory*.

Observation, formulation of a theory, and testing of a theory by additional observation is called the scientific method. In biology, a key aspect to evaluate the validity of a trial or experiment is the presence of a *control group*. Generally, treatment is withheld from the control group but given to the *experimental group*.

First we will make an observation and then use deductive reasoning to create an appropriate hypothesis which will result in an experimental design. Consider the following: trees grow well in the sunlight. Hypothesis: exposure to light is directly related to tree growth. Experiment: two groups of trees are grown in similar conditions except one group (*experimental*) is exposed to light while the other group (*control*) is not exposed to light. Growth is carefully measured and the two groups are compared. Note that tree growth (*dependent variable*) is dependent on light (*independent variable*).

There are experiments where it is important to expose the control group to some factor different from the factor given to the experimental group (= *positive control*); as opposed to not giving the control group any exposure at all (= *negative control*). Exposure for a control group is used in medicine and dentistry because of the "Placebo Effect."

Experiments have shown that giving a person a pill that contains no biologically active material will cure many illnesses in up to 30% of individuals. Thus if Drug X is developed using a traditional control group, and the "efficacy" is estimated at 32%, it may be that the drug is no more effective than a sugar pill! In this case, the control group must be exposed to an unmedicated preparation to negate the Placebo Effect. To be believable the experiment must be well-grounded in evidence (= *valid,* based on the scientific method) and then one must be able to reproduce the results.

2.5.1 The Experiment

A lab in Boston reports 15% cell death when maximally stimulating the APO-1 receptor. In order to appropriately interpret the results, it must first be compared to:

A. data from other labs.
B. the attrition rate of other cell types.
C. the actual number of APO-1 cells dying in the tissue culture.
D. the rate of cell death without stimulation of APO-1.

- The experiment: stimulating a specific receptor on cells led to a 15% rate of cell death.
- Treatment is the stimulation of a receptor.
- The control (*group without treatment*): under the same conditions, do not stimulate the receptor (choice **D.**).

Choice **C.** does not answer the question. Choices **A.** and **B.** are most relevant if the initial data is shown to be significant. To prove that the data is significant or valid, one must first compare to a control group (choice **D.**).

GOLD STANDARD WARM-UP EXERCISES

CHAPTER 2: Microbiology

1) The blood of hepatitis B chronically infected people contains numerous particles of a harmless protein component of the virus called HBsAg. HBsAg is likely a component of:

A. the capsid of the virus.
B. the nucleic acid core of the virus.
C. the tail of the virus.
D. the slimy mucoid-like capsule on the outer surface of the virus.

2) Both bacteria and eukaryotic cells may share all of the following features EXCEPT:

A. phospholipid bilayer.
B. cell wall.
C. ribosomes.
D. nuclear membrane.

3) What features does the HIV virus share in common with all viruses?

I. RNA as genetic material
II. The ability to infect lymphocytes
III. Obligate intracellular parasite

A. I only
B. III only
C. II and III only
D. I, II and III

4) Once teeth appear, the bacteria comprising the microbial flora of the tissues surrounding the teeth are mainly:

A. gram-negative, aerobes.
B. gram-positive, aerobes.
C. gram-positive, facultative anaerobes.
D. gram-negative, obligate anaerobes.

5) Streptococcus mutans is associated with the tooth surface and appears to be the major causative agent of dental caries, or tooth decay. Streptococcus mutans produces glucan, a sticky polymer of glucose that acts like a cement and binds the bacterial cells together and to the tooth surface. The enzyme which catalyzes the formation of glucan is likely located:

A. in the cytosol of the cocci.
B. in lysosomes within the cytoplasm of the cocci.
C. in the nuclei of the cocci.
D. on the cell surface membrane of the cocci.

6) The difference between the bacterium E. coli and the fungus Aspergillus is:

A. Aspergillus contains ribosomes.
B. E. coli has a cell wall.
C. Aspergillus can undergo anaerobic metabolism.
D. E. coli does not have a nucleus.

7) Streptococcus mutans and Lactobacillus are, respectively:

A. spherical and helical.
B. spherical and cylindrical.
C. cylindrical and helical.
D. helical and cylindrical.

8) The high number of bacteria in dental plaque result from the proliferation of bacteria by all of the following methods, EXCEPT:

A. translocation.
B. transduction.
C. transformation.
D. binary fission.

9) Given that the time for one TS type E. coli to divide at 30 °C is approximately 15 minutes, if 10 bacteria should begin dividing in ample culture media, approximately how many would be present 2 hours later?

A. 500
B. 1000
C. 2500
D. 5000

10) Given unlimited resources, which of the following graphs shows the population growth curve for the yeast Candida albicans once infection occurs?

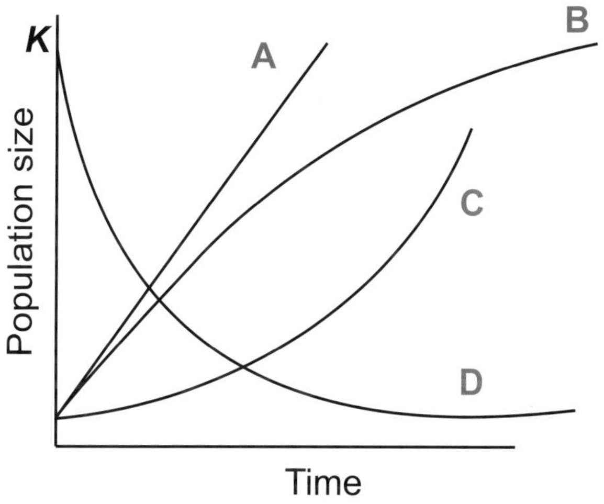

11) Yeast cells used for cloning the gene for HBsAg could be propagated by all but which of the following methods?

A. Budding
B. Transduction
C. Fusion
D. Meiotic division

12) Nitrogen fixation is accomplished by:

A. plants.
B. animals.
C. bacteria.
D. viruses.

GS ANSWER KEY

Chapter 2

		Cross-Reference			Cross-Reference
1.	A	BIO 2.1	7.	B	BIO 2.2
2.	D	BIO 2.2	8.	A	BIO 2.2, 15.5
3.	B	BIO 2.1	9.	C	BIO 1.3, 2.2
4.	C	BIO 2.2, 4.5	10.	C	BIO 2.3
5.	D	BIO 1.1, 2.2, 4.1	11.	B	BIO 2.3
6.	D	BIO 2.2-2.3	12.	C	BIO 2.2

*** Explanations can be found at the back of the book.**

APPENDIX

CHAPTER 2

Topic: Chimeric Plasmid

Muscular dystrophy is one of the most frequently encountered genetic diseases, affecting one in every 4000 boys (but much less commonly girls) born in America. Muscular dystrophy results in the progressive degeneration of skeletal and cardiac muscle fibers, weakening the muscle and leading ultimately to death from respiratory or cardiac failure.

The gene responsible for a major form of muscular dystrophy has been identified. This gene codes for a protein known as dystrophin, which is absent or present in a nonfunctional form in patients with the disease. Dystrophin is located on the inner surface of the plasma membrane in normal muscle protein.

The cloning of a fragment of DNA allows indefinite amounts of dystrophin to be produced from even a single original molecule. An insertion generates a hybrid or chimeric plasmid or phage, consisting in part of the additional "foreign" sequences. These chimeric elements replicate in bacteria just like the original plasmid or phage and so can be obtained in large amounts. Copies of the original foreign fragment can be retrieved from the progeny. Since the properties of the chimeric species usually are unaffected by the particular foreign sequences that are involved, almost any sequence of DNA can be cloned in this way. Because the phage or plasmid is used to "carry" the foreign DNA as an inert part of the genome, it is often referred to as the cloning vector.

13) The functions of dystrophin likely include all of the following EXCEPT one. Which is the EXCEPTION?

A. Recognition of protein hormones important to the functioning of the cells
B. Maintenance of the structural integrity of the plasma membrane
C. Keeping ion channels within the cells open
D. Protection of elements within the membrane during contraction of the cells

14) In order for cloning of foreign DNA to take place:

A. plasmids must incorporate the foreign DNA into the DNA in their capsids.
B. there must be several sites at which DNA can be inserted.
C. bacteria must be able to resume their usual life cycle after additional sequences of DNA have been incorporated into their genomes.
D. bacteria must divide meiotically, so no two daughter cells are exactly alike.

15) Plasmid genomes are circular and a single cleavage converts the DNA into a linear molecule. The two ends can be joined to the ends of a linear foreign DNA to regenerate a circular chimeric plasmid. Which of the following rules would be most important in allowing this process to occur?

A. DNA replication occurs in a semi-conservative manner.
B. The genetic code is composed of triplets of bases which correspond to the 20 amino acids used in protein structure.
C. The stability of the DNA helix is dependent on the number of C-G bonds present.
D. Phosphodiester bonds must link the plasmid DNA to the foreign DNA.

16) One possible method of treating muscular dystrophy using cloning techniques would be to:

A. Splice the nonfunctional genes out of dystrophic muscle cells and clone them in bacterial plasmids.
B. Determine the amino acid sequence of dystrophin and introduce the protein into muscle cells artificially.
C. Clone the gene responsible for coding dystrophin and insert the normal gene into dystrophic muscle cells.
D. Prevent skeletal and cardiac muscle tissue degradation by cloning and inserting the genes for troponin and tropomyosin into dystrophic muscle cells.

17) If the gene which codes for troponin was absent from muscle cells, all of the following processes would be inhibited EXCEPT one. Which is the EXCEPTION?

A. The movement of tropomyosin to a new position on the actin molecules
B. The uncovering of the active sites for the attachment of actin to the cross bridges of myosin
C. The hydrolysis of ATP in the myosin head to produce ADP, P_i, and energy
D. The release of Ca^{2+} ions from the sarcoplasmic reticulum

ANSWER KEY

ADVANCED TOPICS - CHAPTER 2

		Cross-Reference
13.	A	P2, S3
14.	C	P3, S3, S5; BIO 2.2, BIO 15.7
15.	D	BIO 1.2.2, BCM 1.5, BIO 15.7
16.	C	deduce, BIO 15.7
17.	D	BIO 5.2

P = paragraph; *S* = sentence; *E* = equation; *T* = table; *F* = figure

Go online to MCAT-prep.com/forum to join the discussion about our GS chapter review questions.

PROTEIN SYNTHESIS

Chapter 3

Memorize

* The genetic code (triplet)
* Central Dogma: DNA ➔ RNA ➔ protein
* Definitions: mRNA, tRNA, rRNA
* Codon-anticodon relationship
* Initiation, elongation and termination

Understand

* Mechanism of transcription
* Mechanism of translation
* Roles of mRNA, tRNA, rRNA
* Role and structure of ribosomes
* One-gene–one-enzyme hypothesis
* The biosynthetic pathway

Clinical Correlation

Antibiotics often work as protein synthesis inhibitors which can result in the death of the microorganism. Generally, protein synthesis is inhibited at various stages of prokaryotic mRNA translation into proteins, like initiation, elongation (including aminoacyl tRNA entry, proofreading, peptidyl transfer, etc.) and termination.

MCAT-Prep.com

Introduction

Protein synthesis is the creation of proteins using DNA and RNA. Individual amino acids are connected to each other in peptide linkages in a specific order given by the sequence of nucleotides in DNA. Thus the process occurs through a precise interplay directed by the genetic code and involving mRNA, tRNA and amino acids - all in an environment provided by a ribosome.

Optional Gold Standard Resources

Free Online Q&A + Forum

Online Videos

Flashcards

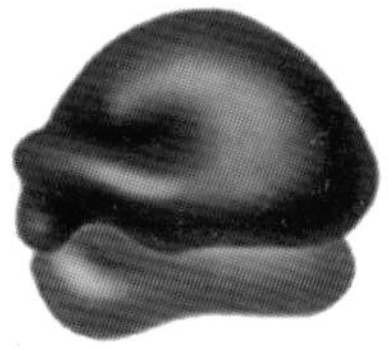

Special Guest

Building Proteins

Proteins (which comprise many hormones, enzymes, antibodies, etc.) are long chains formed by peptide bonds between combinations of twenty amino acid subunits. Each amino acid is encoded in a sequence of three nucleotides (a triplet code = the *genetic code*). A gene is a conglomeration of such codes and thus is a section of DNA which encodes for a protein (or a polypeptide which is exactly like a protein but much smaller).

DNA Transcription

The information in DNA is rewritten (transcribed) into a messenger composed of RNA (= mRNA); the reaction is catalyzed by the enzyme RNA polymerase. The newly synthesized mRNA is elongated in the 5′ to 3′ direction. It carries the complement of a DNA sequence.

Transcription can be summarized in 4 or 5 steps for prokaryotes or eukaryotes, respectively:

1. RNA polymerase moves the transcription bubble, a stretch of unpaired nucleotides, by breaking the hydrogen bonds between complementary nucleotides (see BCM 1.5 for nucleoside phosphates - nucleotides - and the binding of nitrogen bases).
2. RNA polymerase adds matching RNA nucleotides that are paired with complementary DNA bases.
3. The extension of the RNA sugar-phosphate backbone is catalyzed by RNA polymerase.
4. Hydrogen bonds of the untwisted RNA +

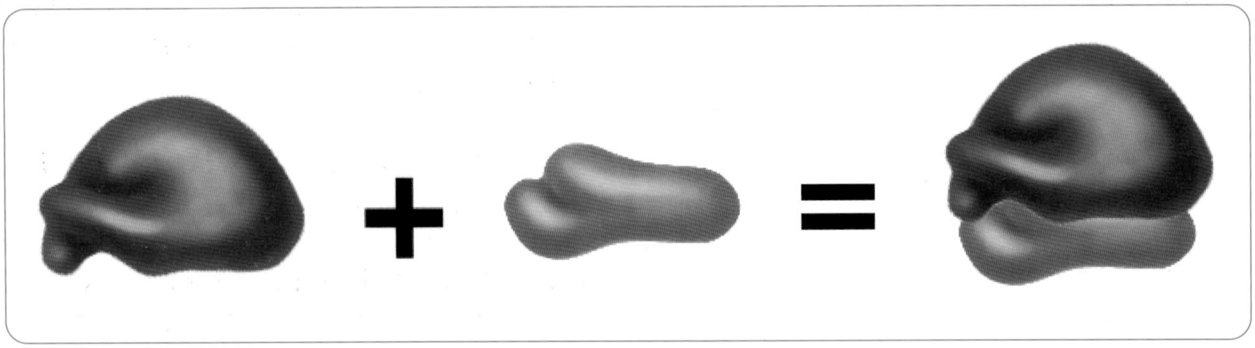

Figure IV.A.3.1: A ribosome provides the environment for protein synthesis. Ribosomes are composed of a large and a small subunit. The unit of measurement used is called the "Svedberg unit" (S) which is a measure of the rate of sedimentation in a centrifuge as opposed to a direct measurement of size. For this reason, fragment names do not add up (70S is made of 50S and 30S). Prokaryotes have 70S ribosomes, each comprised of a small (30S) and a large (50S) subunit. Eukaryotes have 80S ribosomes, each comprised of a small (40S) and large (60S) subunit. The ribosomes found in chloroplasts and mitochondria of eukaryotes also consist of large and small subunits bound together with proteins into one 70S ribosome. These organelles are believed to be descendants of bacteria ("Endosymbiotic theory") thus their ribosomes are similar to those of bacteria (see BIO 16.6.3).

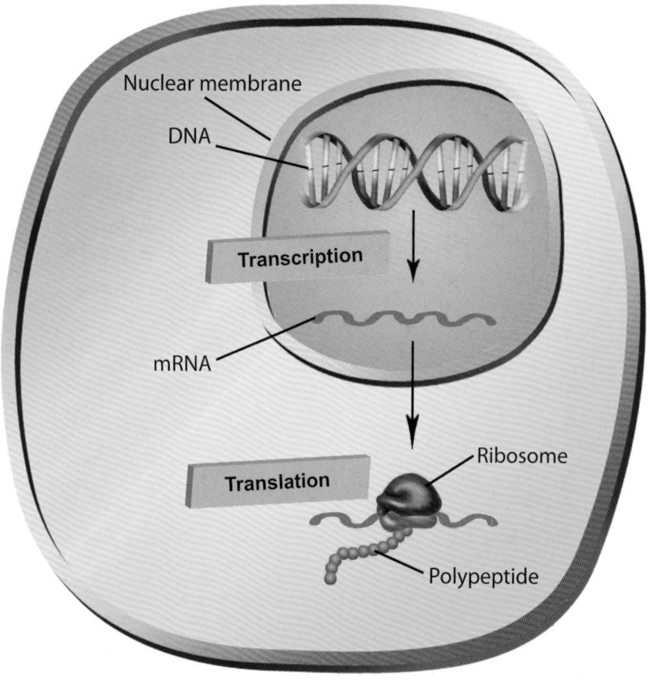

Figure IV.A.3.2: The central dogma of protein synthesis.

DNA helix break, freeing the newly synthesized RNA strand.

5. If the cell has a nucleus, the RNA is further processed [addition of a 5′ cap and a 3′ poly(A) tail] and then exits through the nuclear pore to the cytoplasm.

The mRNA synthesis in eukaryotes begins with the binding of RNA polymerase at a specific DNA sequence known as promoters. Elongation continues until the RNA polymerase reaches a termination signal. The initially formed primary mRNA transcript, also called pre-mRNA, contains regions called introns that are not expressed in the synthesized protein.The introns are removed and the regions that are expressed (exons) are spliced together to form the final functional mRNA molecule. {EXons EXpressed; INtrons IN the garbage!}

Post-transcriptional processing of mRNA occurs in the nucleus. Even before transcription is completed, a 7-methylguanosine cap is added to the 5′ end of the growing mRNA serving as attachment site for protein synthesis and protection against degradation. The 3′ end is added with a poly(A) tail consisting of 20 to 250 adenylate residues as protection. Of course, "A" refers to adenine and the nucleotide is thus adenosine monophosphate or AMP (BCM 1.5, 1.6) which *poly*merizes to create the tail of residues. The messenger

Note the following summary of protein synthesis[1]:

DNA —TRANSCRIBED (in the nucleus)—> mRNA —TRANSLATED (in the cytosol)—> protein

[1] for eukaryotes; in prokaryotes, some of the above-mentioned events occur simultaneously since they contain no nucleus. In fact, in bacterial cells it is common to have several ribosomes working in parallel on a single mRNA, forming what is called polyribosomes or polysome.

then leaves the nucleus with the information necessary to make a protein.

RNA Translation

The mRNA is constantly produced and degraded, which is the main method through which cells regulate the amount of a particular protein they synthesize. It attaches to a small subunit of a ribosome which will then attach to a larger ribosomal subunit thus creating a full ribosome. A ribosome is composed of a complex of protein and ribosomal RNA (= rRNA). The rRNA is the most abundant of all RNA types.

Floating in the cytoplasm is yet another form of RNA; this RNA specializes in taking amino acids and transfering them onto other amino acids when contained within the environment of the ribosome. More specifically, this transfer RNA (tRNA) molecule can be charged with a specific amino acid by aminoacyl-tRNA synthetase enzyme, bring the amino acid to the environment of ribosome, recognize the triplet code (= codon) on mRNA via its own triplet code anticodon, which is a three nucleotide sequence on tRNA that recognizes the complementary codon in mRNA; and finally, tRNA can transfer its amino acid onto the preceding one thus elongating the polypeptide chain. In a way, tRNA translates the code that mRNA carries into a sequence of amino acids which can produce a protein.

Translation of mRNA into a protein involves three stages: initiation, elongation and termination. The direction of synthesis of the protein chain proceeds from the amino end/terminus to the carboxyl end/terminus. Synthesis begins when the ribosome scans the mRNA until it binds to a start codon (AUG), which specifies the amino acid methionine. During elongation, a peptide bond is formed between the existing amino acid in the protein chain and the incoming amino acid. Following peptide bond formation, the ribosome shifts by one codon in the 5′ to 3′ direction along mRNA and the uncharged tRNA is expelled and the peptidyl-tRNA grows by one amino acid. Protein synthesis terminates when the ribosome binds to one of the three mRNA termination codons (UAA, UAG or UGA; notice the similarity with the DNA stop codons in Table IV.A.3.1 except that U replaces T in this RNA molecule).

The 20 Amino Acids	The 64 DNA Codons
Alanine	GCT, GCC, GCA, GCG
Arginine	CGT, CGC, CGA, CGG, AGA, AGG
Asparagine	AAT, AAC
Aspartic acid	GAT, GAC
Cysteine	TGT, TGC
Glutamic acid	GAA, GAG
Glutamine	CAA, CAG
Glycine	GGT, GGC, GGA, GGG
Histidine	CAT, CAC
Isoleucine	ATT, ATC, ATA
Leucine	CTT, CTC, CTA, CTG, TTA, TTG
Lysine	AAA, AAG
Methionine	ATG
Phenylalanine	TTT, TTC
Proline	CCT, CCC, CCA, CCG
Serine	TCT, TCC, TCA, TCG, AGT, AGC
Threonine	ACT, ACC, ACA, ACG
Tyrosine	TAT, TAC
Tryptophan	TGG
Valine	GTT, GTC, GTA, GTG
Stop codons	TAA, TAG, TGA

Table IV.A.3.1: The 20 standard amino acids.

The 20 standard amino acids are encoded by the genetic code of 64 codons. Notice that since there are 4 bases (A, T, G, C), if there were only two bases per codon, then only 16 amino acids could be coded for ($4^2=16$). However, since at least 21 codes are required (20 amino acids plus a stop codon) and the next largest number of bases is three, then 4^3 gives 64 possible codons, meaning that some degeneracy exists.

Degeneracy is the redundancy of the genetic code. Degeneracy occurs because there are more codons than encodable amino acids. This makes the genetic code more tolerant to point mutations (BIO 15.5). For example, in theory, fourfold degenerate codons can tolerate any point mutation at the third position (see valine, alanine, glycine, etc. in Table IV.A.3.1 and notice that any 3rd base codes for the same amino acid). The structure of amino acids was discussed in BCM 1.1.

A nonsense mutation is a point mutation (BIO 15.5) in a sequence of DNA that results in a premature stop codon (UAA, UAG, UGA), or a nonsense codon in the transcribed mRNA. Either way, an incomplete, and usually nonfunctional protein is the result. A missense mutation is a point mutation where a single nucleotide is changed to cause substitution of a different amino acid. Some genetic disorders (i.e. thalassemia) result from nonsense mutations.

Protein made on free ribosomes in the cytoplasm may be used for intracellular purposes (i.e. enzymes for glycolysis, etc.). Whereas proteins made on rER ribosomes are usually modified by both rER and the Golgi apparatus en route to the plasma membrane or exocytosis (i.e. antibodies, intestinal enzymes, etc.).

Key Points

Note the following: i) the various kinds of RNA are single stranded molecules which are produced using DNA as a template; ii) hormones can have a potent regulatory effect on protein synthesis (esp. enzymes); iii) allosteric enzymes (= proteins with two different configurations - each with different biological prop-

DNA	Coding Strand (codons)	5′→ →------ T T C ------→ → 3′
	Template Strand (anticodons)	3′← ←------ A A G ------← ← 5′
mRNA	The Message (codons)	5′ → →------ U U C ------→ → 3′
tRNA	The Transfer (anticodons)	3′ ← ← A A G ← ← 5′
Protein	Amino Acid	**N-terminus** → → Phenylalanine → → **C-terminus**

Table IV.A.3.2. DNA, RNA and protein strands with directions of synthesis. For both DNA and RNA, strands are synthesized from the **5′** ends → → to the **3′** ends. Protein chains are synthesized from the **N-terminus** → → to the **C-terminus**. Color code: the **old** end is **cold blue**; the **new** end is **red hot** where new residues are added. As shown in the table, mRNA is synthesized complementary and antiparallel to the **template strand (anticodons)** of DNA, so the resulting mRNA consists of codons corresponding to those in the coding strand of DNA. The **anticodons of tRNA** read each three-base mRNA codon and thus transfers the corresponding **amino acid** to the growing **polypeptide chain** or **protein** according to the genetic code.

erties) are important regulators of transcription; iv) there are many protein factors which trigger specific events in the initiation (using a start codon, AUG), elongation and termination (using a stop codon) of the synthesis of a protein; v) one end of the protein has an amine group ($-NH_2$, which projects from the first amino acid), while the other end has a carboxylic acid group (-COOH, which projects from the last amino acid). {Amino acids and protein structure were explored in BCM 1.1 and 1.2}

Note that the free amine group end, the start of the protein, is also referred to as: N-terminus, amino-terminus, NH_2-terminus, N-terminal end or amine-terminus. The free carboxylic acid end, which is the end of the protein, is also referred to as: C-terminus, carboxyl-terminus, carboxy-terminus, C-terminal tail, C-terminal end, or COOH-terminus.

Differences in translation between prokaryotes and eukaryotes:

1) Ribosomes: in prokaryotes it is 70S, in eukaryotes it is 80S
2) Start codon: the start codon AUG specifies formyl-methionine [f-Met] in prokaryotes, in eukaryotes it is methionine
3) Location of translation: in prokaryotes translation occurs at the same compartment and same time as transcription, in eukaryotes transcription occurs in the nucleus while translation occurs in the cytosol.

Because of the incredible variety of organisms that use the genetic code, it was thought to be a *truly* 'universal' code but that is not quite accurate. Variant codes have evolved. For example, protein synthesis in human mitochondria relies on a genetic code that differs from the standard genetic code.

Furthermore, not all genetic information is stored using the genetic code. DNA also has regulatory sequences, chromosomal structural areas and other non-coding DNA that can contribute greatly to phenotype. Such elements operate under sets of rules that are different from the codon-to-amino acid standard underlying the genetic code.

3.1 One Gene, One Enzyme, and the Biosynthetic Pathway

Duchenne muscular dystrophy (DMD) is a disease caused by a mutation in the DNA (X-linked recessive mutation; BIO 15.3). DMD patients have a mutation in the gene coding for the protein dystrophin. This protein connects the cytoskeleton to the extracellular matrix (thus through the plasma membrane) in muscle cells and appears to stabilize the muscle during contraction. Without dystrophin, the plasma membrane ruptures during muscle contraction and degeneration of the muscle tissue occurs (most DMD patients become wheelchair-dependent early in life). One gene, one protein and we can see how it is expressed in the organism (phenotype; BIO 15.1).

Experiments done in the 1940s, that would later give birth to Molecular Biology, used the bread mold *Neurospora* (a fungus; BIO 2.3) to conclude the following:

- Molecules are synthesized in a series of steps (= biosynthetic pathway, or, more generally: metabolic pathway)
- Each step is catalyzed by a unique enzyme (of course, enzymes are proteins)
- Each enzyme is specified by a unique gene ("one gene, one enzyme").

As we have seen in Biochemistry chapters 3 and 4, in a metabolic pathway, a principal chemical is modified by a series of chemical reactions. Enzymes catalyze these reactions. Because of the many chemicals (= "metabolites") that may be involved, metabolic pathways can be complex. Consider the following straightforward synthetic pathway (Int = Intermediate):

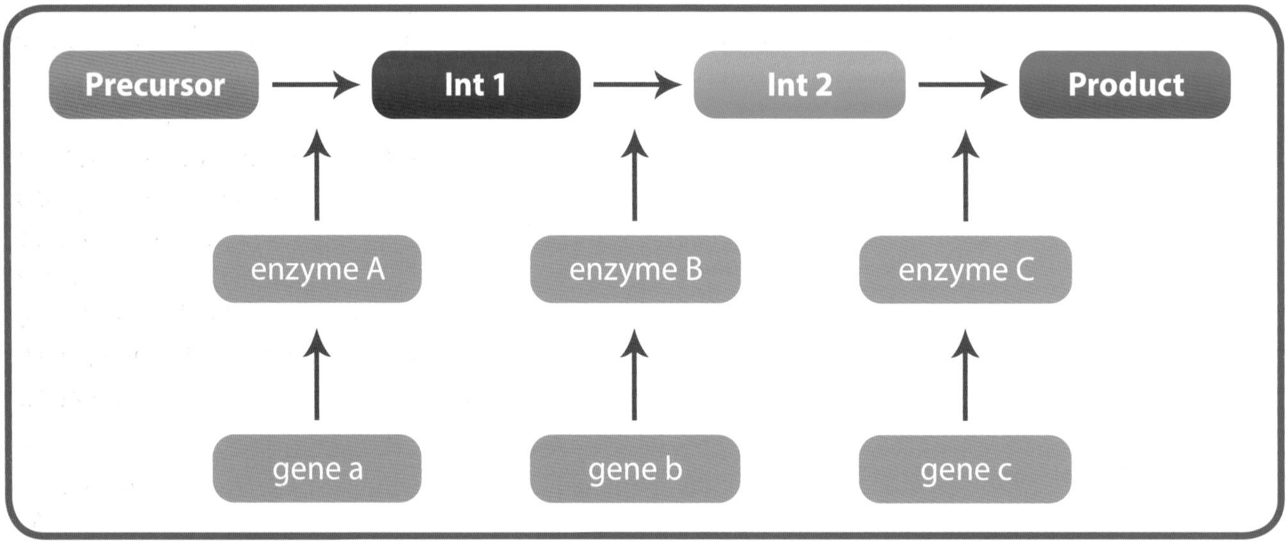

Consider the following questions:

1. Imagine that there was a mutation (or inactivation) in gene c, would any Product be produced? Would you expect the intermediates to be produced? Would their concentrations go up or down?

2. What would be the consequences of a mutation in gene b?

3. What happens if we add Intermediate 1 or Intermediate 2 to the media of a gene b mutation? Would either case result in Product? {Note: "media" is plural and refers to a growth medium or culture medium which is a liquid or gel designed to support the growth of cells}

Consider your answers before continuing. You can expect questions like this on the real exam.

1. If there is a mutation at gene c then enzyme C is blocked (i.e. it is either not being produced or it is not functioning normally) which means the Product would not be produced and we would expect Intermediate 2 to increase in concentration (imagine a production line where one worker stops working but there continues to be items arriving at their desk, the result is accumulation at that point and non-production beyond that point).

2. A mutation at gene b stops the function of enzyme B thus the production of Intermediate 2 is blocked thus no Product is formed. Intermediate 1 begins to accumulate.

3. Adding Intermediate 1 just leads to its accumulation since we are presented with one way arrows so the reaction can only move forward but it is blocked because of the gene b mutation [had the arrows been double sided, which is quite normal in nature, then Le Chatelier's principle (CHM 9.9) would suggest that Precursor would be produced because of the stress of increasing Intermediate 1].

However, if Intermediate 2 is added to the media with the gene b mutation, since gene c is not mutated, the Product will be formed. Being beyond the 'blockage' caused by enzyme B dysfunction, the medium supplemented with Intermediate 2 bypasses the problem and is able to produce Product because there are no issues with gene c.

It should be noted that the one gene-one enzyme hypothesis predated the understanding of the genetic code and our modern understanding of enzymes – many of which are composed of multiple polypeptides (BCM 1.2), each of which is coded for by one gene. Thus "one gene-one polypeptide" would be more accurate but even so, remains incomplete because of more recent discoveries outside the scope of this exam.

Peptide: The result of the moon pulling on the Pepsi. ;)

GOLD STANDARD WARM-UP EXERCISES

CHAPTER 3: Protein Synthesis

1) Which of the following enzymes is most important in RNA synthesis during transcription?
   - A. DNA polymerase
   - B. RNA replicase
   - C. RNA polymerase
   - D. Reverse transcriptase

2) The last step in translation, termination, in addition to the termination codon, requires release factors (RFs). Where would the RFs be expected to be found in the cell?
   - A. Within the nuclear membrane
   - B. Floating in the cytosol
   - C. In the matrix of the mitochondria
   - D. Within the lumen of the smooth endoplasmic reticulum

3) During the period of time that primary oocytes remain in prophase I of meiosis, they undergo an extended period of growth, including accelerated synthesis and accumulation of rRNA. The increased rate of rRNA synthesis is accompanied by:
   - A. disassembly of ribosomes into their component parts.
   - B. thickening of the nuclear membrane.
   - C. an increase in the size and/or number of nucleoli.
   - D. a decrease in nuclear chromatin material.

4) The 3 base pair sequence found on an mRNA strand is called which of the following?
   - A. Codon
   - B. Anticodon
   - C. Genome
   - D. Gene

5) A ribosome is:
   - A. one of three binding sites for tRNA during translation.
   - B. a sequence of nucleotides in DNA that marks the end of a gene and signals RNA polymerase to release the newly made RNA molecule and detach from the DNA.
   - C. a noncoding, intervening sequence within a primary transcript that is removed from the transcript during RNA processing.
   - D. a complex of rRNA and protein molecules that functions as a site of protein synthesis.

6) The triplet code of CAT in DNA is represented as ______ in mRNA and ______ in tRNA.
   - A. GUA, CAU
   - B. CAT, CAT
   - C. GAA, CAT
   - D. GTA, CAU

7) Transcription occurs along a ____ template forming an mRNA in the ____ direction.
   - A. 3′ to 5′; 3′ to 5′
   - B. 5′ to 3′; 3′ to 5′
   - C. 5′ to 3′; 5′ to 3′
   - D. 3′ to 5′; 5′ to 3′

8) What is the meaning of the degeneracy of the genetic code?
   - A. A single codon may specify more than one amino acid.
   - B. A single amino acid may have more than one codon.
   - C. AUG is a single start codon.
   - D. The first two bases specify the amino acid.

GS ANSWER KEY

CHAPTER 3

		Cross-Reference			Cross-Reference
1.	C	BIO 3.0	5.	D	BIO 3.0
2.	B	BIO 1.2.1, 3.0	6.	A	BIO 1.2.2, 3.0
3.	C	BIO 3.0, 1.2.1	7.	D	BIO 1.2.2, 3.0
4.	A	BIO 3.0	8.	B	BIO 3.0

*** Explanations can be found at the back of the book.**

Go online to MCAT-prep.com/forum to join the discussion about our GS chapter review questions.

APPENDIX

CHAPTER 3: Protein Synthesis

Topic: Release Factor Recognition

The last step in translation involves the cleavage of the ester bond that joins the complete peptide chain to the tRNA corresponding to its C-terminal amino acid. This process of termination, in addition to the termination codon, requires release factors (RFs). The freeing of the ribosome from mRNA during this step requires the participation of a protein called ribosome releasing factor (RRF).

Cells usually do not contain tRNAs that can recognize the three termination codons. In E. coli, when these codons arrive on the ribosome they are recognized by one of three release factors. RF-1 recognizes UAA and UAG, while RF-2 recognizes UAA and UGA. The third release factor, RF-3, does not itself recognize termination codons but stimulates the activity of the other two factors.

The consequence of release factor recognition of a termination codon is to alter the peptidyl transferase center on the large ribosomal subunit so that it can accept water as the attacking nucleophile rather than requiring the normal substrate, aminoacyl-tRNA.

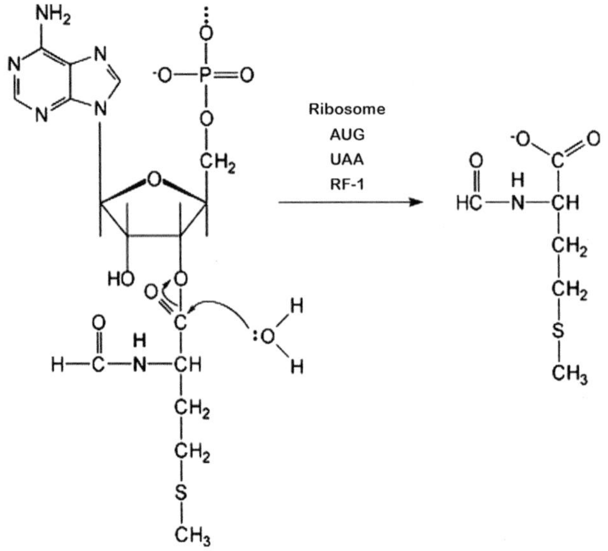

Figure 1

9) The alteration to the peptidyl transferase center during the termination reaction serves to convert peptidyl transferase into a(n):

A. exonuclease
B. lyase.
C. esterase.
D. ligase.

10) Sparsomycin is an antibiotic that inhibits peptidyl transferase activity. The effect of adding this compound to an in vitro reaction in which E. coli ribosomes are combined with methionine aminoacyl-tRNA complex, RF-1 and the nucleotide triplets, AUG and UAA, would be to:

A. inhibit hydrolysis of the amino acid, allowing polypeptide chain extension.
B. inhibit peptide bond formation causing the amino acid to be released.
C. induce hydrolysis of the aminoacyl-tRNA complex.
D. inhibit both hydrolysis of the aminoacyl-tRNA complex and peptide bond formation.

11) If the water in the reaction in Fig. 1 was labeled with ^{18}O, which of the following molecules would contain ^{18}O at the end of the reaction?

A. The free amino acid
B. The phosphate group of the tRNA molecule
C. Oxygen-containing molecules in the cytoplasm
D. The ribose moiety of the tRNA molecule

ANSWER KEY

ADVANCED TOPICS - CHAPTER 3

		Cross-Reference
9.	C	P1; E; BIO 4.1, ORG 9.4
10.	D	P3; E; BIO 3.0, 4.2, 20.2.1
11.	A	BIO 20.2.1, ORG 8.1, 9.4

P = paragraph; *S* = sentence; *E* = equation; *T* = table; *F* = figure

Chapter 4

Memorize

* Only the most basic features of biotechnol-gy from this chapter should be memorized as vell as DNA basics found in Biochemistry Chapter 1; and Biology Chapters 1, 14 and 15.

Understand

* DNA recombination, restriction fragments
* Gene cloning, restriction enzymes, methylation, sticky/blunt ends
* DNA libraries, cDNA, gene function and expression
* Annealing, PCR, sex determination, DNA sequencing, Sanger method
* Gel electrophoresis, Southern blotting
* SDS-PAGE, chromatography, applications of DNA technology, RFLP
* Stem cells, safety/ethics of DNA technology

Clinical Correlation

Gene and stem cell therapy are 2 very exciting branches of medicine recently born from biotechnology. The former involves introducing a new gene into a person to compensate for the incorrect expression of their own gene, or to stimulate an inactive gene, or restrict an overactive one. For the latter, stem cells can be used to replace or supplement particular tissue in a person with a medical condition.

MCAT-Prep.com

Introduction

Biotechnology is the use of living systems and/or organisms (or derivatives of organisms) to develop or make useful products. Memorizing specifics is much less important than to gain a general understanding of these various biotechnology tools that are very likely to be discussed during the MCAT to test your reasoning skills. Having exposure and comprehension before the exam will make you more time-efficient during the exam.

Optional Gold Standard Resources

Free Online Q&A + Forum

Flashcards

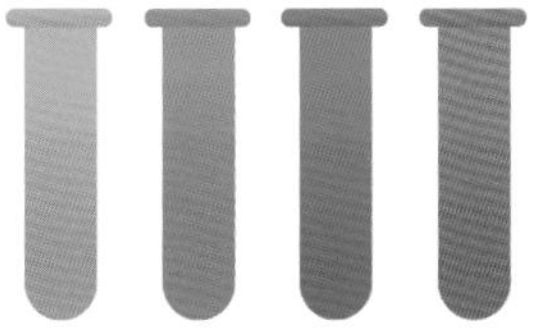

Special Guest

4.1 DNA Recombination and Genetic Technology

DNA recombination involves DNA that contains segments or genes from different sources. The foreign DNA can come from another DNA molecule, a chromosome, or from a complete organism. Much of this DNA transfer is done artificially using DNA recombination techniques, which use restriction enzymes to cut pieces of DNA. These enzymes originate from bacteria and are extremely specific because they only cut DNA at specific recognition sequences along the strand. These recognition sites correspond to different nucleotide sequences and produce *sticky* and *blunt* ends when a double stranded DNA segment is cut.

The sticky end is the unpaired part of the DNA that is ready to bind with a complementary codon (sequence of three adjacent nucleotides; BIO 3.0). These cut pieces or **restriction fragments** are often inserted into plasmids (circular piece of DNA that is able to replicate independently of the chromosomal DNA) which are then able to be introduced into the bacteria via transformation (*see* BIO 2.2).

Treating the plasmid, or *replicon* (BIO 1.2.2), with the same restriction enzymes used on the original fragment produces the same sticky ends in both pieces allowing base pairing to occur when they are mixed together. This attachment is stabilized by DNA ligase (BIO 1.2.2). After the ends are joined and the recombinant plasmid is incorporated into bacteria, the bacteria become capable of producing copious amounts of a specific protein that was not native to its species (i.e. bacteria with recombinant DNA producing insulin to treat diabetes).

To understand the role that biotechnology plays in creating recombinant DNA, we can walk through the various steps required to clone a piece of foreign DNA into a plasmid vector.

Bacterium and Vector Plasmid

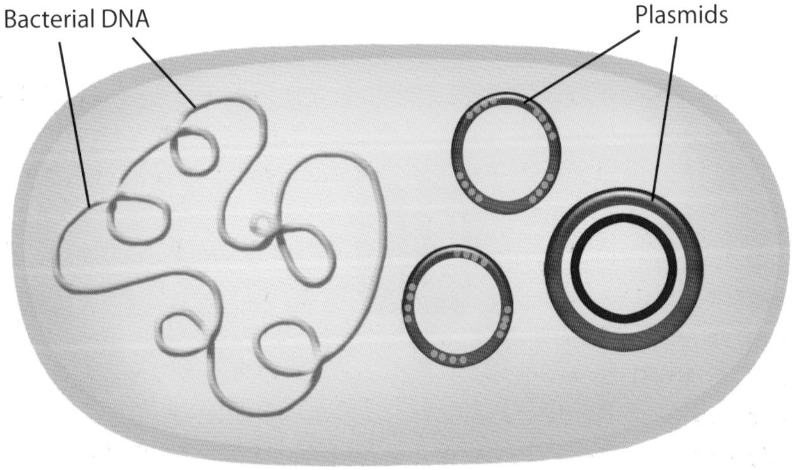

4.1.1 Gene Cloning

Cloning vectors are chosen carefully based on the size of foreign DNA they can carry. Whether a researcher chooses a plasmid, a bacteriophage, a virus, or some other system, all cloning vectors have one thing in common - they must contain at least one unique cloning site, cleavable by a restriction enzyme, where a gene of interest can be inserted. Many commercial and artificially modified cloning vectors often have several cloning sites lumped together in an artificially-engineered region called a Multiple Cloning Site, which allows the researcher to pick restriction sites that are (1) unique to the vector and (2) ensure that translation occurs in-frame. Many cloning vectors also contain an origin of replication (ori) to allow for self-replication. Often, cloning vectors are modified to carry genes that provide resistance to an antibiotic like ampicillin or kanamycin.

For applications such as the large-scale screening of genomic DNA, bacteriophage vectors like bacteriophage λ are commonly used for their highly efficient transfection rates and ease of screening (*transfection* is the deliberate introduction of nucleic acids into cells). To select for appropriately-sized fragments, genomic DNA is partially digested with a restriction enzyme, such that there are still undigested sites, which results in DNA products of varying length. The λ vector is also digested with the same enzyme; both it and the genomic DNA fragments are ligated together, then packaged into phage particles. To select for recombinant phages, plates of densely populated *E. coli* are infected with the phage particles, which produce cleared areas of lysed cells, called *plaques*.

4.1.2 Restriction Enzymes

Restriction endonucleases, or restriction enzymes, generally come in three types. They are classified based on their structure, as well as how they cleave their DNA substrate. These enzymes are naturally found in bacteria and archaea (BIO 2.2), and serve as the organism's own natural defense mechanism - when foreign DNA enters a bacteria, it is cleaved at specific recognition sites by these enzymes. In the meantime, the organism's own DNA is protected by selective methylation of these sites, a process aided by methylase enzymes.

In the laboratory, Type II enzymes are generally the restriction endonucleases used, as they cleave within, or near, specific recognition sites - short, specific, palindromic DNA sequences where cleavage occurs under the right conditions (a *palindrome* is

***Bam*HI**	5'... GGATCC...3' 3'... CCTAGG...5'
***Eco*RI**	5'...GAATTC...3' 3'...CTTAAG...5'
***Pvu*II**	5'...CAGCTG...3' 3'...GTCGAC...5'

Figure IV.A.4.1: Examples of common restriction enzymes and their restriction sites. The first two show examples that will result in sticky ends after cleavage, while digesting with PvuII results in blunt ends.

a sequence that reads the same backward as forward). Depending on the restriction enzyme and its respective restriction site, digestion with the enzyme will produce sticky ends - those with single-stranded extensions at either end - or blunt ends.

The sticky end overhangs the vector DNA base-pair to complementary sticky ends on the target DNA. Once paired, they are covalently joined in a process catalyzed by the enzyme DNA ligase.

4.1.3 DNA Libraries

Once the vector + insert DNA products have been purified and isolated, they can be collected into a genomic DNA library - a collection of recombinant DNA that represents the entire genome of an organism. Each piece of the library is generated in the same manner as summarized in section 4.1.1 and contains a fragment of genomic DNA ligated into a vector. By only doing a partial digest of the genomic DNA, this not only ensures that each insert is of an appropriate size, but it makes sure that the library contains all the genes in a genome. Placement of special filters on top of the phage-containing plates allows DNA or protein to bind to the filters so that they can be screened via hybridization.

cDNA (complementary DNA) libraries can also be generated, which contain double-stranded DNA that is reverse transcribed from an mRNA template. To do this, mRNA must first be purified from cells. In eukaryotes, this is carried out using an oligodeoxythymidylate (oligo dT) cellulose filter, which selectively binds to poly A-tail-containing mRNA. The oligo dT then functions as a primer to synthesize the cDNA. The mRNA is cut up with the RNA-nicking RNase H, and the resulting fragments are used by DNA polymerase I as primers to synthesize DNA. The resulting double-stranded cDNA is then digested and inserted into cloning vectors. The advantage of using cDNA libraries is that unlike genomic DNA, they do not include introns or flanking sequences.

In order to correctly find and locate the gene of interest, researchers screen DNA libraries using a hybridization probe - a molecule that recognizes a specific DNA sequence or protein product, such as a cDNA fragment that closely resembles the predicted sequence of the gene of interest. Typically, probes are labeled with a compound that allows for easy detection, such as a radioactive isotope, a reactive enzyme that produces a color response, or a fluorescent dye. The sensitivity, or "stringency," of the hybridization reaction can be increased or decreased by altering a number of experimental variables, such as the salt concentration and temperature. Once positive hits are detected, the corresponding cDNA or genomic DNA can be isolated from the phage plates.

Once a gene of interest has been identified and isolated, it can be amplified using the polymerase chain reaction, or PCR.

4.1.4 Polymerase Chain Reaction

The polymerase chain reaction (PCR) is a powerful biological tool that allows the rapid amplification of any fragment of DNA without purification. In PCR, DNA primers are made to flank the specific sequence to be amplified. These primers are then extended to the end of the DNA molecule with the use of a heat-resistant DNA polymerase. The newly synthesized DNA strand is then used as the template to undergo another round of replication.

The first step in PCR is the melting of the target DNA into two single strands by heating the reaction mixture to approximately 94 °C, and then rapidly cooling the mixture to allow annealing of the primers to their specific locations (note: *annealing* is the sticking together of complementary single strands which, of course, involves the formation of hydrogen bonds between the base pairs; BIO 1.2.2). Once the primer has annealed, the temperature is elevated to 72 °C to allow optimal activity of the DNA polymerase. The polymerase will

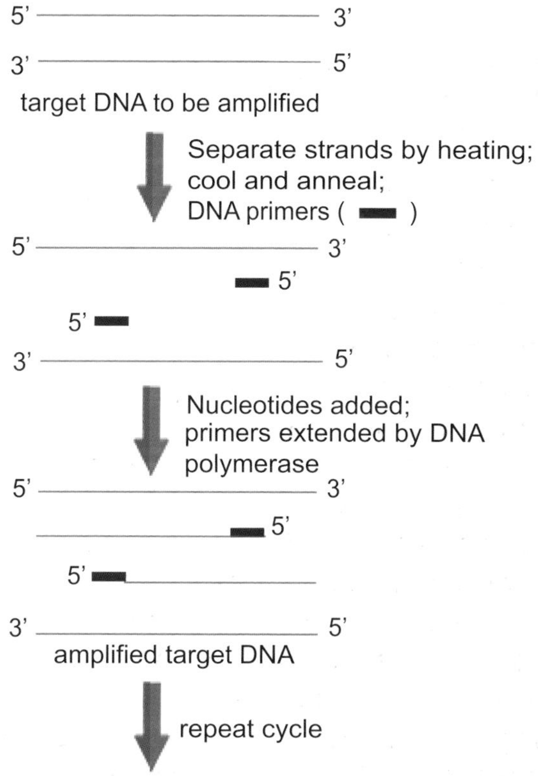

Figure IV.A.4.2: Polymerase chain reaction. There are three main steps in PCR: denaturing (heating to 95 °C), annealing (cooling), and extending (heating to 72 °C). These steps are repeated between 20-35 times until the DNA segment of interest has been sufficiently amplified.

continue to add nucleotides until the entire complementary strand of the template is completed, at which point the cycle is repeated (Figure IV.A.4.2).

One of the uses of PCR is sex determination, which requires amplification of intron 1 of the amelogenin gene. This gene found on the X-Y homologous chromosomes has a 184 base pair deletion on the Y homologue. Therefore, by amplifying intron 1, females can be distinguished from males by the fact that males will have two different sizes of the amplified DNA while females will only have one unique fragment size.

PCR can also be used to introduce specific mutations into a gene for a variety of research purposes, including deleting entire fragments, changing specific amino acids, adding peptide tags (i.e. peptide sequences grafted onto a protein), and more.

4.1.5 DNA Sequencing

To ensure that the gene insert of interest does not contain any mistakes, the DNA can be sequenced. These days, many researchers make use of sequencing machines and commercially available services, but many are based on the Sanger method of DNA sequencing. Four preparations of the DNA molecule are made; each is incubated with a labeled sequencing primer, DNA polymerase, all four DNA triphosphates, and one of the nucleotides in its dideoxy form (ddATP, ddCTP, ddGTP, or ddTTP).

New strands of DNA are synthesized, beginning at the primer, and continue until a dideoxyribonucleotide (ddNTP) is inserted, which stalls the synthesis. Because the reaction mixture also includes the unmodified nucleotides, the ddNTPs are inserted at random, thus resulting in a mixture of DNA fragments of varying length. The DNA mixture is separated by gel electrophoresis, and the radio-labeled fragments are "read" one nucleotide at a time (see Figure IV.A.4.3).

4.2 Protein Expression Using Recombinant DNA

Recombinant DNA can be used to express protein, which allows researchers to characterize its function, molecular interactions, enzyme activity, three-dimensional structure, and more. This often requires the DNA to be cloned into an expression vector, a vector that has been engineered to robustly produce protein in large quantities. These vectors can include a variety of features, such as ribosome-binding sites, strong promoters, transcription termination sequences, and a means of induction, such that protein expression only

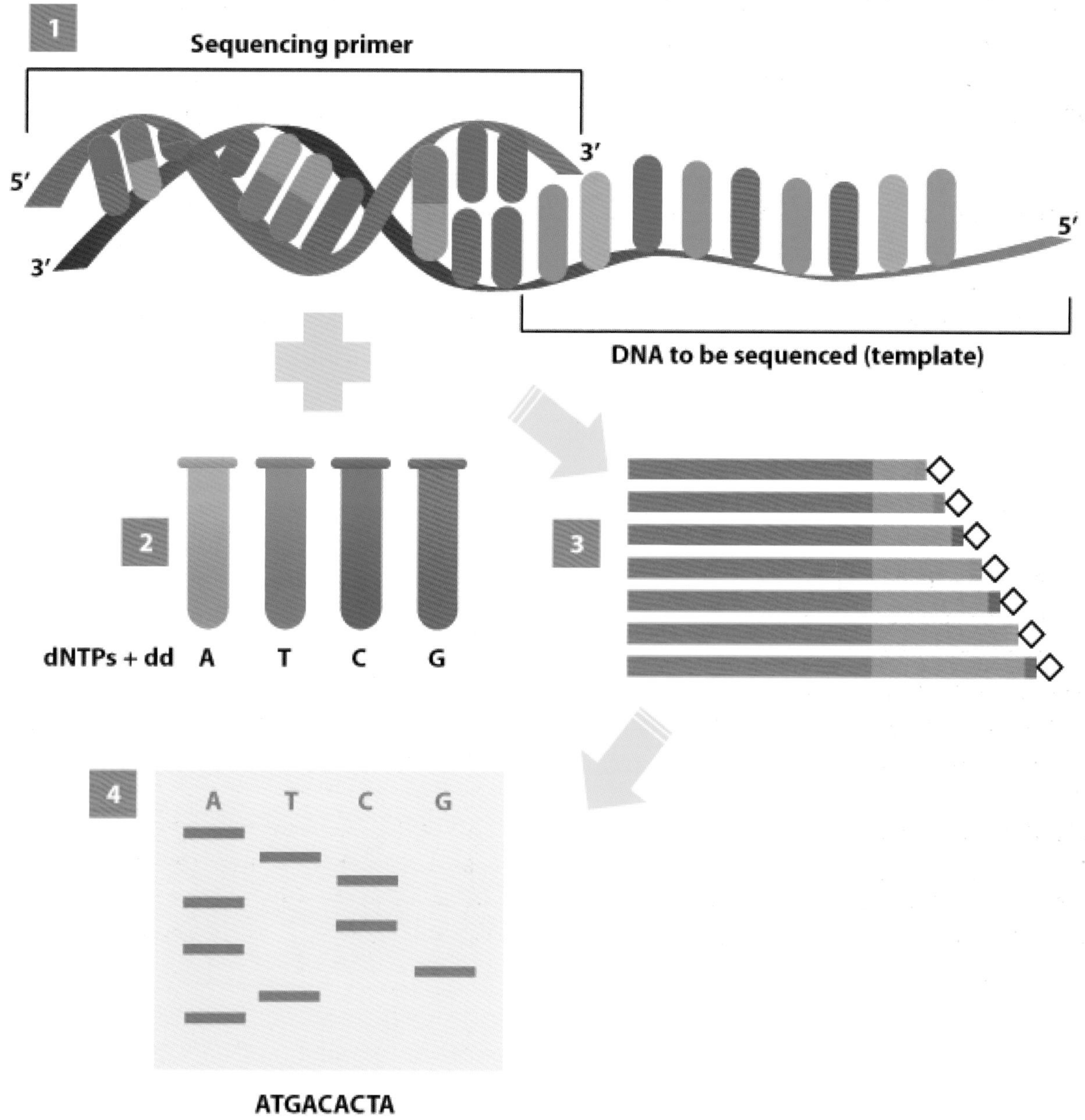

Figure IV.A.4.3: The steps in the Sanger method of DNA sequencing. (1+2) Four separate preparations are made, each including: the DNA to be sequenced, labeled sequencing primer, DNA polymerase, all four DNA triphosphates. Each preparation also includes one of the nucleotides in its dideoxy form (ddATP, etc). The synthesis reaction continues until a ddNTP is inserted (3), at which point the synthesis stops. The DNA mixture is separated by gel electrophoresis (4), allowing the sequence to be pieced together base by base. Because shorter DNA fragments travel the fastest in gel electrophoresis, they are closer to the end. Thus, the sequence is read from the bottom up.

begins upon the addition of a specific inducer such as IPTG or arabinose. Depending on the intended host, the vectors may also include elements such as Shine-Dalgarno sequences in prokaryote expression vectors, or Kozak consensus sequences in eukaryote expression vectors.

Protein expression can be optimized at the gene level, by altering its amino acid sequence in such a way that allows for less toxic expression or more accurate folding, or at the host level. Some *E. coli* strains have been carefully engineered to maximize protein expression, such as with the constitutive expression of T7 RNA polymerase (for use with expression vectors containing a T7 phage promoter), or the ability to recognize rare codons. The expression protocol itself can be highly optimized as well - because cells are living systems, there is no one standard protocol for protein expression. Some proteins require certain temperatures to fold properly, while the over-accumulation of others may lead to the rapid death of their hosts.

While many eukaryotic proteins can be functionally expressed in prokaryotic hosts, this is not always the case. Some eukaryotic proteins must be post-translationally modified, which is not always possible in hosts that lack the necessary enzymes. Thus, there are a variety of eukaryotic expression vectors available, which contain different selection markers, different transcription and translation regulation sequences, polyadenylation signals, and more.

The requirements for a gene expression system largely depends on the end goal. Proteins meant to just be characterized in various assays may not need to be expressed in large amounts, while other applications, such as macromolecular crystallography and therapeutics, require large quantities of very pure protein.

4.2.1 DNA Techniques and Analysis of Gene Expression

There are a variety of tools and techniques that can be used to determine the fidelity of DNA or a protein product once it has been isolated.

Gel electrophoresis is a method of separating DNA fragments of differing lengths based on their size. The DNA fragments are passed through an electrically-charged agarose gel. Since DNA is negatively charged, it will move towards the cathode (positive electrode). The shorter fragments move faster than the longer ones and can be visualized as a banding pattern using autoradiography techniques.

Southern blotting, named after Dr. E. Southern, is the process of transferring DNA fragments from the electrophoresis agarose gel onto filter paper where they are identified with probes. The procedure begins by digesting DNA in a mixture with *restriction*

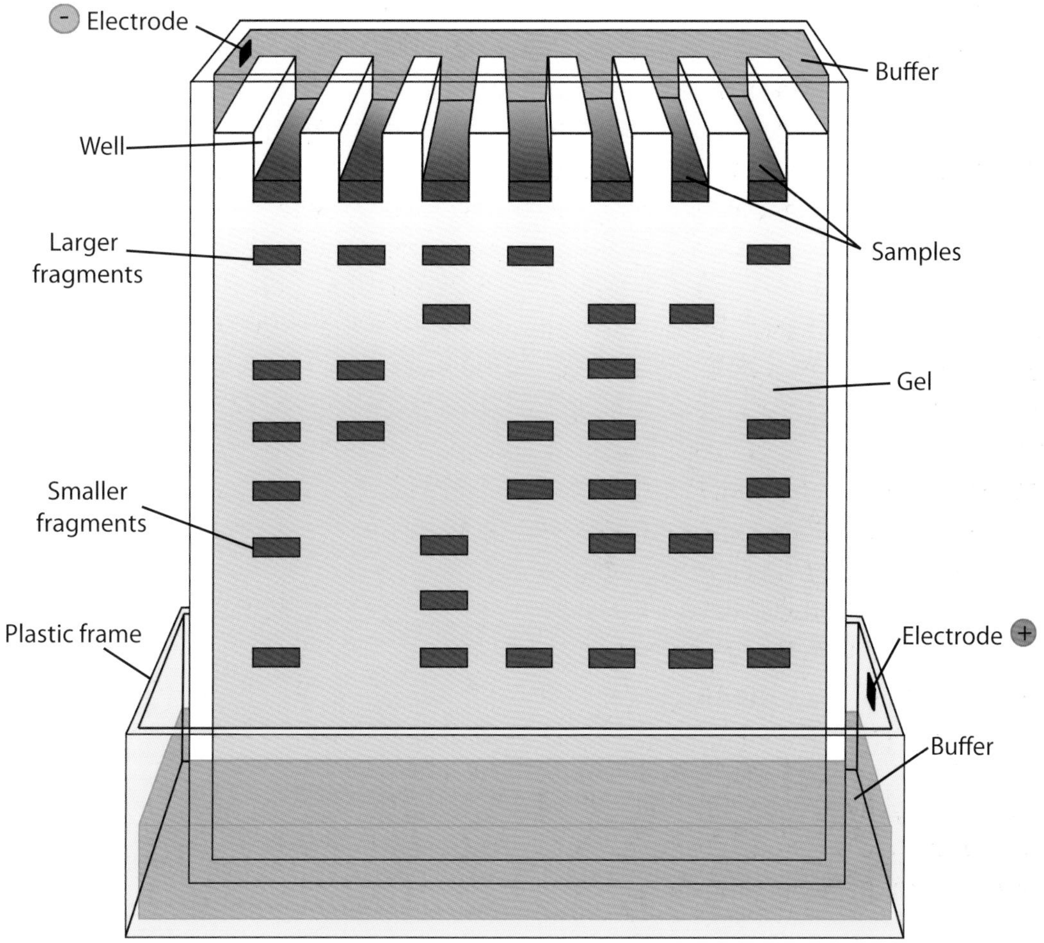

Figure IV.A.4.4: Gel Electrophoresis.

endonucleases to cut out specific pieces of DNA. The DNA fragments are then subjected to gel electrophoresis. The now separated fragments are bathed in an alkaline solution where they immediately begin to denature. These fragments are then placed (or blotted) onto nitrocellulose paper and then incubated with a specific probe whose location can be visualized with autoradiography.

Northern blotting is adapted from the Southern blot to detect specific sequences of RNA by hybridization with cDNA. Similarly, *Western blotting* is used to identify specific amino-acid sequences in proteins. Some students prefer to remember the blotting techniques with the mnemonic SNOW DROP.

SNOW	DROP
Southern	**D**NA
Northern	**R**NA
O	**O**
Western	**P**rotein

DNA microarray technology (= DNA chip or biochip or "laboratory-on-a-chip") helps to determine which genes are active and which are inactive in different cell types. This technology evolved from Southern blotting and can also be used to genotype multiple regions of a genome. DNA microarrays are created by robotic machines that arrange incredibly small amounts of hundreds or thousands of gene sequences on a single microscope slide. These sequences can be a short section of a gene or other DNA element that is used to hybridize a cDNA or cRNA (also called antisense RNA) sample. The hybridization is usually observed and quantified by the detection of fluorescent tag.

NB: The molecular biology techniques of FRAP (BIO 1.5) and ELISA (BIO 8.4) were described elsewhere in this book. Electrophoresis and chromatography are discussed in Organic Chemistry Chapter 13.

4.2.2 Protein Quantification

Protein expression can be quantified and analyzed using a variety of techniques. Quantification techniques allow researchers to determine basic information about the expressed product - concentration, amount, size - while functional assays allow researchers to characterize the protein's function and activity, as well as assess whether or not an expressed protein product is properly folded or correctly post-translationally modified.

SDS-PAGE, sodium dodecyl sulfate polyacrylamide gel electrophoresis (ORG 13), also separates proteins according to their electrophoretic mobility. SDS is an anionic detergent (i.e. negatively charged) which has the following effect: (1) denature proteins and (2) give an additional negative charge to the now-linearized proteins. In most proteins, the binding of SDS to the polypeptide chain gives an even distribution of charge per unit mass, thus fractionation will approximate size during electrophoresis (i.e. not dependent on charge).

The preparation of protein samples for SDS-PAGE analysis denatures the protein, destroying information about the protein's oligomerization status. In contrast, researchers can run native gels, which do not include SDS or other denaturing compounds in either the sample treatment buffer or the gel itself.

Proteins can also be quantified using Western blotting, a technique used to detect specific proteins either in homogenized tissue, in chromatography fractions, or cellular extracts. Proteins are separated by gel electrophoresis on an SDS-PAGE gel, and detected using labeled antibodies specific to the protein, or part of the protein.

4.2.3 Column Chromatography

Applications that require homogenous protein samples first require the purification of said protein. Proteins can be purified based on several traits, including size, overall charge, hydrophobicity, and more. Techniques such as *Fast Protein Liquid Chromatography* (FPLC) allow the rapid and selective separation of protein based on these traits.

Affinity chromatography allows the rapid purification of biological molecules based on certain affinities, such as those between antigen and antibody, enzyme and substrate, or genetically engineered protein tags and specific matrices. An example of the latter is the inclusion of a poly-His tag during the cloning process. His-tagged protein can be extracted from crude cellular extract by introducing nickel - or cobalt-agarose beads, which selectively bind the poly-His proteins. The protein is then bonded (or *chelated*) with a competing compound, such as imadazole.

Ion chromatography allows the purification of biomolecules based on overall charge - cation chromatography selectively binds positively-charged molecules, while anion chromatography binds negatively-charged molecules. Proteins are removed by washing (*eluted*) using increasing concentrations of salt.

Proteins can also be purified based on size using *size exclusion chromatography*

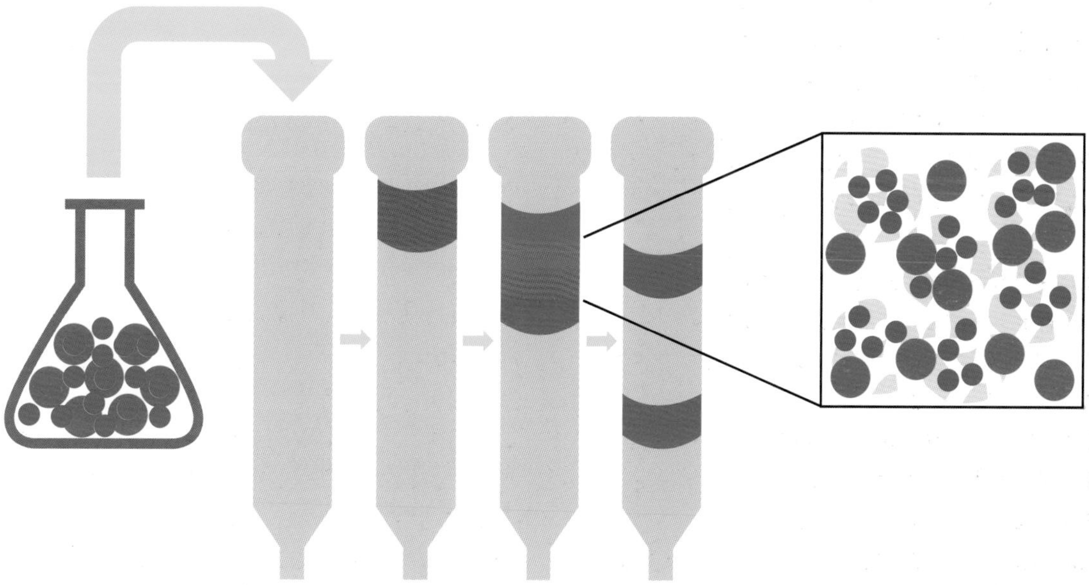

Figure IV.A.4.5. Size-exclusion chromatography. A mixture of proteins is applied to a column packed with porous beads. As the proteins travel through the column, smaller proteins are slowed down by the pores, while larger proteins avoid the beads entirely. As a result, larger proteins are eluted first.

(SEC), or gel filtration. A mixed protein solution is applied to the top of a long column packed with porous polymer beads. As the solution filters through the beads, smaller molecules are slowed down by the pores in the beads, while larger molecules will be allowed to flow through at a faster rate. Thus, larger molecules are eluted first (*see* Figure IV.A.4.5).

4.2.3 Functional Assays

Just because a protein is successfully expressed and purified, does not mean that it is functional. Researchers perform functional assays to help determine whether or not a protein is properly folded and error-free. If the function of an enzyme is already known, enzyme assays can aid in ensuring that the purified enzyme is functional, as well as characterize the kinetic profile and specific activity of the enzyme.

Spectrophotometric assays measure the change in wavelength absorption of certain molecules (e.g.: both NADH and NADPH absorb UV light, but not NAD^+ or $NADP^+$), while fluorometric assays measure the emission of certain wavelengths after specific light absorption (NADH and NADPH are fluorescent, but not NAD^+ or $NADP^+$). Thus, a researcher interested in studying the function of an oxidoreductase could use NADH as a substrate and measure the resulting change in UV absorption or fluorescence.

Protein function can also be measured using techniques like isothermal titration calorimetry (ITC), which determines the thermodynamic properties of binding interactions; or thermal shift assays (also known as Differential Scanning Fluorimetry [DSF]), which measures the thermal stability of proteins with and without specific ligands.

Despite the numerous scientific discoveries being made every day, there still remains plenty of genes and proteins that are still yet uncharacterized. One way to determine gene function is by removing or disabling the gene either in cells or in live animal models, and observing the consequences.

***In vitro* mutagenesis** introduces mutations into a gene, thus changing or disabling the expressed protein product. Careful observation of the resulting cellular phenotype can help pinpoint the function of the wildtype gene (i.e. the typical gene of a species as it occurs in nature). Likewise, the introduction of mutated genes, or the reduction of the expression (i.e. *knockdown*) of genes, in animal models can help determine their functionality.

4.3 Practical Applications of DNA Technology

Medical Applications. The diagnosis of infectious diseases has been simplified through DNA and protein technology. Medical professionals can detect the presence of viruses and other disease vectors in tissues and blood using techniques like enzyme-linked immunosorbent assays (ELISA), which use antibodies to detect the presence of antigens in liquid samples (BIO 8.4). It can also be used to test for the presence of specific allergens in food.

Scientists have also used gene markers to identify hereditary diseases in individuals before their symptomatic onset, or predict the likelihood that an individual might develop certain cancers. In both cases, preventative measures can be taken, such as the preemptive removal of target organs, or early treatment for symptoms. Medical professionals can also identify recessive carriers of potentially debilitating genetic disorders, predicting whether or not the offspring of two individuals will carry the disease.

Human Gene Therapy. Thanks in large part to our growing knowledge of genetic disorders, gene functions, and DNA manipulation, gene therapy is an increasingly viable treatment option for individuals suffering from genetic disorders. Theoretically, the replacement of defective genes in patients with normal alleles can reverse, prevent, or slow diseases. These normal alleles are inserted into somatic cells that multiply throughout the body, such as bone marrow cells, and express the normal gene. Such bone marrow transplants are a form of stem cell therapy, a practice that uses stem cells to treat or prevent illnesses.

Over the past couple of decades, researchers have examined the possibility of using stem cell therapy for other applications. Examples include using neural stem cells to treat degenerative brain diseases like Parkinson's and Alzheimer's, and using stem cells to treat heart disease. Because stem cells have the ability to differentiate into different types of specialized cells, they have been extensively researched for their reparative capabilities.

Recent advances have also been made in the field of *optogenetics*, an area of biomedical engineering that uses photostimulation to precisely control the activity of electrically excitable cells. Animal studies have shown that light-activated cation channels, such as channelrhodopsin-2 from the green algae *Chlamydomonas reinhardtii,* can be artificially expressed in excitable cells such as neuronal cells, muscle cells, and cardiac cells, which can then be forcefully depolarized by exposure to pulses of blue light. Scientists hope that optogenetics can offer answers for a variety of medical issues such as Parkinson's disease, neurological diseases, retinal degeneration, depression, and addiction problems.

Pharmaceuticals. A large number of therapeutic gene products are produced commercially using recombinant DNA and large-scale protein expression and purification techniques. Products include insulin, interferons, growth hormones, erythropoietin, tissue plasminogen activator, blood clotting factors, and more. Using host systems like *E. coli,* yeast, and other fast-growing organisms, vast quantities of protein can be expressed, including those with human origins.

Other pharmaceutical applications include the production of vaccines. Two types of vaccines are typically used - active viral particles of a nonpathogenic viral strain, and inactivated particles of pathogenic viruses. Both work by triggering an immune response in the body, which generates antibodies against the virus particles.

Forensic Evidence. DNA testing allows forensic scientists to positively identify criminals based on biological evidence left at crime scenes, such as blood, tissue, hair, or semen. Because every (non-identical twin) individual has wholly unique DNA, DNA fingerprinting techniques like RFLP analysis allow scientists to compare DNA samples from the crime scene to the DNA of the suspect and victim.

Restriction fragment length polymorphisms or RFLP is a technique that exploits variations in restriction fragments from one individual to another that differ in length due to polymorphisms, or slight differences in DNA sequences. The process involves digesting DNA sequences with different restriction enzymes, detecting the resulting restriction fragments by gel electrophoresis, and comparing their lengths. In DNA fingerprinting, commonly used to analyze DNA left at crime scenes, RFLP's are produced and compared to RFLP's of known suspects in order to catch the perpetrator.

DNA fingerprinting can also be used for paternity testing. In addition to RFLP analysis, DNA fingerprinting can also be performed using simple tandem repeats (STRs), satellite DNA of varying lengths present in each individual.

Environmental Cleanup. Genetic engineering is also being used to tackle environmental issues, such as sewage treatment, oil spill cleanup, heavy metal decontamination, and other issues. By utilizing the innate ability of some organisms to metabolize certain compounds, bacteria have been engineered to degrade a wide variety of organic and inorganic products, such as those found after toxic spills or dumps. Those used for heavy metal decontamination have been engineered to extract metals such as copper and lead, and convert them into more readily-disposable salt forms. The bacteria used in wastewater treatment plants break down organic compounds into non-toxic components.

Agriculture Uses. While selective breeding over millions of years has allowed humans to fine-tune crops to be more productive, more drought-resistant, faster growing, or tastier, advances in biotechnology over the last few decades has allowed scientists to play an even greater role in plant agriculture. Genetic engineering has been used to confer resistance to herbicides and insecticides, while others have even been engineered to combat pest damage by expressing insect toxins. Others, like beta-carotene-expressing rice, have been engineered to produce certain nutrients.

One way that transgenic plants are created is through the usage of **Ti plasmids**, taken from the soil bacterium *Agrobacterium tumefaciens*. Recombinant Ti plasmids infect plant cells, inserting a foreign gene of interest into the plant's chromosome. However, not all plants are susceptible to Ti plasmid infection - monocots (plants with one seed leaf) such as corn and wheat are resistant to Agrobacterium, meaning DNA must be introduced via electroporation or other methods.

Animals have been subjected to bioengineering as well, speeding up the process that traditional breeding practices have accomplished for millennia. Transgenic livestock can be created to develop larger muscles, softer wool, more marbled meat, or other traits. A desirable gene from one organism is identified, then cloned into the nuclei of an *in vitro* fertilized egg taken from a female of the same, or similar, species. The eggs are then implanted into a surrogate mother, who gives birth to a transgenic animal.

Other animals are modified to produce protein products and antibodies, such as hormones, meant for human usage. The genes that encode for such products are typically added to the animal's genome in a manner that allows the protein product to be secreted in the animal's milk, which allows larger quantities to be made.

Ethics of DNA Technology. There are ongoing debates about the ethical merits of DNA technology, ranging from stem cell research, transgenic research, to gene therapy. Much has been made in recent years about genetically modified organisms, or GMOs. Ongoing controversy surrounds the issue, with anti-GMO advocates voicing concerns about food safety, livestock farming practices, and accidental genetic transfer from transgenic plants to surrounding flora. Controversy regarding stem cell research largely revolves around the harvesting and usage of embryonic stem cells; however, stem cells can also be harvested from adults in the form of somatic stem cells, pluripotent stem cells, and amniotic stem cells.

GOLD STANDARD WARM-UP EXERCISES

CHAPTER 4: Biotechnology

1) The polymerase chain reaction resembles which of the following cellular process?

   A. Transcription of DNA
   B. Protein synthesis
   C. DNA replication
   D. Translation

2) Why is a heat resistant DNA polymerase required for successive replication in the polymerase chain reaction, rather than simply a human DNA polymerase?

   A. The high temperatures required to melt the DNA double strand may denature a normal human cellular DNA polymerase.
   B. The high temperatures required to melt the DNA would cause human DNA polymerase to remain bound to the DNA strand.
   C. Heat resistant DNA polymerase increases the rate of the polymerase chain reaction at high temperatures whereas human DNA polymerase lowers the rate.
   D. Heat resistant DNA polymerase recognizes RNA primers whereas human DNA polymerase does not.

3) The use of PCR for sex determination relies on the fact that:

   A. the amelogenin gene is responsible for an autosomal recessive trait.
   B. the X and Y homologous chromosomes have different sizes of intron 1 of the amelogenin gene.
   C. females have an X and Y chromosome and males have two X chromosomes.
   D. intron 1 has a different nucleotide length than intron 2.

4) What would PCR amplification of an individual's intron 1 of the amelogenin gene reveal if the individual were male?

   A. One type of intron 1 since the individual has one X chromosome and one Y chromosome.
   B. Two types of intron 1 since the individual has only one X chromosome.
   C. One type of intron 1 since the individual has only one X chromosome.
   D. Two types of intron 1 since the individual has one X chromosome and one Y chromosome.

5) The technique that utilizes probes to detect specific DNA sequences is known as which of the following?

   A. Southern blot
   B. RFLP
   C. Western blot
   D. PCR

6) A DNA plasmid with one unique restriction site that is improperly digested with the corresponding restriction enzyme may result in:

   A. an inability to be ligated.
   B. gel electrophoresis results that show multiple bands.
   C. DNA with some blunt, some sticky ends.
   D. susceptibility to methylation.

7) The inclusion of antibiotic resistance genes in DNA cloning vectors allows for all of the following EXCEPT:

A. positive selection of potentially viable clones.
B. protection against contamination from non-transfected or foreign *E. coli.*
C. protection against bacteriophages.
D. negative selection against empty plasmids missing the target gene insert.

8) The following components are all required for polymerase chain reaction EXCEPT:

A. DNA ligase.
B. a DNA template.
C. deoxynucleotide triphosphates.
D. DNA polymerase.

9) During the screening of cDNA libraries, prior to adding the labeled hybridization probe, researchers often first incubate the DNA to be analyzed with sheared salmon sperm. What does this step accomplish?

A. It raises the efficiency of the hybridization probe.
B. It increases non-specific binding between the hybridization probe and the DNA fragments in the library.
C. It reduces non-specific binding between the hybridization probe and the DNA fragments in the library.
D. It provides nucleotides for the reaction.

10) A mixture of weakly and strongly negatively-charged proteins is applied to an anion exchange chromatography column using a buffer with neutral pH. If a gradient with an increasing salt concentration is applied, which protein(s) will be eluted first?

A. The protein with the highest isoelectric point.
B. The protein with the lowest isoelectric point.
C. The protein with the largest mass.
D. The protein with the smallest mass.

11) The unified atomic mass unit (symbol: u = amu) or dalton (symbol: Da) is the standard unit that is used for indicating mass on an atomic or molecular scale. A recombinant protein that expresses as both a 50 kDa monomer and a 100 kDa dimer in a 1:1 ratio is eluted from a size exclusion column as two distinct samples. When both samples are combined and run on a denaturing SDS-PAGE gel, one would expect to observe:

A. one single band at 100 kDa.
B. one single band at 50 kDa.
C. distinct bands at 50 kDa and 100 kDa.
D. several bands of varying sizes.

12) Light-activated cation channels such as channelrhodopsin-2, used in the field of optogenetics, cause the rapid depolarization of excitable cells. This depolarization is caused by:

A. the sudden influx of anions.
B. the sudden influx of salts.
C. the sudden influx of cations.
D. the sudden efflux of cations.

GS ANSWER KEY

CHAPTER 4

		Cross-Reference			*Cross-Reference*
1.	C	BIO 1.2.2, 4.1.4	7.	C	BIO 2.2, 4.1.1, 4.1.3
2.	A	BIO 1.2.2, BCM 2.9, deduce	8.	A	BIO 1.2.2, 4.1.4
3.	B	BIO 15.3, BCM 4.1.4	9.	D	BIO 4.1.3
4.	D	BIO 15.3, BCM 4.1.4	10.	A	BIO 4.2.3, BCM 1.1.2, BCM 1.2
5	A	BIO 15.7, BCM 4.1.4	11.	B	BIO 4.2.2
6.	B	BIO 1.2.2, 2.2, 4.1.2, 4.2.1	12.	C	BIO 1.1.2, 4.3

*** Explanations can be found at the back of the book.**

Go online to MCAT-prep.com/forum to join the discussion about our GS chapter review questions.

GO[illegible]D NOTES

SPECIALIZED EUKARYOTIC CELLS AND TISSUES
Chapter 5

Memorize

* Neuron: basic structure and function
* Reasons for the membrane potential
* Structural characteristics of striated, smooth, and cardiac muscle
* Basic structure/function: epithelial cells, sarcomeres, connective tissue cells

Understand

* Resting potential: electrochemical gradient/action potential, graph
* Excitatory and inhibitory nerve fibers: summation, frequency of firing
* Organization of contractile elements: actin and myosin filaments
* Cross bridges, sliding filament model; calcium regulation of contraction

Not Required

* Advanced level college info
* Memorizing details about epithelial cells, connective tissue

MCAT-Prep.com

Introduction

To build a living organism, with all the various tissues and organs, cells must specialize. Communication among cells and organs, movement, protection and support are achieved to a great degree by neurons, muscle cells, epithelial cells and the cells of connective tissue, respectively.

Optional Gold Standard Resources

Free Online Q&A + Forum

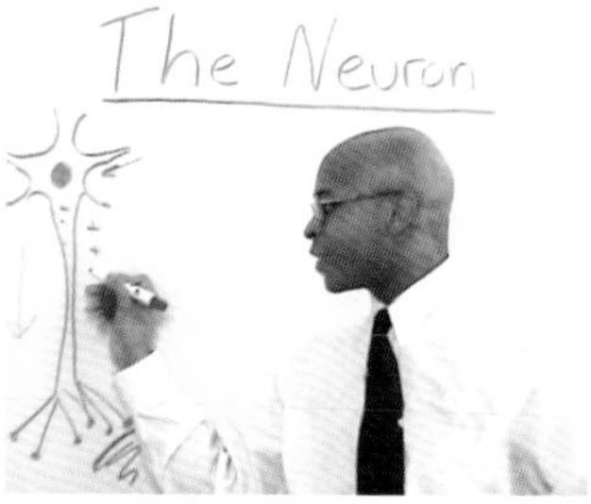

Online Videos

Flashcards

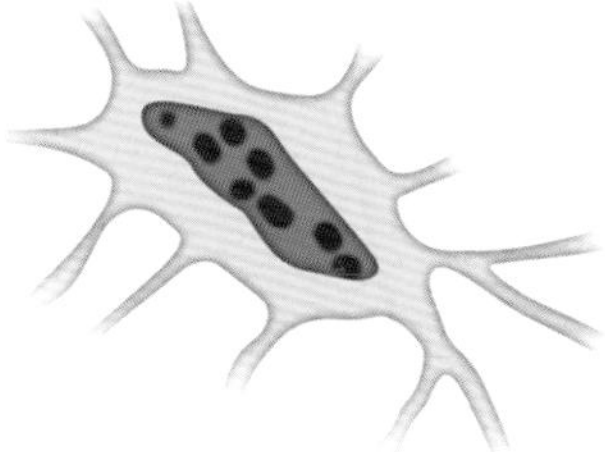

Special Guest

5.1 Neural Cells and Tissues

The brain, spinal cord and peripheral nervous system are composed of nerve tissue. The basic cell types of nerve tissue is the *neuron* and the *glial cell*. Glial cells support and protect neurons and participate in neural activity, nutrition and defense processes. Neurons (= nerve cells) represent the functional unit of the nervous system. They conduct and transmit nerve impulses.

Neurons can be classified based on the shape or *morphology*. Unipolar neurons possess a single process. Bipolar neurons possess a single axon and a single dendrite. Multipolar neurons possess a single axon and more than one dendrite and are the most common type. Pseudounipolar neurons possess a single process that subsequently branches out into an axon and dendrite (note that in biology "pseudo" means "false"). Neurons can also be classified based on function. Sensory neurons receive stimuli from the environment and conduct impulses to the CNS. Motor neurons conduct impulses from the CNS to other neurons, muscles or glands. Interneurons connect other neurons and regulate transmitting signal between neurons.

Each neuron consists of a nerve cell body (*perikaryon or soma*), and its processes, which usually include multiple *dendrites* and a single *axon*. The cell body of a typical neuron contains a nucleus, *Nissl* material which is rough endoplasmic reticulum, free ribosomes, Golgi apparatus, mitochondria, many neurotubules, neurofilaments and pigment inclusions. The cell processes of neurons occur as axons and dendrites.

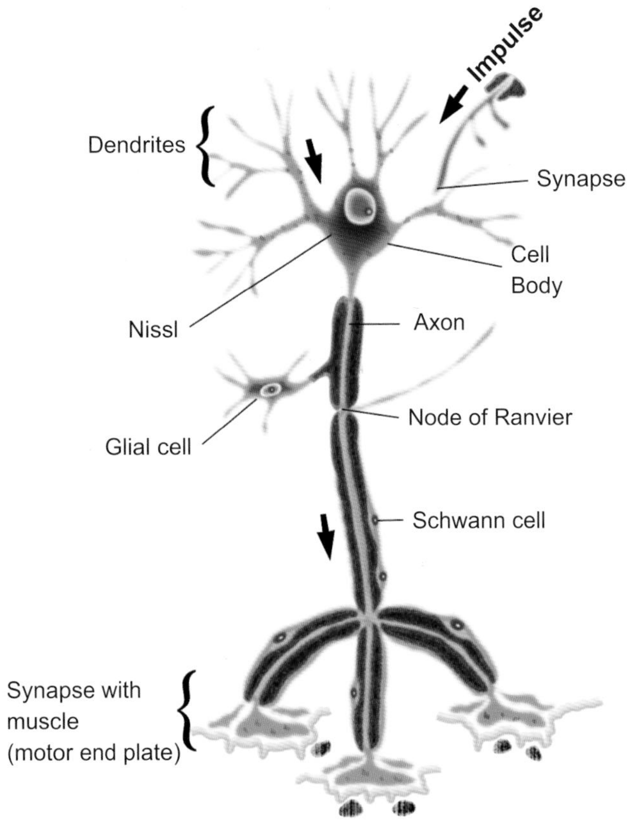

Figure IV.A.5.1: A neuron and other cells of nerve tissue, showing the neuromuscular junction, or motor end plate.

Dendrites contain most of the components of the cell, whereas axons contain major structures found in dendrites except for the Nissl material and Golgi apparatus. As a rule, dendrites receive stimuli from sensory cells, axons, or other neurons and conduct these impulses to the cell body of neurons and ultimately through to the axon. Axons are long cellular processes that conduct impulses away from the cell body of neurons. These originate from the axon hillock, a specialized region that contains many microtubules and neurofilaments. At the synaptic (terminal) ends of axons, the presynaptic process contains vesicles from which are elaborated excitatory or inhibitory substances.

Unmyelinated fibers in peripheral nerves lie in grooves on the surface of the neurolemma (= plasma membrane) of a type of glial cell (*Schwann cell*). **Myelinated** peripheral neurons are invested by numerous layers of plasma membrane of Schwann cells or oligodendrocytes that constitute a *myelin sheath*, which allows axons to conduct impulses faster. The myelin sheath is produced by oligodendrocytes in the CNS and by Schwann cells in the PNS. In junctional areas between adjacent Schwann cells or oligodendrocytes there is a lack of myelin. These junctional areas along the myelinated process constitute the nodes of Ranvier.

The neurons of the nervous system are arranged so that each neuron stimulates or inhibits other neurons and these in turn may stimulate or inhibit others until the functions of the nervous system are performed. The area between a neuron and the successive cell (i.e. another neuron, muscle fiber or gland) is called a *synapse*. Synapses can be classified as either a chemical synapse or an electrical synapse. A chemical synapse involves the release of a neurotransmitter by the presynaptic cell which then diffuses across the synapse and can act on the postsynaptic cell to generate an action potential. Signal transmission is delayed due to the time required for diffusion of the neurotransmitter across the synapse onto the membrane of the postsynaptic cell. An electrical synapse involves the movement of ions from one neuron to another via gap junctions (BIO 1.4.1). Signal transmission is immediate. Electrical synapses are often found in neural systems that require the fastest possible response, such as defensive reflexes.

When a neuron makes a synapse with muscle, it is called a *motor end plate* (see Fig. IV.A.5.1). The terminal endings of the nerve filament that synapse with the next cell are called presynaptic terminals, synaptic knobs, or more commonly - synaptic boutons. The postsynaptic terminal is the membrane part of another neuron or muscle or gland that is receiving the impulse. The synaptic cleft is the narrow space between the presynaptic and postsynaptic membrane.

At the synapse there is no physical contact between the two cells. The space between the dendrite of one neuron and the axon of another neuron is called the synaptic cleft and it measures about 200 - 300 angstroms (1 angstrom = 10^{-10} m) in a chemical synapse and about a tenth of that distance in an electrical synapse. The mediators in a chemical synapse, known as neurotransmitters, are housed in the presynaptic terminal and are exocytosed in response to an increase in intracellular Ca^{2+} concentration. The mediators or transmitters diffuse through the synaptic cleft when an impulse reaches the terminal and bind to receptors in the postsynaptic membrane. This transmitter substance may either excite the *postsynaptic* neuron or inhibit it. They are therefore called either excitatory or inhibitory transmitters (examples include *acetylcholine* and *GABA*, respectively).

5.1.1 The Membrane Potential

A membrane or resting potential (V_m) occurs across the plasma membranes of all cells. In large nerve and muscle cells this potential amounts to about 70 millivolts with positivity outside the cell membrane and negativity inside (V_m = -70 mV). The development of this potential occurs as follows: every cell membrane contains a Na^+ - K^+ ATPase that pumps each ion to where its concentration is highest. The concentration of K^+ is higher inside the neuron and the concentration of Na^+ is higher outside; therefore, Na^+ is pumped to the outside of the cell and K^+ to the inside. However, more Na^+ is pumped outward than K^+ inward ($3Na^+$ per $2K^+$). Also, the membrane is relatively permeable to K^+ so that it can leak out of the cell with relative ease. Therefore, the net effect is a loss of positive charges from inside the membrane and a gain of positive charges on the outside. The resulting membrane potential is the basis of all conduction of impulses by nerve and muscle fibers.

5.1.2 Action Potential

The action potential is a sequence of changes in the electric potential that occurs within a small fraction of a second when a nerve or muscle membrane impulse spreads over the surface of the cell. An excitatory stimulus on a postsynaptic neuron depolarizes the membrane and makes the membrane potential less negative. Once the membrane potential reaches a critical threshold, the voltage-gated Na^+ channels become fully open, permitting the inward flow of Na^+ into the cell. The membrane potential is at the critical threshold when it is in a state where an action potential is inevitable. As a result, the positive sodium ions on the outside of the membrane now flow rapidly to the more negative interior. Therefore, the membrane potential suddenly becomes reversed with positivity on the inside and negativity on the outside. This state is called *depolarization* and is caused by an inward Na^+ current.

Depolarization also leads to the inactivation of the Na^+ channel and slowly opens the K^+ channel. The combined effect of the two preceding events repolarizes the membrane back to its resting potential. This is called *repolarization*. In fact, the neuron may shoot past the resting membrane potential and become even more negative, and this is called hyperpolarization. The depolarized nerve goes on depolarizing the adjacent nerve membrane in a wavy manner which is called an impulse. In other words, an impulse is a wave of depolarization. Different axons can propagate impulses at different speeds. The increasing diameter of a nerve fiber or degree of myelination results in a faster impulse. The impulse is fastest in myelinated fibers since the wave of depolarization "jumps" from node to node of Ranvier: this is called *saltatory* conduction because an action potential can be generated only at nodes of Ranvier.

Immediately following an action potential, the neuron will pass through three stages in the following order: a) it can no longer elicit

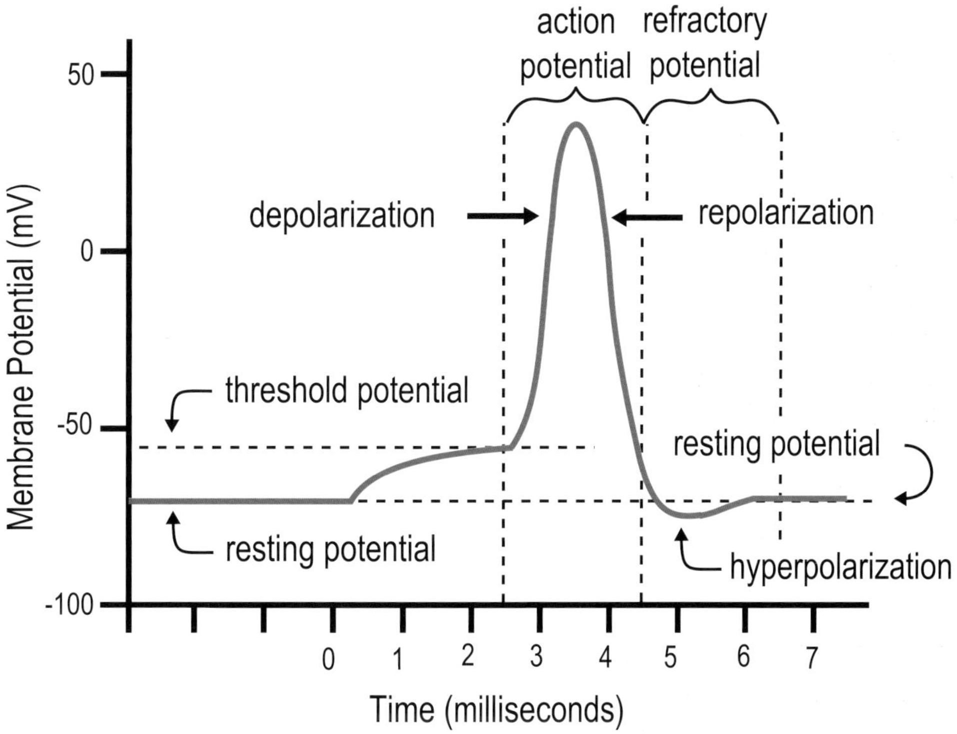

Figure IV.A.5.2: Action potential.

another action potential no matter how large the stimulus is = *absolute refractory period*; b) it can elicit another action potential only if a larger than usual stimulus is provided = *relative refractory period*; c) it returns to its original resting potential and thus can depolarize as easily as it originally did.

The action potential is an all-or-none event. The magnitude or strength of the action potential is not graded according to the strength of the stimulus. It occurs with the same magnitude each time it occurs, or it does not occur at all.

5.1.3 Action Potential: A Positive Perspective

To better understand the action potential it is useful to take a closer look at what occurs to the positive ions Na^+ and K^+. To begin with, there are protein channels in the plasma membrane that act like gates which guard the passage of specific ions. Some gates open or close in response to V_m and are thus called *voltage gated channels.*

Once a threshold potential is reached, the voltage gated Na^+ channels open allowing the permeability or *conductance* of Na^+ to increase. The Na^+ ions can now diffuse across their chemical gradient: from an area of high concentration (*outside the membrane*) to an area of low concentration (*inside the membrane*). The Na^+ ions will also diffuse across their electrical gradient: from an area of relative positivity (*outside the membrane*) to an area of relative negativity (*inside the membrane*). Thus the inside becomes positive and the membrane is depolarized. Repolarization occurs as the Na^+ channels close and the voltage gated K^+ channels open. As K^+ conductance increases to the outside (where K^+ concentration is lowest), the membrane repolarizes to once again become relatively negative on the inside.

5.2 Contractile Cells and Tissues

There are three types of muscle tissue: smooth, skeletal and cardiac. All three types are composed of muscle cells (fibers) that contain myofibrils possessing contractile filaments of actin and myosin.

Smooth muscle:- Smooth muscle cells are spindle shaped and are organized chiefly into sheets or bands of smooth muscle tissue. They contain a single nucleus and actively divide and regenerate. This tissue is found in blood vessels and other tubular visceral structures (i.e. intestines). Smooth muscles contain both actin and myosin filaments but actin predominates. The filaments are not organized into patterns that give cross striations as in cardiac and skeletal muscle. Filaments course obliquely in the cells and attach to the plasma membrane. Contraction of smooth muscle is involuntary and is innervated by the autonomic nervous system.

Skeletal muscle:- Skeletal muscle fibers are characterized by their peripherally located multiple nuclei and striated myofibrils. Myofibrils are longitudinally arranged bundles of thick and thin myofilaments. Myofilaments are composed of thick and thin filaments present in an alternating arrangement responsible for the cross-striation pattern. The striations in a sarcomere consists of an A-band (dark), which contains both thin and thick filaments. These are bordered toward the Z-lines by I-bands (light), which contain thin filaments only. The mid-region of the A-band contains an H-band (light), which contains thick filaments only and is bisected by an M-line. The Z lines are dense regions bisecting each I-band and anchor the thin filaments. The filaments interdigitate and are cross-bridged in the A-band with myosin filaments forming a hexagonal pattern of one myosin filament surrounded by six actin filaments. In the contraction of a muscle fiber,

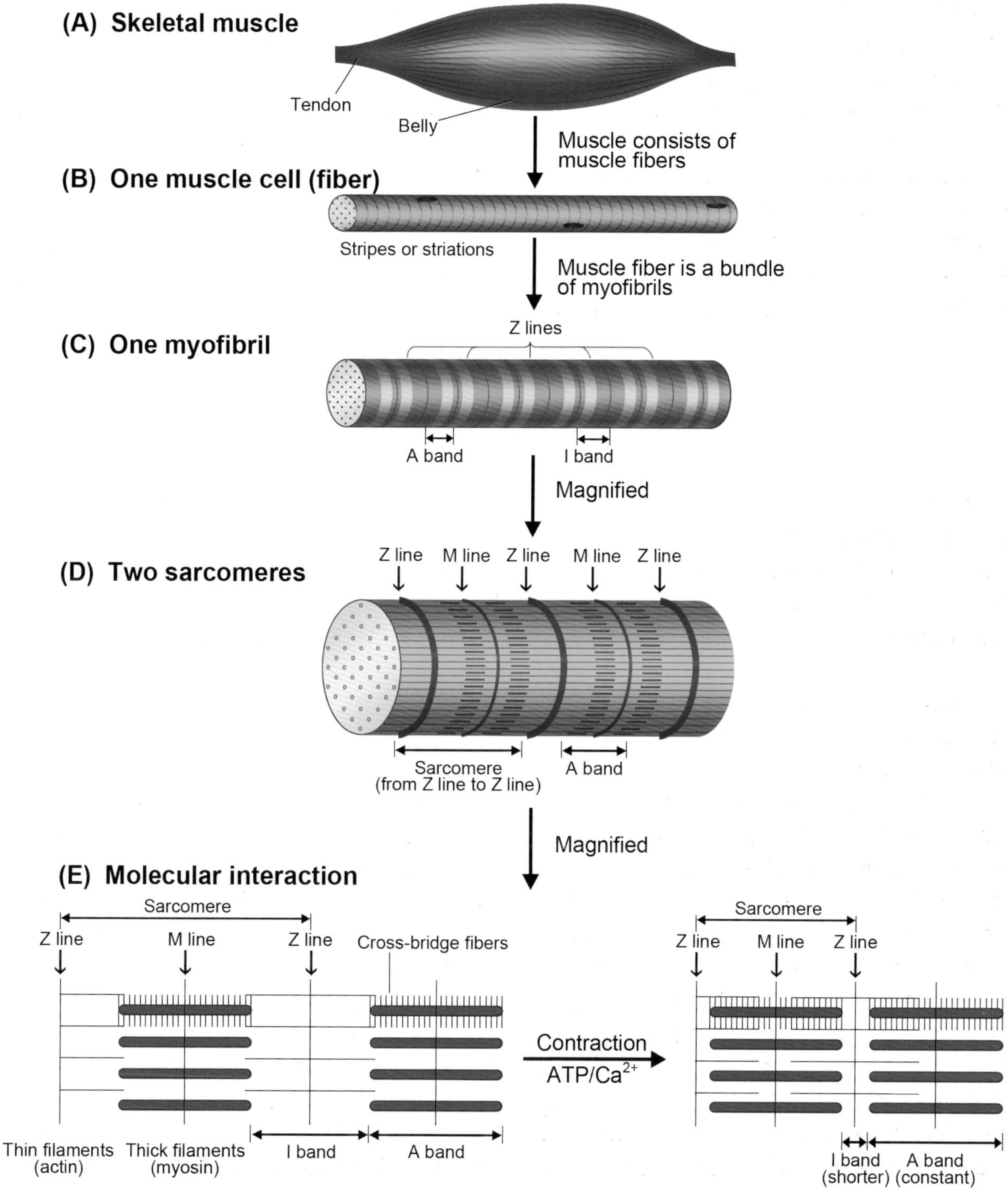

Figure IV.A.5.3: A schematic view of the molecular basis for muscle contraction. Note: the "H zone" is the central portion of an A band and is characterized by the presence of myosin filaments.

thick and thin filaments do not shorten but increase their overlap. The actin filaments of the I-bands move more deeply into the A-band, resulting in a shortening of the H-band and the I-bands as Z disks are brought closer. However, the A-band remains constant in length. {Mnemonic: "HI" bands shorten}

Each skeletal muscle fiber is invested with a sarcolemma (= plasmalemma = plasma membrane) that extends into the fiber as numerous small transverse tubes called T-tubules. These tubules ring the myofibrils at the A-I junction and are bounded on each side by terminal cisternae of the endoplasmic (sarcoplasmic) reticulum. The T-tubules, together with a pair of terminal cisternae form a triad. The triad helps to provide a uniform contraction throughout the muscle cell as it provides channels for ions to flow freely and helps to propagate action potentials. There are thousands of triads per skeletal muscle fiber.

The sarcoplasmic reticulum is a modified endoplasmic reticulum that regulates muscle contraction by either transporting Ca^{2+} into storage (muscle relaxation) or releasing Ca^{2+} during excitation-contraction coupling (muscle contraction).

The thick filaments within a myofibril are composed of about 250 myosin molecules arranged in an antiparallel fashion and some associated proteins. The myosin molecule is composed of two identical heavy chains and two pairs of light chain. The heavy chain consists of two "heads" and one "tail". The head contains an actin binding site which is involved in muscle contraction. The thin filaments within a myofibril are composed of actin and to a lesser degree two smaller proteins: *troponin and tropomyosin*. An action potential in the muscle cell membrane initiates depolarization of the T tubules, which causes the nearby sarcoplasmic reticulum to release its Ca^{2+} ions and thus an increase in intracellular [Ca^{2+}]. Calcium then attaches to a subunit of troponin resulting in the movement of tropomyosin and the uncovering of the active sites for the attachment of actin to the cross bridging heads of myosin. Due to this attachment, ATP in the myosin head hydrolyses, producing energy, Pi and ADP which results in a bending of the myosin head and a pulling of the actin filament into the A-band. These actin-myosin bridges detach again when myosin binds a new ATP molecule and attaches to a new site on actin toward the plus end as long as Ca^{2+} is bound to troponin. Finally, relaxation of muscle occurs when Ca^{2+} is sequestered by the sarcoplasmic reticulum. Thus calcium is pumped out of the cytoplasm and calcium levels return to normal, tropomyosin again binds to actin, preventing myosin from binding.

There are three interesting consequences to the preceding:

i) neither actin nor myosin change length during muscle contraction; rather, shortening of the muscle fiber occurs as the filaments slide over each other increasing the area of overlap.

ii) initially a dead person is very stiff (*rigor mortis*) since they can no longer produce the ATP necessary to detach the actin-myosin bridges thus their muscles remain locked in position.

iii) Ca^{2+} is a critical ion both for muscle contraction and for transmitter release from presynaptic neurons.

Cardiac muscle:- Cardiac muscle contains striations and myofibrils that are similar to those of skeletal muscle. Contraction of cardiac muscle is involuntary and is innervated by the autonomic nervous system. It differs from skeletal muscle in several major ways. Cardiac muscle fibers branch and contain centrally located nuclei (characteristically, one nucleus per cell) and large numbers of mitochondria. Individual cardiac muscle cells are attached to each other at their ends by *intercalated* disks. These disks contain several types of membrane junctional complexes, the most important of which is the *gap junction* (BIO 1.4.1). Cardiac muscle cells do not regenerate: injury to cardiac muscle is repaired by fibrous connective tissue.

The gap junction electrically couples one cell to its neighbor (= *syncytium*) so that electric depolarization is propagated throughout the heart by cell-to-cell contact rather than by nerve innervation to each cell. The sarcoplasmic reticulum - T-tubule system is arranged differently in cardiac muscle than in skeletal muscle. In cardiac muscle each T-tubule enters at the Z-line and forms a diad with only one terminal cisterna of sarcoplasmic reticulum.

5.3 Epithelial Cells and Tissues

Epithelia have the following characteristics:

1. they cover all body surfaces (i.e. skin, organs, etc.)
2. they are the principal tissues of glands
3. their cells are anchored by a nonliving layer (= the basement membrane)
4. they lack blood vessels and are thus nourished by diffusion.

Epithelial tissues are classified according to the characteristics of their cells. Tissues with elongated cells are called *columnar*, those with thin flattened cells are *squamous*, and those with cube-like cells are *cuboidal*. They are further classified as **simple** if they have a single layer of cells and **stratified** if they have multiple layers of cells. As examples of the classification, skin is composed of a stratified squamous epithelium while various glands (i.e. thyroid, salivary, etc.) contain a simple cuboidal epithelium. The former epithelium serves to protect against microorganisms, loss of water or heat, while the latter epithelium functions to secrete glandular products.

5.4 Connective Cells and Tissues

Connective tissue connects and joins other body tissue and parts. It also carries substances for processing, nutrition, and waste release. Connective tissue is characterized by the presence of relatively few cells surrounded by an extensive network of extracellular matrix, consisting of ground substance, extracellular fluid, and fibers.

The adult connective tissues are: connective tissue proper, cartilage, bone and blood (see *The Circulatory System*, section 7.5). Connective tissue proper is further classified into loose connective tissue, dense connective tissue, elastic tissue, reticular tissue and adipose tissue.

5.4.1 Loose Connective Tissue

Loose connective tissue is found in the superficial fascia. It is generally considered as the *packaging material* of the body, in part, because it frequently envelopes muscles. Fascia - usually a clear or white sheet (or band) of fibrous connective tissue - helps to bind skin to underlying organs, to fill spaces between muscles, etc. Loose connective tissue contains most of the cell types and all the fiber types found in the other connective tissues. The most common cell types are the fibroblast, macrophage, adipose cell, mast cell, plasma cell and wandering cells from the blood (which include several types of white blood cells).

Fibroblasts are the predominant cell type in connective tissue proper and have the capability to differentiate into other types of cells under certain conditions.

Macrophages are part of the *reticulo-endothelial system* (tissue which predominately destroys foreign particles). They are responsible for phagocytosing foreign bodies and assisting the immune response. They possess large lysosomes containing digestive enzymes which are necessary for the digestion of phagocytosed materials. Mast cells reside mostly along blood vessels and contain granules which include *heparin* and *histamine*. Heparin is a compound which prevents blood clotting and histamine is associated with allergic reactions. Mast cells mediate type I hypersensitivity.

Plasma cells are part of the immune system in that they produce circulatory antibodies (BIO 7.5, 8.2). They contain extensive amounts of rough endoplasmic reticulum (rER).

Adipose cells are found in varying quantities, when they predominate, the tissue is called adipose (fat) tissue.

Fibers are long protein polymers present in different types of connective tissue. Common types of fibers include collagen fiber, reticular fiber and elastic fiber.

Collagen fibers are usually found in bundles and provide **strength** to the tissue. Many different types of collagen fibers are identified on the basis of their molecular structure. Of the five most common types, collagen type I is the most abundant, being found in dermis, bone, dentine, tendons, organ capsules, fascia and sclera. Type II is located in hyaline and elastic cartilage. Type III is probably the collagenous component of reticular fibers. Type IV is found in a specific part (*the basal lamina*) of basement membranes. Type V is a component of placental basement membranes. **Reticular fibers** are smaller, more delicate fibers that form the basic framework of reticular connective tissue. **Elastic fibers** branch and provide elasticity and support to connective tissue.

Ground substance is the gelatinous material that fills most of the space between the cells and the fibers. It is composed of acid mucopolysaccharides and structural glycoproteins and its properties are important in determining the permeability and consistency of the connective tissue.

5.4.2 Dense Connective Tissue

Dense irregular connective tissue is found in the dermis, periosteum, perichondrium and capsules of some organs. All of the fiber types are present, but collagenous fibers predominate. Dense regular connective tissue occurs as aponeuroses, ligaments and tendons. In most ligaments and tendons collagenous fibers are most prevalent and are oriented parallel to each other. Fibroblasts are practically the only cell type present.

5.4.3 Cartilage

Cartilage is composed of chondrocytes (= cartilage cells) embedded in an intercellular (= extracellular) matrix, consisting of fibers and an amorphous firm ground substance. In cases of injury, cartilage repairs slowly since it has no direct blood supply. Three types of cartilage are distinguished on the basis of the amount of ground substance and the relative abundance of collagenous and elastic fibers. They are hyaline, elastic and fibrous cartilage.

Hyaline Cartilage is found as costal (rib) cartilage, articular cartilage and cartilage of the nose, larynx, trachea and bronchi. The extracellular matrix consists primarily of collagenous fibers and a ground substance rich in chondromucoprotein, a copolymer of a protein and chondroitin sulphates.

Elastic Cartilage is found in the pinna of the ear, auditory tube and epiglottis, and some laryngeal cartilage. Elastic fibers predominate and thus provide greater flexibility. Calcification of this type of cartilage is rare.

Fibrous Cartilage occurs in the anchorage of tendons and ligaments, in intervertebral disks, in the symphysis pubis, and in some interarticular disks and in some ligaments. Chondrocytes occur singly or in rows between large bundles of collagenous fibers. Compared with hyaline cartilage, only small amounts of hyaline matrix surround the chondrocytes of fibrous cartilage.

5.4.4 Bone

Bone tissue consists of three **cell types** and a calcified **extracellular matrix** that contains organic and inorganic components. The three cell types are: *osteoblasts* which synthesize the organic components of the matrix (osteoid) and become embedded in lacunae; *osteocytes* which are mature bone cells entrapped in their own lacunae within the matrix and maintain communication with each other via gap junctions; and *osteoclasts* which are large multinucleated cells functioning in resorption and remodeling of bone.

The organic matrix consists of dense collagenous fibers (primarily type I collagen) which is important in providing flexibility and tensile strength to bone. The inorganic component is responsible for the *rigidity* of the bone and is composed chiefly of calcium phosphate and calcium carbonate with small amounts of magnesium, fluoride, hydroxide, sulphate and hydroxyapatite.

Compact bone contains haversian systems (osteons), interstitial lamellae and circumferential lamellae. The Haversian system is the structural unit for bone and each osteon consists of a central Haversian canal surrounded by a number of concentric deposits of bony matrix called lamellae. Haversian systems consist of extensively branching haversian canals that are oriented chiefly longitudinally in long bones. Each canal contains blood vessels and is surrounded by 8 to 15 concentric lamellae and osteocytes.

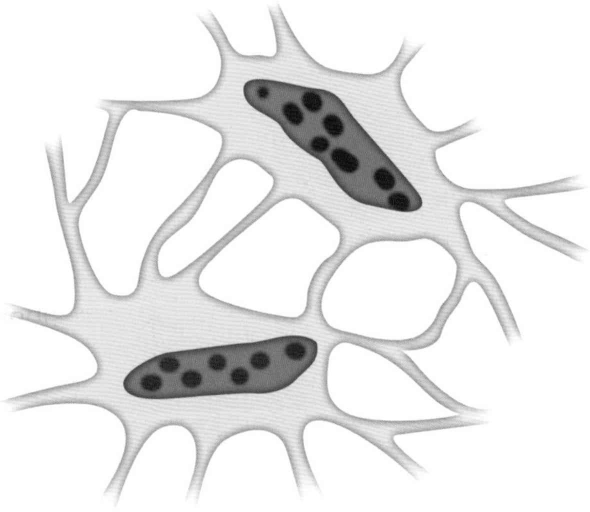

Figure IV.A.5.4: Osteocytes.

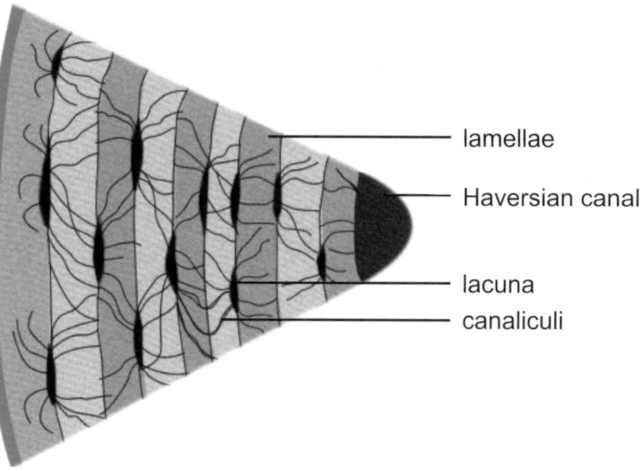

Figure IV.A.5.5: Schematic drawing of part of a haversian system.

Nutrients from blood vessels in the haversian canals pass through canaliculi and lacunae to reach all osteocytes in the system. Volkmann's canals traverse the bone transversely and interconnect the haversian systems. They enter through the outer circumferential lamellae and carry blood vessels and nerves which are continuous with those of the haversian canals and the periosteum. The periosteum is the connective tissue layer which envelopes bone. The endosteum is the connective tissue layer which lines the marrow cavities and supplies osteoprogenitor cells and osteoblasts for bone formation.

Figure IV.A.5.6
Schematic drawing of the wall of a long bone.

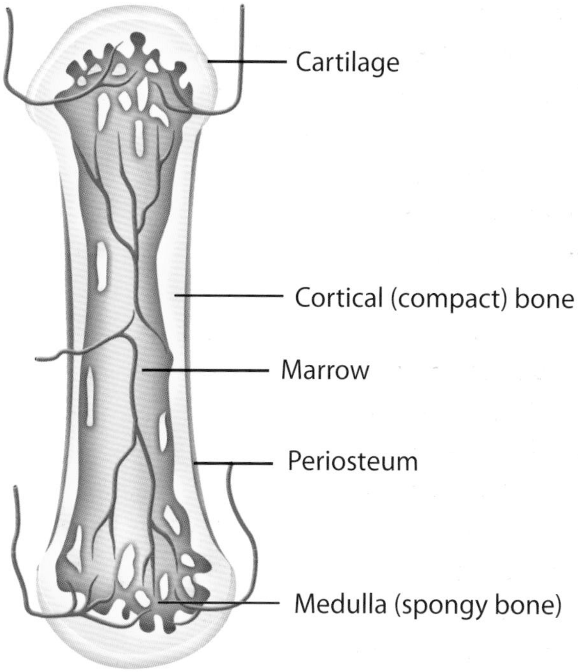

Figure IV.A.5.7
Schematic drawing of adult bone structure.

Bones are supplied by a loop of blood vessels that enter from the periosteal region, penetrate the cortical bone, and enter the medulla before returning to the periphery of the bone. Long bones are specifically supplied by arteries which pass to the marrow through diaphyseal, metaphyseal and epiphyseal arteries (for bone structure, see BIO 11.3.1).

Bone undergoes extensive remodelling, and harvesian systems may break down or be resorbed in order that calcium can be made available to other parts of the body. Bone resorption occurs by osteocytes engaging in osteolysis or by osteoclastic activity.

GOLD STANDARD WARM-UP EXERCISES

CHAPTER 5: Specialized Eukaryotic Cells and Tissues

1) Which of the following is NOT part of a neuron?

A. Synapse
B. Dendrite
C. Axon
D. Nissl bodies

2) The ATP-dependent dopamine transporter can be found at the presynaptic terminal of nerve cells. The dopamine transporter is most likely a:

A. protein in the neurolemma.
B. protein in the outer membrane of mitochondria.
C. protein in the neural nuclear membranes.
D. phospholipid in the plasma membrane.

3) Consider the following Table.

Table 1: Concentration of Na^+, K^+, and Cl^- inside and outside mammalian motor neurons.

Ion	Concentration (mmol/L H_2O)		Equilibrium potential (mV)
	Inside cell	Outside cell	
Na^+	15.0	150.0	+60
K^+	150.0	5.5	-90
Cl^-	9.0	125.0	-75
Resting membrane potential (V_m) = −70 mV			

At resting membrane potential, in what direction will K^+ ions move spontaneously in a cell?

A. From the cytosol to the nucleus
B. From the cytosol to the cell exterior
C. From the cell exterior to the cytosol
D. From the mitochondria to the cytosol

4) All of the following explain the ionic concentrations in Table 1 EXCEPT:

A. Na^+ and Cl^- ions passively diffuse more quickly into the extracellular fluid than K^+ ions.
B. Na^+ ions are actively pumped out of the intracellular fluid.
C. the negative charge of the cell contents repels Cl^- ions from the cell.
D. the cell membrane is more freely permeable to K^+ ions than to Na^+ and Cl^- ions.

5) At inhibitory synapses, a hyperpolarization of the membrane known as an inhibitory postsynaptic potential is produced rendering V_m more negative. This occurs as a result of (data from Table 1 can be considered):

A. an increase in the postsynaptic membrane's permeability to Na^+ and K^+ ions.
B. an increase in the permeability of the presynaptic membrane to Ca^{2+} ions.
C. the entry of Cl^- ions into the synaptic knob.
D. an increase in the permeability of the postsynaptic membrane to Cl^- ions.

6) Diisopropylfluorophosphate (DFP) acts as an irreversible inhibitor at the active site of acetylcholinesterase. This enzyme deactivates the chemical transmitter acetylcholine. The main effect of DFP would be to:

A. prevent the passage of nerve impulses along the postsynaptic neuron.
B. prevent the entry of Ca^{2+} into the synaptic knob.
C. initiate muscular tetany.
D. generate a very large action potential.

7) According to the following diagram, which ion channel opens and closes more quickly?

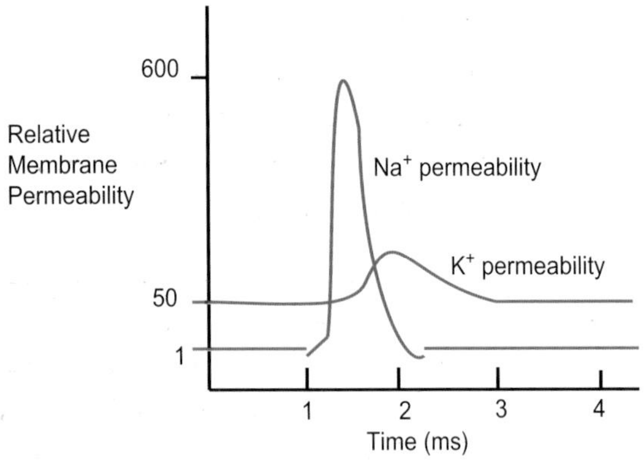

A. The K^+ channel because its relative membrane permeability is lower than for Na^+.
B. The Na^+ channel because its extracellular concentration is greater than for K^+.
C. The K^+ channel because it remains permeable for a longer period of time.
D. The Na^+ channel because its permeability increases and decreases at a faster rate.

8) An experiment is performed in which an inhibitor is applied to a single neuron. Upon stimulating the neuron and measuring both the intracellular and extracellular ion concentrations, it is found that the levels of K^+ and Na^+ have reached equilibrium. Based on these results, the inhibitor most likely inhibits the:

A. ATPase.
B. Cl^- channel.
C. K^+ channel.
D. Na^+ channel.

9) What would happen to the action potential in the previous diagram if K^+ channels were hindered but not completely blocked following depolarization?

A. The action potential would not repolarize.
B. The action potential would repolarize at a faster rate.
C. The duration of the action potential would be more than 1 ms.
D. The action potential would repolarize to less than -70 mV.

10) If cyanide was added to nerve cells, what would be expected to happen to the ionic composition of the cells?

A. Na^+ ions would be actively pumped into the cell and K^+ ions would be pumped out.
B. Intracellular Na^+ would increase since the sodium pump would stop functioning.
C. The potential of the cell membrane would not be reversed so that Cl^- ions would freely enter the cell.
D. The cell membrane would become freely permeable to Na^+ and Cl^- ions.

11) The temporary increase in the sarcolemma's permeability to Na^+ and K^+ ions that occurs at the motor end plate of a neuromuscular junction is immediately preceded by which of the following?

A. The release of acetylcholine from the motor neuron into the synaptic gap.
B. The release of adrenaline from the motor neuron into the synaptic gap.
C. The passage of a nerve impulse along the axon of a motor neuron.
D. The release of noradrenaline from a sensory neuron into the synaptic gap.

12) The overall reaction which takes place at the sodium pump is given by the equation:

$$3Na^+_{(inside)} + 2K^+_{(outside)} + ATP^{4-} + H_2O \rightarrow 3Na^+_{(outside)} + 2K^+_{(inside)} + ADP^{3-} + P_i + H^+$$

When a muscle is very active, at the end of glycolysis, pyruvate is converted to lactate by the addition of H^+ ions. During vigorous exercise, how many ions of K^+ could be pumped into a cell per molecule of glucose?

A. 2
B. 4
C. 8
D. 12

13) Stimulating electrodes were placed on a nerve and a recording electrode was placed near the motor end plate. First curare and then eserine were added to the solution bathing the muscle. The action potentials produced by stimulating the nerve were recorded and the results are shown.

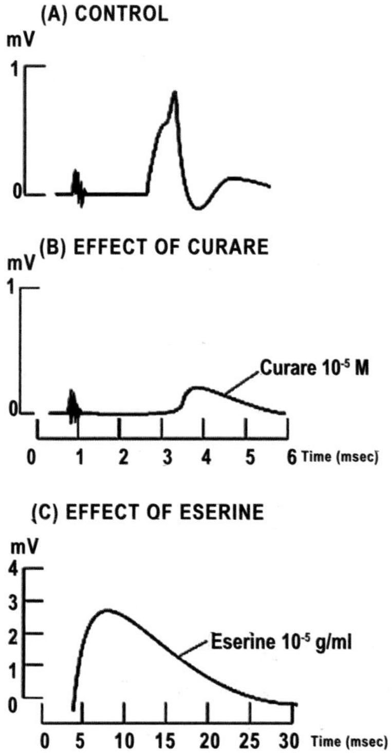

According to the results of the experiment, curare and eserine could act by, respectively:

A. blocking ion channels and binding to the receptors on ACh-activated channels.
B. blocking ion channels and preventing the hydrolysis of acetylcholinesterase.
C. initiating the entry of calcium ions into the synaptic knob and initiating the passage of a nerve impulse along the muscle cell.
D. binding to ACh receptor sites on the post-synaptic membrane and preventing the hydrolysis of acetylcholine.

14) In the control in the graph for the previous question, the part of the curve between 4 and 5 msec represents:

A. the absolute refractory period.
B. the relative refractory period.
C. the depolarization of the membrane.
D. saltatory conduction.

15) The depolarization across the muscle membrane triggers an all-or-none action potential in the muscle cell. This suggests that an increase in the amount of transmitter released at the neuromuscular junction would change:

A. the amplitude of the action potential.
B. the frequency of the nerve impulses.
C. the direction of the action potential.
D. the speed at which nerve impulses travel along the muscle cell.

16) Which of the following is true about muscle contraction?

A. Troponin and tropomyosin slide past one another allowing the muscle to shorten.
B. Decreased intracellular $[Ca^{++}]$ enhances the degree of muscular contraction.
C. Cardiac muscle fibers contain centrally located nuclei.
D. Neither actin nor myosin change length during muscle contraction.

17) In muscle cells, the actin filaments are:

A. thin and associated with the proteins troponin and collagen.
B. thin and associated with the proteins troponin and tropomyosin.
C. thick and associated with the proteins troponin and collagen.
D. thick and associated with the proteins troponin and tropomyosin.

18) If the gene which codes for troponin was absent from muscle cells, which of the following processes would NOT be inhibited?

A. The movement of tropomyosin to a new position on the actin molecules
B. The uncovering of the active sites for the attachment of actin to the cross bridges of myosin
C. The hydrolysis of ATP in the myosin head to produce ADP, P_i, and energy
D. The release of Ca^{2+} ions from the sarcoplasmic reticulum

19) Contraction of a muscle occurs when:

A. myosin binds and releases actin.
B. actin binds and releases myosin.
C. tropomyosin binds and releases actin.
D. actin binds and releases tropomyosin.

20) All of the following contain a phospholipid bilayer EXCEPT:

A. sarcolemma.
B. neurolemma.
C. basement membrane.
D. plasma membrane.

21) At the neuromuscular junction, the receptors on the acetylcholine-activated channels are likely located:

A. on the tubule of the T system.
B. in the sarcolemma.
C. on the muscle surface.
D. in the synaptic cleft.

22) Glycoproteins are found in all cellular compartments and are also secreted from the cell. Collagen, a secreted glycoprotein of the extracellular matrix, has simple carbohydrates - the disaccharide Glc beta (1,2) Gal linked to hydroxylysine. If a base mutation occurred in cells so that all the hydroxylysine residues were replaced by asparagine residues in the amino acid side chains, which of the following would result?

A. Glycoprotein formation would cease.
B. The strength of loose connective tissue might be affected.
C. Protein folding could not occur.
D. Protein recognition would be impossible.

23) What type of tissue is bone tissue?

A. Muscle
B. Epithelial
C. Connective
D. Nervous

24) Muscle is surrounded by what tough sheet of whitish connective tissue?

A. Tendon
B. Ligament
C. Marrow
D. Fascia

25) The organic portion of bone consists of which one of the following proteins?

A. Collagen
B. Fibrin
C. Actin
D. Myosin

GS ANSWER KEY

CHAPTER 5

		Cross-Reference			Cross-Reference
1.	A	BIO 5.1	14.	B	BIO 5.1.2
2.	A	BIO 5.1, 1.1, 1.1.3	15.	B	BIO 5.1.1-5.1.2
3.	B	BIO 5.1.1-5.1.3, deduce	16.	D	BIO 5.2
4.	A	BIO 1.2.2, 5.1.1-5.1.3, deduce	17.	B	BIO 5.2
5.	D	BIO 5.1.1-5.1.3, deduce	18.	D	BIO 5.2
6.	C	BIO 4.2, 5.1, 11.2	19.	A	BIO 5.2
7.	D	BIO 5.1.1-5.1.3, deduce	20.	C	BIO 1.1, 5.2-5.3
8.	A	BIO 4.2, 5.1.1-5.1.3, deduce	21.	B	BIO 1.1, 5.2 paragraph 4
9.	C	BIO 5.1.1, 5.1.2	22.	B	BIO 5.4.1
10.	B	BIO 4.4, 4.9, 5.1.1	23.	C	BIO 5.4
11.	A	BIO 5.1.1-5.1.3	24.	D	BIO 5.4.1, 5.4.2
12.	B	BIO 4.4, 5.1.1; CHM 1.5	25.	A	BIO 5.4.4
13.	D	BIO 5.1.2, deduce			

*** Explanations can be found at the back of the book.**

Go online to MCAT-prep.com/forum to join the discussion about our GS chapter review questions.

APPENDIX

CHAPTER 5: Specialized Eukaryotic Cells and Tissues

Passage: The Nernst Equation

When movement of ions is considered, two factors will influence the direction in which they diffuse: one is concentration, the other is electrical charge. An ion will usually diffuse from a region of its high concentration to a region of its low concentration. It will also generally be attracted towards a region of opposite charge, and move away from a region of similar charge. Thus ions are said to move down electrochemical gradients, which are the combined effects of both electrical and concentration gradients. Strictly speaking, active transport of ions is their movement against an electrochemical gradient powered by an energy source.

Consider the data in the following Table.

Table 1: Concentration of Na^+, K^+, and Cl^- inside and outside mammalian motor neurons. The sign of the potential (mV) is inside relative to the outside of the cell.

Ion	Concentration (mmol/L H_2O)		Equilibrium potential (mV)
	Inside cell	Outside cell	
Na^+	15.0	150.0	+60
K^+	150.0	5.5	-90
Cl^-	9.0	125.0	-75
Resting membrane potential (V_m) = −70 mV			

The value of the equilibrium potential for any ion depends upon the concentration gradient for that ion across the membrane. The equilibrium potential for any ion can be calculated using the Nernst equation.

$$E_{cell} = E^o_{cell} - (RT/nF)\ln Q$$

- E_{cell} = cell potential under nonstandard conditions (V); CHM 10.1
- E^o_{cell} = cell potential under standard conditions
- R = gas constant, which is 8.31 (volt-coulomb)/(mol-K); CHM 4.1.8
- T = temperature (K); CHM 4.1.1
- n = number of moles of electrons exchanged in the electrochemical reaction (mol)
- F = Faraday's constant (96,500 coulombs/mol); CHM 10.5
- Q = reaction quotient, which is the equilibrium expression with prevailing concentrations rather than, necessarilly, with equilibrium concentrations (= K_{eq}; CHM 9.8)
- ln = the natural logarithm which is log base e; CHM 6.5.1

Once the relevant values have been

inserted, the Nernst equation can be simplified for specific ions. For example, the following is an approximation of the Nernst equation for the equilibrium potential for potassium (E_k in mV) at room temperature:

$$E_k = 60 \log_{10} \frac{[K^+]_o}{[K^+]_i}$$

- $[K^+]_o$ = extracellular K^+ concentration in mM
- $[K^+]_i$ = intracellular K^+ concentration in mM

The Goldman–Hodgkin–Katz voltage equation (= the Goldman equation) also determines the equilibrium potential across a cell's membrane. However, as opposed to the Nernst equation, the Goldman equation takes into account all of the ions that are permeant through that membrane.

26) If the concentration of potassium outside a mammalian motor neuron were changed to 0.55 mol/L, what would be the predicted change in the equilibrium potential for potassium?

A. 12 mV
B. 120 mV
C. 60 mV
D. 600 mV

27) A graph of E_k vs $\log_{10}[K^+]_o$ would be:

A. a straight line.
B. a logarithmic curve
C. an exponential curve.
D. a sigmoidal curve.

ANSWER KEY

ADVANCED TOPICS - CHAPTER 5

Cross-Reference

26. B E; T; CHM 6.5.1; QR Appendix
27. A E; QR Appendix

P = paragraph; *S* = sentence; *E* = equation; *T* = table; *F* = figure

NERVOUS AND ENDOCRINE SYSTEMS

Chapter 6

Memorize

* Nervous system: basic structure, major functions
* Basic sensory reception and processing
* Basic ear, eye: structure and function
* Define: endocrine gland, hormone
* Major endocrine glands: names, locations, major hormones

Understand

* Organization of the nervous system; sensor and effector neurons
* Feedback loop, reflex arc: role of spinal cord, brain
* Endocrine system: specific chemical control at cell, tissue, and organ level
* Cellular mechanisms of hormone action, transport of hormones
* Integration with nervous system: feedback control

Clinical Correlation

A pituitary tumor can present as a result of its anatomy (causing visual prolems by pressing on the optic nerves) or its function – causing increased homone levels. For example, a prolactin tumor can present with breast milk even in males.

MCAT-Prep.com

Introduction

The nervous and endocrine systems are composed of a network of highly specialized cells that can communicate information about an organism's surroundings and itself. Thus together, these two systems can process incoming information and then regulate and coordinate responses in other parts of the body.

Optional Gold Standard Resources

Free Online Q&A + Forum

Online Videos

Flashcards

Special Guest

6.1 Organisation of the Vertebrate Nervous System

The role of the nervous system is to control and coordinate body activities in a rapid and precise mode of action. The nervous system is composed of central and peripheral nervous systems.

The **central nervous system** (CNS) is enclosed within the cranium (skull) and vertebral (spinal) canal and consists respectively of the brain and spinal cord. The **peripheral nervous system** (PNS) is outside the bony encasement and is composed of peripheral nerves, which are branches or continuations of the spinal or cranial nerves. The PNS can be divided into the **somatic nervous system** and the **autonomic nervous system** which are *anatomically* a portion of both the central and peripheral nervous systems.

The somatic nervous system contains sensory fibers that bring information back to the CNS and motor fibers that innervate skeletal muscles. The autonomic nervous system (ANS) contains motor fibers that innervate smooth muscle, cardiac muscle and glands. The ANS is then divided into *sympathetic* and *parasympathetic* divisions, which generally act against each other. The sympathetic division acts to prepare the body for an emergency situation (fight or flight) while the parasympathetic division acts to conserve energy and restore the body to resting level (rest and digest).

As a rule, a collection of nerve cell bodies in the CNS is called a *nucleus* and outside the CNS it is called a *ganglion*. Neurons that carry information from the environment to the brain or spinal cord are called *afferent neurons*. Neurons that carry motor commands from the brain or spinal cord to the different parts of body are called *efferent neurons*. Neurons that connect sensory and motor neurons in neural pathways are called *interneurons*.

The spinal cord is a long cylindrical structure whose hollow core is called the *central canal*. The central canal is surrounded by a gray matter which is in turn surrounded by a white matter (the reverse is true for the brain: outer gray matter and inner white matter). Basically, the gray matter consists of the cell bodies of neurons whereas the white matter consists of the nerve fibers (axons and dendrites). There are 31 pairs of spinal nerves each leaving the spinal cord at various levels: 8 cervical (neck), 12 thoracic (chest), 5 lumbar (abdomen), 5 sacral and 1 coccygeal (these latter 6 are from the pelvic region). The lower end of the spinal cord is cone shaped and is called the *conus medullaris*.

The brain can be divided into three main regions: the forebrain which contains the telencephalon and the diencephalon; the midbrain; and the hindbrain which contains the cerebellum, the pons and the medulla. The **brain stem** includes the latter two structures and the midbrain.

The telencephalon is the **cerebral hemispheres** (cerebrum) which contain an outer surface (cortex) of gray matter. Its function is in higher order processes (i.e. learning, memory, emotions, voluntary motor activity, processing sensory input, etc.). For

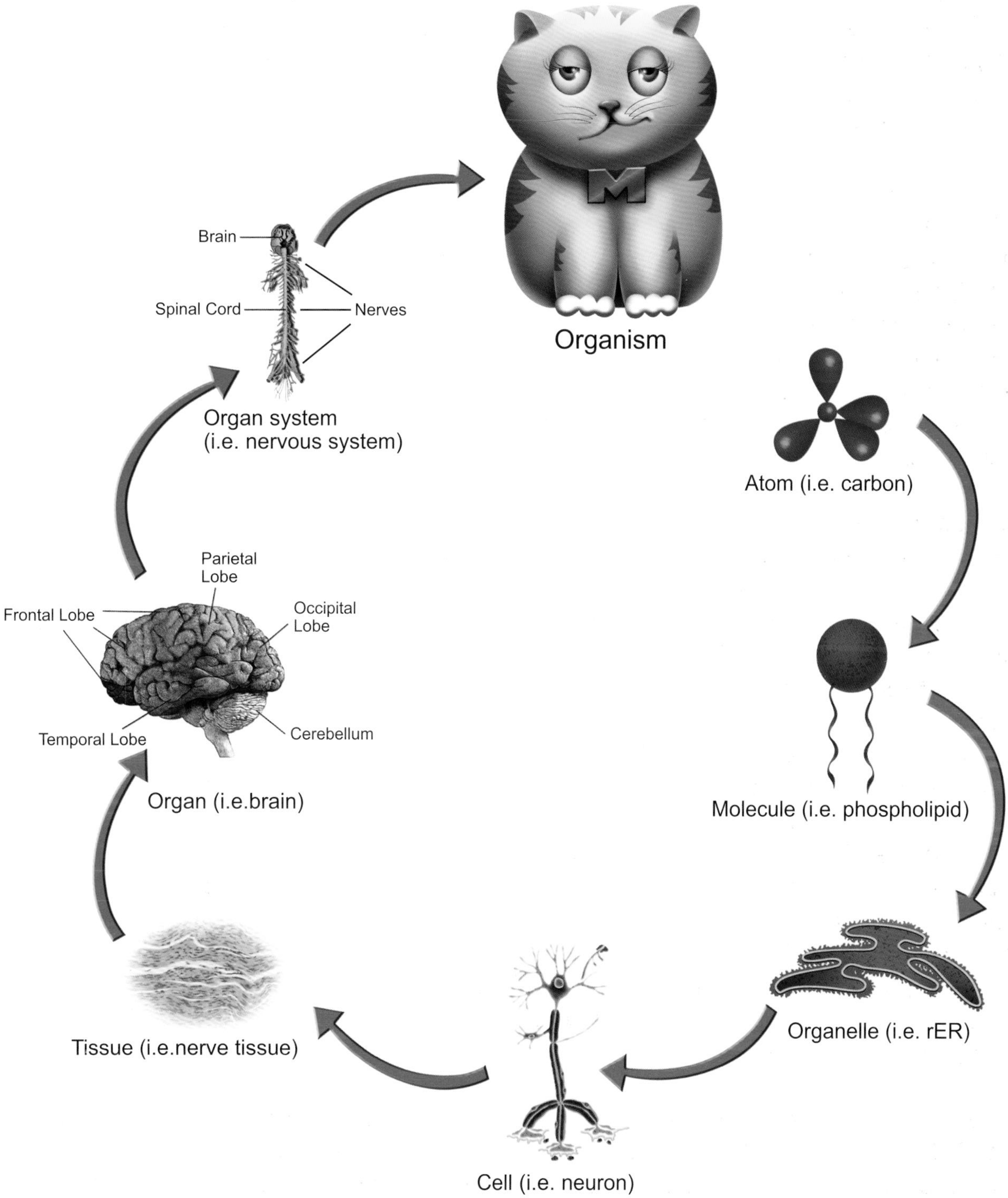

Figure IV.A.6.0: Levels of organization.

most people, the left hemisphere specializes in language, while the right hemisphere specializes in patterns and spatial relationships.

Each hemisphere is subdivided into four lobes: *occipital* which receives input from the optic nerve for vision; *temporal* which receives auditory signals for hearing; *parietal* which receives somatosensory information from the opposite side of the body (= heat, cold, touch, pain, and the sense of body movement); and *frontal* which is involved in problem solving and controls voluntary movements for the opposite side of the body.

The diencephalon contains the **thalamus** which is a relay center for sensory input, and the **hypothalamus** which is crucial for homeostatic controls (heart rate, body temperature, thirst, sex drive, hunger, etc.). Protruding from its base and greatly influenced by the hypothalamus is the **pituitary** which is an endocrine gland. The limbic system, which functions to produce emotions, is composed of the diencephalon and deep structures of the cerebrum (esp. basal ganglia).

The midbrain is a relay center for visual and auditory input and also regulated motor function.

The hindbrain consists of the cerebellum, the pons and the medulla. The cerebellum plays an important role in coordination and the control of muscle tone. The pons acts as a relay center between the cerebral cortex and the cerebellum. The medulla controls many vital functions such as breathing, heart rate, arteriole blood pressure, etc.

There are 12 pairs of cranial nerves which emerge from the base of the brain (esp. the brain stem): *olfactory* (I) for smell; *optic* (II) for vision; *oculomotor* (III), *trochlear* (IV) and *abducens* (VI) for eye movements; *trigeminal* (V) for motor (i.e. *mastication* which is chewing) and sensory activities (i.e. pain, temperature, and pressure for the head and face); *facial* (VII) for taste (sensory) and facial expression (motor); *vestibulo-cochlear* (VIII) for the senses of equilibrium (vestibular branch) and hearing (cochlear branch); *glosso-pharyngeal* (IX) for taste and swallowing; *vagus* (X) for speech, swallowing, slowing the heart rate, and many sensory and motor innervations to smooth muscles of the viscera (internal organs) of the thorax and abdomen; *accessory* (XI) for head rotation and shoulder movement; and *hypoglossal* (XII) for tongue movement.

Both the brain and the spinal cord are surrounded by three membranes (= meninges). The outermost covering is called the dura mater, the innermost is called the pia mater (which is in direct contact with nervous tissue), while the middle layer is called the arachnoid mater. {DAP = **d**ura - **a**rachnoid - **p**ia, repectively, from out to in}.

6.1.1 The Sensory Receptors

The sensory receptors include any type of nerve ending in the body that can be stimulated by some physical or chemical stimulus either outside or within the body. These receptors include the rods and cones of the eye, the cochlear nerve endings of the ear, the taste endings of the mouth, the olfactory endings in the nose, sensory nerve endings in the skin, etc. Afferent neurons carry sense signals to the central nervous system.

6.1.2 The Effector Receptors

These include every organ that can be stimulated by nerve impulses. An important effector system is skeletal muscle. Smooth muscles of the body and the glandular cells are among the important effector organs. Efferent neurons carry motor signals from the CNS to effector receptors. {The term "effector" in biology refers to an organ, cell or molecule that *acts* in response to a stimulus (cause-effect).}

6.1.3 Reflex Arc

One basic means by which the nervous system controls the functions in the body is the reflex arc, in which a stimulus excites a receptor, appropriate impulses are transmitted into the CNS where various nervous reactions take place, and then appropriate effector impulses are transmitted to an effector organ to cause a reflex effect (i.e. removal of one's hand from a hot object, the knee-jerk reflex, etc.). The preceding can be processed at the level of the spinal cord.

Example of knee-jerk reflex: tapping on the patellar tendon causes the thigh muscle (quadriceps) to stretch. The stretching of muscle stimulates the afferent fibers, which synapse on the motoneuron (= motor neuron; BIO 5.1) in the spinal cord. The activation of the motoneuron causes contraction of the muscle that was stretched. This contraction makes the lower leg extend.

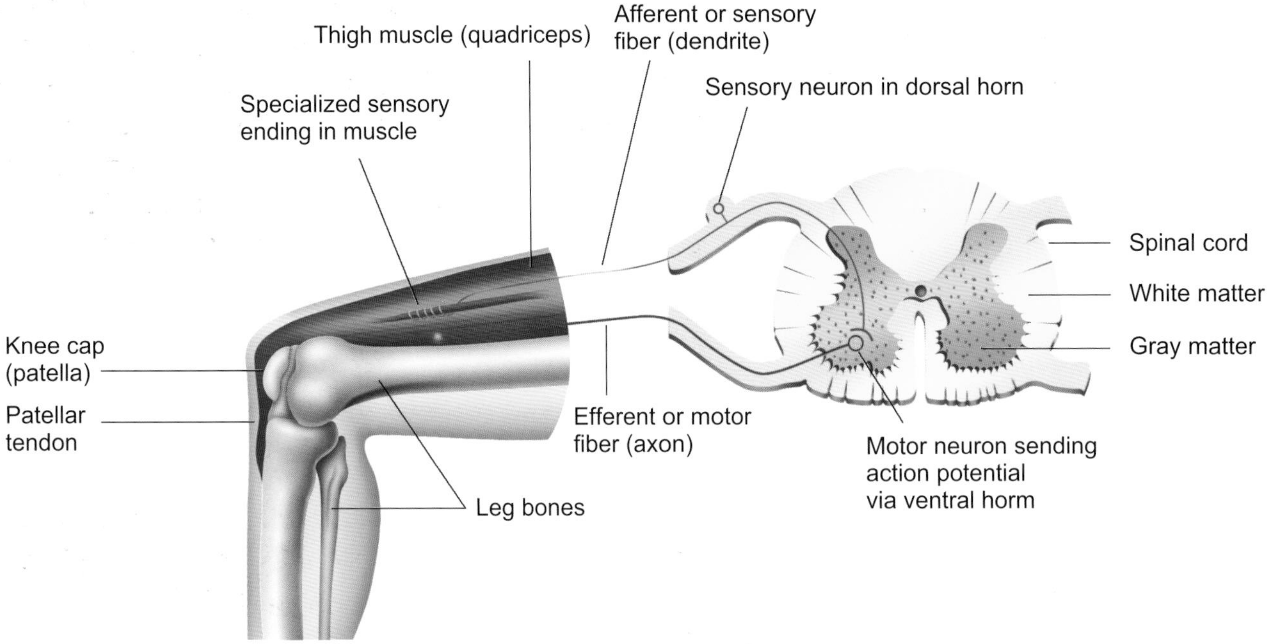

Figure IV.A.6.1: Schematic representation of the basis of the knee jerk reflex.

6.1.4 Autonomic Nervous System

While the Somatic Nervous System controls voluntary activities (i.e. innervates skeletal muscle), the Autonomic Nervous System (ANS) controls involuntary activities. The ANS consists of two components which often antagonize each other: the sympathetic and parasympathetic nervous systems.

The **Sympathetic Nervous System** originates in neurons located in the lateral horns of the gray matter of the spinal cord. Nerve fibers pass by way of anterior (ventral) nerve roots first into the spinal nerves and then immediately into the sympathetic chain. From here fiber pathways are transmitted to all portions of the body, especially to the different visceral organs and to the blood vessels.

The sympathetic nervous system uses norepinephrine as its primary neurotransmitter. This division of the nervous system is crucial in the "fight, fright or flight" responses (i.e. pupillary dilation, increase in breathing, blood pressure and heart rate, increase of blood flow to skeletal muscle, decrease of visceral function, etc.).

Parasympathetic Nervous System: The parasympathetic fibers pass mainly through the *vagus nerves*, though a few fibers pass through several of the other cranial nerves and through the anterior roots of the sacral segments of the spinal cord. Parasympathetic fibers do not spread as extensively through the body as do sympathetic fibers, but they do innervate some of the thoracic and abdominal organs, as well as the pupillary sphincter and ciliary muscles of the eye and the salivary glands.

The parasympathetic nervous system uses acetylcholine as its primary neurotransmitter. This division of the nervous system is crucial for vegetative responses (i.e. pupillary constriction, decrease in breathing, blood pressure and heart rate, increase in blood flow to the gastro-intestinal tract, etc.).

6.1.5 Autonomic Nerve Fibers

The nerve fibers from the ANS are primarily motor fibers. Unlike the motor pathways of the somatic nervous system, which usually include a single neuron between the CNS and an effector, those of the ANS involve *two* neurons. The first neuron has its cell body in the brain or spinal cord but its axon (= *preganglionic fiber*) extends outside of the CNS. The axon enters adjacent sympathetic chain ganglia, where they synapse with the cell body of a second neuron or travel up or down the chain to synapse with that of a remote second neuron (*recall: a ganglion is a collection of nerve cell bodies outside the CNS*). The axon of the second neuron (= *postganglionic fiber*) extends to a visceral effector.

The sympathetic ganglia form chains which, for example, may extend longitudinally along each side of the vertebral column. Conversely, the parasympathetic ganglia are located *near* or *within* various visceral organs (i.e. bladder, intestine, etc.) thus requiring relatively short postganglionic fibers. Therefore, sympathetic nerve fibers are characterized by short preganglionic fibers and long postganglionic fibers while parasympathetic nerve fibers are characterized by long preganglionic fibers and short postganglionic fibers.

Both divisions of the ANS secrete *acetylcholine* from their preganglionic fibers. Most sympathetic postganglionic fibers secrete *norepinephrine* (= nor*adren*alin), and for this reason they are called ***adren**ergic* fibers. The parasympathetic postganglionic fibers secrete acetyl**choline** and are called ***cholinergic** fibers.*

There are two types of acetylcholine receptors (AChR) that bind acetylcholine and transmit its signal: muscarinic AChRs and nicotinic AChRs, which are named after the agonists muscarine and nicotine, respectively. The two receptors are functionally different, the muscarinic type is a G-protein coupled receptor that mediates a slow metabolic response via second messenger cascades (involving cAMP), while the nicotinic type is a ligand-gated ionotropic channel that mediates a fast synaptic transmission of the neurotransmitter (no use of second messengers).

6.2 Sensory Reception and Processing

Each modality of sensation is detected by a particular nerve ending. The most common nerve ending is the free nerve ending. Different types of free nerve endings result in different types of sensations such as pain, warmth, pressure, touch, etc. In addition to free nerve endings, skin contains a number of specialized endings that are adapted to respond to some specific type of physical stimulus.

Sensory endings deep in the body are capable of detecting proprioceptive sensations such as joint receptors, which detect the degree of angulation of a joint, Golgi tendon organs which detect the degree of tension in the tendons, and muscle spindles which detect the degree of stretch of a muscle fiber (see diagram of reflex with muscle spindle in BIO 6.1.2).

6.2.1 Olfaction

Olfaction (the sense of smell) is perceived by the brain following the stimulation of the olfactory epithelium located in the nostrils. The olfactory epithelium contain large numbers of neurons with chemoreceptors called olfactory cells which are responsible for the detection of different types of smell. Odorant molecules bind to the receptors located on the cilia of olfactory receptor neurons and produce a depolarizing receptor potential. Once the depolarization passes threshold, an action potential is generated and is conducted into CNS. It is believed that there might be seven or more primary sensations of smell which combine to give various types of smell that we perceive in life.

6.2.2 Taste

Taste buds in combination with olfaction give humans the taste sensation. Taste buds are primarily located on the surface of the tongue with smaller numbers found in the roof of the mouth and the walls of the pharynx (throat). Taste buds contain chemoreceptors which are activated once the chemical is dissolved in saliva which is secreted by the salivary glands. Contrary to olfactory receptor cells, taste receptors are not true neurons: they are chemical receptors only.

Four different types of taste buds are known to exist, each of these responding principally to saltiness, sweetness, sourness and bitterness.

When a stimulus is received by either a taste bud or an olfactory cell for the second time, the intensity of the response is diminished. This is called sensory *adaptation*.

6.2.3 Ears: Structure and Function

Ears function in both hearing and balance. It consists of three parts: the *external ear* which receives sound waves; the air-filled *middle ear* which transmits and amplifies sound waves; and the fluid-filled *inner ear* which transduces sound waves into nerve impulse. The vestibular organ, located in the inner ear, is responsible for equilibrium.

The external ear is composed of the external cartilaginous portion, the pinna or *auricle*, and the external auditory meatus or canal. The external auditory meatus connects the auricle and the middle ear or *tympanic cavity*. The tympanic cavity is bordered on the outside by the tympanic membrane, and inside the air-filled cavity are the auditory ossicles - the *malleus* (hammer), *incus* (anvil), and *stapes* (stirrup). The stapes is held by ligaments to a part of inner ear called the *oval window*. The auditory ossicles function in amplifying the sound vibration and transmitting it from the tympanic membrane to the oval window.

The inner ear or *labyrinth* consists of an osseous (= bony) labyrinth containing a membranous labyrinth. The bony labyrinth houses the semicircular canals, the cochlea and the vestibule. The semicircular canals contain the semicircular ducts of the membranous labyrinth, which can detect angular acceleration. The vestibule contains the saccule and utricle, which are sac-like thin connective tissue lined by vestibular hair cells which are responsible for the detection of linear acceleration. Together, the semicircular canals and the vestibule, known as the vestibular system,

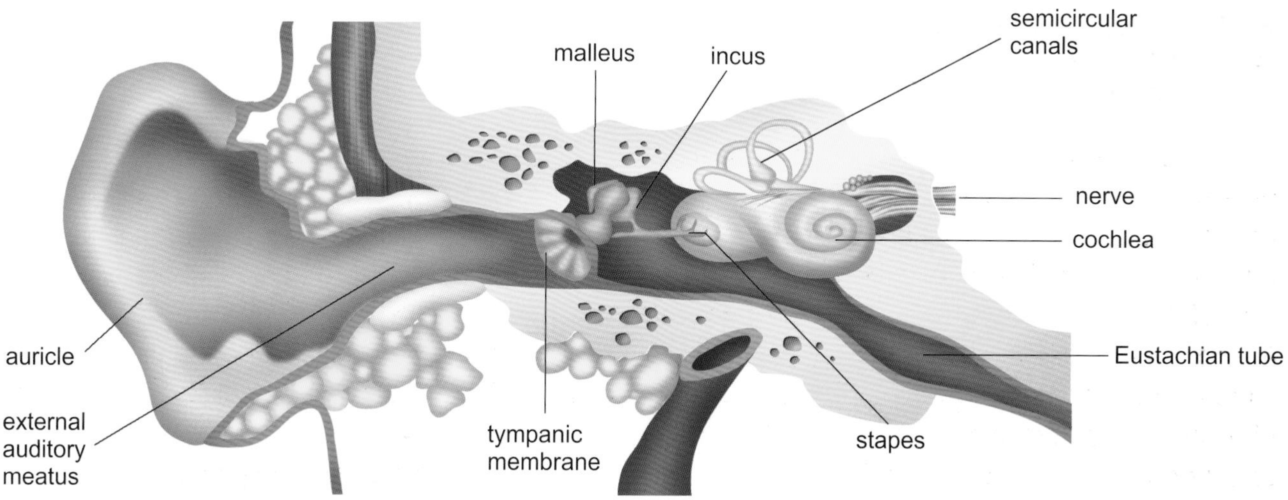

Figure IV.A.6.2: Structure of the external, middle and inner ear.

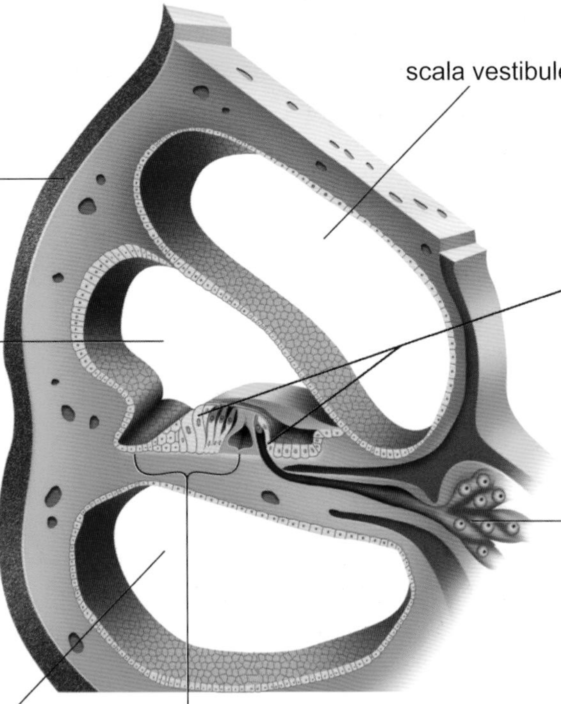

Figure IV.A.6.3: Cross-section of the cochlea.

are responsible for detection of linear and angular acceleration of the head. The cochlea is divided into three spaces: the scala vestibule, scala tympani and the scala media, or cochlear duct. The cochlear duct contains the spiral organ of Corti, which functions in the reception of sound and responds to different sound frequencies.

The eustachian tube connects the middle ear to the pharynx. This tube is important in maintaining equal pressure on both sides of the tympanic membrane. During ascent in an airplane, there is a decrease in cabin air pressure, leading to a relative increase in the pressure of the middle ear. Swallowing or yawning opens the eustachian tube allowing an equalization of pressure in the middle ear.

Mechanism of hearing: Sound is caused by the compression of waves that travel through the air. Each compression wave is funneled by the external ear to strike the tympanic membrane (ear drum). Thus the sound vibrations are transmitted through the osseous system which consists of three tiny bones (the malleus, incus, and stapes) into the cochlea at the oval window. Movement of the stapes at the oval window causes disturbance in the lymph of cochlea and stimulates the hair cells found in the basilar membrane which is called the *organ of Corti*. Bending of the hair cells causes depolarization of the basilar membrane. From here the auditory nerves carry the impulses to the auditory area of the brain (*temporal lobe*) where it is interpreted as sound.

6.2.4 Vision: Eye Structure and Function

The eyeball consists of three layers: i) an outer fibrous tunic composed of the sclera and cornea; ii) a vascular coat (uvea) of choroid, the ciliary body and iris; and iii) the retina formed of pigment and sensory (nervous) layers. The anterior chamber lies between the cornea anteriorly (in front) and the iris and pupil posteriorly (behind); the posterior chamber lies between the iris anteriorly and the ciliary processes and the lens posteriorly.

The transparent cornea constitutes the anterior one sixth of the eye and receives light from external environment. The sclera forms

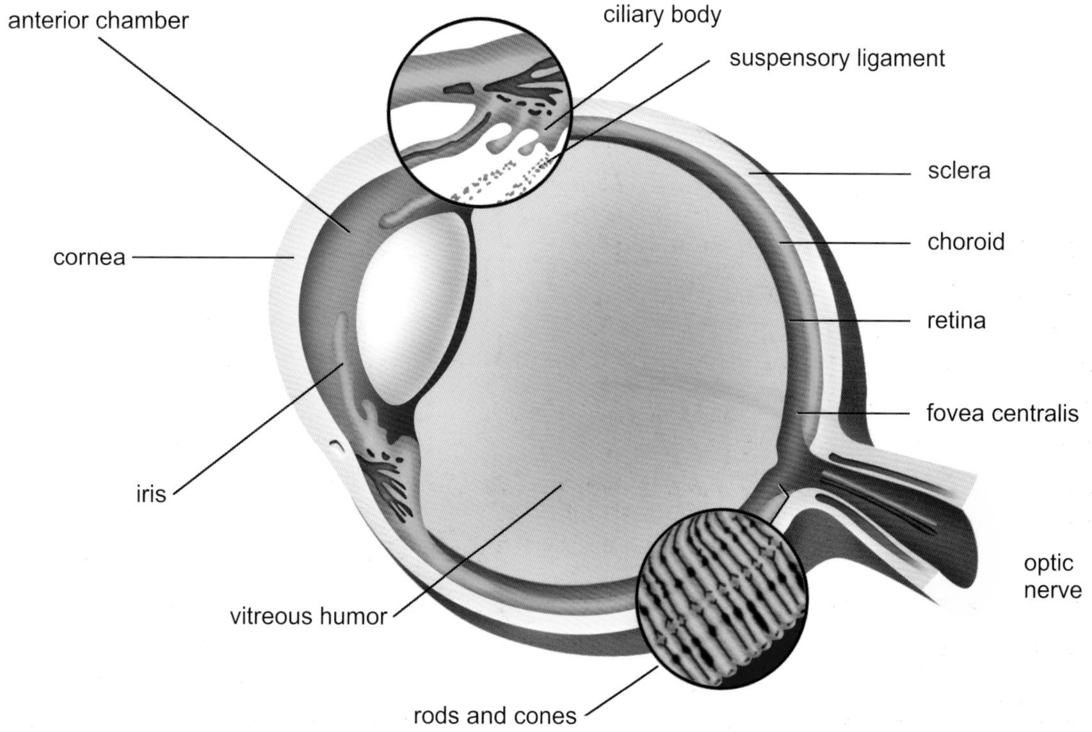

Figure IV.A.6.4: Structure of the eye.

the posterior five sixths of the fibrous tunic and is composed of dense fibrous connective tissue. The choroid layer consists of vascular loose connective tissue. The ciliary body is an anterior expansion of the choroid that encircles the lens. The lens can focus light on the retina by the contraction or relaxation of muscles in the ciliary body which transmit tension along suspensory ligaments to the lens.

Contraction of the ciliary muscle makes the lens become more convex, thereby allowing the eye to focus on nearby objects. Relaxation of the ciliary muscle allows the eye to focus on far objects. The iris separates the anterior and the posterior chamber and forms an aperture called the "pupil" whose diameter is continually adjusted by the pupillary muscles. This helps to control the intensity of light impinging on the retina.

The retina is divisible into ten layers. Layers two to five contain the rod and cone receptors of the light pathway.

Rods and Cones: The light sensitive receptors (*photoreceptors*) of the retina are millions of minute cells called rods and cones. The rods (*"night vision"*) distinguish only the black and white aspects of an image and are sensitive to light of low intensity (*"high sensitivity"*). The cones (*"day vision"*) are capable of distinguishing three colors: red, green and blue and are sensitive to light of high intensity (*"low sensitivity"*). From different combinations of these three colors, all colors can be seen.

Photoreceptors contain photosensitive pigments. For example, rods contain the membrane protein *rhodopsin* which is covalently linked to a form of vitamin A. Light causes an isomerization of *retinal* (an aldehyde form of vitamin A) which can affect Na^+ channels in a manner as to start an action potential.

The central portion of the retina which is called the fovea centralis has only cones, which allows this portion to have very sharp vision, while the peripheral areas, which contain progressively more and more rods, have progressively more diffuse vision. Since acuity and color vision are mediated by the same cells (cones), visual acuity is much better in bright light than dim light.

Each point of the retina connects with a discrete point in the visual cortex which is in the back of the brain (i.e. the occipital lobe). The image that is formed on the retina is upside down and reversed from left to right. This information leaves the eye via the optic nerve en route to the visual cortex which corrects the image.

Defects of vision

1. Myopia (short-sighted or nearsighted): In this condition, an image is formed in front of the retina because the lens converges light too much since the eyeballs are long. A diverging (concave) lens helps focus the image on the retina and it is used for the correction of myopia.

2. Hyperopia (long-sighted or farsighted): In this condition, an image is formed behind the retina since the eyeballs are too short. A converging (convex) lens helps focus the image on the retina.

3. Astigmatism: In this condition, the curvatures of either the cornea or the lens are different at different angles. A cylindrical lens helps to improve this condition.

4. Presbyopia: This condition is characterized by the inability to focus (especially objects which are closer). This condition, which is often seen in the elderly, is corrected by using a converging lens.

6.3 Endocrine Systems

The endocrine system is the set of glands, tissues and cells that secrete hormones directly into circulatory system (ductless). The hormones are transported by the blood system, sometimes bound to plasma proteins, en route to having an effect on the cells of a target organ. Thus hormones control many of the body's functions by acting - predominantly - in one of the following major ways:

1. By controlling transport of substances through cell membranes

2. By controlling the activity of some of the specific genes, which in turn determine the formation of specific enzymes

3. By controlling directly some metabolic systems of cells.

Steroid hormones can diffuse across the plasma membrane and bind to specific receptors in the cytosol or nucleus, thus forming a direct intracellular effect (i.e. on DNA; ORG 12.4.1). Non-steroid hormones do not diffuse across the membrane. They tend to bind plasma membrane receptors, which leads to the production of a second messenger.

Secondary messengers are a component of signal transduction cascades which amplify the strength of a signal (i.e. hormone, growth factors, neurotransmitter, etc.). Examples include cyclic AMP (cAMP), phosphoinositol, cyclic GMP and arachidonic acid systems.

In all four cases, a hormone (= the primary messenger or *agonist*) binds the receptor exposing a binding site for a G-protein (the *transducer*). The G-protein, named for its ability to exchange GDP on its alpha subunit for a GTP (BIO 4.4-4.10), is bound to the inner membrane. Once the exchange for GTP takes place, the alpha subunit of the G-protein transducer breaks free from the beta and gamma subunits, all parts remaining membrane-bound. The alpha subunit is now free to move along the inner membrane and eventually contacts another membrane-bound protein - the *primary effector*.

The primary effector has an action which creates a signal that can diffuse within the cell. This signal is the *secondary messenger*.

Calcium ions are important intracellular messengers which can regulate calmodulin and are responsible for many important physiological functions, such as in muscle contraction (BIO 5.2). The enzyme phospholipase C (primary effector) produces diacylglycerol and inositol trisphosphate (secondary messenger), which increases calcium ion (secondary effector) membrane permeability. Active G-protein can also open calcium channels. The other product of phospholipase C, diacylglycerol (secondary messenger), activates protein kinase C (secondary effector), which assists in the activation of cAMP (another second messenger).

The agonist epinephrine (hormone, BIO 6.1.3) can bind a receptor activating the transducer (G-protein) and using a primary effector (adenylyl cyclase) produces a secondary messenger (cAMP) which, in turn, brings about target cell responses that are recognized as the hormone's actions.

Of the following hormones, if there is no mention as to its chemical nature, then it is a non-steroidal hormone (i.e. protein, polypeptide, etc.).

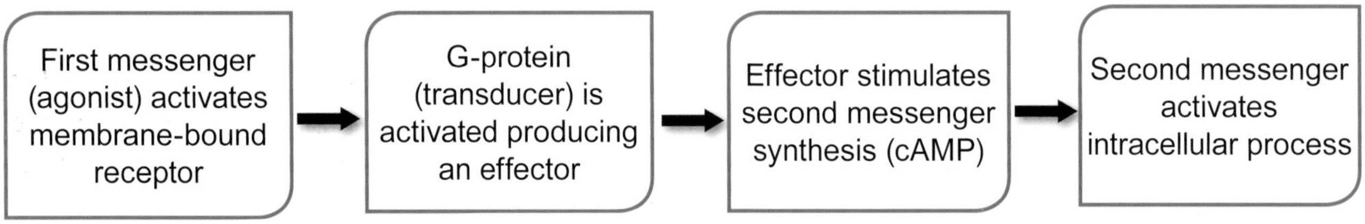

6.3.1 Pituitary Hormones

The **pituitary gland** secretes hormones that regulate a wide variety of functions in the body. This gland is divided into two major divisions: the anterior and the posterior pituitary gland. Six hormones are secreted by the anterior pituitary gland whereas two hormones are secreted by the posterior gland. The **hypothalamus** influences the secretion of hormones from both parts of the pituitary in different ways: i) it secretes specific *releasing factors* into special blood vessels (a *portal system* called hypothalamic-hypophysial portal system) which carries these factors (hormones) that affect the cells in the anterior pituitary by either stimulating or inhibiting the release of anterior pituitary hormones; ii) the hypothalamus contains neurosecretory cell bodies that synthesize, package and transport their products (esp. the two hormones oxytocin and ADH) down the axons directly into the posterior pituitary where they can be released into circulation.

The hormones secreted by the anterior pituitary gland are as follows:

1. Growth hormone (GH)
2. Thyroid Stimulating Hormone (TSH)
3. Adrenocorticotropic hormone (ACTH)
4. Prolactin
5. Follicle Stimulating Hormone (FSH) or Interstitial Cell Stimulating Hormone (ICSH)
6. Luteinizing Hormone (LH)

[N.B. these latter two hormones will be discussed in the section on Reproduction, see BIO 14.2, 14.3]

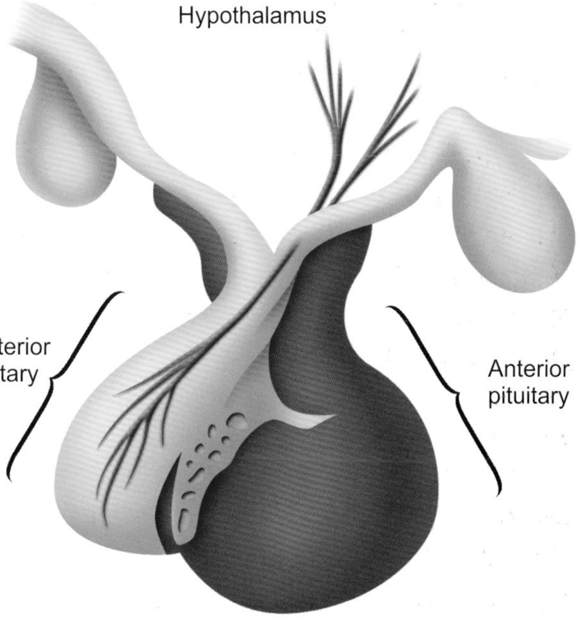

Figure IV.A.6.5: The pituitary gland.

Growth Hormone causes growth of the body. It causes enlargement and proliferation of cells in all parts of the body. Ultimately, the epiphyses of the long bones unite with the shaft of the bones (BIO 11.3.1). After adolescence, growth hormone continues to be secreted lower than the pre-adolescent rate. Though most of the growth in the body stops at this stage, the metabolic roles of the growth hormone continue such as the enhancement of protein synthesis and lean body mass, increasing blood glucose concentration, increasing lipolysis, etc.

Abnormal increase in the secretion of growth hormone at a young age results in a condition called gigantism, while a reduction in the production of growth hormone leads to dwarfism. Abnormal increase in the secretion of growth hormone in adults results in a condition called acromegaly, a disorder characterized by a disproportionate bone enlargement, especially in the face, hands and feet.

Thyroid Stimulating Hormone stimulates the thyroid gland. The hormones produced by the thyroid gland (*thyroxine:* T_4, *triiodothyronine:* T_3) contain four and three iodine atoms, respectively. They increase the basal metabolic rate of the body (BMR). Therefore, indirectly, TSH increases the overall rate of metabolism of the body.

Adrenocorticotropic hormone strongly stimulates the production of cortisol by the adrenal cortex, and it also stimulates the production of the other adrenocortical hormones, but to a lesser extent.

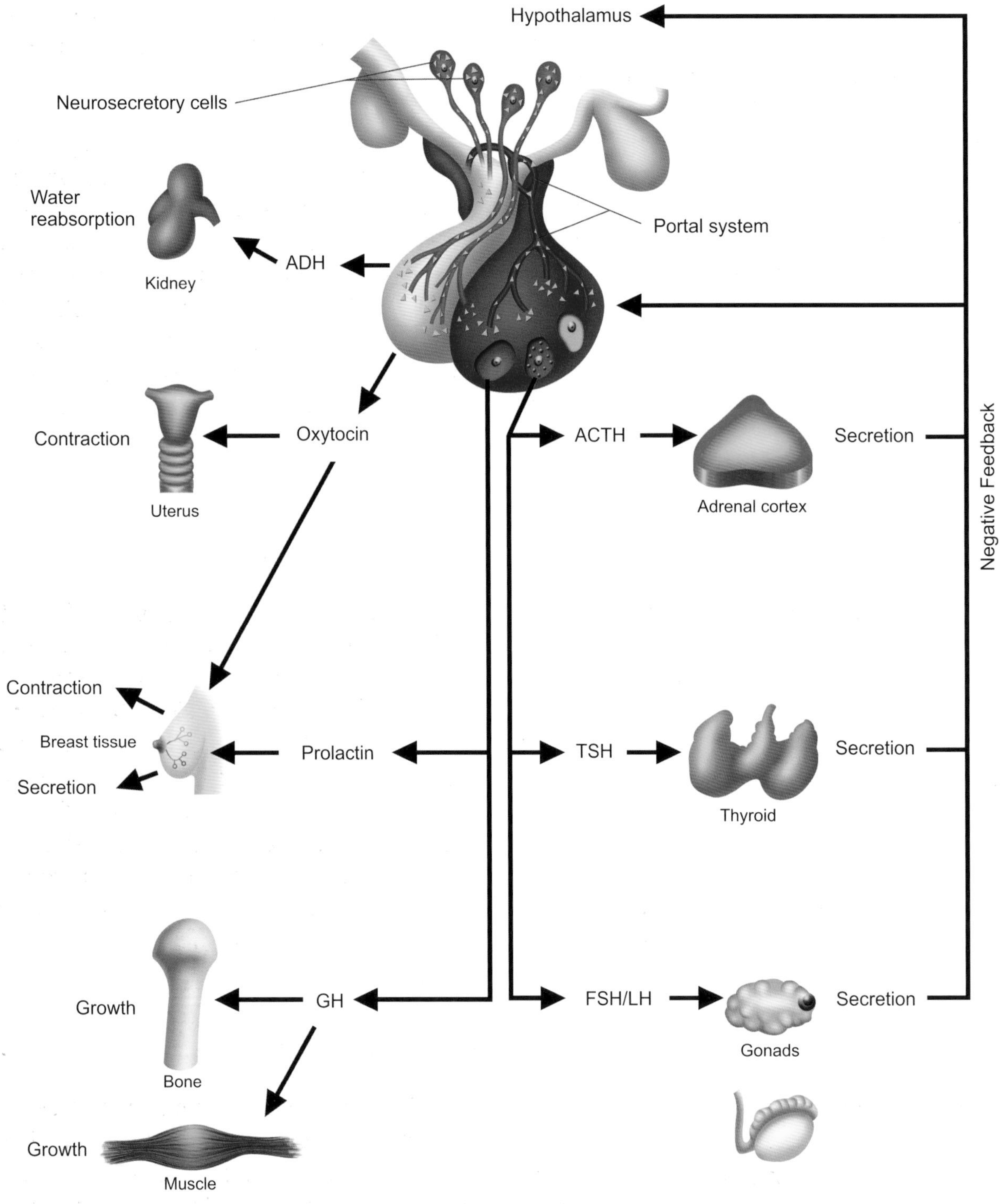

Figure IV.A.6.6: Pituitary hormones and their target organs.

Prolactin plays an important role in the development of the breast during pregnancy and promotes milk production in the breast. In addition, a high level of prolactin can inhibit ovulation.

Antidiuretic hormone (ADH) is synthesized by neurosecretory cells in the hypothalamus and then travels down the axons to the posterior pituitary for secretion. Antidiuretic hormone enhances the rate of water reabsorption from the renal tubules leading to the concentration of urine (BIO 10.3). ADH also constricts the arterioles and causes a rise in arterial pressure and hence it is also called *vasopressin*.

Similar to ADH, *oxytocin* originates in the hypothalamus and then travels down the axons to the posterior pituitary for secretion. Oxytocin causes contraction of the uterus and, to a lesser extent, the other smooth muscles of the body. It also stimulates the myoepithelial cells of the breast in a manner that makes the milk flow into the ducts. This is termed milk ejection or milk *let-down*.

6.3.2 Adrenocortical Hormones

On the top of each kidney lies an adrenal gland which contains an inner region (*medulla*) and an outer region (*cortex*). The adrenal cortex secretes three different types of steroid hormones that are similar chemically but vary widely in a physiological manner.

These are:

1. Mineralocorticoids - e.g., Aldosterone
2. Glucocorticoids - e.g., Cortisol, Cortisone
3. Sex Hormones e.g., Androgens, Estrogens

Mineralocorticoids - Aldosterone

The mineralocorticoids influence the electrolyte balance of the body. Aldosterone is a mineralocorticoid which is secreted and then enhances sodium transport from the renal tubules into the peritubular fluids, and at the same time enhances potassium transport from the peritubular fluids into the tubules. In other words, aldosterone causes conservation of sodium in the body and excretion of potassium in the urine. As a result of sodium retention, there is an increased passive reabsorption of chloride ions and water from the tubules. Overproduction of aldosterone will result in excessive retention of fluid, which leads to hypertension.

Glucocorticoids - Cortisol

Several different glucocorticoids are secreted by the adrenal cortex, but almost all of the glucocorticoid activity is caused by cortisol, also called hydrocortisone. Glucocorticoids affect the metabolism of carbohydrates, proteins and lipids. It causes an increase in the blood concentration of glucose by stimulation of gluconeogenesis (generation of glucose from non-carbohydrate carbon substrates). It causes degradation of proteins and causes increased use of fat for energy. Long term use of glucocorticoids suppresses the immune system. It also has an anti-inflammatory effect by inhibiting the release of inflammatory mediators.

Sex hormones

Androgens (i.e. testosterone) are the masculinizing hormones in the body. They are responsible for the development of the secondary sexual characteristics in a male (i.e. increased body hair). On the contrary estrogens have a feminizing effect in the body and they are responsible for the development of the secondary sexual characteristics in a female (i.e. breast development). The proceeding hormones supplement secretions from the gonads which will be discussed later (see "*Reproduction*"; BIO 14.2, 14.3).

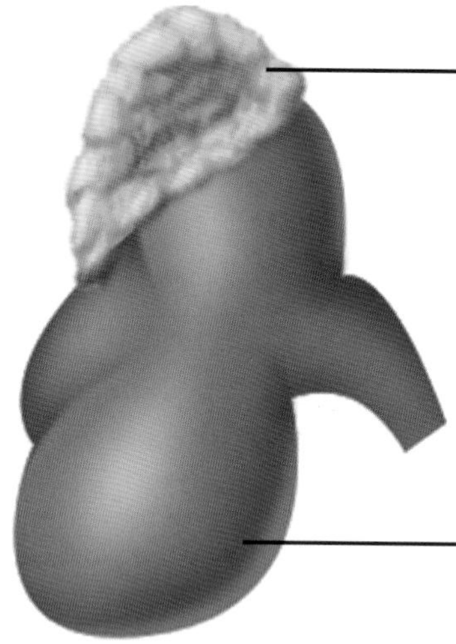

Figure IV.A.6.7: The adrenal gland sits on top of the kidney.

The Adrenal Medulla

The adrenal medulla synthesizes epinephrine (= *adrenaline*) and norepinephrine which: i) are non-steroidal stimulants of the sympathetic nervous system; ii) raise blood glucose concentrations; iii) increase heart rate and blood pressure; iv) increase blood supply to the brain, heart and skeletal muscle; and v) decrease blood supply to the skin, digestive system and renal system.

6.3.3 Thyroid Hormones

The thyroid gland is located anteriorly in the neck and is composed of follicles lined with thyroid glandular cells. These cells secrete a glycoprotein called thyroglobulin. The tyrosine residue of thyroglobulin then reacts with iodine forming mono-iodotyrosine (MIT) and di-iodotyrosine (DIT). When two molecules of DIT combine, thyroxine (T_4) is formed. When one molecule of DIT and one molecule of MIT combine, tri-iodothyronine (T_3) is formed. The rate of synthesis of thyroid hormone is influenced by TSH from the pituitary.

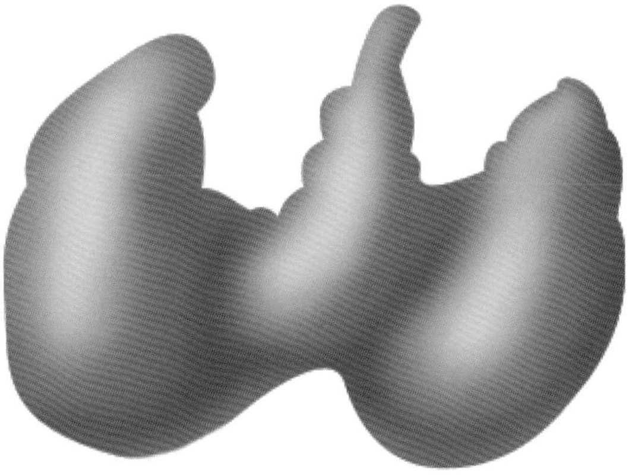

Figure IV.A.6.8: The thyroid gland.

Once thyroid hormones have been released into the blood stream they combine with several different plasma proteins. Then they are released into the cells from the blood stream. They play a vital role in maturation of CNS as thyroid hormone deficiency leads to irreversible mental retardation. They increase heart rate, ventilation rate and O_2 consumption. They also increase the size and numbers of mitochondria and these in turn increase the rate of production of ATP, which is a factor that promotes cellular metabolism; glycogenolysis and gluconeogenesis both increase; lipolysis increases; and protein synthesis also increases. The overall effect of thyroid hormone on metabolism is catabolic.

Hyperthyroidism is an excess of thyroid hormone secretion above that needed for normal function. Basically, an increased rate of metabolism throughout the body is observed. Other symptoms include fast heart rate and respiratory rate, weight loss, sweating, tremor, and protruding eyes.

Hypothyroidism is an inadequate amount of thyroid hormone secreted into the blood stream. Generally it slows down the metabolic rate and enhances the collection of mucinous fluid in the tissue spaces, creating an edematous (fluid filled) state called myxedema. Other symptoms include slowed heart rate and respiratory rate, weight gain, cold intolerance, fatigue, and mental slowness.

The thyroid and parathyroid glands affect blood calcium concentration in different ways. The thyroid produces *calcitonin* which inhibits osteoclast activity and stimulates osteoblasts to form bone tissue; thus blood $[Ca^{2+}]$ decreases. The parathyroid glands produce parathormone (= parathyroid hormone = PTH), which stimulates osteoclasts to break down bone, thus raising $[Ca^{2+}]$ and $[PO_4^{3-}]$ in the blood (BIO 5.4.4).

6.3.4 Pancreatic Hormones

The pancreas contains clusters of cells (= *islets of Langerhans*) closely associated with blood vessels. The islets of Langerhans, which perform the endocrine function of the pancreas, contain alpha cells that secrete *glucagon* and beta cells that secrete *insulin*. Glucagon increases blood glucose concentration by promoting the following events in the liver: the conversion of glycogen to glucose (*glycogenolysis*) and the production of glucose from amino acids (*gluconeogenesis*). Insulin decreases blood glucose by increasing cellular uptake of glucose, promoting glycogen formation and decreasing gluconeogenesis. A deficiency in insulin or insensitivity to insulin results in *diabetes mellitus*.

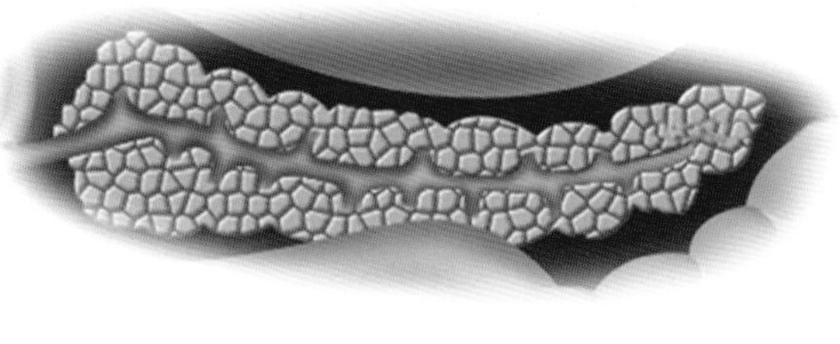

Figure IV.A.6.9: The pancreas.

6.3.5 Kidney Hormones

The kidney produces and secretes *renin*, *erythropoietin* and it helps in the activation of vitamin D. Renin is an enzyme that catalyzes the conversion of angiotensinogen to angiotensin I. Angiotensin I is then converted to angiotensin II by angiotensin-converting enzyme (ACE). Angiotensin II acts on the adrenal cortex to increase the synthesis and release of aldosterone, which increases Na^+ reabsorption, and causes vasoconstriction of arterioles leading to an increase in both blood volume and blood pressure. Erythropoietin increases the production of *erythrocytes* by acting on red bone marrow.

Vitamin D is a steroid which is critical for the proper absorption of calcium from the small intestine; thus it is essential for the normal growth and development of bone and teeth. Vitamin D can either be ingested or produced from a precursor by the activity of ultraviolet light on skin cells. It must be further activated in the liver and kidney by hydroxylation.

6.3.6 A Negative Feedback Loop

In order to maintain the internal environment of the body in equilibrium (= *homeostasis*), our hormones engage in various negative feedback loops. Negative feedback is self-limiting: a hormone produces biologic actions that, in turn, directly or indirectly inhibit further secretion of that hormone.

For example, if the body is exposed to extreme cold, the hypothalamus will activate systems to conserve heat (see *Skin as an Organ System*, BIO 13.1) and to produce heat. Heat production can be attained by increasing the basal metabolic rate. To achieve this, the hypothalamus secretes a releasing factor (thyrotropin releasing factor - TRF) which stimulates the anterior pituitary to secrete TSH. Thus the thyroid gland is stimulated to secrete the thyroid hormones.

Body temperature begins to return to normal. The high levels of circulating thyroid hormones begin to *inhibit* the production of TRF and TSH (= *negative feedback*) which in turn ensures the reduction in the levels of the thyroid hormones. Thus homeostasis is maintained.

6.3.7 A Positive Feedback Loop

As opposed to negative feedback, a positive feedback loop is where the body senses a change and activates mechanisms that accelerate or increase that change. Occasionally this may help homeostasis by working in conjunction with a larger negative feedback loop, but unfortunately it often produces the opposite effect and can be life-threatening.

An example of a beneficial positive feedback loop is seen in childbirth, where stretching of the uterus triggers the secretion of oxytocin (BIO 6.3.1), which stimulates uterine contractions and speeds up labor. Of course, once the baby is out of the mother's body, the loop is broken.

Often, however, positive feedback produces the very opposite of homeostasis: a rapid loss of internal stability with potentially fatal consequences. For example, most human deaths from SARS and the bird flu (H5N1) epidemic were caused by a "cytokine storm" which is a positive feedback loop between immune cells and cytokines (signalling molecules similar to hormones). Thus, in many cases, it is the body's exaggerated response to infection that is the cause of death rather than the direct action of the original infecting agent. Many diseases involve dangerous positive feedback loops.

GOLD STANDARD WARM-UP EXERCISES

CHAPTER 6: Nervous and Endocrine Systems

1) How many PAIRS of nerves leave the vertebrate brain?

A. 3
B. 6
C. 8
D. 12

2) The structure in the brain responsible for maintaining homeostasis (i.e. body temperature, heart rate, etc.) is the:

A. pituitary.
B. thalamus.
C. hypothalamus.
D. cerebellum.

3) Damage to which pair of nerves comprising the descending pathways, would likely cause persons with spinal-cord damage to have no control over the micturition process (i.e. urination)?

A. Vagus
B. Abducans
C. Trigeminal
D. Hypoglossal

4) Increased physical activity results in raising the heart rate and blood pressure. The nervous system specifically implicated is:

A. somatic.
B. peripheral.
C. parasympathetic.
D. sympathetic.

5) A collection of nerve cell bodies in the central nervous system is generally referred to as a:

A. nerve.
B. conus.
C. ganglion.
D. nucleus.

6) All of the following are correct concerning the autonomic nervous system EXCEPT:

A. nicotinic receptors operate through a second messenger system involving the regulation of cAMP.
B. both divisions of the ANS secrete acetylcholine from their preganglionic fibers.
C. the parasympathetic postganglionic fibers are cholinergic.
D. the sympathetic ganglia form chains which may extend longitudinally along each side of the vertebral column.

7) The vertebrate eyeball is bounded anteriorly by what convex, transparent tissue?

A. Sclera
B. Choroid
C. Cornea
D. Vitreous humor

8) What is the name given to the jelly-like substance filling the chamber behind the lens of the human eye?

A. Vitreous humor
B. Fovea centralis
C. Ciliary body
D. Choroid

9) All of the following are necessary for directing light onto the retina EXCEPT:

A. cornea.
B. iris.
C. lens.
D. aqueous humor.

10) The name of the ductless glands which secrete their products into the circulatory system are:

A. holocrine.
B. apocrine.
C. exocrine.
D. endocrine.

11) All of the following would be symptoms of hypothyroidism, EXCEPT:

A. hypothermia.
B. dry skin.
C. hyperactivity.
D. myxedema.

12) Which of the following endocrine glands would have the most direct antagonistic effect on the action of calcitonin?

A. Adrenal cortex
B. Thyroid
C. Pancreas
D. Parathyroid

13) Which of the following is the target organ of TRH?

A. Anterior pituitary
B. Posterior pituitary
C. Parathyroid
D. Thyroid

14) Increased levels of hormones in the adrenal gland would have which of the following effects?

A. Increased synthesis of proteins
B. Increased levels of sodium in the nephron
C. Increased metabolism of glycogen
D. Decreased blood volume

15) A certain compound has been found to strengthen bone by increasing calcium deposition in the bones. This compound would most likely stimulate which of the following?

A. Osteoclast activity
B. Calcitonin secretion
C. Parathyroid hormone secretion
D. Thyroxine secretion

16) The hypothalamus is best characterized as:

I. an endocrine gland.
II. a nexus of somatic receptor cells.
III. a producer of gonadotropin hormone.

A. I only
B. II only
C. II and III only
D. I, II, and III

17) This question refers to Fig. 1.

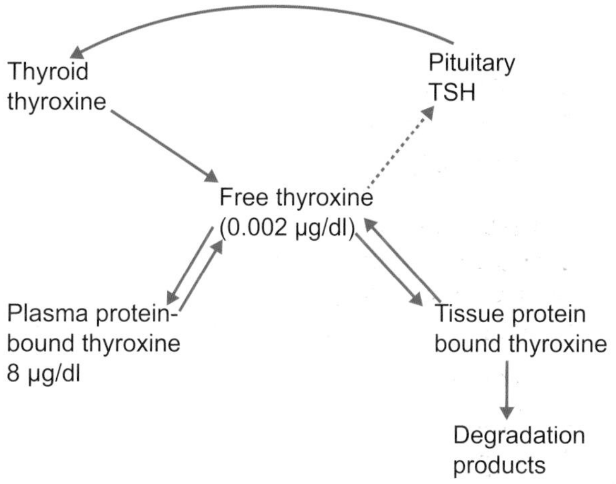

Figure 1

According to the equilibrium shown in Fig. 1, an elevation in the concentration of free thyroid hormone in the plasma is followed by:

A. an increase in tissue protein-bound thyroxine.
B. an increase in tissue protein-bound thyroxine and plasma protein-bound thyroxine.
C. an increase in the amount of TSH secreted from the pituitary gland.
D. an increase in both the amount of TSH secreted from the pituitary gland and the release of thyroxine from the thyroid gland.

18) Symptoms of hypothyroidism and hyperthyroidism, respectively, include:

A. a fine tremor and diminished concentration.
B. brittle nails and kidney stones.
C. rapid heart beat and increased irritability.
D. lethargy and nervous agitation.

19) Which of the following cell types would be expected to be maximally stimulated in a patient with hyperparathyroidism?

A. Osteoclasts
B. Osteoblasts
C. Fibroblasts
D. Chondrocytes

20) Parathormone influences calcium homeostasis by reducing tubular reabsorption of PO_4^{3-} in the kidneys. Which of the following, if true, would clarify the adaptive significance of this process?

A. PO_4^{3-} and Ca^{2+} feedback positively on each other.
B. Elevated levels of extracellular PO_4^{3-} result in calcification of bones and tissues.
C. Increased PO_4^{3-} levels cause an increase in parathormone secretion.
D. Decreased extracellular PO_4^{3-} levels cause a decrease in calcitonin production.

21) On a very hot day, the bladder would likely contain:

A. a large amount of urine hypertonic to blood plasma.
B. a large amount of urine hypotonic to blood plasma.
C. a small amount of urine hypertonic to blood plasma.
D. a small amount of urine hypotonic to blood plasma.

22) Which of the following best represents a possible series of physiological events following the detection by the hypothalamus of a cold environment?

A. heat promoting center → parasympathetic nerves → adrenal medulla → epinephrine production
B. heat promoting center → sympathetic nerves → sweat glands → stimulating local secretion
C. heat promoting center → sympathetic nerves → adrenal medulla → epinephrine production
D. heat promoting center → parasympathetic nerves → heart → dilated coronary vessels

23) Low blood pressure would normally result in which of the following?

A. Increased production of oxytocin in the hypothalamus.
B. Decreased levels of prolactin in the anterior pituitary.
C. Increased levels of parathyroid hormone.
D. Increased production of aldosterone in the adrenal cortex.

24) After radioactive iodine ^{131}I is injected into the vein of a patient, where would ^{131}I concentration be highest?

A. Liver
B. Parathyroid
C. Thyroid
D. Muscle cells

25) The hormone which exerts the most control on the concentration of the urine in the bladder is:

A. vasopressin.
B. oxytocin.
C. thyroxine.
D. prolactin.

26) Which of the following is an example of positive feedback?

A. An elevated body temperature of 101 °F causes a further increase.

B. Elevated TSH results in elevated thyroxine.

C. Calcitonin and parathromone regulate calcium levels.

D. Increased thyroid releasing factor (TRH) leads to increased TSH.

GS ANSWER KEY

CHAPTER 6

		Cross-Reference			*Cross-Reference*
1.	D	BIO 6.1	14.	C	BIO 6.3.1, 6.3.2
2.	C	BIO 6.1	15.	B	BIO 6.3.3
3.	A	BIO 6.1, 6.1.4	16.	A	BIO 6.3, 6.3.1
4.	D	BIO 6.1.4	17.	B	CHM 9.9, BIO 6.3.3, 6.3.6
5.	D	BIO 6.1	18.	D	BIO 6.3.3
6.	A	BIO 6.1.5	19.	A	BIO 5.4.4, 6.3.3
7.	C	BIO 6.2.4	20.	B	BIO 5.4.4, 6.3.3
8.	A	BIO 6.2.4	21.	C	BIO 1.1.1, 6.3.1 and F
9.	B	BIO 6.2.4	22.	C	BIO 6.1, 6.1.4, 6.3.2, 6.3.3
10.	D	BIO 6.3	23.	D	BIO 6.3.1, 6.3.2
11.	C	BIO 6.3.1, 6.3.3	24.	C	BIO 6.3.1
12.	D	BIO 6.3.3	25.	A	BIO 6.3, 6.3.1
13.	A	BIO 6.3.1, 6.3.3	26.	A	BIO 6.3.6, 6.3.7

* Explanations can be found at the back of the book.

Go online to MCAT-prep.com/forum to join the discussion about our GS chapter review questions.

THE CIRCULATORY SYSTEM

Chapter 7

Memorize

Circ. and lymphatic systems: basic structures and functions
Composition of blood, lymph, purpose of lymph nodes
RBC production and destruction; spleen, bone marrow
Basics: coagulation, clotting mechanisms

Understand

* Circ: structure/function; 4 chambered heart: systolic/diastolic pressure
* Oxygen transport; hemoglobin, oxygen content/affinity
* Substances transported by blood, lymph
* Source of lymph: diffusion from capillaries by differential pressure

Clinical Correlation

If the heart muscle does not grow with its 'normal' shape, it can lead to a change in the flow characteristics of blood. The continuity and Bernouilli's equations (PHY 6.1) can be used to explain how some young athletes have sudden and unexpected heart conditions due to abnormal flow of blood.

MCAT-Prep.com

Introduction

The circulatory system is concerned with the movement of nutrients, gases and wastes to and from cells. The circulatory or cardiovascular system (closed) distributes blood while the lymphatic system (open) distributes lymph.

Optional Gold Standard Resources

Free Online Q&A + Forum

Online Videos

Flashcards

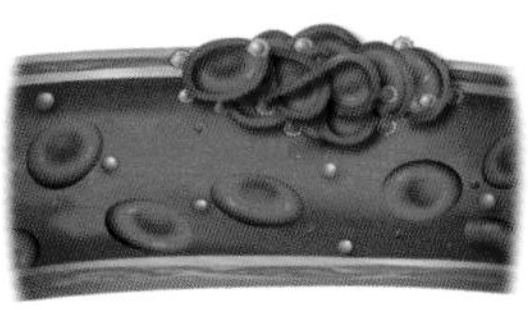

Special Guest

7.1 Generalities

The circulatory system is composed of the heart, blood, and blood vessels. The heart (which acts like a pump) and its blood vessels (which act like a closed system of ducts) are called the *cardiovascular system* which moves the blood throughout the body.

The following represents some important functions of blood within the circulatory system.

* It transports:

- hormones from endocrine glands to target tissues
- molecules and cells which are components of the immune system
- nutrients from the digestive tract (usu. to the liver)
- oxygen from the respiratory system to body cells
- waste from the body cells to the respiratory and excretory systems.

* It aids in temperature control (*thermoregulation*) by:

- distributing heat from skeletal muscle and other active organs to the rest of the body
- being directed to or away from the skin depending on whether or not the body wants to release or conserve heat, respectively.

7.2 The Heart

The heart is a muscular, cone-shaped organ about the size of a fist. The heart is composed of connective tissue (BIO 5.4) and cardiac muscle (BIO 5.2) which includes a region that generates electrical signals (see BIO 11.2 for SA node). The heart contains four chambers: two thick muscular walled *ventricles* and two thinner walled *atria*. An inner wall or *septum* separates the heart (and therefore the preceding chambers) into left and right sides. The atria contract or *pump* blood more or less simultaneously and so do the ventricles.

Deoxygenated blood returning to the heart from all body tissues except the lungs (= *systemic circulation*) enters the right atrium through large veins (= *venae cavae*). The blood is then pumped into the right ventricle through the tricuspid valve (which is one of many one-way valves in the cardiovascular system). Next the blood is pumped to the lungs (= *pulmonary circulation*) through semilunar valves (pulmonary valves) and pulmonary arteries {remember: blood in arteries goes away from the heart}.

The blood loses CO_2 and is **oxygenated** in the lungs and returns through pulmonary veins to the left atrium. Now the blood is pumped through the mitral (= bicuspid) valve into the largest chamber of the heart: the left ventricle. This ventricle's task is to return

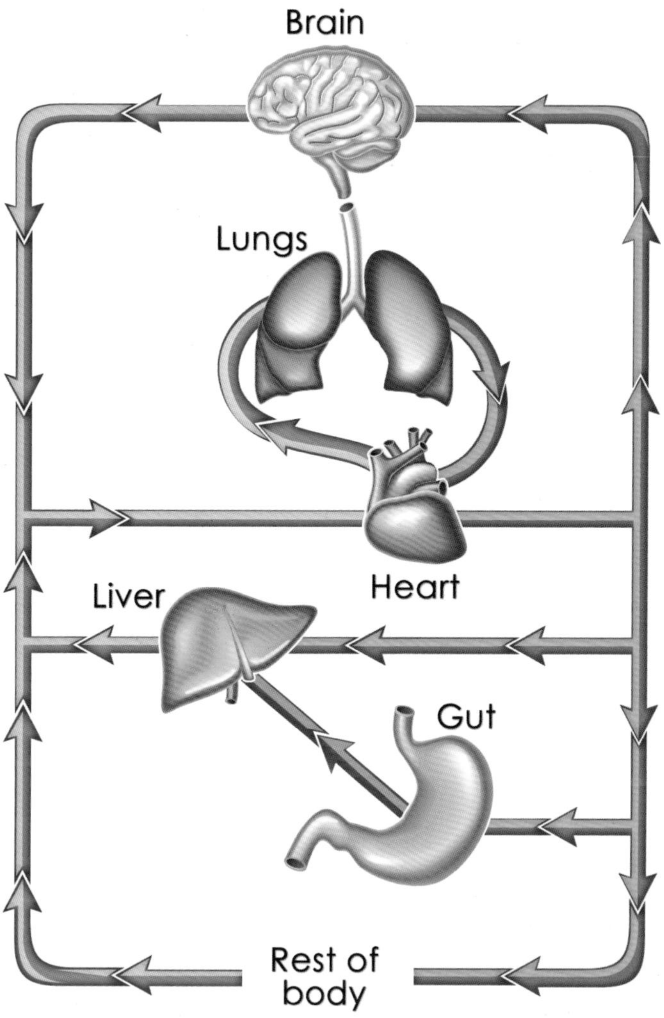

Figure IV.A.7.0: Overview of vascular anatomy.

The vascular anatomy of the human body or for an individual organ is comprised of both in-series and in-parallel vascular components. Blood leaves the heart through the aorta (high in oxygen, red in color) from which it is distributed to major organs by large arteries, each of which originates from the aorta. Therefore, these major distributing arteries are in parallel with each other. Thus the circulations of the head, arms, gastrointestinal systems, kidneys, and legs are all parallel circulations. There are some exceptions, notably the gastrointestinal (gut) and hepatic (liver) circulations, which are partly in series because the venous drainage from the intestines become the hepatic portal vein which supplies most of the blood flow to the liver. Vessels transporting from one capillary bed to another are called portal veins (besides the liver, note the portal system in the anterior pituitary, BIO 6.3.1).

blood into the systemic circulation by pumping into a huge artery: the *aorta* (its valve is the aortic valve).

The mitral (= bicuspid = 2 leaflets) and tricuspid (tri = 3 leaflets) valves are prevented from everting into the atria by strong fibrous cords (*chordae tendineae*) which are attached to small mounds of muscle (*papillary muscles*) in their respective ventricles. A major cause of heart murmurs is the inadequate functioning of these valves.

7.3 Blood Vessels

Blood vessels include arteries, arterioles, capillaries, venules and veins. Whereas arteries tend to have thick, smooth muscular walls and contain blood at high pressure, veins have thinner walls and low blood pressure. However, veins contain the highest proportion of blood in the cardiovascular system (about 2/3rds). The wall of a blood vessel is composed of an outer adventitia, an inner intima and a *m*iddle *m*uscle layer, the *media*.

Oxygenated blood entering the systemic circulation must get to all the body's tissues. The aorta must divide into smaller and smaller arteries (small artery = **arteriole**) in order to get to the level of the capillary which i) is the smallest blood vessel; ii) often forms branching networks called *capillary beds*; and iii) is the level at which the exchange of wastes and gases (i.e. O_2 and CO_2) occurs by diffusion.

In the next step in circulation, the newly deoxygenated blood enters very small veins (= **venules**) and then into larger and larger veins until the blood enters the venae cavae and then the right atrium. There are two venae cavae: one drains blood from the upper body while the other drains blood from the lower body (*superior* and *inferior* venae cavae, respectively).

Since the walls of veins are thin and somewhat floppy, they are often located in muscles. Thus movement of the leg squeezes the veins, which pushes the blood through 1-way bicuspid valves toward the heart. This is referred to as the *muscle pump*.

Coronary arteries branch off the aorta to supply the heart muscle.

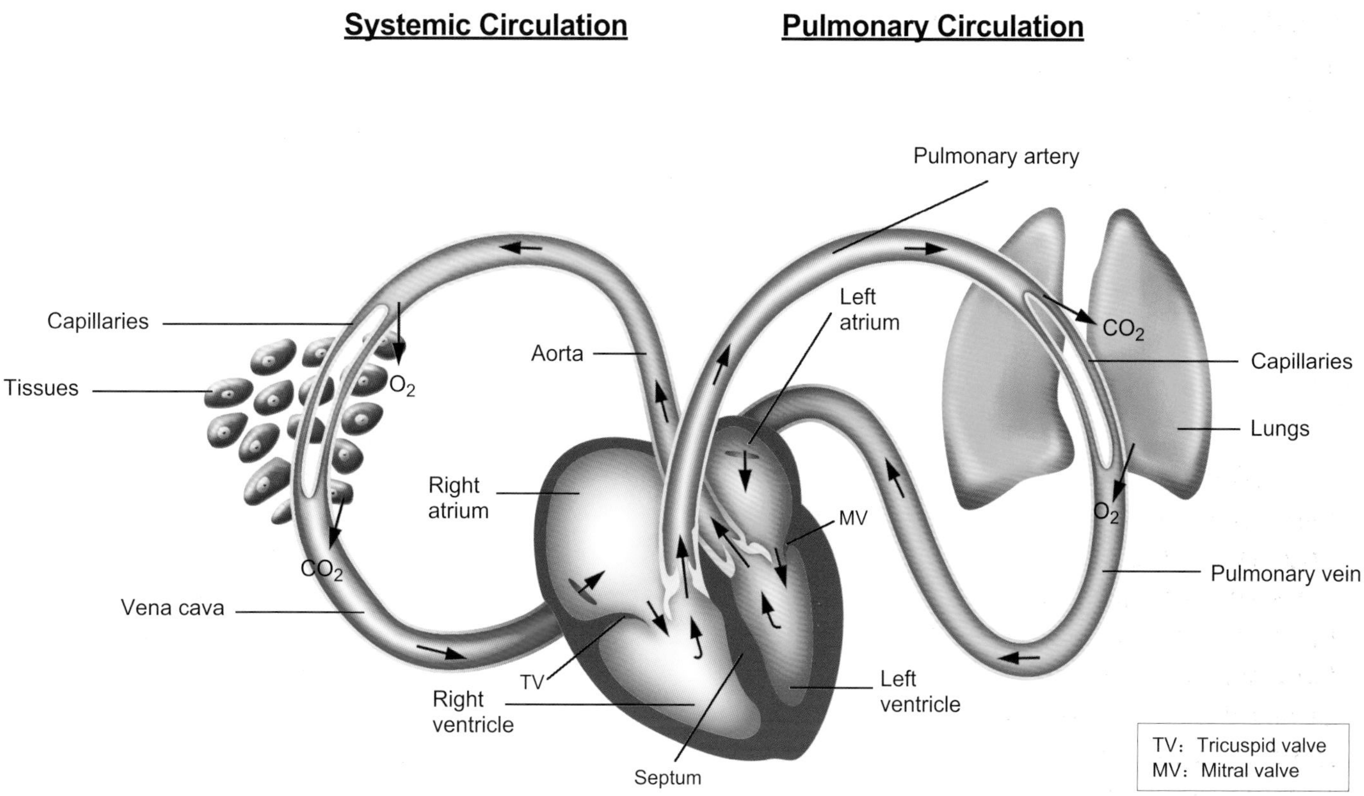

Figure IV.A.7.1: Schematic representation of the circulatory system.

Systemic circulation: transports blood from the left ventricle into the aorta then to all parts of the body and then returns to the right atrium from the superior and inferior venae cavae. *Pulmonary circulation:* transports blood from the right ventricle into pulmonary arteries to the lungs for exchange of oxygen and carbon dioxide and returns blood to the left atrium from pulmonary veins.

7.4 Blood Pressure

Blood pressure is the force exerted by the blood against the inner walls of blood vessels (esp. arteries). Maximum arterial pressure is measured when the ventricle contracts and blood is pumped into the arterial system (= *systolic pressure*). Minimal arterial pressure is measured when the ventricle is relaxed and blood is returned to the heart via veins (= *diastolic pressure*). Pulse pressure is the difference between the systolic pressure and the diastolic pressure. Blood pressure is usually measured in the brachial artery in the arm. A pressure of 120/80 signifies a systolic pressure of 120 mmHg and a diastolic pressure of 80 mmHg. The *pulse pressure* is the difference (i.e. 40 mmHg).

Peripheral resistance is essentially the result of arterioles and capillaries which resist the flow of blood from arteries to veins (the narrower the vessel, the higher the resistance). Arterioles are the site of the highest resistance in the cardiovascular system. An increase in peripheral resistance causes a rise in blood pressure. As blood travels down the systemic circulation, blood pressure decreases progressively due to the peripheral resistance to blood flow.

7.5 Blood Composition

Blood contains plasma (55%) and *formed elements* (45%). Plasma is a straw colored liquid which is mostly composed of water (92%), electrolytes, and the following plasma proteins:

* **Albumin** which is important in maintaining the osmotic pressure and helps to transport many substances in the blood

* **Globulins** which include both transport proteins and the proteins which form antibodies

* **Fibrinogen** which polymerizes to form the insoluble protein *fibrin* which is essential for normal blood clotting. If you take away fibrinogen and some other clotting factors from plasma you will be left with a fluid called *serum*.

The formed elements of the blood originate from precursors in the bone marrow which produce the following for the circulatory system: 99% red blood cells (= *erythrocytes*), then there are platelets (= *thrombocytes*), and white blood cells (= *leukocytes*). Red blood cells (RBCs) are biconcave cells without nuclei (*anucleate*) that circulate for 110-120 days before their components are recycled by macrophages. Interestingly, mature RBCs do not possess most organelles such as mitochondria, Golgi nor ER because RBCs are packed with hemoglobin. The primary function of hemoglobin is the transport of O_2 and CO_2 to and from tissue.

Platelets are cytoplasmic fragments of large bone marrow cells (*megakaryocytes*) which are involved in blood clotting by adhering to the collagen of injured vessels, releasing mediators which cause blood vessels to constrict (= *vasoconstriction*), etc.

Calcium ions (Ca^{2+}) are also important in blood clotting because they help in signaling platelets to aggregate.

White blood cells help in the defense against infection; they are divided into *granulocytes* and *agranulocytes* depending on whether or not the cell does or does not contain granules, respectively.

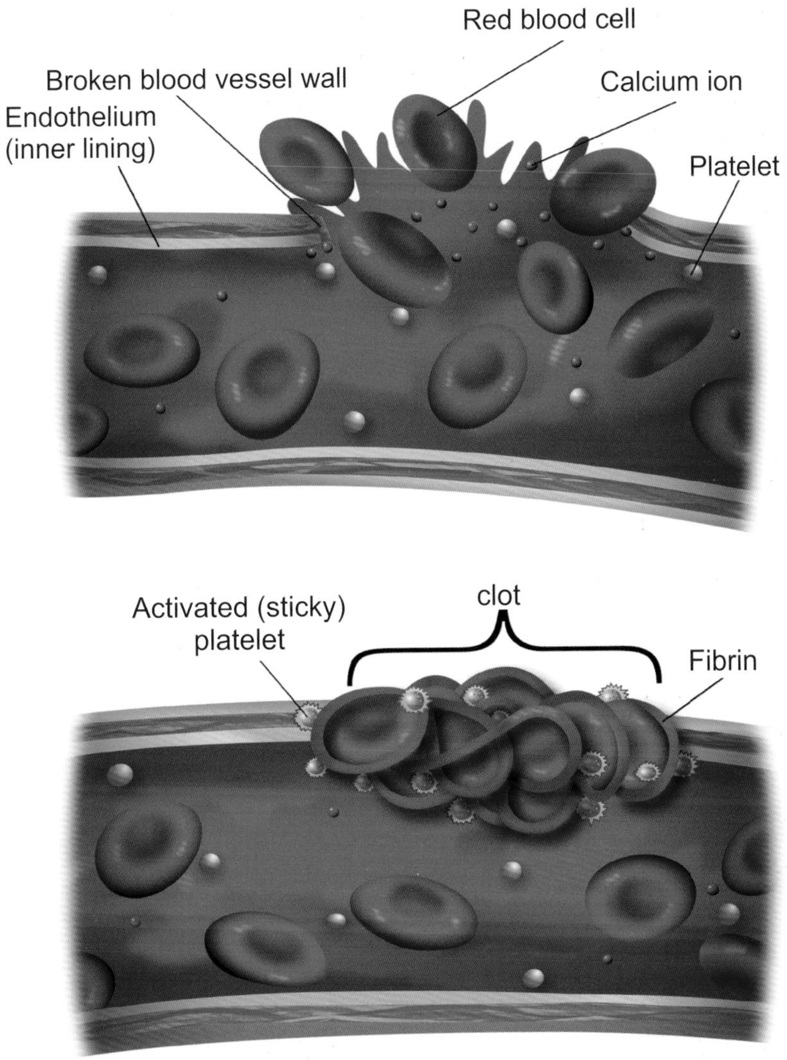

Figure IV.A.7.1.1: Schematic representation of blood clotting.

Granulocytes (= *polymorphonuclear leukocytes*) possess varying number of azurophilic (burgundy when stained) granules and are divided into: i) neutrophils which are the first white blood cells to respond to infection, they are important in controlling bacterial infection by phagocytosis - killing and digesting bacteria - and are the main cellular constituent of pus; ii) eosinophils which, like neutrophils, are phagocytic and also participate in allergic reactions and the destruction of parasites; iii) basophils which can release both anticoagulants (heparin) and substances important in hypersensitivity reactions (histamine).

Agranulocytes (= *mononuclear leukocytes*)) lack specific granules and are divided into: i) *lymphocytes* which are vital to the immune system (see *Immune System*, chapter 8); and monocytes (often called *phagocytes* or *macrophages* when they are outside of the circulatory system) which can phagocytose large particles.

The hematocrit measures how much space (volume) in the blood is occupied by red blood cells and is expressed as a percentage. Normal hematocrit in adults is about 45%.

{*See* BIO 15.2 *for ABO Blood Types*}

7.5.1 Hemoglobin

Each red blood cell carries hundreds of molecules of a substance which is responsible for their red color: **hemoglobin**. Hemoglobin (Hb) is a complex of *heme*, which is an iron-containing porphyrin ring, and *globin*, which is a tetrameric (= has 4 subunits) protein consisting of two α-subunits and two β-subunits. The iron from the heme group is normally in its reduced state (Fe^{2+}); however, in the presence of O_2, it can be oxidized to Fe^{3+}.

In the lungs, oxygen concentration or *partial pressure* is high, thus O_2 dissolves in the blood; oxygen can then quickly and reversibly combine with the iron in Hb forming bright red *oxyhemoglobin*. The binding of oxygen to hemoglobin is cooperative. In other words, each oxygen that binds to Hb facilitates the binding of the next oxygen. Consequently, the dissociation curve for oxyhemoglobin is sigmoidal as a result of the change in affinity of hemoglobin as each O_2 successively binds to the globin subunit (see BIO 4.3).

Examine the hemoglobin curve in Figure IV.A.7.2 carefully. Notice that at a PO_2 of 100 mmHg (e.g. arterial blood), the percentage of saturation of hemoglobin is almost 100%, which means all four heme groups on the four hemoglobin subunits are bound with O_2. At a PO_2 of 40 mmHg (e.g. venous blood), the percentage of saturation of hemoglobin is about 75%, which means three of the four heme groups on the four hemoglobin subunits are bound with O_2. At a PO_2 of 27 mmHg, the percentage of saturation of hemoglobin is only 50%, which means half of the four heme groups on the four hemoglobin subunits are bound with O_2. The partial pressure of oxygen (PO_2) at 50% saturation is called P50.

The curve can: (i) shift to the left which means that for a given PO_2 in the tissue capillary there is decreased unloading (release) of oxygen and that the affinity of hemoglobin for O_2 is increased; or (ii) shift to the right which means that for a given PO_2 in the tissue capillary there is increased

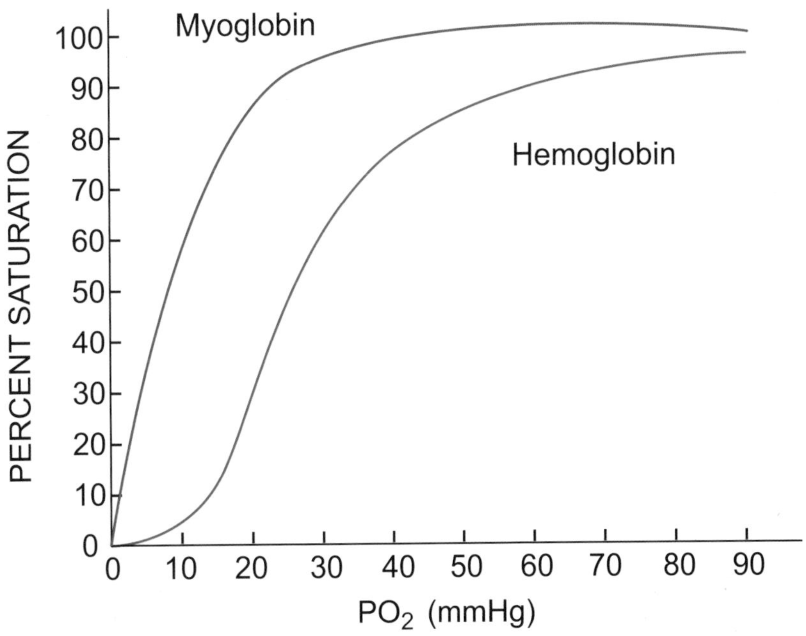

Figure IV.A.7.2: Oxygen dissociation curve: percent O_2 saturation versus O_2 partial pressure.

unloading of oxygen and that the affinity of hemoglobin for O_2 is decreased. The latter occurs when the tissue (i.e. muscle) is very active and thus requires more oxygen.

Thus a right shift occurs when the muscle is hot (↑ temperature during exercise), acid (↓ pH due to lactic acid produced in exercising muscle, see BIO 4.4. and 4.5), hypercarbic (↑CO_2 as during exercise, tissue produces more CO_2, see BIO 4.4. and 12.4.1), or contains high levels of organic phosphates (esp. increased synthesis of 2,3 DPG in red blood cells as a means to adapt to chronic hypoxemia).

In the body tissues where the partial pressure of O_2 is low and CO_2 is high, O_2 is released and CO_2 combines with the protein component of Hb forming the darker colored *carbaminohemoglobin* (also called: deoxyhemoglobin).

The red color of muscle is due to a different heme-containing protein concentrated in muscle called myoglobin. Myoglobin is a monomeric protein containing one heme prosthetic group. The O_2 binding curve for myoglobin is hyperbolic, which means that it lacks cooperativity (BCM 2.9).

7.5.2 Capillaries: A Closer Look

Capillary fluid movement can occur as a result of two processes: diffusion (dominant role) and filtration (secondary role but critical for the proper function of organs, especially the kidney; BIO 10.3). Osmotic pressure (BIO 1.1.1, CHM 5.1.3) due to proteins in blood plasma is sometimes called colloid osmotic pressure or oncotic pressure. The Starling equation is an equation that describes the role of hydrostatic and oncotic forces (= Starling forces) in the movement of fluid across capillary membranes as a result of filtration.

When blood enters the arteriole end of a capillary, it is still under pressure produced by the contraction of the ventricle. As a result of this pressure, a substantial amount of water (hydrostatic) and some plasma proteins filter through the walls of the capillaries into the tissue space. This fluid, called interstitial fluid (BIO 7.6), is simply blood plasma minus most of the proteins.

Interstitial fluid bathes the cells in the tissue space and substances in it can enter the cells by diffusion (mostly) or active transport. Substances, like carbon dioxide, can diffuse out of cells and into the interstitial fluid.

Near the venous end of a capillary, the blood pressure is greatly reduced. Here another force comes into play. Although the composition of interstitial fluid is similar to that of blood plasma, it contains a smaller concentration of proteins than plasma and thus a somewhat greater concentration of water.

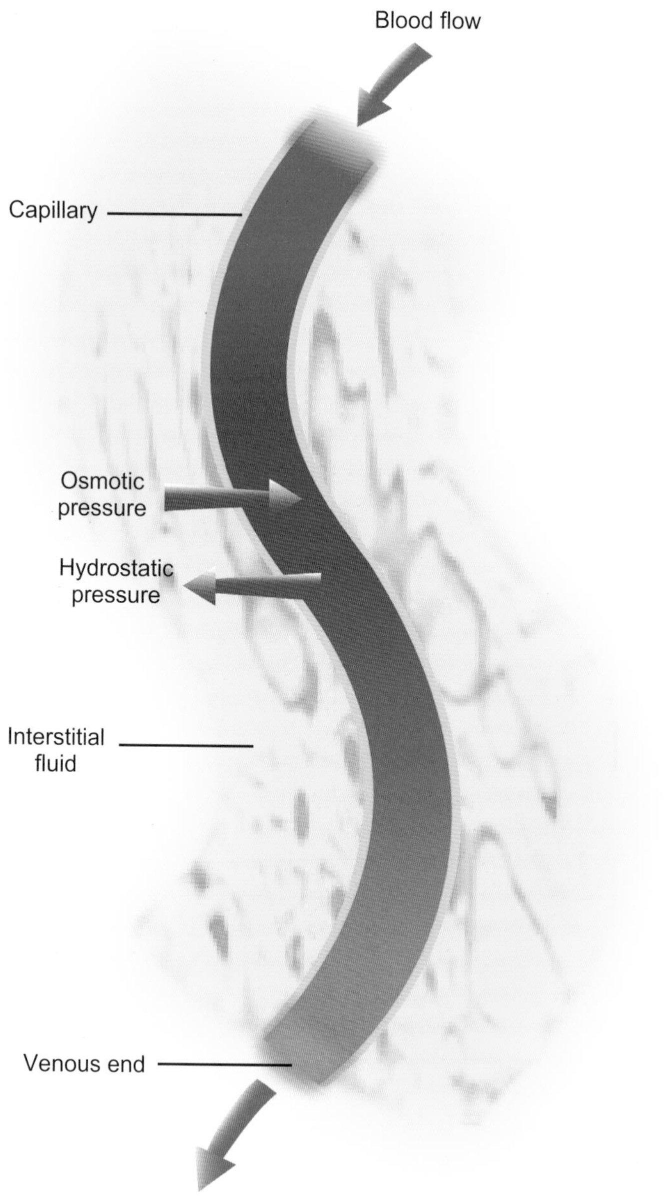

Figure IV.A.7.2b: Circulation at the level of the capillary. The exchange of water, oxygen, carbon dioxide, and many other nutrient and waste chemical substances between blood and surrounding tissues occurs at the level of the capillary.

This difference sets up an osmotic pressure. Although the osmotic pressure is small, it is greater than the blood pressure at the venous end of the capillary. Thus the fluid reenters the capillary here.

To summarize: when the blood pressure is greater than the osmotic pressure, filtration is favored and fluid tends to move out of the capillary; when the blood pressure is less than the osmotic pressure, reabsorption is favored and fluid tends to enter into the capillary.

7.6 The Lymphatic System

Body fluids can exist in blood vessels (intravascular), in cells (intracellular) or in a 3rd space which is intercellular (between cells) or extracellular (outside cells). Such fluids are called interstitial fluids. The **lymphatic system** is a network of vessels which can circulate fluid from the 3rd space to the cardiovascular system.

Aided by osmotic pressure, interstitial fluids enter the lymphatic system via small closed-ended tubes called *lymphatic capillaries* (in the small intestine they are called *lacteals*). Once the fluid enters it is called **lymph**. The lymph continues to flow into larger and larger vessels propelled by muscular contraction (esp. skeletal) and one-way valves. Then the lymph will usually pass through *lymph nodes* and then into a large vessel (esp. *the thoracic duct*) which drains into one of the large veins which eventually leads to the right atrium.

Lymph functions in important ways. Most protein molecules which leak out of blood capillaries are returned to the bloodstream by lymph. Also, microorganisms which invade tissue fluids are carried to lymph nodes by lymph. Lymph nodes contain *lymphocytes* and macrophages which are components of the immune system.

GOLD STANDARD WARM-UP EXERCISES

CHAPTER 7: The Circulatory System

1) In humans which of the following orders of blood circulation is correct?

A. Vena cava → right atrium → right ventricle → pulmonary arteries → pulmonary veins → left atrium
B. Vena cava → left atrium → left ventricle → pulmonary veins → pulmonary arteries → right ventricle
C. Vena cava → right ventricle → left ventricle → pulmonary veins → pulmonary arteries → left atrium
D. Vena cava → left atrium → left ventricle → pulmonary vein → pulmonary artery → right atrium

2) The rate of respiration is primarily dependent on the concentration of carbon dioxide in the blood. As carbon dioxide levels rise, chemoreceptors in blood vessels are stimulated to discharge neuronal impulses to the respiratory center in the medulla oblongata in the brain stem. These chemoreceptors are likely located in the:

A. vena cava.
B. pulmonary artery.
C. femoral vein.
D. aorta.

3) Veins tend to have ALL the following EXCEPT:

A. very elastic walls.
B. increasing size toward the heart.
C. thin walls.
D. valves for unidirectional flow.

4) Blood in the pulmonary veins is rich in:

A. myoglobin.
B. carbaminohemoglobin.
C. oxyhemoglobin.
D. lymph.

5) A biologically active agent, which completely diffuses through capillary beds, is injected into the brachiocephalic vein of the left arm. Which of the following would be most affected by the agent?

A. Heart
B. Lung
C. Left arm
D. Right arm

6) If the partial pressure of O_2 was increased to make up the total pressure of gas in blood which of the following would occur?

A. There would be a decrease in HbO_2.
B. There would be an increase in HbO_2.
C. The concentrations of Hb would equal HbO_2.
D. No answer can be determined from the information given.

7) Which of the following best explains why 97% of oxygen in blood is in the HbO_2 form?

A. Oxygen binds irreversibly to the iron atoms in hemoglobin.
B. Oxygen does not dissolve well in blood plasma.
C. There are allosteric interactions between hemoglobin subunits
D. Hemoglobin consists of four proteinacious subunits.

8) Which of the following graphs best represents the relationship between percent saturation of hemoglobin and pO_2 (mmHg) at different temperatures?

A.

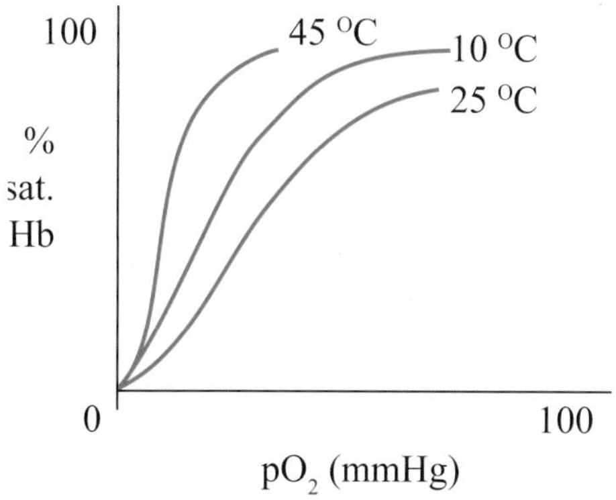

B.

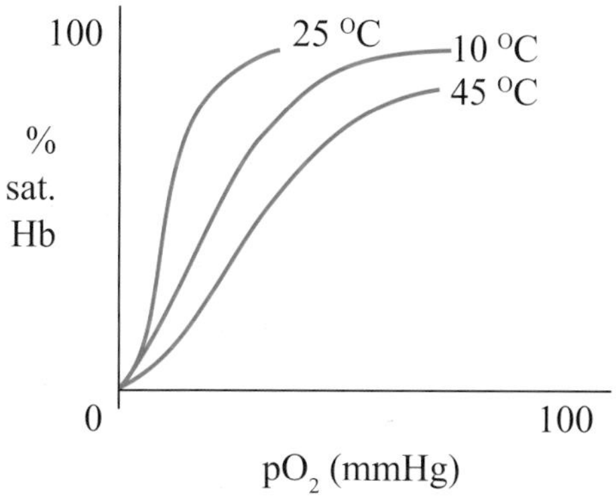

C.

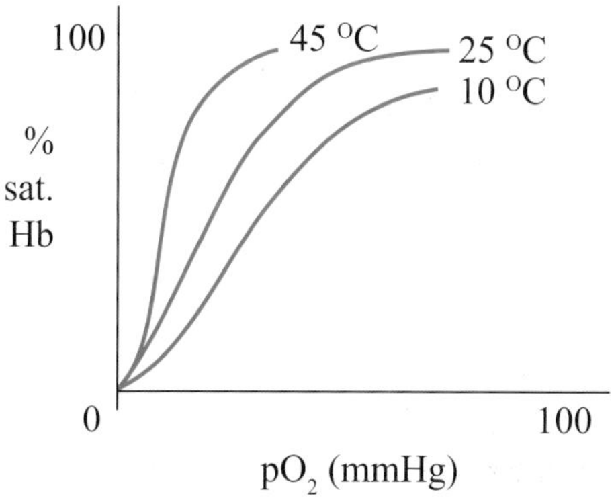

D.

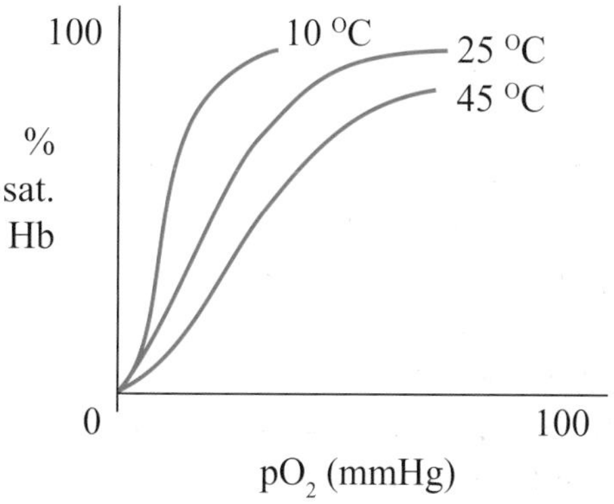

9) Which of the following body systems in humans is implicated in thermoregulation and transportation of components of the immune and endocrine systems?

A. The lymphatic system
B. Skin
C. The excretory system
D. The circulatory system

10) Once the erythrocytes enter the blood in humans, it is estimated that they have an average lifetime of how many days?

A. 75 days
B. 120 days
C. 220 days
D. 365 days

11) The net effect of the glycerate 2,3-biphosphate (GBP) is to shift the hemoglobin oxygen binding curve to higher oxygen tensions. Which of the following graphs represents the oxygen-binding curve in the presence of GBP?

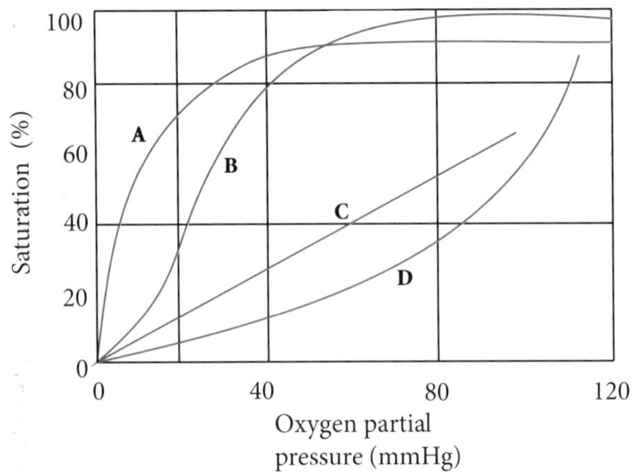

12) Glycerate 2,3-biphosphate functions to shift the oxygen binding curve by:

A. increasing the carbon carbon-dioxide concentration in the red blood cells.
B. altering the pH of the tissue fluid surrounding the red blood cells.
C. reducing the affinity between oxygen and hemoglobin at low oxygen concentrations.
D. forming a complex with oxygen at low oxygen concentrations.

13) Which of the following tissues most benefits from the shifts in the oxygen-binding curves caused by GBP and myoglobin?

A. Cardiac muscle tissue
B. Skeletal muscle tissue
C. Loose connective tissue
D. Intestinal wall tissue

14) In regions with an increased partial pressure of carbon dioxide, the oxygen dissociation curve is shifted to the right. This is known as the Bohr effect or shift. What is the physiological significance of this shift?

A. It counteracts the shift in the oxygen-binding curve caused by the presence of GBP.
B. It counteracts the shift in the oxygen-binding curve caused by the presence of myoglobin.
C. It increases the pH of actively respiring tissue.
D. It facilitates the delivery of increased quantities of oxygen from the blood to cells which produce energy.

15) Protons, like GBP, bind preferentially to deoxyhemoglobin. Thus, which of the following equations best explains the Bohr shift?

A. $CO_2 + H_2O \leftrightarrow H_2CO_3 \leftrightarrow H^+ + HCO_3^-$ (tissues)
B. $H^+ + HbO_2 \leftrightarrow HHb^+ + O_2$ (tissues)
C. $HCO_3^- + H^+ \leftrightarrow H_2CO_3 \leftrightarrow CO_2 + H_2O$ (lungs)
D. $HHb^+ + O_2 + HCO_3^- \leftrightarrow HbO_2 + CO_2 + H_2O$ (lungs)

16) Would the walls of the atria or ventricles expected to be thicker?

A. Atria, because blood ejection due to atrial contraction is high.
B. Atria, because blood ejection due to atrial contraction is low.
C. Ventricles, because ventricular stroke volume is high.
D. Ventricles, because ventricular stroke volume is low.

GS ANSWER KEY

CHAPTER 7

		Cross-Reference
1.	A	BIO 7.2, 7.3
2.	D	BIO 7.3
3.	A	BIO 7.3
4.	C	BIO 7.2, 7.3, 7.5.1
5.	B	BIO 7.3
6.	B	BIO 7.5.1
7.	C	BIO 3.0, 4.3, 7.5.1
8.	D	BIO 7.5.1
9.	D	BIO 7.1
10.	B	BIO 7.5
11.	B	BIO 7.5.1
12.	C	BIO 7.5.1
13.	B	BIO 4.2, 11.2
14.	D	BIO 4.4-4.5, 7.5.1, 12.4.1
15.	B	BIO 7.5.1
16.	C	BIO 7.2

*** Explanations can be found at the back of the book.**

Go online to MCAT-prep.com/forum to join the discussion about our GS chapter review questions.

APPENDIX

CHAPTER 7: The Circulatory System

Passage: The Cardiac Cycle

The cardiac cycle is the series of events comprising a complete contraction and relaxation of the heart's four chambers. The process of depolarization in the SA node (BIO 11.2) triggers the cardiac cycle which normally lasts about 0.22 seconds. The electronics of the cycle can be monitored by an electrocardiogram (EKG). The cycle is divided into two major phases, both named for events in the ventricle: the period of ventricular contraction and blood ejection, *systole*, followed by the period of ventricular relaxation and blood filling, *diastole*.

During the very first part of systole, the ventricles are contracting but all valves in the heart are closed thus no blood can be ejected. Once the rising pressure in the ventricles becomes great enough to open the aortic and pulmonary valves, the ventricular ejection or systole occurs. Blood is forced into the aorta and pulmonary trunk as the contracting ventricular muscle fibers shorten. The volume of blood ejected from a ventricle during systole is termed *stroke volume*. The total volume of blood pumped by the heart in one minute is the *cardiac output* (Q) and can be calculated as follows:

$$Q = \text{Stroke Volume} \times \text{Heart rate}$$

An average resting cardiac output would be 4.9 L/min for a human female and 5.6 L/min for a male.

During the very first part of diastole, the ventricles begin to relax, and the aortic and pulmonary valves close. No blood is entering or leaving the ventricles since once again all the valves are closed. Once ventricular pressure falls below atrial pressure, the atrioventricular (AV) valves open (i.e. mitral and tricuspid valves). Atrial contraction occurs towards the end of diastole, after most of the ventricular filling has taken place. The ventricle receives blood throughout most of diastole, not just when the atrium contracts. When the left ventricle is filled to capacity, it is known as End Diastolic Volume (EDV). Ejection fraction (EF) is the fraction of blood ejected by the left ventricle during systole and is usually given as a percentage:

$$EF = (\text{Stroke Volume})/(EDV) \times 100\%$$

17) Position P on the EKG of Fig. 1 probably correspond to:

A. atrial contraction.
B. ventricular contraction.
C. the beginning of ventricular systole.
D. the beginning of ventricular diastole.

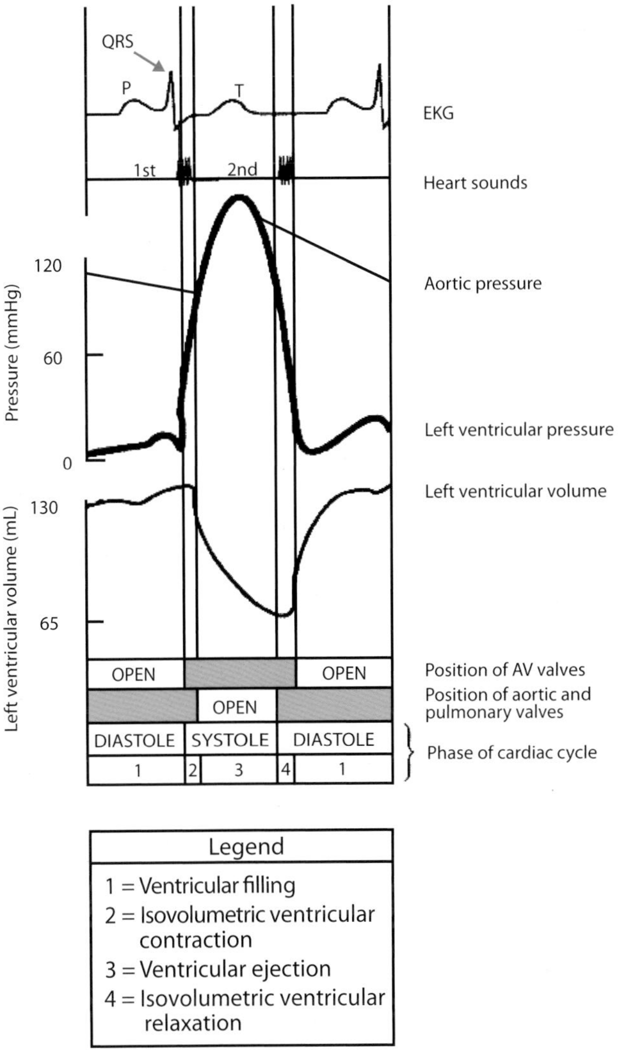

Figure 1: Electronic and pressure changes in the heart and aorta during the cardiac cycle.

18) The first heart sound represented in Fig. 1 is probably made when:

A. during ventricular systole, blood in the ventricle is forced against the closed atrioventricular valve.
B. during ventricular diastole, blood in the arteries is forced against the aortic and pulmonary artery pocket valves.
C. during ventricular diastole, blood in the ventricle is forced against the closed atrioventricular valve.
D. during ventricular systole, blood in the arteries is forced against the aortic and pulmonary artery pocket valves.

19) The graph below shows the effects on stroke volume of stimulating the sympathetic nerves to the heart.

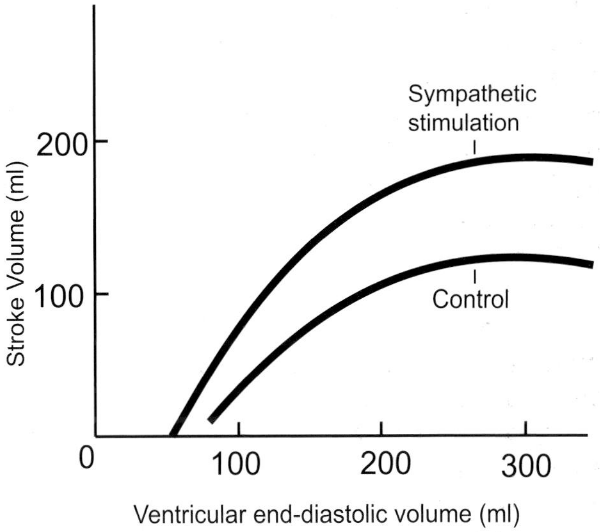

According to the graph, the net result of sympathetic stimulation on ejection fraction is to:

A. approximately double ejection fraction at any given end diastolic volume.
B. decrease ejection fraction at any given end diastolic volume.
C. increase ejection fraction at any given end diastolic volume.
D. leave ejection fraction relatively unchanged.

20) According to Fig. 1, the opening of the aortic and pulmonary valves is associated with all of the following EXCEPT one. Which one is the EXCEPTION?

A. Ventricular systole
B. A rise and fall in aortic pressure
C. A drop and rise in left ventricular volume
D. The third phase of the cardiac cycle

21) Stroke Volume / End Diastolic Volume is equal to which of the following?

A. Cardiac output
B. Ejection fraction
C. Stroke volume
D. End systolic volume

22) Which of the following correctly defines stroke volume (SV)?

A. SV = cardiac output - end systolic volume
B. SV = end diastolic volume - ejection fraction
C. SV = end systolic volume - end diastolic volume
D. SV = end diastolic volume - end systolic volume

ANSWER KEY

ADVANCED TOPICS - CHAPTER 7

		Cross-Reference
17.	A	F, BIO 7.2-7.4
18.	A	F, BIO 7.2-7.4
19.	C	F, BIO 6.1.4, 7.2-7.5
20.	C	F, BIO 7.2-7.4
21	B	Ch 12
22	D	Appendix Ch 12, deduce

P = paragraph; *S* = sentence; *E* = equation; *T* = table; *F* = figure

Explanations can be found at the back of the book.

THE IMMUNE SYSTEM

Chapter 8

Memorize	Understand	Clinical Correlation
* Roles in immunity: T-lymphocytes; * B-lymphocytes * Tissues in the immune system including bone marrow * Spleen, thymus, lymph nodes	* Concepts of antigen, antibody, interaction * Structure of antibody molecule * Mechanism of stimulation by antigen	The immune system is finely tuned to defeat invaders but it is far from perfect. Asthma and Crohn's disease are common examples of an over active immune system. The often fatal cytokine storm is caused by a positive feedback loop (BIO 6.3.7) between cytokines and white blood cells.

MCAT-Prep.com

Introduction

The immune system protects against disease. Many processes are used in order to identify and kill various microbes (see Microbiology, Chapter 2, for examples) as well as tumor cells. There are 2 acquired responses of the immune system: cell-mediated and humoral.

Optional Gold Standard Resources

Free Online Q&A + Forum

Online Videos

Flashcards

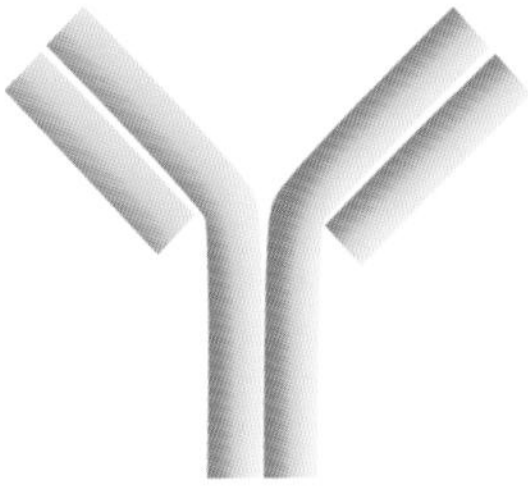

Special Guest

8.1 Overview

The immune system is composed of various cells and organs which defend the body against pathogens, toxins or any other foreign agents. Substances (usu. proteins) on the foreign agent causing an immune response are called **antigens**. There are two acquired responses to an antigen: (1) the **cell mediated response** where T-lymphocytes are the dominant force and act against microorganisms, tumors, and virus infected cells; and (2) the **humoral response** where B-lymphocytes are the dominant force and act against specific proteins present on foreign molecules.

8.2 Cells of the Immune System

B-lymphocytes originate in the bone marrow. Though T-lymphocytes also originate in the bone marrow, they go on to mature in the thymus gland. T-lymphocytes learn with the help of macrophages to recognize and attack only foreign substances (i.e. antigens) in a direct cell to cell manner (= *cell-mediated* or *cellular immunity*). T-lymphocytes have two major subtypes: T-helper cells and T-cytotoxic cells. Some T-cells (T_8, T_C, or T cytotoxic) mediate the apoptosis of foreign cells and virus-infected cells. Some T-cells (T_4, T_H or T *h*elper) mediate the cellular response by secreting substances to activate macrophages, other T-cells and even B-cells. {T_H-cells are specifically targeted and killed by the HIV virus in AIDS patients}

B-lymphocytes act indirectly against the foreign agent by producing and secreting <u>antigen-specific</u> proteins called **antibodies**, which are sometimes called immunoglobulins = *humoral immunity*). Antibodies are "designer" proteins which can specifically attack the antigen for which it was designed. The antibodies along with other proteins (i.e. complement proteins) can attack the antigen-bearing particle in many ways:

- **Lysis** by digesting the plasma membrane of the foreign cell

- **Opsonization** which is the altering of cell membranes so the foreign particle is more susceptible to phagocytosis by neutrophils and macrophages

- **Agglutination** which is the clumping of antigen-bearing cells

- **Chemotaxis** which is the attracting of other cells (i.e. phagocytes) to the area

- **Inflammation** which includes migration of cells, release of fluids and dilatation of blood vessels.

The activated antibody secreting B-lymphocyte is called a *plasma cell*. After the first or *primary* response to an antigen, both T- and B-cells produce *memory cells* which are formed during the initial response to an anti-

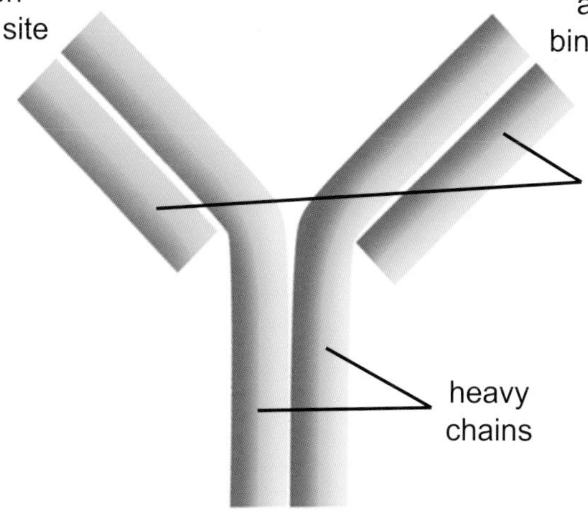

Figure IV.A.8.1: Schematic representation of an antibody. Antibodies are composed of disulfide bond-linked heavy and light chains. The unique part of the antigen recognized by an antibody is called the epitope. The antigen binding site on the antibody is extremely variable (= hypervariable).

Antibody (= Immunoglobulin = Ig)	Description
IgA	Found in saliva, tears and breast milk. Found in mucosal areas, such as the GI, respiratory and urogenital tracts thus prevents colonization by pathogens.
IgD	Functions mainly as an antigen receptor on B-cells that have not been exposed to antigens. Activates mast cells and basophils (BIO 7.5) to produce antimicrobial factors.
IgE	Binds to particles that induce allergic reactions (= allergens) and triggers histamine release from mast cells and basophils. Also protects against parasitic worms.
IgG	In its four forms, provides the majority of antibody-based immunity against invading germs or pathogens. The only antibody capable of crossing the placenta (BIO 14.6) to give passive immunity to the fetus.
IgM	Expressed on the surface of B-cells (monomer) and in a secreted form (pentamer = complex of 5 monomers). Eliminates pathogens in the early stages of B-cell mediated (humoral) immunity before there is sufficient IgG.

Table IV.A.8.1: Antibody isotypes of mammals. Antibodies are grouped into different "isotypes" based on which heavy chain they possess. The five different antibody isotypes known in mammals are displayed in the table.

genic challenge. These memory cells remain in the circulation and will make the next or secondary response much faster and much greater. {Note: though lymphocytes are vital to the immune system, it is the neutrophil which responds to injury first; BIO 7.5}

T-cells cannot recognise, and therefore react to, 'free' floating antigen. T-cells can only recognize an antigen that has been processed and presented by cells in association will a special cell surface molecule called the major histocompatibility complex (MHC). In fact, "antigen presenting cells", through the use of MHC, can teach both B-cells and T-cells which antigens are safe (*self*) and which are dangerous and should be attacked (*nonself*). MHC Class I molecules present to T_C cells while MHC Class II molecules present to T_H cells.

8.3 Tissues of the Immune System

The important tissues of the immune system are the bone marrow, and the lymphatic organs which include the thymus, the lymph nodes and the spleen. The roles of the bone marrow and the thymus have already been discussed. It is of value to add that the thymus secretes a hormone (= *thymosin*) which appears to help stimulate the activity of T-lymphocytes.

Lymph nodes are often the size of a pea and are found in groups or chains along the paths of the larger lymphatic vessels. Their functions can be broken down into three general categories: i) a non-specific filtration of bacteria and other particles from the lymph using the phagocytic activity of macrophages; ii) the storage and proliferation of T-cells, B-cells and antibody production; (iii) initiate immune response on the recognition of antigen.

The **spleen** is the largest lymphatic organ and is situated in the upper left part of the abdominal cavity. Within its lobules it has tissue called red and white pulp. The white pulp of the spleen contains all of the organ's lymphoid tissue (T-cells, B-cells, macrophages, and other antigen presenting cells) and is the site of active immune responses via the proliferation of T- and B-lymphocytes and the production of antibodies by plasma cells. The red pulp is composed of several types of blood cells including red blood cells, platelets and granulocytes. Its main function is to filter the blood of antigen and phagocytose damaged or aged red blood cells (the latter has a lifespan of approximately 110-120 days). In addition, the red pulp of the spleen is a site for red blood cell storage (i.e. a blood storage organ).

Autoimmunity!

Figure IV.A.8.2: Actually, "autoimmunity" refers to a disease process where the immune system attacks one's own cells and tissues as opposed to one's own car.

8.4 Advanced Topic: ELISA

ELISA, enzyme-linked-immunosorbent serologic assay, is a rapid test used to determine if a particular protein is in a sample and, if so, to quantify it (= assay). ELISA relies on an enzymatic conversion reaction and an antibody-antigen interaction which would lead to a detectable signal – usually a color change. Consequently, ELISA has no need of any radioisotope nor any radiation-counting apparatus.

There are 2 forms of ELISA: (1) direct ELISA uses monoclonal antibodies to detect antigen in a sample; (2) indirect ELISA is used to find a specific antibody in a sample (i.e. HIV antibodies in serum). {Notice the similarity with the concept of "direct" and "indirect" immunofluorescence, BIO 1.5.1}

GOLD STANDARD WARM-UP EXERCISES

CHAPTER 8: The Immune System

1) Helper T-cells are required to activate:

A. hemoglobin and T lymphocytes.
B. thrombocytes and B lymphocytes.
C. B lymphocytes and T lymphocytes.
D. erythrocytes and thrombocytes.

2) The retrovirus HIV infects primarily the helper T cells by making specific interactions with the cell's receptors. What must first occur in order for the retrovirus to infect the cell?

A. The protein coat of the virus fuse with the helper T cell plasma membrane.
B. The viral envelope must make contact and be recognized by helper T cell receptors.
C. The viral RNA must be translated.
D. The helper T cell must engulf the virus via phagocytosis.

3) Before being injected into humans as a vaccine, the hepatitis B virus (HBV) would first have to:

A. be cloned in yeast cells to ensure that enough of the virus had been injected to elicit an immune response.
B. have its protein coat removed.
C. be purified.
D. be inactivated.

4) The following graph shows the immune response for an initial injection of Hepatitis B Surface Antigen (HBsAg) and a subsequent injection of the HBV virus. Which of the following best explains the differences in the two responses?

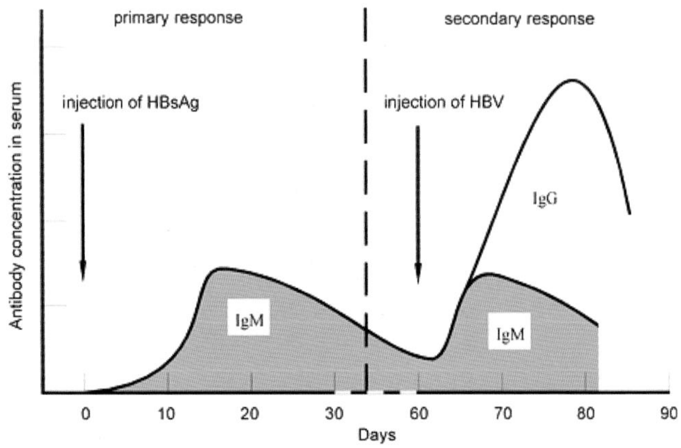

A. During the initial response, the immune response was carried out primarily by macrophages and B-lymphocytes.
B. During the secondary response, T-cells possessing membrane receptors, recognized and attacked the viral antigens.
C. Memory cells produced by T- and B-cells during the first exposure made the second response faster and more intense.
D. Memory cells produced by macrophages during the first infection recognized the viral antigens more quickly during the second infection, causing antibody production to be increased.

5) In terms of immunity, what is the major disadvantage of injecting monoclonal antibodies directly into the circulatory system instead of an inactivated form of the antigen?

A. Activated antigens can cause infection.
B. The immune response is faster when the inactivated antigen is injected.
C. The antibodies injected are often recognized as antigens by the immune system, thereby eliciting an immune response.
D. No memory cells are produced when the monoclonal antibody is directly injected into the circulatory system.

6) Which of the following biological processes would be inhibited by the removal of an adult human spleen?

A. The production of erythrocytes
B. The production of macrophages
C. The production of T-lymphocytes
D. The destruction of erythrocytes

7) Tissue transplantation is a technique which also can stimulate an immune response in recipients. Several methods are used to prevent rejection. These might include all but which of the following?

A. Exposure of the tissue to be transplanted to X-irradiation to prevent infection from occurring
B. Exposure of bone marrow and lymph tissues to X-irradiation
C. Immunosuppression
D. Tissue matching

8) Each antibody molecule is made up of how many PAIR of polypeptide chains joined together by disulfide bonds?

A. 1
B. 2
C. 3
D. 4

9) The immune system normally discriminates between which types of antigens?

A. Primary and secondary
B. Humoral and cell-mediated
C. B and T cells
D. Self and non-self

10) Surplus red blood cells, needed to meet an emergency, are MAINLY stored in what organ of the human body?

A. Spleen
B. Liver
C. Yellow marrow
D. Pancreas

GS ANSWER KEY

Chapter 8

		Cross-Reference			Cross-Reference
1.	C	BIO 8.2	6.	D	BIO 8.3
2.	B	BIO 2.1, 2.1.1, 8.2	7.	A	BIO 8.2, deduce
3.	D	BIO 2.1, 8.2	8.	B	BIO 8.2
4.	C	BIO 8.1, 8.2	9.	D	BIO 8.1, 8.2
5.	D	BIO 8.1, 8.2	10.	A	BIO 8.3

* Explanations can be found at the back of the book.

Go online to MCAT-prep.com/forum to join the discussion about our GS chapter review questions.

GO D NO S

THE DIGESTIVE SYSTEM

Chapter 9

Memorize

sic anatomy of the upper GI and lower
tracts
iva as lubrication and enzyme source
mach low pH, gastric juice, mucal
tection against self-destruction
es for production of digestive enzymes,
s of digestion
er: nutrient metabolism, vitamin storage;
od glucose regulation, detoxification

Understand

* Basic function of the upper GI and lower GI tracts
* Bile: storage in gallbladder, function
* Pancreas: production of enzymes; transport of enzymes to small intestine
* Small intestine: production of enzymes, site of digestion, neutralize stomach acid
* Peristalsis; structure and function of villi, microvilli

Clinical Correlation

Crohn's disease is a chronic inflammatory disease that can affect any part of the GI tract, from the mouth to the anus. Diarrhea, rectal bleeding and abdominal pain are common symptoms. Usually immune suppressing medications and surgery are both eventually required but neither is curative.

MCAT-Prep.com

Introduction

The digestive system is involved in the mechanical and chemical break down of food into smaller components with the aim of absorption into, for example, blood or lymph. Thus digestion is a form of catabolism.

Optional Gold Standard Resources

Free Online Q&A + Forum

Online Videos

Flashcards

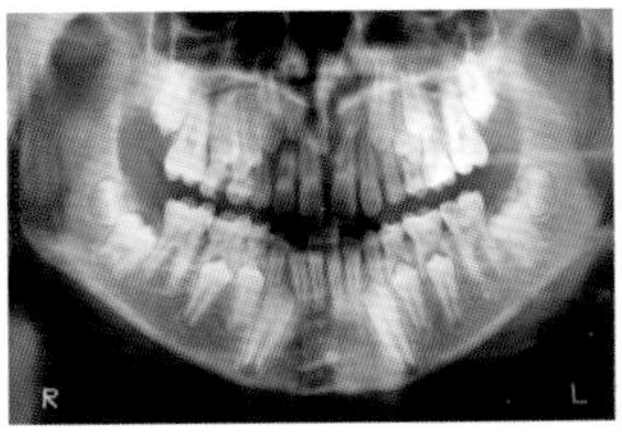

Special Guest

9.1 Overview

The digestive or *gastrointestinal* (= GI) system is principally concerned with the intake and reduction of food into subunits for absorption. These events occur in five main phases which are located in specific parts of the GI system: i) **ingestion** which is the taking of food or liquid into the mouth; ii) **fragmentation** which is when larger pieces of food are *mechanically* broken down; iii) **digestion** where macromolecules are *chemically* broken down into subunits which can be absorbed; iv) **absorption** through cell membranes; and v) **elimination** of the waste products. The GI system secretes enzymes and hormones that facilitate in the process of ingestion, digestion, absorption as well as elimination.

The GI tract (gut or *alimentary canal*) is a muscular tract about 9 meters long covered by a layer of mucosa which has definable characteristics in each area along the tract. The GI tract includes the oral cavity (mouth), pharynx, esophagus, stomach, small intestine, large intestine, and anus. The GI system includes the accessory organs which release secretions into the tract: the salivary glands, gallbladder, liver, and pancreas (*see Figure IV.A.9.1*).

9.2 The Oral Cavity and Esophagus

Ingestion, fragmentation and digestion begin in the oral cavity. Teeth are calcified, hard structures in the oral cavity used to fragment food (= *mastication*). Children have twenty teeth (= *deciduous*) and adults have thirty-two (= *permanent*). From front to back, each quadrant (= *quarter)* of the mouth contains: two incisors for cutting, one cuspid (= *canine*) for tearing, two bicuspids (= *premolars*) for crushing, and three molars for grinding.

Digestion of food begins in the oral cavity when the 3 pairs of salivary glands (*parotid*, *sublingual*, and *submandibular*) synthesize and secrete saliva. Saliva lubricates the oral cavity, assists in the process of deglutition, controls bacterial flora and initiates the process of digestion. Its production is unique in that it is increased by both sympathetic and parasympathetic innervation. Major components of saliva include salivary amylase, lysozyme, lingual lipase and mucus. Amylase is an enzyme which starts the initial digestion of carbohydrates by splitting starch and glycogen into disaccharide subunits. Lipase is an enzyme which starts the initial digestion of triglyceride (fats). The mucous helps to bind food particles together and lubricate it as it is swallowed.

Swallowing (= *deglutition*) occurs in a coordinated manner in which the tongue and pharyngeal muscles propel the bolus of food into the esophagus while at the same time the upper esophageal sphincter relaxes to permit food to enter. The epiglottis is a small flap of

Basic Dental Anatomy and Pathology

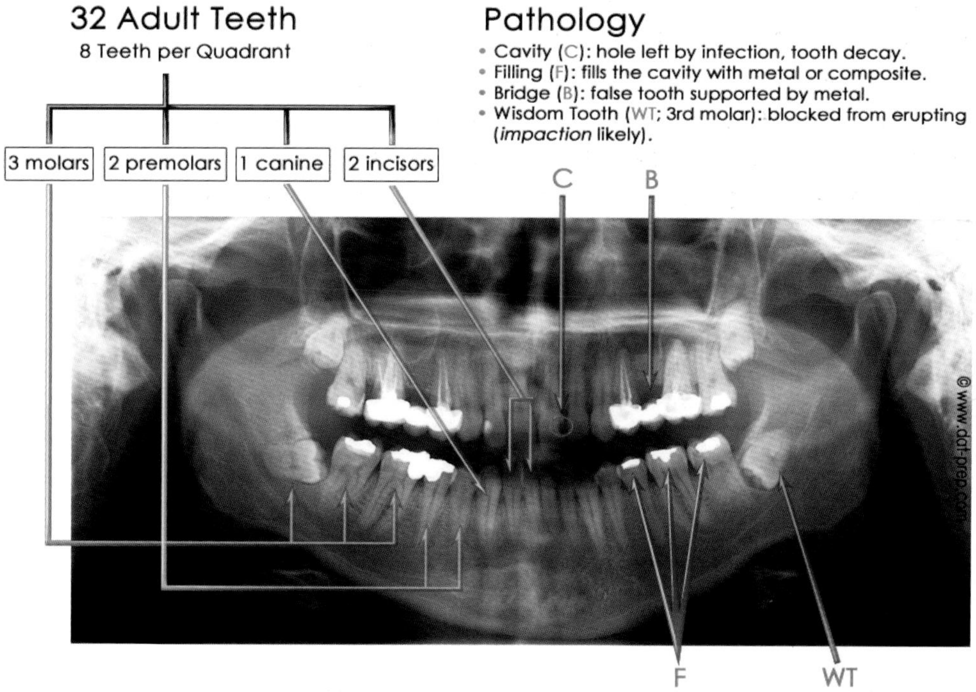

Figure IV.A.9.0a: Dental X-ray of an adult. The pathology of teeth is not prerequisite knowledge for the MCAT and is only presented for your interest.

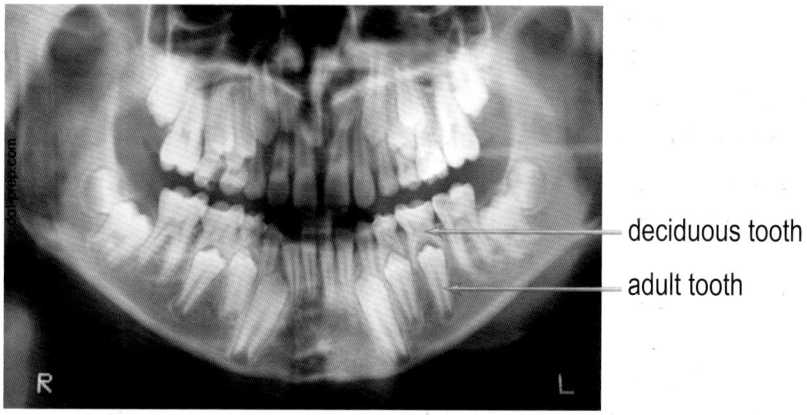

Figure IV.A.9.0b: Dental X-ray of a child showing deciduous (AKA: baby, primary, milk, temporary) teeth and emerging adult (permanent) teeth. Note the "R" on the X-ray indicates the right side of the patient who is facing the observer.

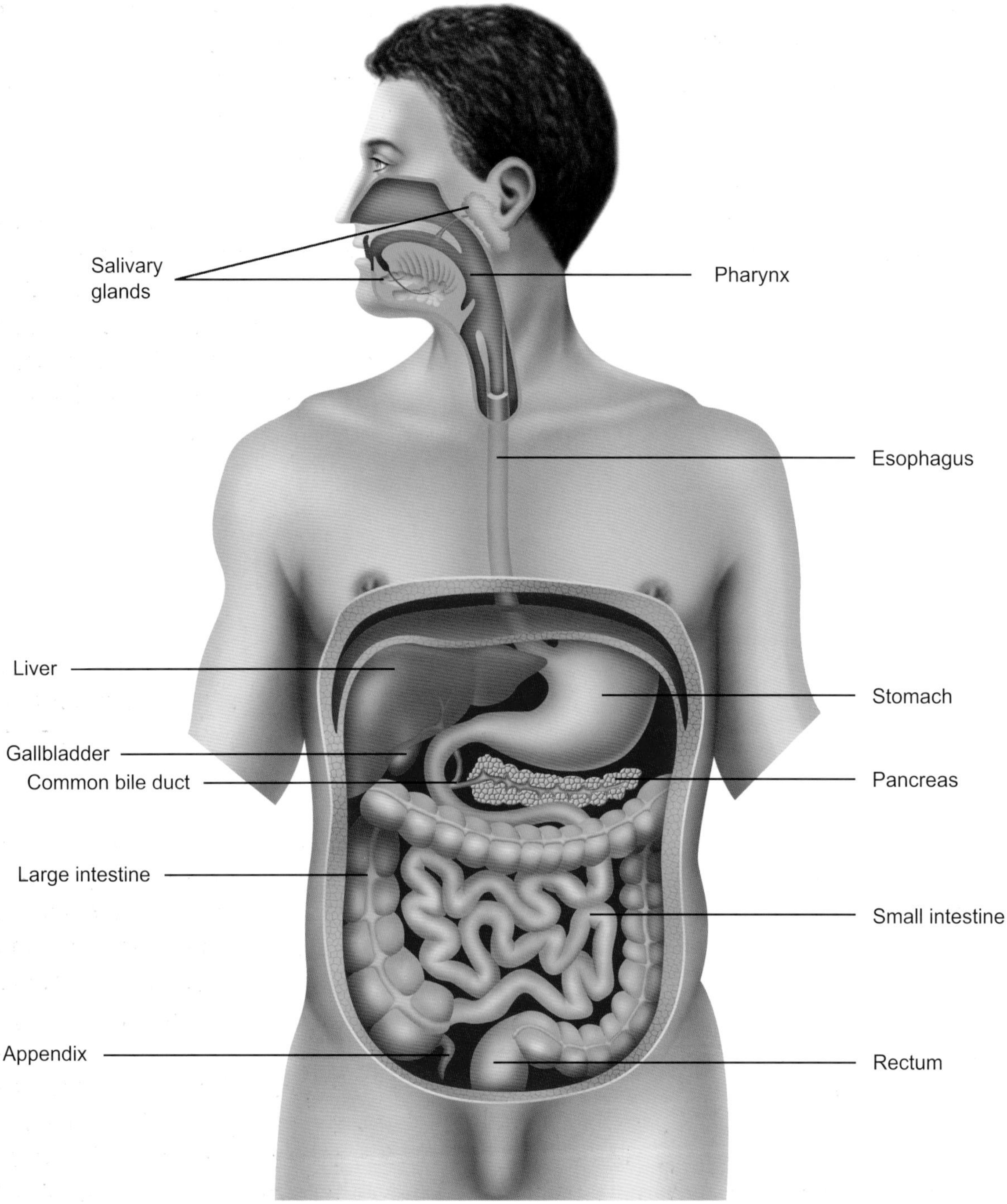

Figure IV.A.9.1: Schematic drawing of the major components of the digestive system.

tissue which covers the opening to the airway (= *glottis*) while swallowing. Gravity and peristalsis help bring the food through the esophagus to the stomach.

The GI system is supplied by both extrinsic innervation and intrinsic innervation. The extrinsic innervation includes the sympathetic and parasympathetic nervous system. The parasympathetic nervous system, mediated by the vagus and pelvic nerves, usually stimulates the functions of the GI tract while the sympathetic nervous system usually inhibits the functions of the GI tract. The intrinsic innervation located in the gut wall includes the *myenteric nerve plexus* and *submucosal nerve plexus* which control GI tract motility including peristalsis.

Peristalsis, which is largely the result of two muscle layers in the GI tract (i.e. the inner circular and outer longitudinal layers), is the sequential wave-like muscular contractions which propell food along the tract. The rate, strength and velocity of muscular contractions are modulated by the ANS.

9.3 The Stomach

The stomach continues in fragmenting and digesting the food with its strong muscular activity, its acidic gastric juice and various digestive enzymes present in the gastric juice. The walls of the stomach are lined by thick mucosa which contains goblet cells. These goblet cells of the GI tract protect the lumen from the acidic environment by secreting mucous.

The important components of gastric juice are: i) HCl which keeps the pH low (approximately = 2) to kill microorganisms, to aid in partial hydrolysis of proteins, and to provide the environment for ii) *pepsinogen*, an inactive form of enzyme (= *zymogen*) secreted by gastric chief cells, which is later converted to its active form *pepsin* in the presence of a low pH. Pepsin is involved in the breakdown of proteins. Both the hormone gastrin, which is produced in the stomach; and parasympathetic impulses can increase the production of gastric juice.

The preceding events turns food into a semi-digested fluid called chyme. Chyme is squirted through a muscular sphincter in the stomach, the *pyloric sphincter*, into the first part of the small intestine, the *duodenum*. Many secretions are produced by exocrine glands in the liver and pancreas and enter the duodenum via the *common bile duct*. Exocrine secretions eventually exit the body through ducts. For example, *goblet cells*, which are found in the stomach and throughout the intestine, are exocrine secretory cells which produce mucus which lines the epithelium of the gastrointestinal tract.

9.4 The Exocrine Roles of the Liver and Pancreas

9.4.1 The Liver

The liver occupies the upper right part of the abdominal cavity. It has many roles including: the conversion of glucose to glycogen; the synthesis of glucose from non-carbohydrates; the production of plasma proteins; the destruction of red blood cells; the deamination of amino acids and the formation of urea; the conversion of toxic ammonia to much less toxic urea (the urea cycle); the storage of iron and certain vitamins; the alteration of toxic substances and most medicinal products (*detoxification*); and its exocrine role - the production of **bile** by liver cells (= *hepatocytes*).

Bile is a yellowish - green fluid mainly composed of water, cholesterol, pigments (from the destruction of red blood cells) and salts. It is the **bile salts** which have a digestive function by the emulsification of fats. Emulsification is the dissolving of fat globules into tiny droplets called *micelles* which have hydrophobic interiors and hydrophilic exteriors (cf. Plasma Membrane, BIO 1.1). Bile salts orient themselves around those lipid droplets with their hydrophilic portions towards the aqueous environment and their hydrophobic portions towards the micelle interior and keep them dispersed. Emulsification also helps in the absorption of the fat soluble vitamins A, D, E, and K.

Thus bile is produced by the liver, stored and concentrated in a small muscular sac, the **gallbladder**, and then secreted into the duodenum via the common bile duct.

9.4.2 The Pancreas

The pancreas is close to the duodenum and extends behind the stomach. The pancreas has both endocrine (*see Endocrine Systems; BIO 6.3.4*) and exocrine functions. It secretes pancreatic juice, which consists of alkaline fluid and digestive enzymes, into the pancreatic duct that joins the common bile duct. Pancreatic juice is secreted both due to parasympathetic and hormonal stimuli. The hormones *secretin* and *CCK* are produced and released by the duodenum in response to the presence of chyme. Secretin acts on the pancreatic ductal cells to stimulate HCO_3^- secretion, whose purpose is to neutralize the acidic chyme. CCK acts on pancreatic acinar cells to stimulate the exocrine pancreatic secretion of digestive enzymes. These enzymes are secreted as enzymes or proenzymes (= *zymogens*; BIO 4.3) that must be activated in the intestinal lumen. The enzymes include pancreatic amylase, which can break down carbohydrates into monosaccharides; pancreatic lipase, which can break down fats into fatty acids and monoglycerides; and nuclease, which can break down nucleic acids. The protein enzymes (proteases) include trypsin, chymotrypsin, carboxypeptidase, which can break down proteins into amino acids, dipeptides or tripeptides.

9.5 The Intestines

The **small intestine** is divided into the duodenum, the jejunum, and the ileum, in that order. It is this part of the GI system that completes the digestion of chyme, absorbs the nutrients (i.e. monosaccharides, amino acids, nucleic acids, etc.), and passes the rest onto the large intestine. Peristalsis is the primary mode of transport. Contraction behind the bolus and simultaneous relaxation in front of the bolus propel chyme forward. Segmentation also aids in small intestine movement - it helps to mix the intestinal contents without any forward movement of chyme. Of course, parasympathetic impulses increase intestinal smooth muscle contraction while sympathetic impulses decrease intestinal smooth muscle contraction.

Absorption is aided by the great surface area involved including the finger-like projections **villi** and **microvilli** (*see the Generalized Eukaryotic Cell*, BIO 1.1F and 1.2). Intestinal villi, which increase the surface area ten-fold, are evaginations into the lumen of the small intestine and contain blood capillaries and a single lacteal (lymphatic capillary). Microvilli, which increase the surface area twenty-fold, contain a dense bundle of actin microfilaments cross-linked by proteins fimbrin and villin.

Absorption of carbohydrates, proteins and lipids is completed in the small intestine. Carbohydrates must be broken down into glucose, galactose and fructose for absorption to occur. In contrast, proteins can be absorbed as amino acids, dipeptides and tripeptides. Specific transporters are required for amino acids and peptides to facilitate the absorption across the luminal membrane. Lipids are absorbed in the form of fatty acids, monoglycerides and cholesterol. In the intestinal cells, they are re-esterified to triglycerides, cholesterol ester and phospholipids.

The lacteals absorb most fat products into the lymphatic system while the blood capillaries absorb the rest taking these nutrients to the liver for processing via a special vein - the *hepatic portal vein* [A portal vein carries blood from one capillary bed to another; BIO 7.3]. Goblet cells secrete a copious amount of mucus in order to lubricate the passage of material through the intestine and to protect the epithelium from abrasive chemicals (i.e. acids, enzymes, etc.).

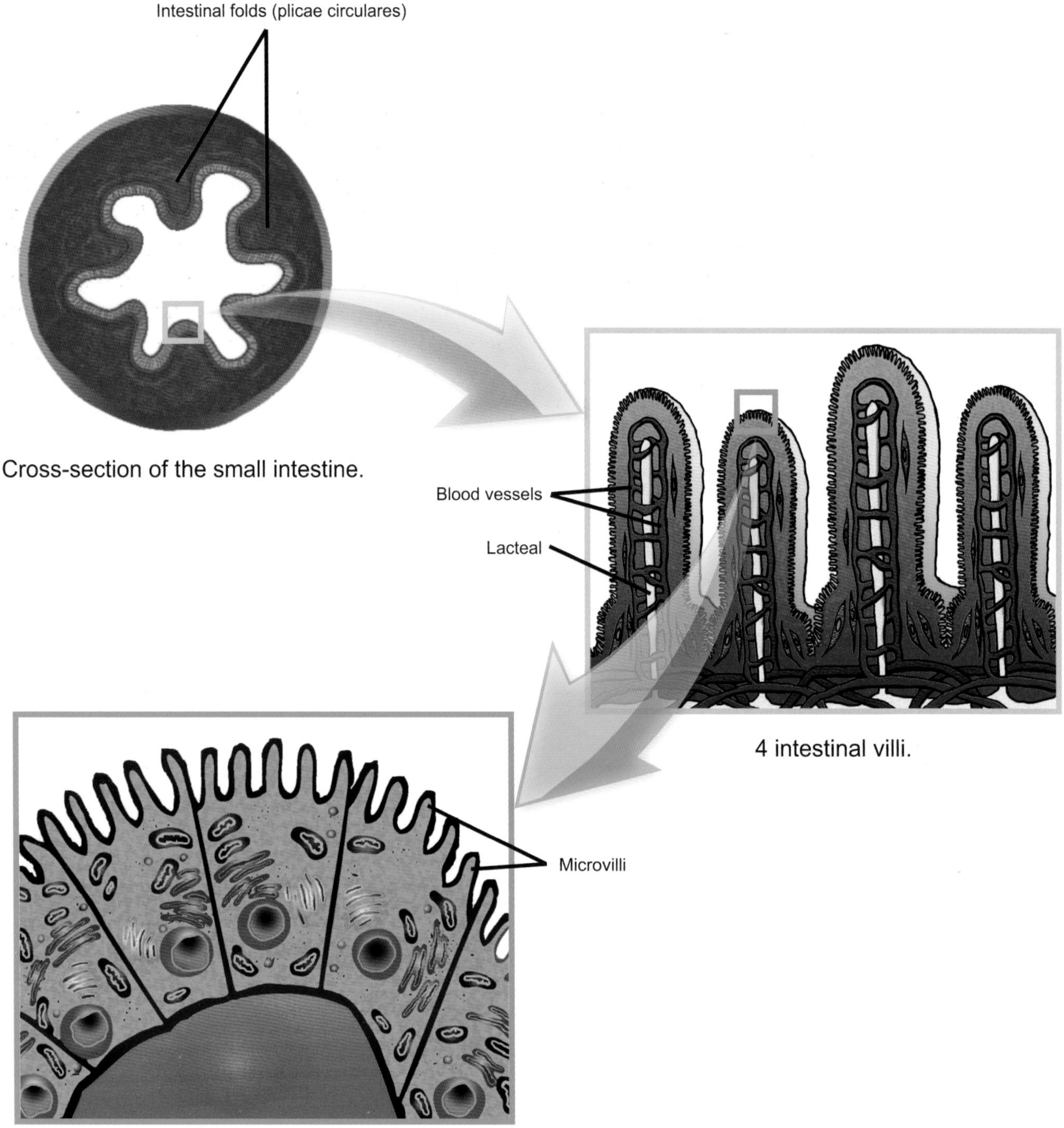

Cross-section of the small intestine.

4 intestinal villi.

Columnar cells (i.e. intestinal cells arranged in columns) with microvilli facing the lumen (brush border).

Figure IV.A.9.2: Levels of organization of the small intestine.

9.5.1 The Large Intestines

The large intestine is divided into: the cecum which connects to the ileum and projects a closed-ended tube - the appendix; the colon which is subdivided into ascending, transverse, descending, and sigmoid portions; the rectum which can store feces; and the anal canal which can expel feces (*defecation*) through the anus with the relaxation of the anal sphincter and the increase in abdominal pressure. The large intestine has little or no digestive functions. It absorbs water and electrolytes from the residual chyme and it forms feces. Feces is mostly water, undigested material, mucous, bile pigments (responsible for the characteristic color) and bacteria (= gut flora = 60% of the dry weight of feces).

Essentially, the relationship between the gut and bacteria is mutualistic and symbiotic (BIO 2.2). Though people can survive with no bacterial flora, these microorganisms perform a host of useful functions, such as fermenting unused energy substrates, training the immune system, preventing growth of harmful species, producing vitamins for the host (i.e. vitamin K), and bile pigments.

GOLD STANDARD WARM-UP EXERCISES

CHAPTER 9: The Digestive System

1) Cellulose is likely not broken down in the small intestine because:

   A. it is actively transported from the lumen of the intestine, across the epithelial lining, in the polysaccharide form.
   B. mastication, salivary amylase and enzymes in the upper part of the stomach completely break it down before it reaches the small intestine.
   C. humans do not possess the enzymes that break down cellulose.
   D. it is needed to propagate the necessary bacterial population in the large intestine.

2) In addition to starch, which of the following substances is also broken down by enzymes in the stomach?

   A. Glucose
   B. Fatty acids
   C. Protein
   D. Glycerol

3) After a meal rich in carbohydrates, monosaccharides are likely transported across the epithelium primarily by:

   A. diffusion.
   B. exocytosis.
   C. endocytosis.
   D. carrier mediated transport.

4) From the lumen of the small intestine, fat products are absorbed by and transported to:

   A. bile salts and the liver, respectively.
   B. bile salts and the lymphatic system, respectively.
   C. lacteals directly to the liver.
   D. lacteals and the lymphatic system, respectively.

5) Along with gastric acid, a zymogen exists in the stomach. The enzyme exists in this form in order to:

   A. prevent the enzyme's degradation while the stomach is empty.
   B. prevent the enzyme from neutralizing the gastric acid in the stomach.
   C. enhance the enzyme's activity.
   D. prevent the enzyme from digesting the cells which produce it.

6) A clogging of the bile duct interferes with the digestion of what category of food?

   A. Fats
   B. Fat soluble vitamins
   C. Triacyl glycerols
   D. All of the above

7) Extracts of the intestinal parasite Ascaris were found to contain irreversible non-competitive inhibitors of human enzymes. The enzymes were likely:

   A. HMG CoA synthetase and lyase.
   B. kinase and carboxypeptidase.
   C. trypsin and pepsin.
   D. hexokinase and vitamin D.

GS ANSWER KEY

CHAPTER 9

		Cross-Reference
1.	C	BIO 9.5; ORG 12.3.3; deduce
2.	C	BIO 9.3
3.	D	BIO 1.1.2
4.	D	BIO 9.5
5.	D	BIO 4.3, 9.3, 9.4
6.	D	BIO 9.4.1; ORG 12.4
7.	C	BIO 9.3, 9.4.2; cf BIO 4.1, 4.2

* Explanations can be found at the back of the book.

Go online to MCAT-prep.com/forum to join the discussion about our GS chapter review questions.

THE EXCRETORY SYSTEM

Chapter 10

Memorize	Understand	Clinical Correlation
Kidney structure: cortex, medulla Nephron structure: glomerulus, Bowman's capsule, proximal tubule, etc. Loop of Henle, distal tubule, collecting duct Storage and elimination: ureter, bladder, urethra	* Roles of the excretory system in homeostasis * Blood pressure, osmoregulation, acid-base balance, N waste removal * Formation of urine: glomerular filtration, secretion and reabsorption of solutes * Concentration of urine; counter-current multiplier mechanism	When the kidneys are damaged, waste products and fluid can build up in the body, causing ankle swelling, weakness, and shortness of breath. If left untreated diseased kidneys may eventually stop functioning completely thus requiring a substitute for its function such as dialysis or a kidney transplantation.

MCAT-Prep.com

Introduction

The excretory system excretes waste. The focus of this chapter is to examine the kidney's role in excretion. This includes eliminating nitrogen waste products of metabolism such as urea. Most excretory organs are discussed in other chapters of this book. In fact, the following is a mnemonic for excretory organs: SKILLs = Skin, Kidneys, Intestines, Liver, Lungs.

Optional Gold Standard Resources

Free Online Q&A + Forum

Online Videos

Flashcards

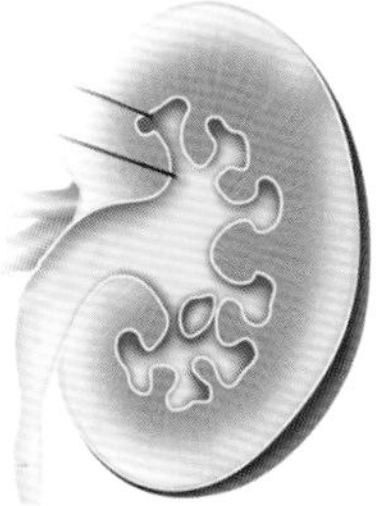

Special Guest

10.1 Overview

Excretion is the elimination of substances (usu. wastes) from the body. It begins at the level of the cell. Broken down red blood cells are excreted as bile pigments into the GI tract; CO_2, an end product of cellular aerobic respiration, is blown away in the lungs; urea and ammonia (NH_3), breakdown products of amino acid metabolism, creatinine, a product of muscle metabolism, and H_2O, a breakdown product of aerobic metabolism, are eliminated by the urinary system. In fact, the urinary system eliminates such a great quantity of waste it is often called the excretory system. It is composed of a pair of kidneys, a pair of ureters and one bladder and urethra.

The composition of body fluids remains within a fairly narrow range. The urinary system is the dominant organ system involved in electrolyte and water homeostasis (*osmoregulation*). It is also responsible for the excretion of toxic nitrogenous compounds (i.e. urea, uric acid, creatinine) and many drugs into the urine. The urine is produced in the kidneys (mostly by the filtration of blood) and is transported, with the help of peristaltic waves, down the tubular ureters to the muscular sack which can store urine, the bladder. Through the process of urination (= *micturition*), urine is expelled from the bladder to the outside via a tubular urethra.

The amount of volume within blood vessels (= *intravascular* or blood volume) and blood pressure are proportional to the rate the kidneys filter blood. Hormones act on the kidney to affect urine formation (see *Endocrine Systems*, BIO 6.3).

10.2 Kidney Structure

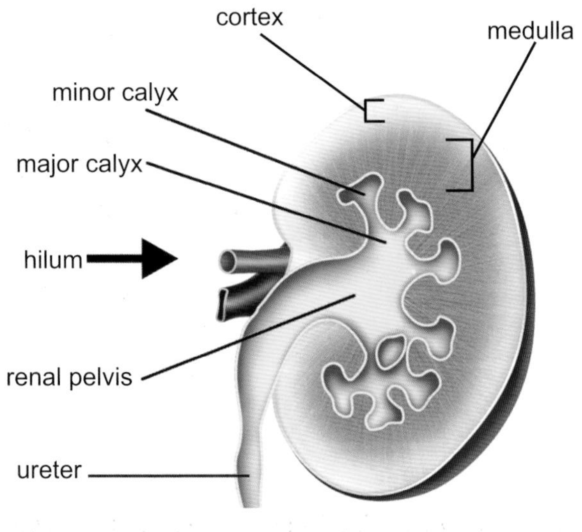

Figure IV.A.10.1: Kidney structure.

The kidney regulates the electrolyte levels in the extracellular fluid and maintains water homeostasis through the production and excretion of urine. The kidney resembles a bean with a concave border (= *the hilum*) where the ureter, nerves, and vessels (blood and lymph) attach. The kidney can be grossly divided into an outer granular-looking **cortex** and an inner dark striated **medulla**. The upper end of the ureter expands into the *renal pelvis* which can be divided into two or three *major calyces*. Each major calyx can be divided into several small branched *minor calyces*. The renal medulla lies deep to the cortex. It is composed of 10-18 medullary pyramids which consist mainly of loop of Henle and collecting tubules. The renal cortex is the superficial layer of the kidney right underneath the capsule. It is composed mainly of renal corpuscles and convoluted tubules.

The kidney is a *filtration-reabsorption-secretion* (excretion) organ. These events are clearly demonstrated at the level of the nephron.

10.3 The Nephron

The nephron is the functional unit of the kidney and consists of the **renal corpuscle** and the **renal tubule**. A renal corpuscle is responsible for the filtration of blood and is composed of a tangled ball of blood capillaries (= *the glomerulus*) and a sac-like structure which surrounds the glomerulus (= *Bowman's capsule*). *Afferent* and *efferent* arterioles lead towards and away from the glomerulus, respectively. The renal tubule is divided into *proximal* and *distal convoluted tubules* with a *loop of Henle* in between. The tube ends in a *collecting duct*.

Blood plasma is **filtered** by the glomerulus through three layers before entering Bowman's capsule. The first layer is formed by the *endothelial cells* of the capillary that possess small holes (= *fenestrae*); the second layer is the *glomerular basement membrane* (BIO 5.3); and the third layer is formed by the negatively charged cells (= *podocytes*) in Bowman's capsule which help repel proteins (most proteins are negatively charged).

The filtration barrier permits passage of water, ions, and small particles from the capillary into Bowman's capsule but prevents pas-

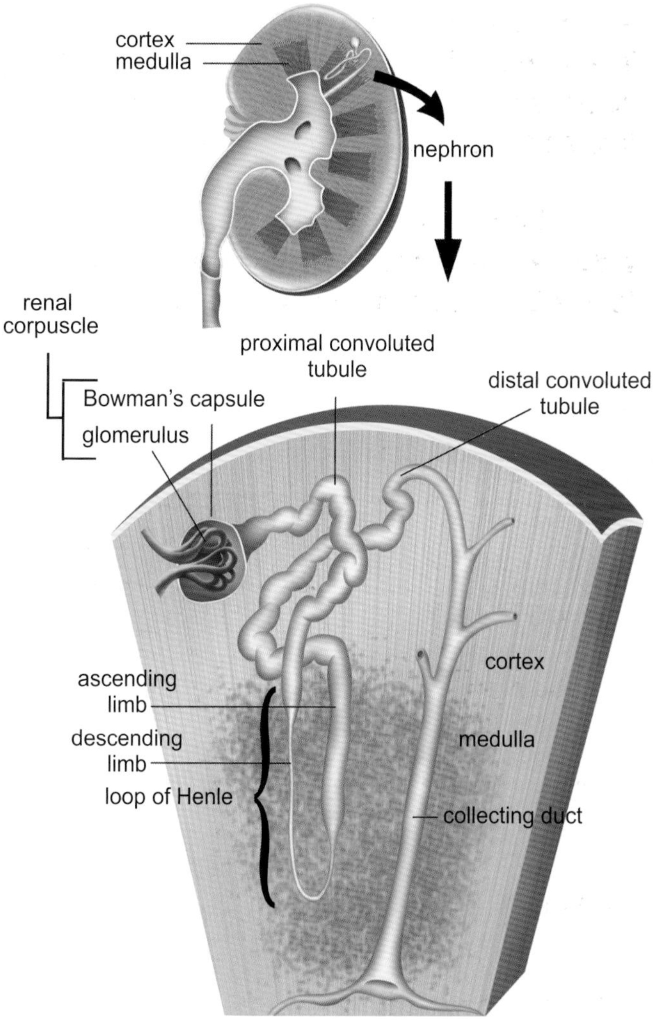

Figure IV.A.10.2: The kidney and its functional unit, the nephron.

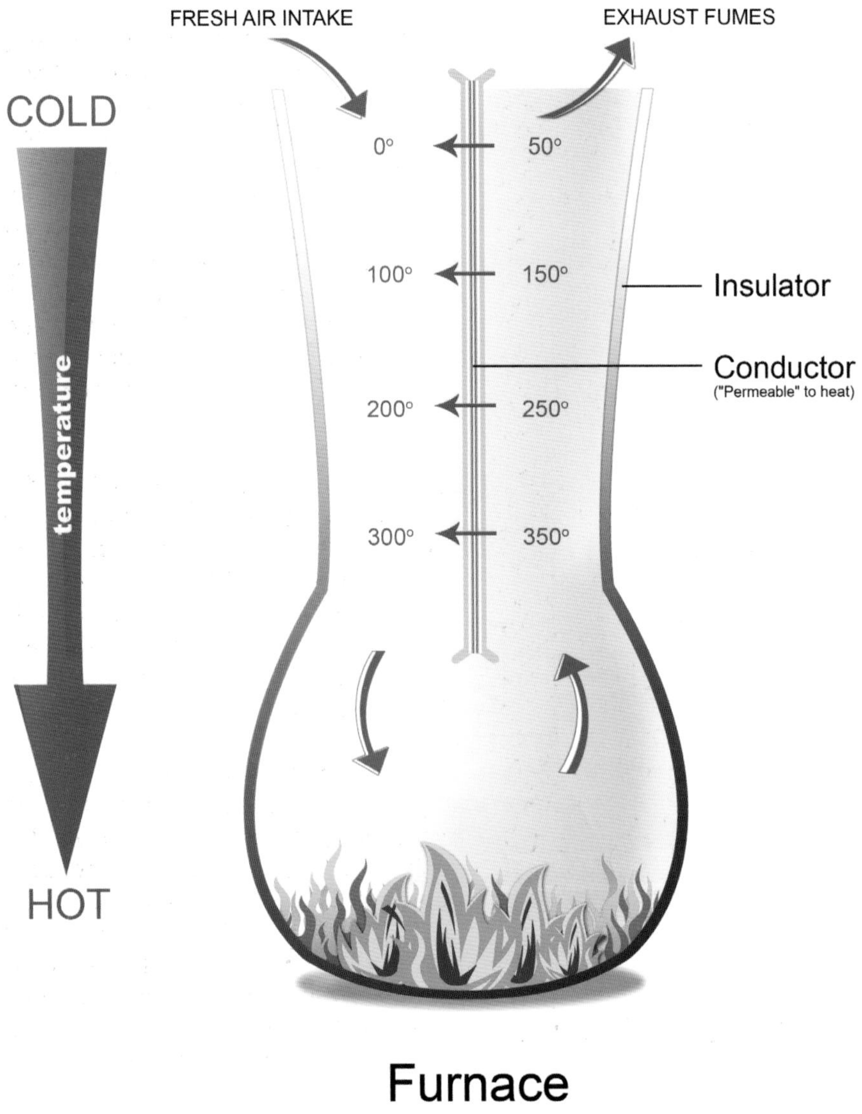

The countercurrent principle depends on a parallel flow arrangement moving in 2 different directions (countercurrent) in close proximity to each other. Our example is that of the air intake and exhaust pipe in this simplified schematic of a furnace.

Heat is transferred from the exhaust fumes to the incoming air.

The small horizontal temperature gradient of only 50° is multiplied longitudinally to a gradient of 300°. This conserves heath that would otherwise be lost.

Figure IV.A.10.3: The countercurrent principle (= counter-current mechanism) using a simplified furnace as an example.

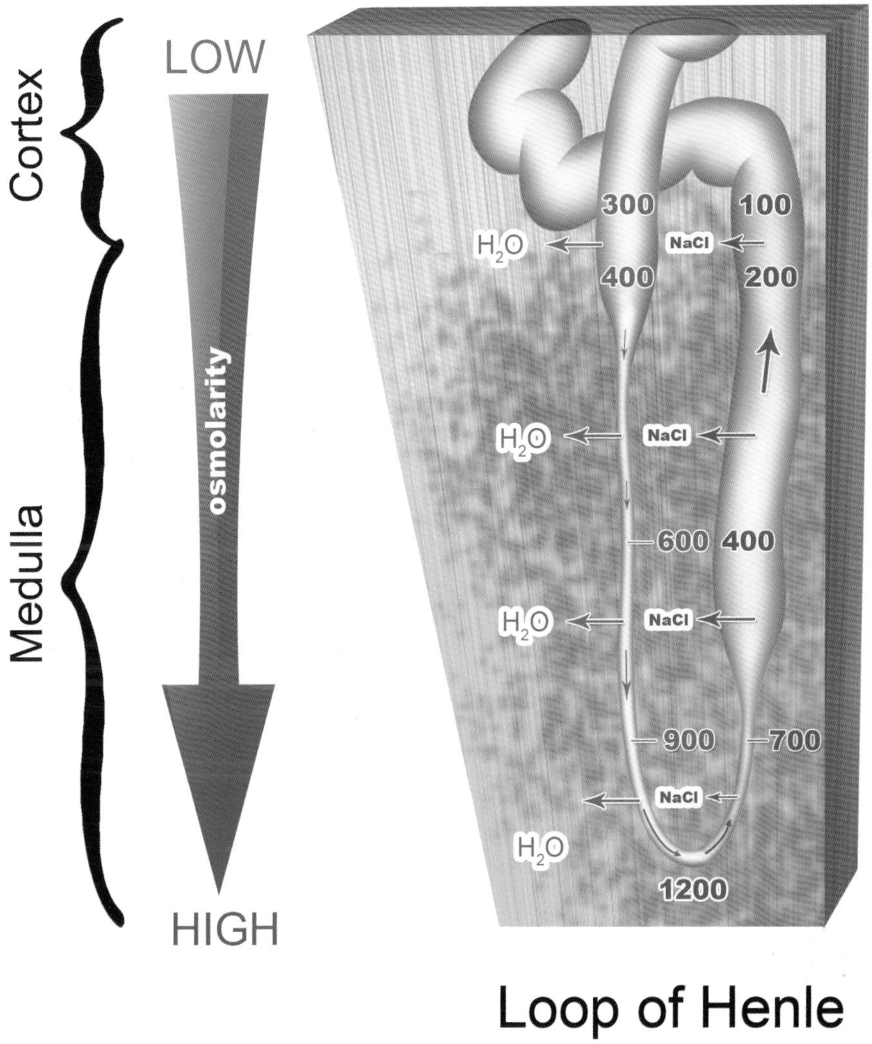

The countercurrent system involving the loop of Henle results in an osmotic gradient increasing from cortex to inner medulla (*juxtamedullary* nephrons). Solutes enter and exit at different segments of the nephron. The descending limb of the loop of Henle is highly permeable to water and relatively impermeable to NaCl (thus the filtrate becomes increasingly hypertonic). The ascending limb is impermeable to water but relatively (through active transport) permeable to NaCl.

Due to the increased osmolarity of the interstitial fluid, water moves out of the descending limb into the interstitial fluid by osmosis. Volume of the filtrate decreases as water leaves. Osmotic concentration of the filtrate increases (1200) as it rounds the hairpin turn of the loop of Henle.

Some of the NaCl leaving the ascending limb moves by diffusion into the descending limb from the interstitial fluid thus increasing the solute concentration in the descending limb. Also, new NaCl in the filtrate continuously enters the tubule inflow to be transported out of the ascending limb into the interstitial fluid. Thus this recycling multiplies NaCl concentration.

Figure IV.A.10.4: The countercurrent principle (= counter-current mechanism) in the loop of Henle.

sage of large/negatively charged particles (= *ultrafiltration*) and forms a filtrate in the Bowman's space. The rate of filtration is proportional to the net ultrafiltration pressure across the glomerular capillaries. This net pressure, which is usually positive and favors fluid filtration out of the capillary, can be derived from the difference between glomerular capillary hydrostatic pressure, which favors fluid out of the capillary, and the combined effect of glomerular capillary oncotic pressure and Bowman's space *hydrostatic* pressure, which favor fluid back into the capillary. {The oncotic pressure of Bowman's space is typically zero, so it is ignored here; keep in mind that 'oncotic pressure' is simply the osmotic pressure caused by proteins; see BIO 7.5.2}

The filtrate, which is similar to plasma but with minimal proteins, now passes into the proximal convoluted tubule (PCT). It is here that the body actively **reabsorbs** compounds that it needs (i.e. proteins, amino acids, and especially glucose); and over 75% of all ions and water are reabsorbed by *obligate* (= required) reabsorption from the PCT. To increase the surface area for absorption, the cells of the PCT have a lot of microvilli (= *brush border*, cf. BIO 1.2). Some substances like H^+, urea and penicillin are **secreted** into the PCT.

From the PCT the filtrate goes through the descending and ascending limbs of the loop of Henle which extend into the renal medulla. The purpose of the loop of Henle is to concentrate the filtrate by the transport of ions (Na^+ and Cl^-) into the medulla which produces an osmotic gradient (= *a countercurrent mechanism*). As a consequence of this system, the medulla of the kidney becomes concentrated with ions and tends to "pull" water out of the renal tubule by osmosis.

The filtrate now passes on to the distal convoluted tubule (DCT) which reabsorbs ions actively and water passively and secretes various ions (i.e. H^+). Hormones can modulate the reabsorption of substances from the DCT (= *facultative* reabsorption). Aldosterone acts at the DCT to absorb Na^+ which is coupled to the secretion of K^+ and the passive retention of H_2O.

Finally the filtrate, now called urine, passes into the collecting duct which drains into larger and larger ducts which lead to renal papillae, calyces, the renal pelvis, and then the ureter. ADH concentrates urine by increasing the permeability of the DCT and the collecting ducts allowing the medulla to draw water out by osmosis. Water returns to the circulation via a system of vessels called the *vasa recta*.

Renin is a hormone (BIO 6.3.5) which is secreted by cells that are "near the glomerulus" (= *juxtaglomerular cells*). At the beginning of the DCT is a region of modified tubular cells which can influence the secretion of renin (= *macula densa*). The juxtaglomerular cells and the macula densa are collectively known as the juxtaglomerular apparatus.

10.4 The Bladder

Urine flow through the ureters to the bladder is propelled by muscular contractions of the ureter wall - peristalsis. The urine is stored in the bladder and intermittently ejected during urination, termed micturition.

The bladder is a balloon-like chamber with walls of muscle collectively termed the detrusor muscle. The contraction of this muscle squeezes the urine into the lumen (= *space inside*) of the bladder to produce urination. That part of the detrusor muscle at the base of the bladder, where the urethra begins, functions as a sphincter - the internal urethral sphincter. Beyond the outlet of the urethra is the external urethral sphincter, the contraction of which can prevent urination even when the detrusor muscle contracts strongly.

The basic micturition reflex is a spinal reflex (BIO 6.1.3), which can be influenced by descending pathways from the brain. The bladder wall contains stretch receptors whose afferent fibers enter the spinal cord and stimulate the parasympathetic nerves that supply and stimulate the detrusor muscle. As the bladder fills with urine, the pressure within it increases and the stretch receptors are stimulated, thereby reflexively eliciting stimulation of the parasympathetic neurons and contractions of the detrusor muscle. When the bladder reaches a certain volume, the induced contraction of the detrusor muscle becomes strong enough to open the internal urethral sphincter. Simultaneously, the afferent input from the stretch receptors inhibits, within the spinal cord, the motor neurons that tonically stimulate the external urethral sphincter to contract. Both sphincters are now open and the contraction of the detrusor muscle is able to produce urination.

In summary:

- The internal sphincter is a continuation of the detrusor muscle and is thus composed of smooth muscle under involuntary or autonomic control. This is the primary muscle for preventing the release of urine.
- The external sphincter is made of skeletal muscle is thus under voluntary control of the somatic nervous system (BIO 6.1.4, 6.1.5, 11.2).

GOLD STANDARD WARM-UP EXERCISES

CHAPTER 10: The Excretory System

1) The functional unit of the kidney is the:

A. renal corpuscle.
B. Bowman's capsule.
C. major calyx.
D. nephron.

2) Through the process of micturition, urine is expelled from the bladder into the:

A. urethra.
B. ureter.
C. major calyx.
D. minor calyx.

3) In studies of the human body, which of the following terms is used to describe the first step in the production of urine?

A. Minor calyces
B. Glomerular filtration
C. Tubular reabsorption
D. Tubular secretion

4) In mammals, the primary function of the loop of Henle is:

A. bicarbonate reabsorption.
B. reabsorption of water.
C. ammonia secretion.
D. water secretion.

5) The internal urethral sphincter is:

A. closed when the detrusor muscle is relaxed.
B. open when the detrusor muscle is relaxed.
C. not under the direct control of the detrusor muscle.
D. innervated directly by motor neurons extending from the descending pathways.

6) Which of the following is the countercurrent multiplier in the kidney?

A. Bowman's capsule around the glomerulus
B. The proximal convoluted tubules
C. The loop of Henle of a juxtamedullary nephron
D. The vasa recta

7) Relative to the capillaries, the fluid in the descending limb of the loop of Henle is which of the following?

A. Strongly hypotonic
B. Weakly hypotonic
C. Hypertonic
D. Isotonic

8) Most tubular reabsorption occurs at the level of the:

A. glomerulus.
B. proximal convoluted tubule.
C. loop of Henle.
D. distal convoluted tubule.

9) The internal and external urethral sphincters consist of:

A. skeletal and smooth muscle, respectively.
B. skeletal muscle and connective tissue, respectively.
C. smooth muscle and skeletal muscle, respectively.
D. smooth muscle and connective tissue, respectively.

GS ANSWER KEY

CHAPTER 10

		Cross-Reference			Cross-Reference
1.	D	BIO 10.3	6.	C	BIO 10.3
2.	A	BIO 10.1	7.	C	BIO 10.3
3.	B	BIO 10.3	8.	B	BIO 10.3, 1.1.1, 7.5.2
4.	B	BIO 10.3	9.	C	BIO 10.4, 11.2
5.	A	BIO 10.4			

*** Explanations can be found at the back of the book.**

Go online to MCAT-prep.com/forum to join the discussion about our GS chapter review questions.

THE MUSCULOSKELETAL SYSTEM
Chapter 11

Memorize

Structure of three basic muscle types: striated, smooth, cardiac
Voluntary/involuntary muscles; sympathetic/parasympathetic innervation
Basics: cartilage, ligaments, tendons
Bone basics: structure, calcium/protein matrix, growth

Understand

* Muscle system, important functions
* Support, mobility, peripheral circulatory assistance, thermoregulation (shivering reflex)
* Control: motor neurons, neuromuscular junctions, motor end plates
* Skeletal system: structural rigidity/support, calcium storage, physical protection
* Skeletal structure: specialization of bone types, basic joint, endo/exoskeleton

Clinical Correlation

Disorders of the musculoskeletal system represent one of the leading causes of disability in the US. Sudden exertion, repetitive strain and awkward posture can result in pain without visible signs of injury. The total cost for treating these disorders is estimated to be more than $125 billion per year.

MCAT-Prep.com

Introduction

The musculoskeletal system (= locomotor system) permits the movement of organisms with the use of muscle and bone. Other uses include providing form and stability for the organism; protection of vital organs (i.e. skull, rib cage); storage for calcium and phosphorous as well as containing a critical component to the production of blood cells (skeletal system).

Optional Gold Standard Resources

Free Online Q&A + Forum

Flashcards

Special Guest

11.1 Overview

The musculoskeletal system supports, protects and enables body parts to move. Muscles convert chemical energy (i.e. ATP, creatine phosphate) into mechanical energy (→ contraction). Thus body heat is produced, body fluids are moved (i.e. lymph), and body parts can move in accordance with lever systems of muscle and bone.

11.2 Muscle

There are many general features of muscle. A latent period is the lag between the stimulation of a muscle and its response. A twitch is a single contraction in response to a brief stimulus which lasts for a fraction of a second. Muscles can either *contract* or *relax* but they cannot actively expand. When muscles are stimulated frequently, they cannot fully relax - this is known as *summation.* Tetany is a sustained contraction (a summation of multiple contractions) that lacks even partial relaxation. If tetany is maintained, the muscle will eventually fatigue or tire. Muscle tone (*tonus*) occurs because even when a muscle appears to be at rest, some degree of sustained contraction is occurring.

The cellular characteristics of muscle have already been described (*see Contractile Cells and Tissues,* BIO 5.2). We will now examine the gross features of the three basic muscle types.

Cardiac muscle forms the walls of the heart and is responsible for the pumping action. Its contractions are continuous and are initiated by inherent mechanisms (i.e., they are myogenic) and modulated by the autonomic nervous system. Its activity is decreased by the parasympathetic nervous system and increased by the sympathetic nervous system. The sinoatrial node (SA node) or *pacemaker* contains specialized cardiac muscle cells in the right atrium which initiate the contraction of the heart (BIO 7.2). The electrical signal then progresses to the atrioventricular node (AV node) in the cardiac muscle (myocardium) - between the atria and ventricles - then through the bundle of His which splits and branches out to Purkinje fibers which can then stimulate the contraction of the ventricles (systole; BIO 7.2).

Smooth Muscle has two forms. One type occurs as separate fibers and can contract in response to motor nerve stimuli. These are found in the iris (*pupillary dilation or constriction*) and the walls of blood vessels (*vasodilation or constriction).* The second and more dominant form occurs as sheets of muscle fibers and is sometimes called *visceral muscle*. It forms the walls of many hollow visceral organs like the stomach, intestines, uterus, and the urinary bladder. Like cardiac muscle, its contractions are inherent, involuntary, and rhythmic. Visceral muscle is responsible for peristalsis. Its contractility is usually slow and can be modulated by the autonomic nervous system, hormones, and local metabolites. The activity of visceral muscle is increased by the parasympathetic nervous system and decreased by the sympathetic nervous system.

Skeletal muscle is responsible for voluntary movements. This includes the skeleton and organs such as the tongue and the globe of the eye. Its cells can form a syncytium which is a mass of cells which merge and can function together. Thus skeletal muscle can contract and relax relatively rapidly (*see the Reflex Arc,* BIO 6.1.3).

It should be noted that there are 2 meanings of the word "syncytium" when describing muscle cells. A classic example is the formation of large multinucleated skeletal muscle cells produced from the fusion of thousands of individual muscle cells (= *myocytes*) as alluded to in the previous paragraph ("true syncytium"). However, "syncytium" can also refer to cells that are interconnected by gap junctions (BIO 1.4), as seen in cardiac muscle cells and certain smooth muscle cells, and are thus synchronized electrically during an action potential ("functional syncytium").

Most skeletal muscles act across joints. Each muscle has a movable end (= *the insertion*) and an immovable end (= *the origin*). When a muscle contracts its insertion is moved towards its origin. When the angle of the joint decreases it is called flexion, when it increases it is called extension. Abduction is movement away from the midline of the body and adduction is movement toward the midline. {Adduction is addicted to the middle (= midline)}

Muscles which assist each other are synergistic (for example: while the deltoid muscle abducts the arm, other muscles hold the shoulder steady). Muscles that can move a joint in opposite directions are antagonistic (for example: at the elbow the biceps can flex while the triceps can extend).

Control of skeletal muscle originates in the cerebral cortex. Skeletal muscle is innervated by the somatic nervous system. Motor (*efferent*) neurons carry nerve impulses from the CNS to synapse with muscle fibers at the *neuro-muscular junction*. The terminal end of the motor neuron (motor end plate) can secrete

Skeletal muscle

acetylcholine which can depolarize the muscle fiber (BIO 5.1, 5.2). One motor neuron can depolarize many muscle fibers (= *a motor unit*).

The autonomic nervous system can supply skeletal muscle with more oxygenated blood in emergencies (sympathetic response) or redirect the blood to the viscera during relaxed states (parasympathetic response).

Skeletal muscle can be categorized as Type I or Type II. Type I fibers (= *cells*) appear red because of the oxygen-binding protein myoglobin (BIO 7.5.1). These fibers are suited for endurance and are slow to fatigue since they use oxidative metabolism to generate ATP (BIO 4.7-4.10). Type II fibers are white due to the absence of myoglobin and a reliance on glycolytic enzymes (BIO 4.5, 4.6). These fibers are efficient for short bursts of speed and power and use both oxidative metabolism and anaerobic metabolism depending on the particular sub-type. Type II myocytes are quicker to fatigue.

11.3 The Skeletal System

The microscopic features of bone and cartilage have already been described (*see Connective Cells and Tissues*, BIO 5.4.3/4). We will now examine the relevant gross features of the skeletal system.

The bones of the skeleton have many functions: i) acting like levers that aid in **body movement**; ii) the **storage** of inorganic salts like calcium and phosphorus (and to a lesser extent sodium and magnesium); iii) the production of blood cells (**= hematopoiesis**) in the metabolically active red marrow of the spongy parts of many bones. Bone also has a yellow marrow which contains fat storage cells.

11.3.1 Bone Structure and Development

Bone structure can be classified as follows: i) long bones which have a long shaft, the diaphysis, that is made up mostly of compact bone and expanded ends, like arm and leg bones; ii) short bones which are shaped like long bones but are smaller and have only a thin layer of compact bone surrounding a spongy bone interior; iii) flat bones which have broad surfaces like the skull, ribs, and the scapula and have two layers of compact bones with a layer of spongy bone in the middle; iv) irregular bones like the vertebrae and many facial bones and consist of a thin layer of compact bone covering a spongy bone

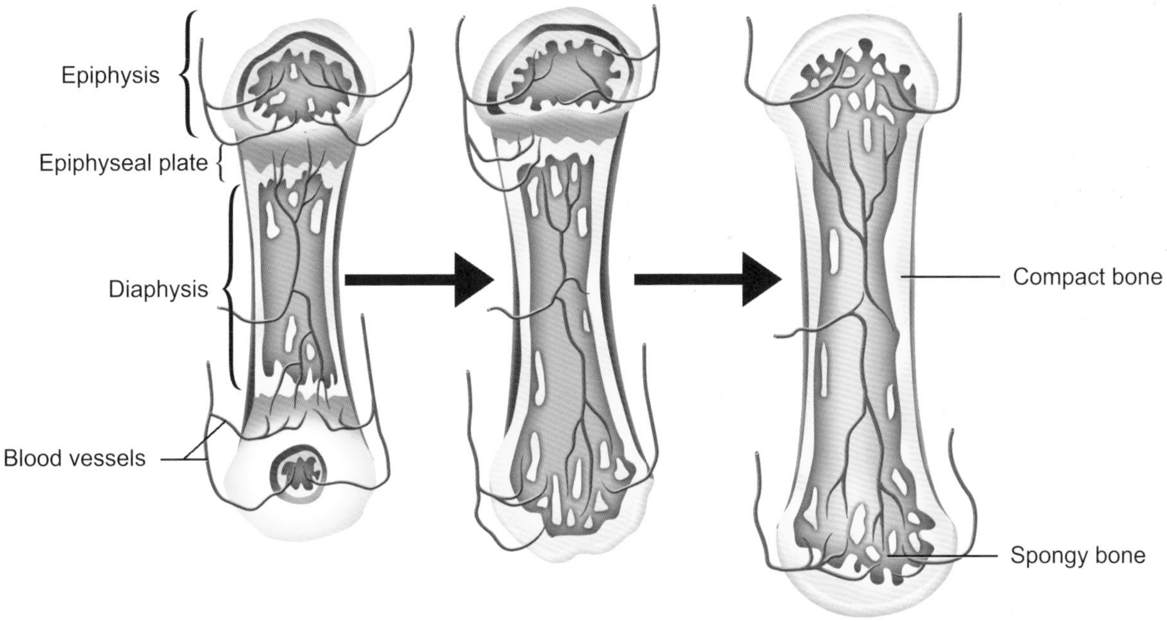

Figure IV.A.11.1: Bone structure and development.

interior. Bone structure can also be classified as: i) primary bone, also known as immature or woven bone, which contains many cells and has a low mineral content; ii) secondary bone, also known as mature or lamellar bone, which has a calcified matrix arranged in regular layers, or lamella.

The rounded expanded end of a long bone is called the *epiphysis* which contains spongy bone. The epiphysis is covered by fibrous tissue (*the periosteum*) and it forms a joint with another bone. Spongy bone contains bony plates called *trabeculae* (= *spicules)*. The shaft of the bone which connects the expanded ends is called the *diaphysis.* It is predominately composed of compact bone. This kind of bone is very strong and resistant to bending and has no trabeculae or bone marrow cavities.

Animals that fly have less dense, more light bones (spongy bone) in order to facilitate flying. Animals that swim do not need to have as strong bones as land animals as the buoyant force of the water takes away from the everyday stress on the bones. In the adult, yellow marrow is likely to be found in the diaphysis while red marrow is likely to be found in the epiphysis.

Bone growth occurs in two ways, intramembranous and endochondral bone formation. Both formations produce bones that are histologically identical. Intramembranous bone formation begins as layers of membranous connective tissue, which are later calcified by osteoblasts. Most of the flat bones are formed by this process. Endochondral bone formation is the process by which most of long bones are formed. It begins with hyaline cartilage that functions as a template for the bone to grow on.

Vascularizaton of the cartilage causes the transformation of cartilage cells to bone cells (osteoblasts), which later form a cartilage-calcified bone matrix. The osteoblasts continue to replace cartilage with bone and the osteoclasts create perforations to form bone marrow cavities. In children one can detect an **epiphyseal growth plate** on X-ray. This plate is a disk of cartilage between the epiphysis and diaphysis where bone is being actively deposited (= *ossification*).

11.3.2 Joint Structure

Articulations or joints are junctions between bones. They can be **immovable** like the dense connective tissue sutures which hold the flat bones of the skull together; **partly movable** like the hyaline and fibrocartilage joints on disks of the vertebrae; or **freely movable** like the synovial joints which are the most prominent joints in the skeletal system. Synovial joints contain a joint capsule composed of outer ligaments and an inner layer (= *the synovial membrane*) which secretes a lubricant (= *synovial fluid*).

Freely movable joints can be of many types. For example, ball and socket joints have a wide range of motion, like the shoulder and hip joints. On the other hand, hinge joints allow motion in only one plane like a hinged door (i.e. the knee, elbow, and interphalangeal joints).

11.3.3 Cartilage

The microscopic aspects of cartilage have already been discussed (*see Dense Connective Tissue*, BIO 5.4.2/3). Opposing and mobile surfaces of bone are covered by various forms of cartilage. As already mentioned, joints with hyaline or fibrocartilage allow little movement.

Ligaments attach bone to bone. They are formed by dense bands of fibrous connective tissue which reinforce the joint capsule and help to maintain bones in the proper anatomical arrangement.

Tendons connect muscle to bone. They are formed by the densest kind of fibrous connective tissue. Tendons allow muscular forces to be exerted even when the body (*or belly*) of the muscle is at some distance from the action.

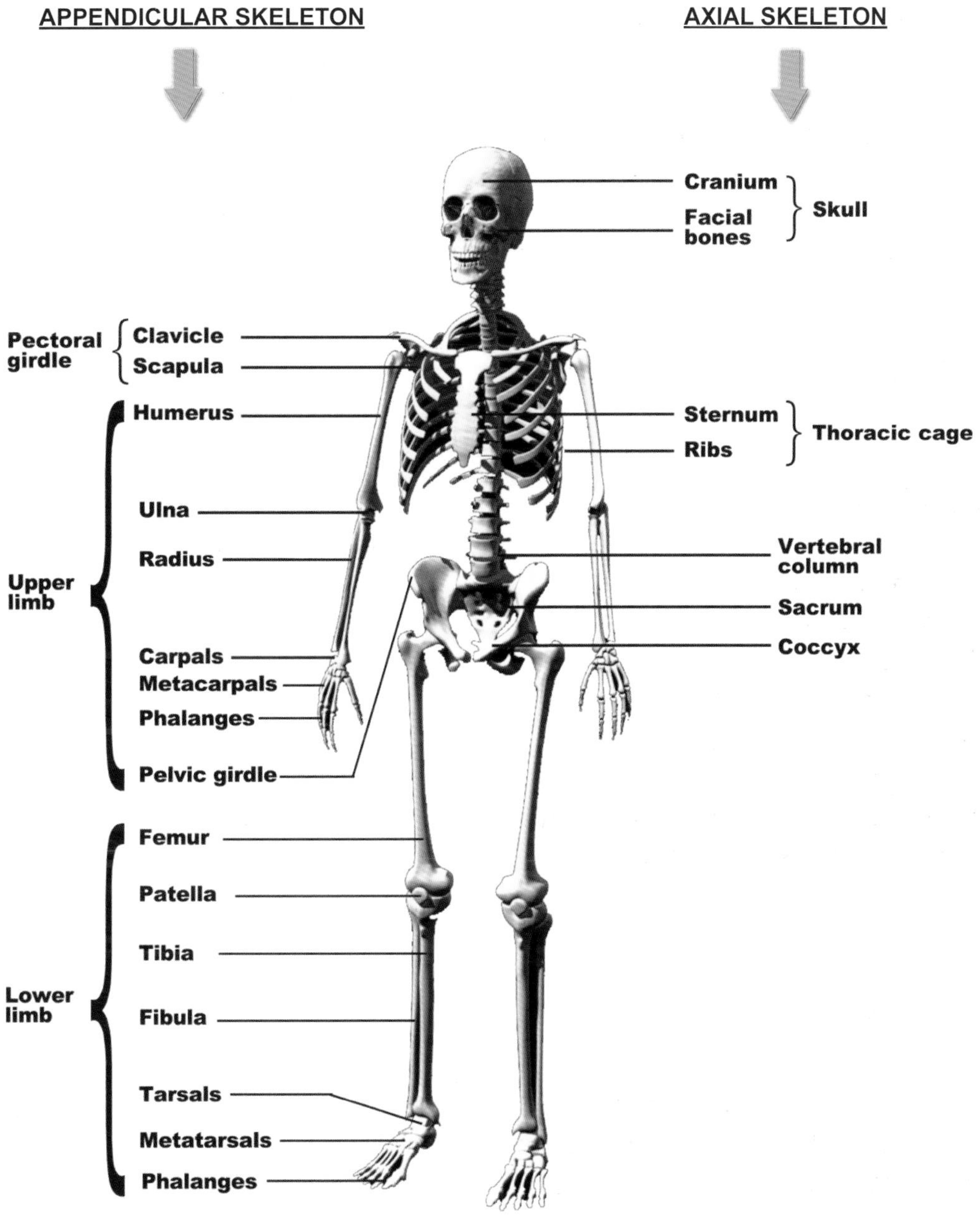

Figure IV.A.11.2: Skeletal structure. Note: in brackets some common relations - scapula (shoulder blade), clavicle (collarbone), carpals (wrist), metacarpals (palm), phalanges (fingers), tibia (shin), patella (kneecap), tarsals (ankle), metatarsals (foot), phalanges (toes), vertebral column (backbone). Note that the appendicular skeleton includes the bones of the appendages and the pectoral and pelvic girdles. The axial skeleton consists of the skull, vertebral column, and the rib cage.

GOLD STANDARD WARM-UP EXERCISES

CHAPTER 11: The Musculoskeletal System

1) As red muscle fibers go from a resting state to a rapidly contracting state, which of the following occurs?

   A. Increased rate of consumption of oxygen
   B. Decreased rate of production of carbon dioxide
   C. Decreased rate of hydrolysis of ATP
   D. Decreased rate of degradation of glucose

2) Suppose that the oxygen supply to continuously contracting red muscles fibers is abruptly cut off. Which of the following processes would occur in the muscles?

   A. Increased rate of synthesis of muscle glycogen
   B. Increased rate of production of ATP
   C. Increased rate of production of carbon dioxide
   D. Increased rate of production of lactic acid

3) Which of the following metabolic processes predominates in rapidly contracting white muscle fibers?

   A. Oxidative phosphorylation
   B. Alcoholic fermentation
   C. Glycolysis
   D. Krebs Citric Acid Cycle reaction

4) Cartilage is likely to be found in all the following adult tissues EXCEPT:

   A. bronchus.
   B. tendons and sternum.
   C. pinna of the ear.
   D. between the epiphysis and diaphysis of long bones.

5) Which of the following refers to a continuous partial contraction of a muscle?

   A. Tetany
   B. Tonus
   C. Twitch
   D. Pacemaker

6) Skeletal muscle is connected to bones by:

   A. joints.
   B. ligaments.
   C. tendons.
   D. loose connective tissue.

7) A joint that allows motion in only one plane (i.e. the knee, elbow) is called a:

   A. ball and socket joint.
   B. synovial joint.
   C. hinged joint.
   D. prominent joint.

8) Which of the following joints is formed by the articulation of the tibia, the malleolus of the fibula, and the tarsals?

A. Ankle
B. Knee
C. Hip
D. Wrist

9) Which of the following is NOT a component of the human axial skeleton?

A. Tarsals
B. Sternum
C. Vertebral column
D. Skull

10) Phalanges are found in the:

A. skull.
B. hip.
C. feet.
D. chest.

GS ANSWER KEY

CHAPTER 11

		Cross-Reference			Cross-Reference
1.	A	BIO 11.2, 4.5, 5.2	6.	C	BIO 11.3.3
2.	D	BIO 11.2, 4.5, 5.2	7.	C	BIO 11.3.2
3.	C	BIO 11.2, 4.5, 5.2	8.	A	BIO 11.3.2, 11.3.3
4.	D	BIO 5.4.3, 11.3.1	9.	A	BIO 11.3.3
5.	B	BIO 11.2	10.	C	BIO 11.3.3

*** Explanations can be found at the back of the book.**

Go online to MCAT-prep.com/forum to join the discussion about our GS chapter review questions.

Chapter 12

Memorize

Basic anatomy and order

Understand

* Basic functions: gas exchange, thermoregulation, . . .
* Protection against disease, particulate matter
* Breathing mechanisms: diaphragm, rib cage, differential pressure
* Resiliency and surface tension effects
* The carbonic-acid-bicarbonate buffer
* Henry's Law

Clinical Correlation

Chronic obstructive pulmonary disease (COPD) includes chronic bronchitis and emphysema (major cause: smoking). It is a progressive disease that makes it increasingly difficult to breath. Asthma is marked by spasms of the bronchi and it is like an allergic reaction against one's own airways. Currently, there is no cure for COPD and asthma.

MCAT-Prep.com

Introduction

The respiratory system permits the exchange of gases with the organism's environment. This critical process occurs in the microscopic space between alveoli and capillaries. It is here where molecules of oxygen and carbon dioxide passively diffuse between the gaseous external environment and the blood.

Optional Gold Standard Resources

Free Online Q&A + Forum

Flashcards

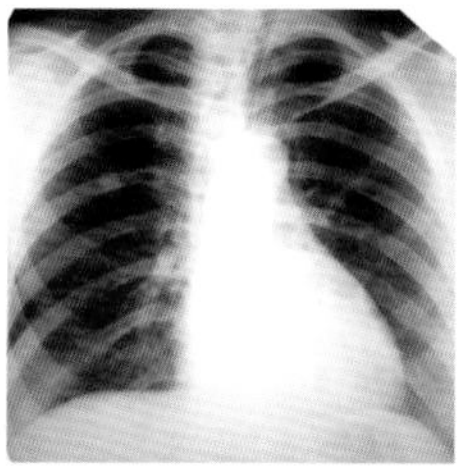

Special Guest

12.1 Overview

There are two forms of respiration: cellular respiration which refers to the oxidation of organic molecules (*see* BCM 3.4-3.7, 4.4-4.7) and mechanical respiration where the gases related to cellular respiration are exchanged between the atmosphere and the circulatory system (O_2 in and CO_2 out).

The respiratory system, which is concerned with mechanical respiration, has the following principal functions:

- providing a conducting system for the exchange of gases
- the filtration of incoming particles
- to help control the water content and temperature (= *thermoregulation*) of the incoming air
- to assist in speech production, the sense of smell, and the regulation of pH.

The respiratory system is composed of the lungs and a series of airways that connect the lungs to the external environment, deliver air to the lungs and perform gas exchange.

12.2 The Upper Respiratory Tract

The respiratory system can be divided into an *upper* and *lower respiratory tract* which are separated by the pharynx. The **upper respiratory tract** is composed of the nose, the nasal cavity, the sinuses, and the nasopharynx. This portion of the respiratory system warms, moistens and filters the air before it reaches the lower respiratory system. The nose (*nares*) has receptors for the sense of smell. It is guarded by hair to entrap coarse particles. The nasal cavity, the hollow space behind the nose, contains a ciliated mucous membrane (= a form of *respiratory epithelium*) to entrap smaller particles and prevent infection (this arrangement is common throughout the respiratory tract; for cilia *see the Generalized Eukaryotic Cell*, BIO 1.2). The nasal cavity adjusts the humidity and temperature of incoming air. The nasopharynx helps to equilibrate pressure between the environment and the middle ear via the eustachian tube (BIO 6.2.3).

12.3 The Lower Respiratory Tract

The **lower respiratory tract** is composed of the larynx which contains the vocal cords, the trachea which divides into left and right main bronchi which continue to divide into smaller airways (→ 2° bronchi → 3° bronchi → bronchioles → terminal bronchioles). The terminal bronchioles are the most distal part of the conducting portion of the respira-

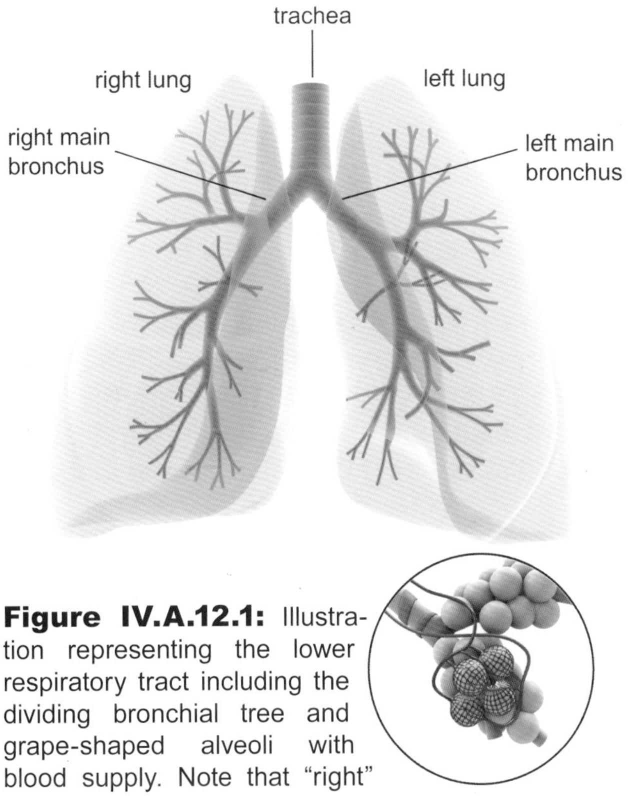

Figure IV.A.12.1: Illustration representing the lower respiratory tract including the dividing bronchial tree and grape-shaped alveoli with blood supply. Note that "right" refers to the patient's perspective which means the left side from your perspective.

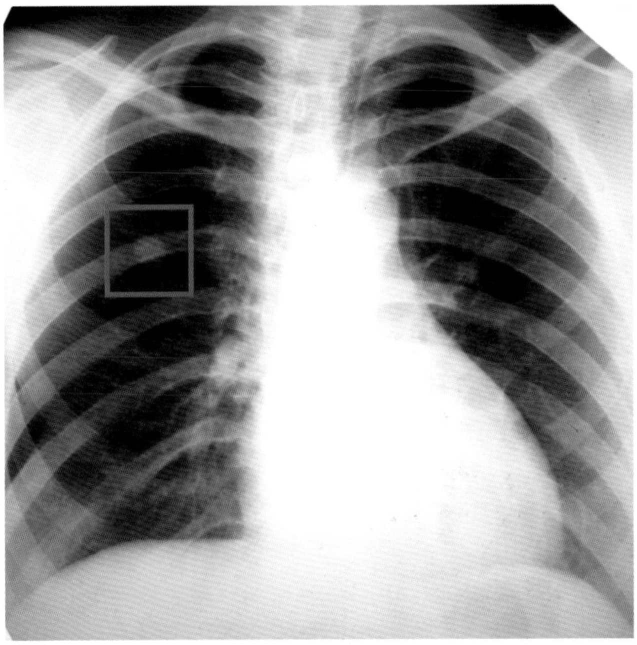

Figure IV.A.12.2: Chest x-ray of an adult male smoker. Notice the coin-shaped shadow in the right lung which presented with coughing blood. Further tests confirmed the presence of a right lung cancer. Cancer-causing chemicals (carcinogens) can irritate any of the cells lining the lower respiratory tract.

tory system. Starting from respiratory bronchioles → alveolar ducts → alveolar sacs until the level of the alveolus, these are considered the respiratory portion of respiratory system, where gas exchange takes place.

It is in these microscopic air sacs called *alveoli* that O_2 diffuses through the alveolar walls and enters the blood in nearby capillaries (where the concentration or *partial pressure* of O_2 is lowest and CO_2 is highest) and CO_2 diffuses from the blood through the walls to enter the alveoli (where the partial pressure of CO_2 is lowest and O_2 is highest). Gas exchange occurs by diffusion across the blood-gas barrier between the alveolar airspace and the capillary lumen. The blood-gas barrier is composed of three layers: type I pneumocyte cells, fused basal laminae and the endothelium of capillaries. *Alveolar macrophages* are phagocytes which help to engulf particles which reach the alveolus. A *surfactant* is secreted into alveoli by special lung cells (*pneumocytes type II*). The surfactant reduces surface tension and prevents the fragile alveoli from collapsing.

Sneezing and coughing, which are reflexes mediated by the medulla, can expel particles from the upper and lower respiratory tract, respectively.

The **lungs** are separated into left and right and are enclosed by the diaphragm and the thoracic cage. It is covered by a membrane (= *pleura*) which secretes a lubricant to reduce friction while breathing. The lungs contain the air passages, nerves, alveoli, blood and lymphatic vessels of the lower respiratory tract.

12.4 Breathing: Structures and Mechanisms

Inspiration is active and occurs according to the following main events: i) nerve impulses from the phrenic nerve cause the muscular diaphragm to contract; as the dome shaped diaphragm moves downward, the thoracic cavity increases; ii) simultaneously, the intercostal (= *between ribs*) muscles and/or certain neck muscles may contract further increasing the thoracic cavity (the muscles mentioned here are called *accessory respiratory muscles* and under normal circumstances the action of the diaphragm is much more important); iii) as the size of the thoracic cavity increases, its internal pressure decreases leaving it relatively negative; iv) the relatively positive atmospheric pressure forces air into the respiratory tract thus inflating the lungs.

Expiration is passive and occurs according to the following main events: i) the diaphragm and the accessory respiratory muscles relax and the chest wall pushed inward; ii) the elastic tissues of the lung, thoracic cage, and the abdominal organs recoil to their original position; iii) this recoil increases the pressure within the lungs (making the pressure relatively positive) thus forcing air out of the lungs and passageways.

12.4.1 Control of Breathing

Though voluntary breathing is possible (!), normally breathing is involuntary, rhythmic, and controlled by the *respiratory center* in the medulla of the brain stem. The respiratory center is sensitive to pH of the cerebrospinal fluid (CSF). An increase in blood CO_2 or consequently, decrease in pH of the CSF, acts on the respiratory center and stimulates breathing, returning the arterial pCO_2 (partial pressure of carbon dioxide) back to normal. The increase in blood CO_2 and the decrease in pH are two interrelated events since CO_2 can be picked up by hemoglobin forming carbamino-hemoglobin (about 20%, BIO 7.5.1), but it can also be converted into carbonic acid by dissolving in blood plasma (about 5%) or by conversion in red blood cells by the enzyme *carbonic anhydrase* (about 75%). The reaction is summarized as follows:

$$CO_2 + H_2O \leftrightarrow \underset{\text{carbonic acid}}{H_2CO_3} \leftrightarrow \underset{\text{bicarbonate}}{HCO_3^-} + H^+$$

According to Henry's Law, the concentration of a gas dissolved in solution is directly proportional to its partial pressure. From the preceding you can see why the respiratory system, through the regulation of the partial pressure of CO_2 in blood, also helps in maintaining pH homeostasis (= a buffer). More generally, the carbonic-acid-bicarbonate buffer is the most important buffer for maintaining acid-base balance in the blood and helps to maintain pH around 7.4.

12.4.2 Henry's Law, Pop and The Bends

Higher gas pressure and lower temperature cause more gas to dissolve in a liquid. When a carbonated drink (soda/pop) is manufactured, water is chilled, optimally to just above freezing, in order to permit the maximum amount of carbon dioxide to dissolve. Then CO_2 is pumped in at high pressure, the pressure is maintained by closing the container (can or bottle), which forces the carbon dioxide to dissolve into the liquid, creating carbonic acid (Le Chatelier's principle; CHM 9.9) and giving 'pop' its tang. Flat soda tastes strange, or at least less pleasant, because of the loss of carbonic acid due to the release of carbon dioxide bubbles/fizz.

So pop is stored in a way to seal pressure, preventing gas escape and maintaining the supersaturation of CO_2 in the solvent. It is pressure and temperature that drive the outgassing process.

Diving underwater exposes the body to increasing pressure (PHY 6.1). A diving cylinder (scuba tank) is used to store and transport high pressure breathing gas. As the dive becomes deeper, inhaled gas is absorbed into body tissue in higher concentrations than normal (Henry's Law). Surfacing from a deep dive underwater, unused gases (inert) like nitrogen try to do the same thing in your bloodstream that happens when you open a container of pop. The release of these bubbles (outgassing) produces the symptoms of decompression sickness (= 'the bends') that can be painful or even fatal.

GOLD STANDARD WARM-UP EXERCISES

CHAPTER 12: The Respiratory System

1) All of the following are in the correct anatomic order EXCEPT:

   A. trachea --> larynx --> bronchus.
   B. bronchus --> bronchioles --> alveolar ducts.
   C. alveolar ducts --> alveolar sacs --> alveolus.
   D. nose --> nasal cavity --> nasopharynx.

2) The vocal cords form part of which of the following?

   A. Pharynx
   B. Larynx
   C. Trachea
   D. Bronchus

3) Which of the following can NOT engage in gas exchange?

   A. Alveolus
   B. Respiratory bronchiole
   C. Alveolar duct
   D. Terminal bronchiole

4) Which of the following secretes surfactant?

   A. Pneumocytes type I
   B. Pneumocytes type II
   C. Alveolar macrophage
   D. Alveolar adipocyte

5) Which of the following factors favors an increase in breathing rate?

   A. Increased blood carbon dioxide
   B. Decreased CSF acidity
   C. Increased CSF pH
   D. Increased blood oxygen

6) One of the the possible injuries during a high speed motor vehicle accident includes a traumatic hemothorax in which blood accumulates in the pleural cavity. With regards to a traumatic hemothorax, which of the following would be of greatest concern?

   A. High oxygenation due to spasms of the diaphragm
   B. Low oxygenation due to blood in the right bronchus
   C. High oxygenation due to hyperventilation
   D. Low oxygenation due to compression of the lung

7) The following are physiological systems which depend on stretch receptors EXCEPT:

   A. the circulatory system.
   B. the respiratory system.
   C. the endocrine system.
   D. the digestive system.

8) Active transport assumes particular importance in all but which of the following structures?

   A. Cells of the large intestine
   B. Alveoli
   C. Nerve and muscle cells
   D. Loop of Henle

GS ANSWER KEY

Chapter 12

		Cross-Reference
1.	A	BIO 12.2, 12.3
2.	B	BIO 12.3
3.	D	BIO 12.3
4.	B	BIO 12.3
5.	A	BIO 12.4.1
6.	D	BIO 12.3
7.	C	BIO 7.2-7.3, 9.1-9.3, 9.5, 12.3-12.4
8.	B	BIO 1.1.2, 12.3

*** Explanations can be found at the back of the book.**

Go online to MCAT-prep.com/forum to join the discussion about our GS chapter review questions.

APPENDIX

CHAPTER 12: The Respiratory System

Passage: Lung Function and Transpulmonary Pressure

The volume of air that flows into or out of an alveolus per unit time is directly proportional to the pressure difference between the atmosphere and alveolus and inversely proportional to the resistance to flow caused by the airways. During normal relaxed breathing, about 500 ml of air flows in and out of the lungs. This is the tidal volume. After expiration, approximately 2.5 liters of air remains in the lungs which is referred to as the functional residual capacity. A spirometer is an instrument for measuring air inhaled and exhaled; it provides a simple way of determining most of the lung volumes and capacities that are measured in pulmonary function tests. The

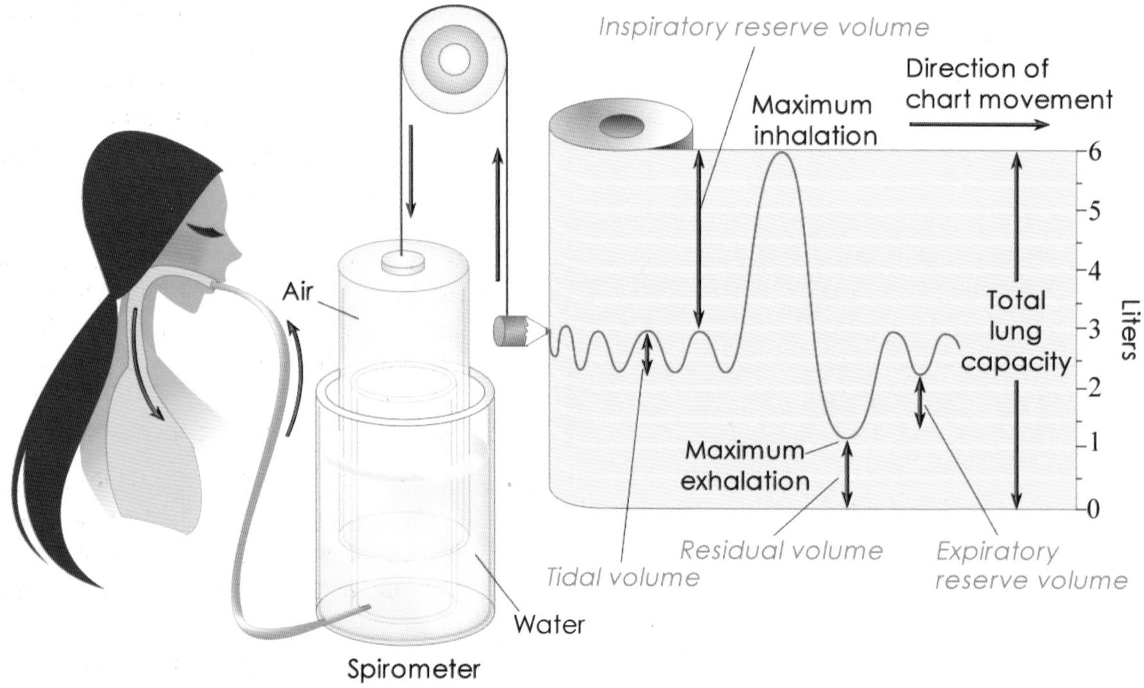

Figure IV.A.12.3: The four lung volumes measured by spirometer. Note that there are 4 key lung capacities: (1) the functional residual capacity which is the sum of the residual volume and the expiratory reserve volume (= ERV which is the maximum volume that can be exhaled following a normal quiet exhalation); (2) the vital capacity (VC) is the maximum volume that can be exhaled following a maximal inhalation; VC = inspiratory reserve volume (IRV) + tidal volume (VT) + ERV; (3) the inspiratory capacity (IC) is the maximum volume that can be inhaled following a normal quiet exhalation; IC = IRV + VT; (4) total lung capacity is the amount of air in the lung after maximal inhalation.

minute ventilation can be calculated as follows:

Minute ventilation =
Tidal volume x Respiratory rate

Airway resistance is: i) directly proportional to the magnitude of the viscosity between the flowing gas molecules; ii) directly proportional to the length of the airway; and iii) inversely proportional to the fourth power of the radius of the airway.

Resistance to air flow in the lung is normally small thus small pressure differences allow large volumes of air to flow. Physical, neural and chemical factors affect airway radii and therefore resistance. Transpulmonary pressure is a physical factor which exerts a distending force on the airways and alveoli. Such a force is critical to prevent small airways from collapsing.

The rate of respiration is primarily dependent on the concentration of carbon dioxide in the blood. As carbon dioxide levels rise, chemoreceptors in blood vessels are stimulated to discharge neuronal impulses to the respiratory center in the medulla oblongata in the brain stem. The respiratory center would then send impulses to the diaphragm causing an increase in the rate of contraction thus increasing the respiratory rate.

9) Given a resting respiratory rate of 12 breaths per minute, give an approximation of the minute ventilation.

A. 2.5 L/min
B. 5.0 L/min
C. 6.0 L/min
D. 30 L/min

10) Which of the following is consistent with the total lung capacity?

A. The amount of air inhaled and exhaled normally at rest
B. The sum of the residual volume and the expiratory reserve volume
C. The maximum volume that can be exhaled following a maximal inhalation
D. The maximum volume of air present in the lungs

11) During inspiration, transpulmonary pressure should:

A. increase, increasing airway radius and decreasing airway resistance.
B. increase, increasing airway radius and increasing airway resistance.
C. decrease, decreasing airway radius and decreasing airway resistance.
D. decrease, decreasing airway radius and increasing airway resistance.

12) Lateral traction refers to the process by which connective tissue fibers maintain airway patency by continuously pulling outward on the sides of the airways. As the lungs expand these fibers become stretched. Thus during inspiration lateral traction acts:

A. in the same direction as transpulmonary pressure, by increasing the viscosity of air.
B. in the opposite direction to transpulmonary pressure, by decreasing the viscosity of air.
C. in the same direction as transpulmonary pressure, by increasing the airway radius.
D. in the opposite direction to transpulmonary pressure, by increasing the airway radius.

13) The Heimlich Maneuver is used to aid individuals who are choking on matter caught in the upper respiratory tract through the application of a sudden abdominal pressure with an upward thrust. The procedure includes:

A. forcing the diaphragm downward, increasing thoracic size and causing a passive expiration.
B. forcing the diaphragm upward, increasing thoracic size and causing a forced expiration.
C. forcing the diaphragm upward, reducing thoracic size and causing a forced expiration.
D. forcing the diaphragm upward, increasing thoracic size and causing a passive expiration.

ANSWER KEY

ADVANCED TOPICS - CHAPTER 12

Cross-Reference

9. C Chap. 12 App.; P1, S3; dimensional analysis
10. D Chap. 12 App.
11. A BIO 12.4, Chap. 12 App. P2; P3, S2
12. C Chap. 12 App.; BIO 12.4
13. B BIO 12.4; deduce

P = paragraph; *S* = sentence; *E* = equation; *T* = table; *F* = figure

GOLD NOTES

THE SKIN AS AN ORGAN SYSTEM

Chapter 13

Memorize

Structure and function of skin, layer differentiation
Sweat glands, location in dermis

Understand

* Skin system: homeostasis and osmoregulation
* Functions in thermoregulation: hair, erectile musculature, fat layer for insulation
* Vasoconstriction and vasodilation in surface capillaries
* Physical protection: nails, calluses, hair; protection against abrasion, disease organisms
* Relative impermeability to water

Clinical Correlation

Autoimmune diseases attacking the skin can be as devastating as severe burns. Genetic disorders where children are born without the protein anchoring the epidermis to the dermis results in skin as fragile as butterfly wings ("Butterfly Children"; epidermolysis bullosa).

MCAT-Prep.com

Introduction

Skin is composed of layers of epithelial tissues which protect underlying muscle, bone, ligaments and internal organs. Thus skin has many roles including protecting the body from microbes, insulation, temperature regulation, sensation and synthesis of vitamin D.

Optional Gold Standard Resources

Free Online Q&A + Forum

Flashcards

Special Guest

13.1 Overview

The skin, or *integument*, is the body's largest organ. The following represents its major functions:

* **Physical protection:** The skin protects against the onslaught of the environment including uv light, chemical, thermal or even mechanical agents. It also serves as a barrier to the invasion of microorganisms.

* **Sensation:** The skin, being the body's largest sensory organ, contains a wide range of sensory receptors including those for pain, temperature, light touch, and pressure.

* **Metabolism:** Vitamin D synthesis can occur in the epidermis of skin (*see Endocrine Systems*, BIO 6.3). Also, energy is stored as fat in subcutaneous adipose tissue.

* **Thermoregulation and osmoregulation:** Skin is vital for the homeostatic mechanism of thermoregulation and to a lesser degree osmoregulation. Hair (*piloerection*, which can trap a layer of warm air against the skin's surface) and especially subcutaneous fat (*adipose tissue*) insulate the body against heat loss. Shivering, which allows muscle to generate heat, and decreasing blood flow to the skin (= *vasoconstriction*) are important in emergencies.

On the other hand, heat and water loss can be increased by increasing blood flow to the multitude of blood vessels (= *vasodilation*) in the dermis (cooling by radiation), the production of sweat, and the evaporation of sweat due to the heat at the surface of the skin; thus the skin cools. {Remember: the **hypothalamus** also regulates body temperature (*see The Nervous System*, BIO 6.1); it is like a thermostat which uses other organs as tools to maintain our body temperatures at about 37 °C (98.6 °F)}.

13.2 The Structure of Skin

Skin is divided into three layers: i) the outer **epidermis** which contains a stratified squamous keratinized epithelium; ii) the inner **dermis** which contains vessels, nerves, muscle, and connective tissues; iii) the innermost **subcutaneous layer**, known as hypodermis, which contains adipose and a loose connective tissue; this layer binds to any underlying organs.

The epidermis is divided into several different layers or *strata*. The deepest layer, *stratum basale*, contains actively dividing cells (keratinocytes) which are nourished by the vessels in the dermis. The mitotic activity of keratinocytes can keep regenerating epidermis approximately every 30 days. As these cells continue to divide, older epidermal cells are pushed towards the surface of the skin - *away from the nutrient providing dermal layer*; thus in time they die. Simultaneously, these cells are actively producing strands of a tough, fibrous, waterproof protein called keratin. This process is called *keratinization*. The two preceding events lead to the formation of an outermost layer (= *stratum corneum*) of keratin-filled dead cells which are devoid of organelles and are continuously shed by a process called *desquamation*.

Melanin is a dark pigment produced by cells (= *melanocytes*) whose cell bodies are usually found in the stratum basale. Melanin absorbs light thus protects against uv light induced cell damage (i.e. sunburns, skin cancer). Individuals have about the same number of melanocytes - regardless of race. Melanin production depends on genetic factors (i.e. race) and it can be stimulated by exposure to sunlight (i.e. tanning).

Langerhans cells have long processes and contain characteristic tennis-racket-shaped Birbeck granules. They function as antigen presenting cells in the immune response (BIO 8.2, 8.3).

Merkel cells are present in the richly innervated areas of stratum basale. They are responsible for receiving afferent nerve impulses and function as sensory mechanoreceptors (BIO 6.1.1).

The dermis is composed of dense irregular connective tissue including type I collagen fibers and a network of elastic fibers. It contains the blood vessels which nourish the various cells in the skin. It also contains motor fibers and many types of sensory nerve fibers such as fine touch receptors, pressure receptors and cold receptors.

13.3 Skin Appendages

The **appendages** of the skin include hair, sebaceous glands and sweat glands. Hair is a modified keratinized structure produced by a cylindrical downgrowth of epithelium (= *hair follicle*). The follicle extends into the dermis (sometimes the subcutaneous tissue as well). The arrector pili muscle attaches to the connective tissue surrounding a hair follicle. When this bundle of smooth muscle contracts (= *piloerection*), it elevates the hair and "goose bumps" are produced.

The sebaceous glands are lobular acinar glands that empty their ducts into the hair follicles. They are most abundant on the face, forehead and scalp. They release an oily/waxy secretion called sebum to lubricate and waterproof the skin.

Sweat glands can be classified as either eccrine sweat glands, which are simple tubular glands present in the skin throughout the body or apocrine sweat glands, which are large specialized glands located only in certain areas of the body (i.e. areola of the nipple, perianal area, axilla which is the "armpit") and will not function until puberty.

We have previously explored endocrine glands and saw how they secrete their products - without the use of a duct - directly into the bloodstream (BIO 6.3). Alternatively, endo-

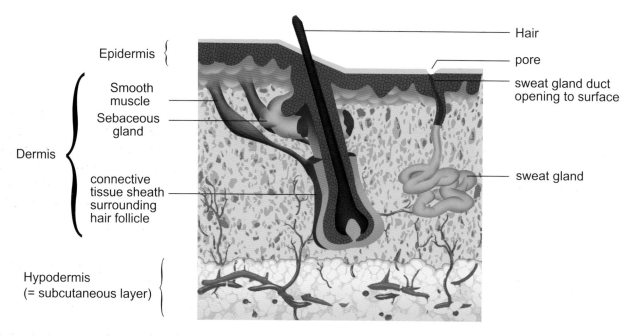

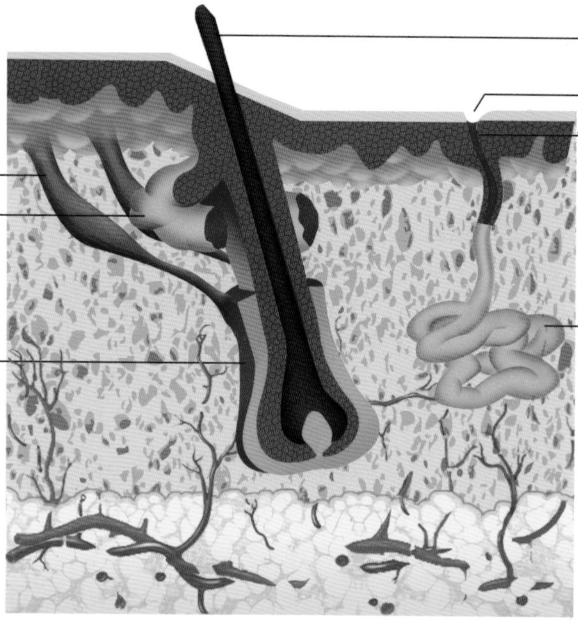

Figure IV.A.13.1: Skin structure with appendages.

crine products may diffuse into surrounding tissue (*paracrine signaling*) where they often affect only target cells near the release site.

An exocrine gland is distinguished by the fact that it excretes its product via a duct to some environment external to itself, either inside the body (BIO 9.3, 9.4) or on a surface of the body. Examples of exocrine glands include the sebaceous glands, sweat glands, salivary glands, mammary glands, pancreas and liver.

Holocrine (= *wholly secretory*) is a type of glandular secretion in which the entire secreting cell, along with its accumulated secretion, forms the secreted matter of the gland; for example, the sebaceous glands. Apocrine concentrates products at the free end of the secreting cell and are thrown off along with a portion of the cytoplasm (i.e. mammary gland, axilla). Eccrine, apocrine and holocrine are subdivisions of exocrine.

13.3.1 Nails, Calluses

Nails are flat, translucent, keratinized coverings near the tip of fingers and toes. They are useful for scratching and fine manipulation (including picking up dimes!).

A callus is a toughened, thickened area of skin. It is usually created in response to repeated friction or pressure thus they are normally found on the hands or feet.

GOLD STANDARD WARM-UP EXERCISES

CHAPTER 13: The Skin As An Organ

1) The skin, the body's largest organ, is divided into 3 layers including the epidermis. The latter contains a waterproof, tough protein called *keratin*. How then is it possible that humans can sweat freely in hot temperatures?

   A. Specialized sweat glands can secrete their products into channels which pass through the epidermis.

   B. Active and passive transport systems carry sweat across the epidermis.

   C. Specialized sebaceous glands can secrete their products into channels which pass through the epidermis.

   D. Osmotic pressure releases sweat across the epidermis.

2) Which of the following best describe why perspiring causes a reduction in body temperature?

   A. Perspiration carries heated water to the surface.

   B. Perspiration removes excess Na^+ and Cl^- ions from cells.

   C. Perspiration evaporates and cools skin.

   D. Perspiration causes vasoconstriction.

3) Which of the following is the best way to reduce body temperature?

   A. Increase kidney function.

   B. Constrict skeletal muscle.

   C. Reduce insulin levels.

   D. Relax smooth muscle of blood vessels.

4) Experiments have now confirmed that sweating only occurs as a result of a rise in core body temperature. Drinking iced water results in a lowering of core body temperature. Thus, exposing the skin to heat while drinking iced water would result in which of the following?

   A. An increase in sweating

   B. A decrease in sweating

   C. An increase in sweating followed by a decrease in sweating

   D. No change in sweat production

5) The name of the process by which oil glands in mammalian skins secrete oils is called:

   A. osmosis.

   B. active transport.

   C. apocrine secretion.

   D. holocrine secretion.

GS ANSWER KEY

CHAPTER 13

		Cross-Reference
1.	A	BIO 13.3
2.	C	BIO 13.1
3.	D	BIO 13.1, 7.3
4.	B	BIO 7.1, 13.1
5.	D	BIO 13.3

*** Explanations can be found at the back of the book.**

Go online to MCAT-prep.com/forum to join the discussion about our GS chapter review questions.

Chapter 14

Memorize

Male and female reproductive structures, functions
Ovum, sperm: differences in formation, relative contribution to next generation
Reproductive sequence: fertilization; implantation; development
Major structures arising out of primary germ layers

Understand

* Gametogenesis by meiosis
* Formation of primary germ layers: endoderm, mesoderm, ectoderm
* Embryogenesis: stages of early development: order and general features of each
* Cell specialization, communication in development, gene regulation in development
* Programmed cell death; basic: the menstrual cycle

Clinical Correlation

"Man and woman" seems crystal clear but genetic and case studies have shown that sex is a biological kaleidoscope. Intersex people include those with PMDS = XY with a male body but internal uterus and fallopian tubes; Swyer syndrome = XY with female body; XX male syndrome, Klinefelter syndrome (XXY), and many more.

MCAT-Prep.com

Introduction

Reproduction refers to the process by which new organisms are produced. The process of development follows as the single celled zygote grows into a fully formed adult. These two processes are fundamental to life as we know it.

Optional Gold Standard Resources

Free Online Q&A + Forum

Online Videos

Flashcards

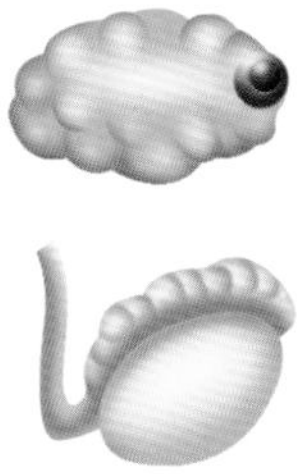

Special Guests

14.1 Organs of the Reproductive System

Gonads are the organs which produce gametes (= germ cells = reproductive cells). The female gonads are the two ovaries which lie in the pelvic cavity. Opening around the ovaries and connecting to the uterus are the Fallopian tubes (= *oviducts*) which conduct the egg (= *ovum*) from the ovary to the uterus. The uterus is a muscular organ. Part of the uterus (= the cervix) protrudes into the vagina or *birth canal*. The vagina leads to the external genitalia. The vulva includes the openings of the vagina, various glands, and folds of skin which are large (= labia majora) and small (= labia minora). The clitoris is found between the labia minora at the anterior end of the vulva. Like the glans penis, it is very sensitive as it is richly innervated. However, the clitoris is unique in being the only organ in the human body devoted solely to sensory pleasure.

The male gonads are the two testicles (= *testes*) which are suspended by spermatic cords in a sac-like scrotum outside the body cavity (this is because the optimal temperature for spermatogenesis is less than body temperature). Sperm (= *spermatozoa*) are produced in the seminiferous tubules in the testes and then continue along a system of ducts including: the epididymis where sperm complete their maturation and are collected and stored; the vas deferens which leads to the ejaculatory duct which in turn leads to the penile urethra which conducts to the exterior. The accessory organs include the seminal vesicles, the bulbourethral and prostate glands. They are exocrine glands whose secretions contribute greatly to the volume of the *ejaculate* (= semen = seminal fluid). The penis is composed of a body or shaft, which contains an erectile tissue which can be engorged by blood; a penile urethra which can conduct either urine or sperm; and a very sensitive head or glans penis which may be covered by foreskin (= *prepuce*, which is removed by circumcision).

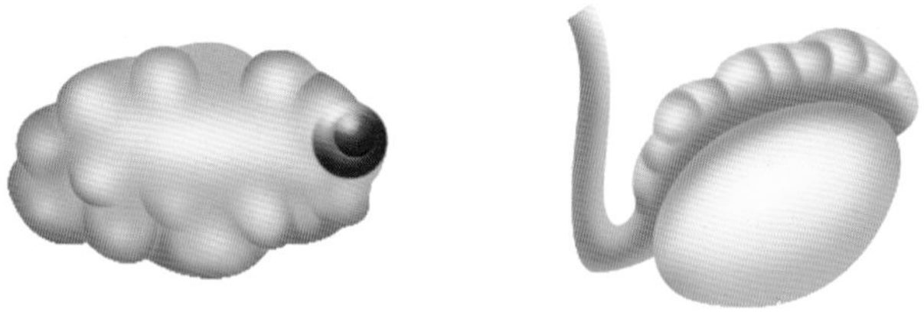

Figure IV.A.14.0: An ovulating ovary and a testicle with spermatic cord.

14.2 Gametogenesis

Gametogenesis refers to the production of gametes (eggs and sperm) which occurs by meiosis (*see Mitosis*, BIO 1.3, *for comparison*). Meiosis involves two successive divisions which can produce four cells from one parent cell. The first division, the reduction division, reduces the number of chromosomes from 2N (= *diploid*) to N (= *haploid*) where N = 23 for humans. This reduction division occurs as follows: i) in **prophase I** the chromosomes appear (= *condensed chromatin*), the nuclear membrane and nucleoli disappear and the spindle fibers become organized. Homologous paternal and maternal chromosomes pair[1] (= *synapsis*) forming a tetrad as each pair of homologous chromosomes consists of four chromatids. The exchange of genetic information (DNA) may occur by crossing over between homologous chromosomes at sites called *chiasmata*, therefore redistributing maternal and paternal genetic information ensuring variability; ii) **in metaphase I** the synaptic pairs of chromosomes line up midway between the poles of the developing spindle (= *the equatorial plate*). Thus each pair consists of 2 chromosomes (= 4 chromatids), each attached to a spindle fiber; iii) in **anaphase I** the homologous chromosomes migrate to opposite poles of the spindle, separating its paternal chromosomes from maternal ones. Thus, each daughter cell will have a unique mixture of paternal and maternal origin of chromosomes. In contrast to anaphase in mitosis, the two chromatids remain held together. Consequently, the centromeres do *not* divide; iv) in **telophase I** the parent cell divides into two daughter cells (= *cytokinesis*), the nuclear membranes and nucleoli reappear, and the spindle fibers are no longer visible. Each daughter cell now contains 23 chromosomes (1N).

The first meiotic division is followed by a short interphase I and then the second meiotic division which proceeds essentially the same as mitosis. Thus prophase II, metaphase II, anaphase II, and telophase II proceed like the corresponding mitotic phases.

Gametogenesis in males (= *spermatogenesis*) proceeds as follows: before the age of sexual maturity only a small number of primordial germ cells (= *spermatogonia*) are present in the testes. There are two types of spermatogonia, type A and type B. Type A spermatogonia (2N) are mitotically active and continuously provide a supply of type A or type B spermatogonia. Type B spermatogonia (2N) undergo meiosis and will give rise to primary spermatocytes. After sexual maturation these cells prolifically multiply throughout a male's life.

In the seminiferous tubules, the type B spermatogonia (2N) enter meiosis I and undergo chromosome replication forming primary spermatocytes with 2N chromosomes. Primary spermatocytes complete meiosis I producing two secondary spermatocytes with 1N chromosomes. Secondary spermatocytes quickly enter meiosis II without an intervening S phase to form four spermatids. Spermatids are haploid (1N) cells.

In summary, each primary spermatocyte results in the production of four spermatids. Spermatids undergo a post-meiotic cytodifferentiation whereby spermatids are transformed into **four** motile sperm (1N) through a process called *spermiogenesis*.

Sperm can be divided into: i) a *head* which is oval and contains the nucleus with its 23 chromosomes {since the nucleus carries either an X or Y sex chromosome, sperm determine the sex of the offspring}. The head is partly surrounded by the acrosome which contains enzymes (esp. hyaluronidase) which help the sperm penetrate the egg. The

[1]synapsing homologous chromosomes are often called *tetrads* or *bivalents*.

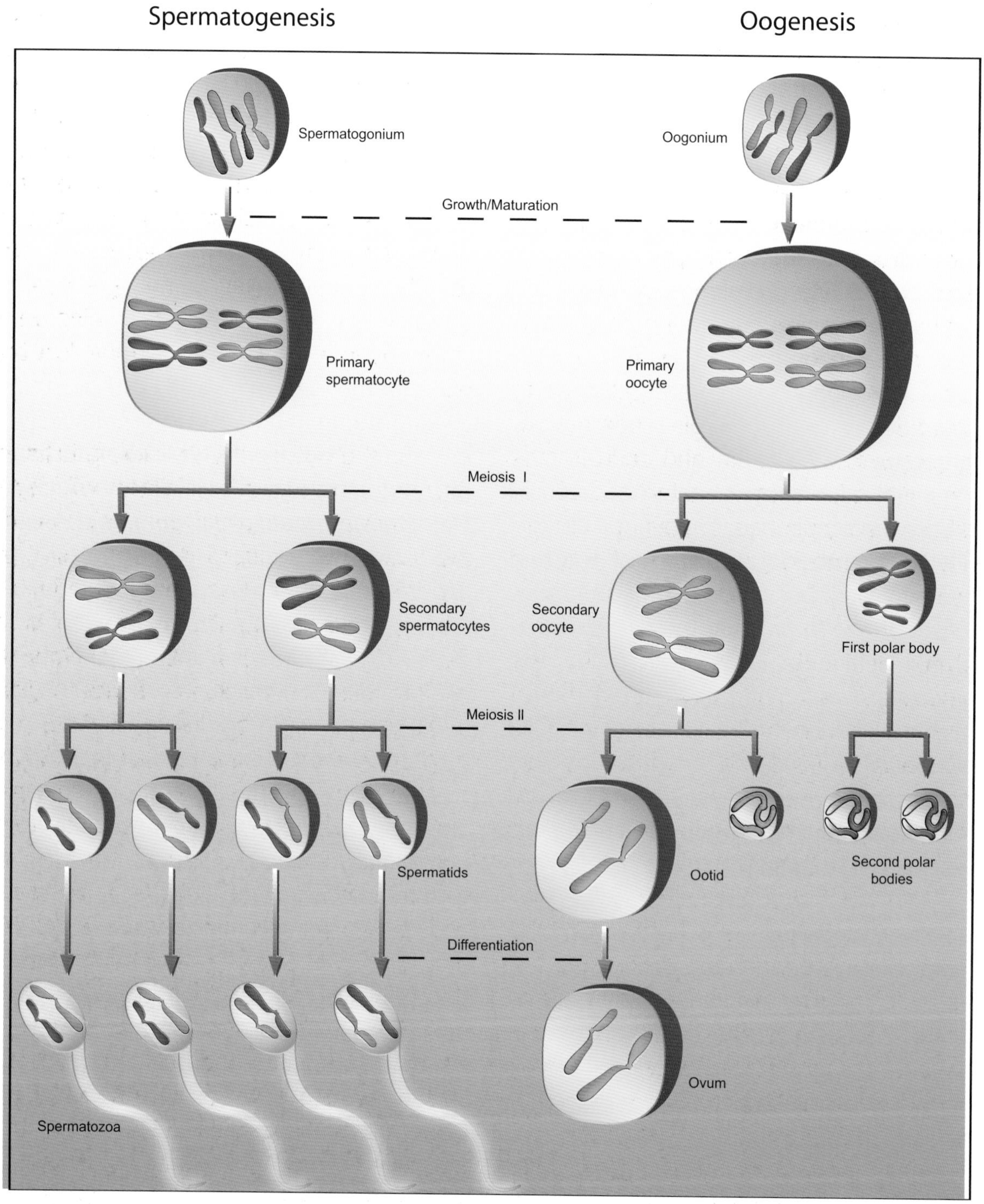

Figure IV.A.14.0a: Gametogenesis.

release of these enzymes is known as the acrosomal reaction; ii) the *body* of the sperm contains a central core surrounded by a large number of mitochondria for power; and iii) the *tail* constitutes a flagellum which is critical for the cell's locomotion. Newly formed sperm are incapable of fertilization until they undergo a process called capacitation, which happens in the female reproductive duct. After removal of its protein coating, the sperm becomes capable of fertilization. Also in the seminiferous tubules are Sertoli cells which support and nourish developing sperm and Leydig cells which produce and secrete testosterone. While LH stimulates the latter, FSH stimulates primary spermatocytes to undergo meiosis. {Remember: LH = Leydig, FSH = spermatogenesis}

Gametogenesis in females (= *oogenesis*) proceeds as follows: in fetal development, groups of cells (= *ovarian or primordial follicles*) develop from the germinal epithelium of the ovary) and differentiate into oogonia (2N). Oogonia (2N) enter meiosis I and undergo DNA replication producing primary oocytes (2N) which are surrounded by epithelia (= *follicular cells*) in the primordial follicle. The oocytes remain arrested in prophase I of meiosis until ovulation which occurs between the ages of about 13 (sexual maturity) and 50 (menopause). Thus, unlike males, all female germ cells are present at birth. Some follicles degenerate and are called *atretic*. During puberty, when the ovarian cycle begins, up to 20 primordial follicles may begin to differentiate to *Graafian follicles*. During this development, meiosis continues. In response to an LH surge from the pituitary gland, the primary oocyte (2N) completes meiosis I just prior to ovulation to form the secondary oocyte (1N) and the first polar body, which will probably degenerate. The secondary oocyte is surrounded by (from the inside out): a thick, tough membrane (= *the zona pellucida*), follicular cells (= *the corona radiata*), and estrogen-secreting thecal cells. It then enters meiosis II and remains arrested in metaphase of meiosis II until fertilization occurs.

Of the twenty or so maturing follicles, all the remaining secondary follicles will degenerate (= *atresia*) except for one which becomes the Graafian (mature) follicle. In response to the LH surge, the secondary oocyte leaves the ruptured Graafian follicle in the process called ovulation. This ovum, along with its zona pellucida and corona radiata, migrate to and through the Fallopian tube (oviduct) where a sperm may penetrate the secondary oocyte (= *fertilization*). If fertilization occurs then the second meiotic division proceeds, forming a mature oocyte, known as ovum, (1N) and a second polar body; if fertilization does not occur, then the ovum degenerates. Unlike in males, each primary germ cell (oocyte) produces one gamete and not four. This is a consequence of the production of *polar bodies* which are degenerated nuclear material. Up to three polar bodies can be formed: one from the division of the primary oocyte, one from the division of the secondary oocyte, and sometimes the first polar body divides.

14.3 The Menstrual Cycle

The "period" or menstrual cycle occurs in about 28 days and can be divided as follows: i) **Menses:** the first four days (days 1-4) of the cycle are notable for the menstrual blood flow. This occurs as a result of an estrogen and progesterone withdrawal which leads to vasoconstriction in the uterus causing the uterine lining (= *endometrium*) to disintegrate and slough away; ii) **Follicular** (ovary) or **Proliferative Phase** (days 5-14): FSH stimulates follicles to mature, and all but one of these follicles will stop growing, and the one dominant follicle in the ovary will continue to mature into a Graafian follicle, which in turn produces and secretes estrogen. Estrogen causes the uterine lining to thicken (= proliferate); iii) **Ovulation**: a very high concentration of estrogen is followed by an LH surge (estrogen-induced LH surge) at about day 15 (midcycle) which stimulates ovulation; iv) **Luteal** or **Secretory Phase** (days 15-28): the follicular cells degenerate into the corpus luteum which secretes estrogen *and* progesterone. Progesterone is responsible for a transient body temperature rise immediately after ovulation and it stimulates the uterine lining to become more vascular and glandular. Estrogen continues to stimulate uterine wall development and, along with progesterone, inhibits the secretion of LH and FSH (= negative feedback).

If the ovum is fertilized, the implanted embryo would produce the hormone *human chorionic gonadotropin* (= hCG) which would stimulate the corpus luteum to continue the secretion of estrogen and progesterone {hCG is the basis for most pregnancy tests}. If there is no fertilization, the corpus luteum degenerates causing a withdrawal of estrogen and progesterone thus the cycle continues [*see* i) *above*].

Estrous vs. menstrual cycles: Mammals with estrous cycles reabsorb the endometrium if conception does not occur during that cycle. Also, they are generally only sexually active during a specific phase of their cycle ("in heat"). In contrast, females of species with menstrual cycles (i.e. humans) can of course be sexually active at any time in their cycle, and the endometrium is shed monthly.

14.4 The Reproductive Sequence

During sexual stimulation parasympathetic impulses in the male lead to the dilatation of penile arteries combined with restricted flow in the veins resulting in the engorgement of the penis with blood (= *an erection*). In the female, the preceding occurs in a similar manner to the clitoris, along with the expansion and increase in secretions in the vagina. Intercourse or copulation may lead to orgasm which includes many responses from the sympathetic nervous system. In the male, the ejaculation of semen accompanies orgasm. In the female, orgasm is accompanied by many reflexes including an increase in muscular activity of the uterus and the Fallopian tubes. The latter may help in the transport of the already motile sperm to reach the tubes where the egg might be.

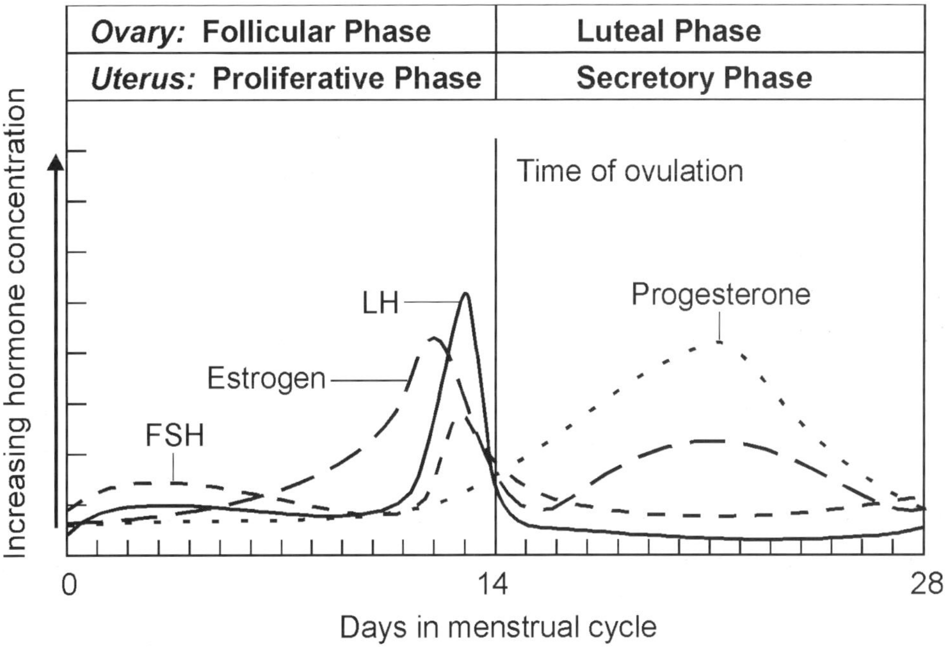

Figure IV.A.14.1: Changing hormone concentration during the menstrual cycle.

14.5 Embryogenesis

The formation of the embryo or *embryogenesis* occurs in a number of steps within two weeks of fertilization. Many parts of the developing embryo take shape during this period (= *morphogenesis*).

Penetration of the zona pellucida leads to the *cortical reaction*, in which the secondary oocyte is no longer permeable to other sperm.

Fertilization is a sequence of events which include: the sperm penetrating the corona radiata and the zona pellucidum due to the release of lytic enzymes from the acrosome known as the acrosome reaction; the fusion of the plasma membranes of the sperm and egg; the egg, which is really a secondary oocyte, becomes a mature ovum by completing the second meiotic division; the nuclei of the ovum and sperm are now called *pronuclei*; the male and female pronuclei fuse forming a zygote (2N). Fertilization, which normally occurs in the Fallopian tubes, is completed within 24 hours of ovulation.

Cleavage consists of rapid, repeated mitotic divisions beginning with the zygote.

Because the resultant daughter cells or blastomeres are still contained within the zona pellucidum, the cytoplasmic mass remains constant. Thus the increasing number of cells requires that each daughter cell be smaller than its parent cell. A morula is a solid ball of about 16 blastomeres which enters the uterus.

Blastulation is the process by which the morula develops a fluid filled cavity (= *blastocoel*) thus converting it to a blastocyst. Since the zona pellucidum degenerates at this point, the blastocyst is free to implant in the uterine lining or endometrium. The blastocyst contains some centrally located cells (= *the inner cell mass*) called the embryoblast which develops into the embryo. The outer cell mass called the trophoblast becomes part of the placenta.

Implantation. The zona pellucida must degenerate before the blastocyst can implant into the endometrium of the uterus. Once implantation is completed, the blastocyst becomes surrounded by layers of cells that further invade the endometrium.

Gastrulation is the process by which the blastula invaginates, and the inner cell mass is converted into a three layered (= *trilaminar*) disk. The trilaminar disk includes the **three primary germ layers**: an outer ectoderm, a middle mesoderm, and an inner endoderm. The ectoderm will develop into the epidermis and the nervous system; the mesoderm will become muscle, connective tissue (incl. blood, bone), and circulatory, reproductive and excretory organs; the endoderm will become the epithelial linings of the respiratory tract, and digestive tract, including the glands of the accessory organs (i.e. the liver and pancreas). During this stage the embryo may be called a gastrula.

Neurulation is the process by which the neural plate and neural folds form and close to produce the neural tube. The neural plate is formed by the thickening of ectoderm which is induced by the developing *notochord*. The notochord is a cellular rod that defines the axis of the embryo and provides some rigidity. Days later, the neural plate invaginates along its central axis producing a central neural groove with neural folds on each side. The neural folds come together and fuse thus converting the neural plate into a neural tube which separates from the surface ectoderm. Special cells on the crest of the neural folds (= *neural crest cells*) migrate to either side of the developing neural tube to a region called the neural crest.

As a consequence, we are left with **three** regions: the surface ectoderm which will become the epidermis; the neural tube which will become the central nervous system (CNS); and the neural crest which will become cranial and spinal ganglia and nerves and the medulla of the adrenal gland. During this stage the embryo may be called a *neurula*.

Mnemonic: Zhat Must Be Good Noodles!
Zygote → **M**orula → **B**lastula → **G**astrula → **N**eurula

14.5.1 Mechanisms of Development

Though this is a subject which is still poorly understood, it seems clear that morphogenesis relies on the coordinated interaction of genetic and environmental factors. When the zygote passes through its first few divisions, the blastomeres remain indeterminate or uncommitted to a specific fate. As development proceeds the cells become increasingly committed to a specific outcome (i.e. neural tube cells → CNS). This is called **determination**.

In order for a cell to specialize it must differentiate into a committed or determined cell. Since essentially all cells in a person's body have the same amount of genetic information, differentiation relies on the *difference* in the way these genes are *activated*. For example, though brain cells (neurons) have the same genes as osteoblasts, neurons do not activate such genes (otherwise we would have bone forming in our brains!). The general mechanism by which cells differentiate is called **induction**.

Induction can occur by many means. If two cells divide unevenly, the cell with more cytoplasm might have the necessary amount of a substance which could *induce* its chromosomes to activate cell-specific genes. Furthermore, sometimes a cell, through contact (i.e. *contact inhibition*) or the release of a chemical mediator, can influence the development of nearby cells (*recall that the notochord induces the development of the neural plate*). The physical environment (pH, temperature, etc.) may also influence the development of certain cells. Irrespective of what form of induction is used, the signal must be translated into an intracellular message which influences the genetic activity of the responding cells.

Programmed cell-death (PCD = apoptosis) is death of a cell in any form, which is controlled by an intracellular program. PCD is carried out in a regulated process directed by DNA which normally confers advantage during an organism's life-cycle. PCD serves fundamental functions during tissue development. For example, the development of the spaces between your fingers requires cells to undergo PCD.

Thus cells specialize and develop into organ systems (morphogenesis). The embryo develops from the second to the ninth week, followed by the fetus which develops from the ninth week to birth (*parturition*).

Reproductive biology is the only science where multiplication and division mean the same thing. :)

14.6 The Placenta

The **placenta** is a complex vascular structure formed by part of the maternal endometrium (= *the decidua basalis*) and cells of embryonic origin (= *the chorion*). The placenta begins to form when the blastocyst implants in the endometrium. A cell layer from the embryo invades the endometrium with fingerlike bumps (= *chorionic villi*) which project into intervillous spaces which contain maternal blood. Maternal spiral arteries enter the intervillous spaces allowing blood to circulate.

The placenta has three main functions: i) the **transfer** of substances necessary for the development of the embryo or fetus from the mother (O_2, H_2O, carbohydrates, amino acids, IgG antibodies - BIO 8.2, vitamins, etc.) and the **transfer** of wastes from the embryo or fetus to the mother (CO_2, urea, uric acid, etc.); ii) the placenta can synthesize substances (i.e. glycogen, fatty acids) to use as an energy source for itself and the embryo or fetus; iii) the placenta produces and secretes a number of hormones including human chorionic gonadotropin (hCG), estrogen and progesterone. The hCG rescues the corpus luteum from regression and stimulates its production of progesterone.

14.7 Fetal Circulation

Consider the following: the fetus has lungs but does not breathe O_2. In fact, the placenta is, metaphorically, the "fetal lung." Oxygenated and nutrient-rich blood returns to the fetus from the placenta via the left umbilical vein. Most of the blood is directed to the inferior vena cava through the ductus venosus. From there, blood joins the deoxygenated and nutrient-poor blood from the superior vena cava and empties into the right atrium. However, most of the blood is diverted from the pulmonary circulation (bypassing the right ventricle) to the left atrium via a hole in the atrial septum: the patent foramen ovale (for adult circulation and anatomy, see chapter 7). Blood then enters the left ventricle and is distributed through the body (systemic circulation) via the aorta.

Some blood in the right atrium enters into the right ventricle and then proceeds into the pulmonary trunk. However, resistance in the collapsed lung is high and the pulmonary artery pressure is higher than it is in the aorta. Consequently, most of the blood bypasses the lung via the ductus arteriosus back to the aorta.

Blood circulates through the body and is sent back to the placenta via right and left umbilical arteries. The placenta re-oxygenates this deoxygenated and nutrient-poor blood and returns it to the fetus through the umbilical vein and the cardiovascular cycle repeats. Notice that in the fetus, oxygenated and nutrient-rich blood can be carried by veins to the right chambers of the heart which cannot occur in normal adult circulation.

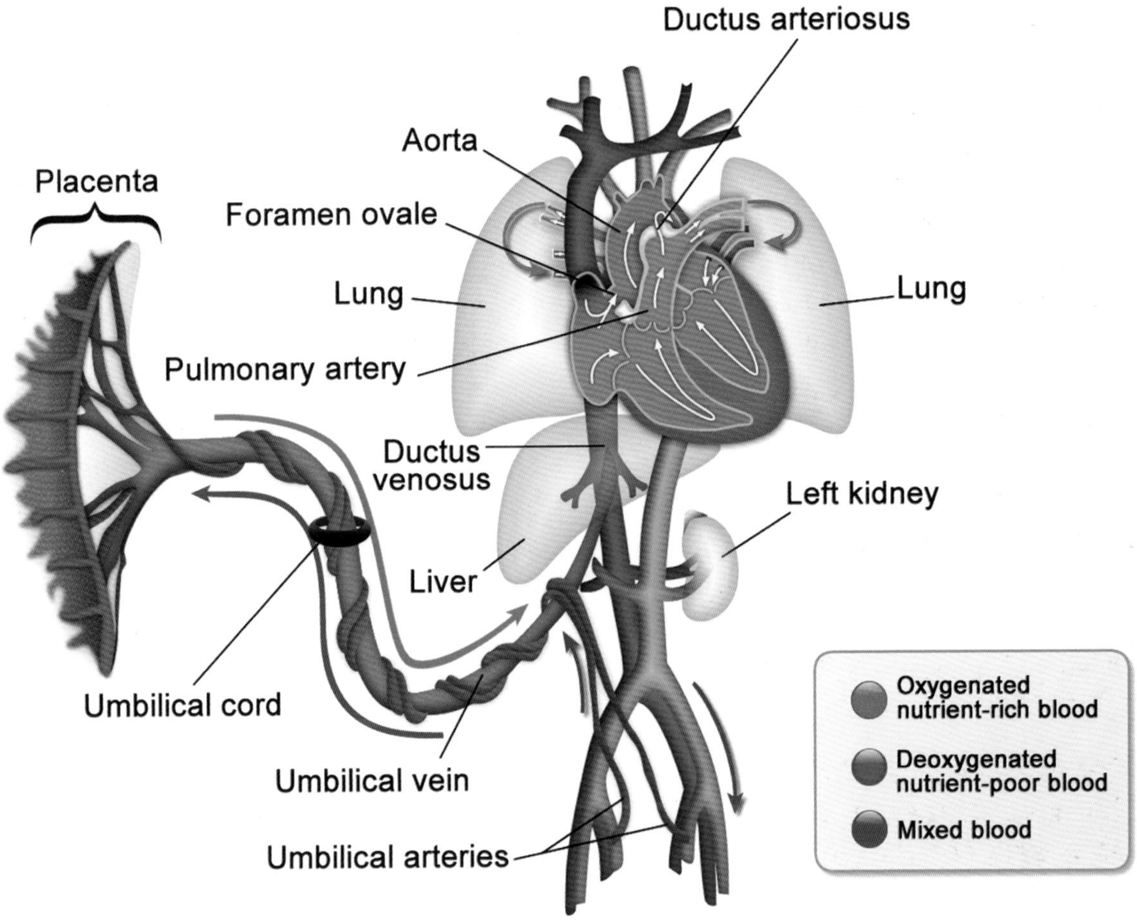

Fig.IV.A.14.2: Fetal circulation.

14.8 Fetal Sexual Development

To begin with, it will be helpful to define two key expressions:

Primary sex characteristics: any anatomical part of the body involved in sexual reproduction and thus part of the reproductive system. Examples: the external sex organs (= genitalia or genitals) and the internal sex organs (= gonads).

Secondary sex characteristics: features that appear during puberty but that are not directly part of the reproductive system. Examples: for females - enlarged breasts, relatively more body fat; for males - facial hair, lower pitched voice and Adam's apple (laryngeal prominence). Of course, it is quite normal for both sexes to develop pubic and underarm hair.

The normal sexual development of the fetus depends on the genotype (XX female, XY male), the morphology of the internal organs and gonads, and the phenotype or external genitalia. Later, these many factors combine to influence the individual's self-perception along with the development of secondary sex characteristics.

Every fetus, regardless of genotype, has the capacity to become a normally formed individual of either sex. Development naturally proceeds towards "female" unless there is a Y chromosome factor present. Thus the XX genotype leads to the maturation of the Müllerian ducts into the uterus, fallopian tubes, and part of the vagina. The primitive gonad will develop into a testis only if the Y chromosome is present and encodes the appropriate factor and eventually the secretion of testosterone. Thus the XY genotype leads to the involution of the Müllerian ducts and the maturation of the Wolffian ducts into the vas deferens, seminiferous tubules and prostate.

When the chromosomes, gonads, or genitals do not allow an individual to be distinctly identified as female or male, they are referred to as *intersex* (see "Clinical Correlation" at the beginning of this chapter).

GOLD STANDARD WARM-UP EXERCISES

CHAPTER 14: Reproduction and Development

1) Fertilization of the ovum by the sperm usually occurs in the:

A. vagina.
B. uterus.
C. oviduct.
D. ovary.

2) Sperm can travel through each of the following EXCEPT one. Which one is the EXCEPTION?

A. Ureter
B. Urethra
C. Vas deferens
D. Epididymis

3) Which of the following does NOT follow the normal anatomic sequence?

I. gametogenesis → seminal vesicles → seminiferous tubules
II. seminiferous tubules → epididymis → vas deferens
III. vas deferens → ejaculatory duct → urethra

A. I only
B. II only
C. I and II only
D. II and III only

4) Which of the following can initiate a second meiotic division?

A. FSH
B. LH
C. Estrogen and progesterone
D. Fertilization

5) The corpus luteum secretes:

A. FSH.
B. LH.
C. progesterone.
D. HCG.

6) The hormone causing growth of the endometrium is:

A. oxytocin.
B. estrogen.
C. luteinizing hormone.
D. prolactin.

7) In the human menstrual cycle, which hormone is preferentially secreted in the follicular phase by the ovary?

A. Estrogen
B. FSH
C. LH
D. Progesterone

8) Which of the following hormones leads to the expulsion of the egg from the ovaries?

A. LH
B. FSH
C. Estrogen
D. Progesterone

9) In vitro fertilization begins by injecting a woman with medications which stimulate multiple egg production in the ovary. Drugs that stimulate multiple egg production probably contain, or increase the production of, which of the following hormones?

I. LH
II. FSH
III. ACTH
IV. Estrogen

A. I only
B. IV only
C. I, II and IV only
D. I, II, III and IV

10) After fertilization, the zygote will develop into a female if:

A. the zygote possesses an X chromosome.
B. the primary oocyte possesses an X chromosome.
C. the egg possesses an X chromosome.
D. the sperm possesses an X chromosome.

11) Damage to the ectoderm during gastrulation will result in an embryo with an underdeveloped:

A. reproductive system.
B. nervous system.
C. excretory system.
D. digestive system.

12) The blastula develops into which of the following?

A. The morula
B. The blastula
C. The gastrula
D. The neurula

13) The developing fetus has a blood vessel called the ductus arteriosus which connects the pulmonary artery to the aorta. When a baby is born, the ductus arteriosus closes permanently. Which is the dominant feature found in a newborn whose ductus arteriosus failed to obliterate?

A. Increased O_2 partial pressure in pulmonary arteries
B. Decreased CO_2 partial pressure in pulmonary arteries
C. Increased O_2 partial pressure in systemic arteries
D. Decreased O_2 partial pressure in systemic arteries

14) The placenta in humans is derived from the:

A. embryo only.
B. uterus only.
C. endometrium and embryo.
D. uterus and fallopian tube.

15) Synapsis and crossing over of chromosomes occurs is which phase of meiosis?

A. Prophase I
B. Prophase II
C. Metaphase I
D. Metaphase II

GS ANSWER KEY

CHAPTER 14

		Cross-Reference			Cross-Reference
1.	C	BIO 14.1, 14.5	9.	C	BIO 14.3
2.	A	BIO 14.1, 10.1, 10.2	10.	D	BIO 14.2, 14.8
3.	A	BIO 14.1	11.	B	BIO 14.5
4.	D	BIO 14.2	12.	C	BIO 14.5
5.	C	BIO 3.0	13.	D	BIO 7.2, 7.3, 14.7
6.	B	BIO 14.3	14.	C	BIO 14.6
7.	A	BIO 6.3.1F, 14.3	15.	C	BIO 14.2
8.	A	BIO 14.3			

*** Explanations can be found at the back of the book.**

Go online to MCAT-prep.com/forum to join the discussion about our GS chapter review questions.

GENETICS

Chapter 15

Memorize

efine: phenotype, genotype, gene, locus,
llele: single and multiple
lomo/heterozygosity, wild type, reces-
iveness, complete/co-dominance
ncomplete dominance, gene pool
ex-linked characteristics, sex determi-
ation
ypes of mutations: random, translation
rror, transcription error, base subs., etc.

Understand

* Importance of meiosis; compare/contrast with mitosis; segregation of genes, assortment, linkage, recombination
* Single/double crossovers; relationship of mutagens to carcinogens
* Hardy-Weinberg Principle, inborn errors of metabolism
* Test cross: back cross, concepts of parental, F1 and F2 generations
* Basics: sections 15.6, 15.6.1

Clinical Correlation

Many scientists would have considered epigenetics (modifying gene expresion rather than the genetic code) and retro-viral gene therapy (replacing a mutated gene using a vector; BIO 2.4) as pure science fiction just decades ago. These rapidly growing fields will likely change the approach to genetic conditions in our lifetimes.

MCAT-Prep.com

Introduction

Genetics is the study of heredity and variation in organisms. The observations of Gregor Mendel in the mid-nineteenth century gave birth to the science which would reveal the physical basis for his conclusions, DNA, about 100 years later.

Optional Gold Standard Resources

Free Online Q&A + Forum

Online Videos

Flashcards

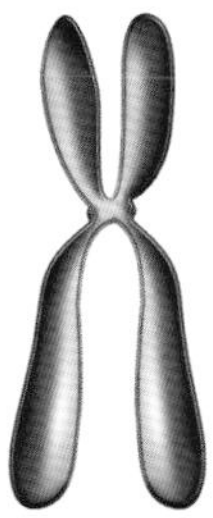

Special Guest

15.1 Background Information

Genetics is a branch of biology which deals with the principles and mechanics of heredity; in other words, the *means* by which *traits* are passed from parents to offspring. To begin, we will first examine some relevant definitions - a few of which we have already discussed.

Chromosomes are a complex of DNA and proteins (incl. histones; BIO 1.2.2). A gene is that sequence of DNA that codes for a protein or polypeptide. A locus is the *position* of the gene on the DNA molecule. Recall that humans inherit 46 chromosomes - 23 from maternal origin and 23 from paternal origin (BIO 14.2). A given chromosome from maternal origin has a counterpart from paternal origin which codes for the same products. This is called a **homologous pair** of chromosomes.

Any homologous pair of chromosomes have a pair of genes which codes for the same product (i.e. hair color). Such pairs of genes are called **alleles**. Thus for one gene product, a nucleus contains one allele from maternal origin and one allele from paternal origin. If both alleles are identical (i.e. they code for the same hair color), then the individual is called **homozygous** for that trait. If the two alleles differ (i.e. one codes for dark hair while the other codes for light hair), then the individual is called **heterozygous** for that trait.

The set of genes possessed by a particular organism is its genotype. The appearance or phenotype of an individual is expressed as a consequence of the genotype and the environment. Consider a heterozygote that expressed one gene (dark hair) but not the other (light hair). The expressed gene would be called dominant while the other unexpressed allele would be called recessive. The individual would have dark hair as their phenotype, yet their genotype would be heterozygous for that trait. The dominant allele is expressed in the phenotype. This is known as Mendel's Law of Dominance.

It is common to symbolize dominant genes with capital letters (A) and recessive genes with small letters (a). From the preceding paragraphs, we can conclude that with two alleles, three genotypes are possible: homozygous dominant (AA), heterozygous (Aa), and homozygous recessive (aa). Note that this only results in two phenotypes since both AA and Aa express the dominant gene, while only aa expresses the recessive gene.

Each individual carries **two** alleles while populations may have many or **multiple alleles**. Sometimes these genes are not strictly dominant or recessive. There may be degrees of blending (= *incomplete dominance*) or sometimes two alleles may be equally dominant (= *codominance*). ABO blood types are an important example of multiple alleles with codominance.

Incomplete dominance occurs when the phenotype of the heterozygote is an intermediate of the phenotypes of the homozygotes. A classic example is flower color in snapdragon: the snapdragon flower color is red for homozygous dominant and white for homozygous recessive. When the red homozygous flower is crossed with the white homozygous flower, the result yields a 100% pink snapdragon flower. The pink snapdragon is the result of the combined effect of both dominant and recessive genes.

Wild type refers to the phenotype of the typical form of a species as it occurs in nature, as opposed to an atypical mutant type.

15.2 ABO Blood Types

Codominance occurs when multiple alleles exist for a particular gene and more than one is dominant. When a dominant allele is combined with a recessive allele, the phenotype of the recessive allele is completely masked. But when two dominant alleles are present, the contributions of both alleles do not overpower each other and the phenotype is the result of the expression of both alleles. A classic example of codominance is the ABO blood type in humans.

Red blood cells can have various antigens or *agglutinogens* on their plasma membranes which aid in blood typing. The important two are antigens A and B. If the red blood cells have only antigen A, the blood type is A; if they have only antigen B, then the blood type is B; if they have both antigens, the blood type is AB; if neither antigen is present, the blood type is O. There are three allelic genes in the population (I^A, I^B, i^O). Two are codominant (I^A, I^B) and one is recessive (i^O). Thus in a given population, there are six possible genotypes which result in four possible phenotypes:

Genotype	*Phenotype*
I^AI^A, I^Ai^O	blood type A
I^BI^B, I^Bi^O	blood type B
I^AI^B	blood type AB
i^Oi^O	blood type O

Blood typing is critical before doing a blood transfusion. This is because people with blood type A have anti-B antibodies, those with type B have anti-A, those with type AB have neither antibody, while type O has both anti-A and anti-B antibodies. If a person with type O blood is given types A, B, or AB, the clumping of the red blood cells will occur (= *agglutination*). Though type O can only receive from type O, it can give to the other blood types since its red blood cells have no antigens {type O = universal donor}. Type AB has neither antibody to react against A or B antigens so it can receive blood from all blood types {type AB = universal recipient}.

The only other antigens which have some importance are the Rh factors which are coded by different genes at different loci from the A and B antigens. Rh factors are either there (Rh^+) or they are not there (Rh^-). 85% of the population are Rh^+. The problem occurs when a woman is Rh^- and has been exposed to Rh^+ blood and then forms anti-Rh^+ antibodies (note: unlike the previous case, exposure is necessary to produce these antibodies). If this woman is pregnant with an Rh^+ fetus her antibodies may cross the placenta and cause the fetus' red blood cells to agglutinate (*erythroblastosis fetalis*). This condition is fatal if left untreated.

15.3 Mendelian Genetics

Recall that in gametogenesis homologous chromosomes separate during the first meiotic division. Thus alleles that code for the same trait are segregated: this is **Mendel's First Law of Segregation. Mendel's Second Law of Independent Assortment** states that different chromosomes (*or factors which carry different traits*) separate independently of each other. For example, consider a primary spermatocyte (2N) undergoing its first meiotic division. It is not the case that all 23 chromosomes of paternal origin will end up in one secondary spermatocyte while the other 23 chromosomes of maternal origin ends up in the other. Rather, each chromosome in a homologous pair separates *independently* of any other chromosome in other homologous pairs.

However, it has been noted experimentally that sometimes traits on the same chromosome assort independently! This non-Mendelian concept is a result of *crossing over* (recall that this is when homologous chromosomes exchange parts, BIO 14.2). In fact, it has been shown that two traits located far apart on a chromosome are more likely to cross over and thus assort independently, as compared to two traits that are close. The propensity for some traits to refrain from assorting independently is called linkage. Double crossovers occur when two crossovers happen in a chromosomal region being studied.

Another exception to Mendel's laws involves **sex linkage**. Mendel's laws would predict that the results of a genetic cross should be the same regardless of which parent introduces the allele. However, it can be shown that some traits follow the inheritance of the sex chromosomes. Humans have one pair of sex chromosomes (XX = female, XY = male), and the remaining 22 pairs of homologous chromosomes are called **autosomes**.

Since females have two X chromosomes and males have only one, a single recessive allele carried on an X chromosome could be expressed in a male since there is no second allele present to mask it. When males inherit one copy of the recessive allele from an X chromosome, they will express the trait. In contrast, females must inherit two copies to express the trait. Therefore, an X-linked recessive phenotype is much more frequently found in males than females. In fact, a typical pattern of sex linkage is when a mother passes her phenotype to all her sons but **none** of her daughters. Her daughters become *carriers* for the recessive allele. Certain forms of hemophilia, colorblindness, and one kind of muscular dystrophy are well-known recessive sex-linked traits. {In what was once known as Lyon's Hypothesis, it has been shown that every female has a condensed, inactivated X chromosome in her body or somatic cells called a Barr body.}

Let us examine the predictions of Mendel's First Law. Consider two parents, one homozygous dominant (AA) and the other homozygous recessive (aa). Each parent can only form one type of gamete with respect to that trait (*either* A *or* a, *respectively*). The next generation (*called first filial or* $\mathbf{F_1}$) must then be uniformly heterozygotes or *hybrids* (Aa). Now the F_1 hybrids can produce gametes that can be either A *half the time* or a *half the time*. When the F_1 generation is self-crossed, i.e. Aa X Aa, the F_2 generation will be more genotypically and phenotypically diverse and we can predict the outcome in the next generation (F_2) using a Punnett square:

	1/2 A	1/2 a
1/2 A	1/4 AA	1/4 Aa
1/2 a	1/4 Aa	1/4 aa

Here is an example as to how you derive the information within the square: when you cross A with A you get AA (i.e. 1/2 A × 1/2 A = 1/4 AA). Thus by doing a simple *mono*hybrid cross (Aa × Aa) with random mating, the Punnett square indicates that in the F_2 generation, 1/4 of the population would be AA, 1/2 would be Aa (1/4 + 1/4), and 1/4 would be aa. In other words the *genotypic* ratio of homozygous dominant to heterozygous to homozygous recessive is 1:2:1. However, since AA and Aa demonstrate the same *phenotype* (i.e. dominant) the ratio of dominant phenotype to recessive phenotype is 3:1.

Now we will consider the predictions of Mendel's Second Law. To examine independent assortment, we will have to consider a case with two traits (usu. on different chromosomes) or a *di*hybrid cross. Imagine a parent which is homozygous dominant for two traits (AABB) while the other is homozygous recessive (aabb). Each parent can only form one type of gamete with respect to those traits (*either* AB *or* ab, *respectively*). The F_1 generation will be uniform for the dominant trait (i.e. *the genotypes would all be* AaBb). In the gametes of the F_1 generation, the alleles will assort independently.

Consequently, an equal amount of all the possible gametes will form: 1/4 AB, 1/4 Ab, 1/4 aB, and 1/4 ab. When the F_1 generation is self-crossed, i.e. AaBb X AaBb, we can predict the outcome in the F_2 generation using the Punnett square:

	1/4 AB	1/4 Ab	1/4 aB	1/4 ab
1/4 AB	1/16 AABB	1/16 AABb	1/16 AaBB	1/16 AaBb
1/4 Ab	1/16 AABb	1/16 AAbb	1/16 AaBb	1/16 Aabb
1/4 aB	1/16 AaBB	1/16 AaBb	1/16 aaBB	1/16 aaBb
1/4 ab	1/16 AaBb	1/16 Aabb	1/16 aaBb	1/16 aabb

Thus by doing a dihybrid cross with random mating, the Punnett square indicates that there are nine possible genotypes (t*he frequency is given in brackets*): AABB (1), AABb (2), AaBb (4), AaBB (2), Aabb (2), aaBb (2), AAbb (1), aaBB (1), and aabb (1). Since A and B are dominant, there are only four phenotypic classes in the ratio 9:3:3:1 which are: the expression of <u>both</u> traits (AABB + AABb + AaBb + AaBB = 9), the expression of only the <u>first</u> trait (AAbb + Aabb = 3), the expression of only the <u>second</u> trait (aaBB + aaBb = 3), and the expression of <u>neither</u> trait (aabb = 1). Now we know, for example, that 9/16 represents that fraction of the population which will have the phenotype of both dominant traits.

15.3.1 A Word about Probability

If you were to flip a quarter, the probability of getting "heads" is 50% (p = 0.5). If you flipped the quarter ten times and each time it came up heads, the probability of getting heads on the next trial is still 50%. After all, previous trials have no effect on the next trial.

Since chance events, such as fertilization of a particular kind of egg by a particular kind of sperm, occur independently, the genotype of one child has no effect on the genotypes of other children produced by a set of parents. Thus in the previous example of the dihybrid cross, the chance of producing the genotype AaBb is 4/16 (25%) irrespective of the genotypes which have already been produced.

15.4 The Hardy-Weinberg Law

The Hardy-Weinberg Law deals with population genetics. A **population** includes all the members of a species which occupy a more or less well defined geographical area and have demonstrated the ability to reproduce from generation to generation. A **gene pool** is the sum of all the unique alleles for a given population. A central component to evolution is the changing of alleles in a gene pool from one generation to the next.

Evolution can be viewed as a changing of gene frequencies within a population over successive generations. The Hardy-Weinberg Law or *equilibrium* predicts the outcome of a randomly mating population of sexually reproducing diploid organisms who are not undergoing evolution.

For the Hardy-Weinberg Law to be applied, the idealized population must meet the following conditions: i) **random mating**: the members of the population must have no mating preferences; ii) **no mutations**: there must be no errors in replication nor similar event resulting in a change in the genome; iii) **isolation**: there must be no exchange of genes between the population being considered and any other population; iv) **large population**: since the law is based on statistical probabilities, to avoid sampling errors, the population cannot be small; v) **no selection pressures**: there must be no reproductive advantage of one allele over the other.

To illustrate a use of the law, consider an idealized population that abides by the preceding conditions and have a gene locus occupied by either A or a. Let p = the frequency of allele A in the population and let q = the frequency of allele a. Since they are the only alleles, p + q = 1. Squaring both sides we get:

$$(p + q)^2 = (1)^2$$

OR

$$p^2 + 2pq + q^2 = 1$$

The preceding equation (= *the Hardy-Weinberg equation*) can be used to calculate genotype frequencies once the allelic frequencies are given. This can be summarized by the following:

	pA	qa
pA	p^2AA	pqAa
qa	pqAa	q^2aa

The Punnett square illustrates the expected frequencies of the three genotypes in the next generation: AA = p^2, Aa = 2pq, and aa= q^2.

For example, let us calculate the percentage of heterozygous individuals in a population where the recessive allele q has a frequency of 0.2. Since p + q = 1, then p = 0.8. Using the Hardy-Weinberg equation and squaring p and q we get:

$$0.64 + 2pq + 0.04 = 1$$

$$2pq = 1 - 0.68 = 0.32$$

Thus the percentage of heterozygous (2pq) individuals is 32%.

A practical application of the Hardy-Weinberg equation is the prediction of how many people in a generation are carriers for a particular recessive allele. The values would have to be recalculated for every generation since humans do not abide by all the conditions of the Hardy-Weinberg Law (i.e. *humans continually evolve*).

15.4.1 Back Cross, Test Cross

A back cross is the cross of an individual (F_1) with one of its parents (P) or an organism with the same genotype as a parent. Back crosses can be used to help identify the genotypes of the individual in a specific type of back cross called a test cross. A test cross is a cross between an organism whose genotype for a certain trait is unknown and an organism that is homozygous recessive for that trait so the unknown genotype can be determined from that of the offspring. For example, for P: AA x aa and F_1: Aa, we get:

Backcross #1: Aa x AA
Progeny #1: 1/2 Aa and 1/2 AA

Backcross #2: Aa x aa
Progeny #2: 1/2 Aa and 1/2 aa

15.5 Genetic Variability

Meiosis and mutations are sources of genetic variability. During meiosis I, crossing over occurs between the parental and maternal genes which leads to a recombination of parental genes yielding unique haploid gametes. Thus recombination can result in alleles of linked traits separating into different gametes. However, the closer two traits are on a chromosome, the more likely they will be linked and thus remain together, and vice versa.

Further recombination occurs during the random fusion of gametes during fertilization.

Consequently, taking Mendel's two laws and recombination together, we can predict that parents can give their offspring combinations of alleles which the parents never had. This leads to **genetic variability**.

Mutations are rare, inheritable, random changes in the genetic material (DNA) of a cell. Mutations are much more likely to be either neutral (esp. *silent mutations*) or negative (i.e. cancer) than positive for an organism's survival. Nonetheless, such a change in the genome increases genetic variability. Only mutations of gametes, and not somatic cells, are passed on to offspring.

The following are some forms of mutations:

- **Point mutation** is a change affecting a single base pair in a gene
- **Deletion** is the removal of a sequence of DNA, the regions on either side being joined together
- **Inversion** is the reversal of a segment of DNA
- **Translocation** is when one chromosome breaks and attaches to another
- **Duplication** is when a sequence of DNA is repeated.
- **Frame shift mutations** occur when bases are added or deleted in numbers other than multiples of three. Such deletions or additions cause the rest of the sequence to be shifted such that each triplet reading frame is altered.

A mutagen is any substance or agent that can cause a mutation. A mutagen is not the same as a carcinogen. Carcinogens are agents that cause cancer. While many mutagens are carcinogens as well, many others are not. The Ames test is a widely used test to screen chemicals used in foods or medications for mutagenic potential.

Mutations can produce many types of genetic diseases including inborn errors of metabolism. These disorders in normal metabolism are usually due to defects of a single gene that codes for one enzyme.

15.6 Genetics and Heredity: A Closer Look

The rest of this chapter begins to push into more advanced topics in genetics. However, these topics continue to represent legitimate exam material.

Epistasis occurs when one gene masks the phenotype of a second gene. This is often the case in pigmentation where one gene turns on (or off) the production of pigment, while a second gene controls the amount of pigment produced. Such is the case in mice fur where one gene codes for the presence or absence of pigmentation and the other codes for the color. If C and c represent the alleles for the presence or absence of color and B and b represent black and brown then a phenotype of CCbb and Ccbb would both correspond to a brown phenotype. Whenever cc is inherited the fur will be white.

Pleiotropy occurs when a single gene has more than one phenotypic expression. This is often seen in pea plants where the gene that expresses round or wrinkled texture of seeds also influences the expression of starch metabolism. For example, in wrinkled seeds there is more unconverted glucose which leads to an increase of the osmotic gradient. These seeds will subsequently contain more water than round seeds. When they mature they will dehydrate and produce the wrinkled appearance.

Polygenic inheritance refers to traits that cannot be expressed in just a few types but rather as a range of varieties. The most popular example would be human height which ranges from very short to very tall. This phenomenon (many genes shaping one phenotype) is the opposite of pleiotropy.

Penetrance refers to the proportion of individuals carrying a particular variant of a gene (allele or genotype) that also express the associated phenotype. Alleles which are highly penetrant are more likely to be noticed. Penetrance only considers whether individuals express the trait or not. *Expressivity* refers to the variation in the degree of expression of a given trait.

Nondisjunction occurs when the chromosomes do not separate properly and do not migrate to opposite poles as in normal anaphase of meiosis (BIO 14.2). This could arise from a failure of homologous chromosomes to separate in meiosis I, or the failure of sister chromatids to separate during meiosis II or mitosis. Most of the time, gametes produced after nondisjunction are sterile; however, certain imbalances can be fertile and lead to genetic defects. Down Syndrome (Trisomy 21 = 3 copies of chromosome 21 due to its nondisjunction, thus the person has an extra chromosome making a total of 47 chromosomes); Turner and Klinefelter Syndrome (nondisjunction of sex chromosomes); and Cri du Chat (deletion in chromosome 5) are well known genetic disorders. Hemophilia and red-green color blindness are common sex-linked disorders and are recessive.

Phenylketonuria, sickle-cell anemia and Tay-Sachs disease are common autosomal recessive disorders.

Gene linkage refers to genes that reside on the same chromosome and are unable to display independent assortment because they are physically connected (BIO 15.3). The further away the two genes are on the chromosome the higher probability there is that they will crossover during synapsis. In these cases recombination frequencies are used to provide a linkage map where the arrangement of the genes can be ascertained. For example, say you have a fly with genotype BBTTYY and the crossover frequency between B and T is 26%, between Y and T is 18% and between B and Y is 8%. Greater recombination frequencies mean greater distances so you know that B and T are the furthest apart. This corresponds to a gene order of B-Y-T and since frequencies are a direct measure of distance you know exactly how far apart each allele is and can easily calculate the map distances.

Twin studies (nature vs. nurture) help to gauge the relative importance of environmental and genetic influences on individuals in a sample. Twins can either be monozygotic ("identical"), meaning that they develop from one zygote (BIO 14.5) that splits and forms two embryos, or dizygotic ("fraternal"), meaning that they develop from two separate eggs, each fertilized by separate sperm cells. Thus fraternal twins are like any 2 siblings from a genetic point of view, but they may share the same environment as they grow up together.

To control for environment, the classical twin study design compares the similarity of monozygotic and dizygotic twins. If identical twins are considerably more similar than fraternal twins (which is found for most traits), this implies that genes play an important role for those specific traits. By comparing hundreds of families of twins, researchers can then understand more about the roles of genetic effects, shared environment, and unique environment in shaping behavior or in the development of disease.

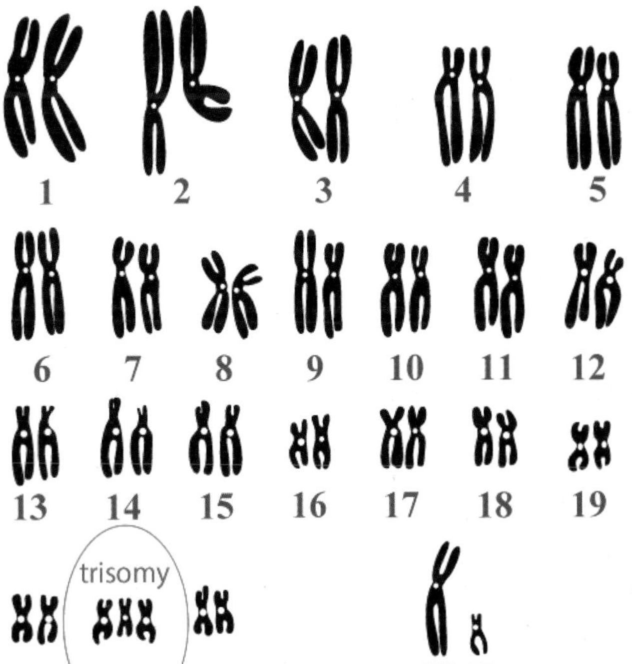

Figure IV.A.15.1: Illustration of a karyotype from a person with Down's syndrome. A karyotype is a picture of one set of chromosomes. First, chromosomes are isolated, then stained, and finally examined under a microscope. A picture of the chromosomes is taken through the microscope. Note the following points regarding the illustration above: 47 chromosomes, male, and trisomy 21.

15.6.1 Mitochondrial DNA

Mitochondrial DNA (mtDNA or mDNA) has become increasingly popular as a tool to determine how closely populations are related as well as to clarify the evolutionary relationships among species (= phylogenetics). Mitochondrial DNA is circular (BIO 1.2.2, 16.6.3) and can be regarded as the smallest chromosome. In most species, including humans, mtDNA is inherited solely from the mother. The DNA sequence of mtDNA has been determined from a large number of organisms and individuals (including some organisms that are extinct).

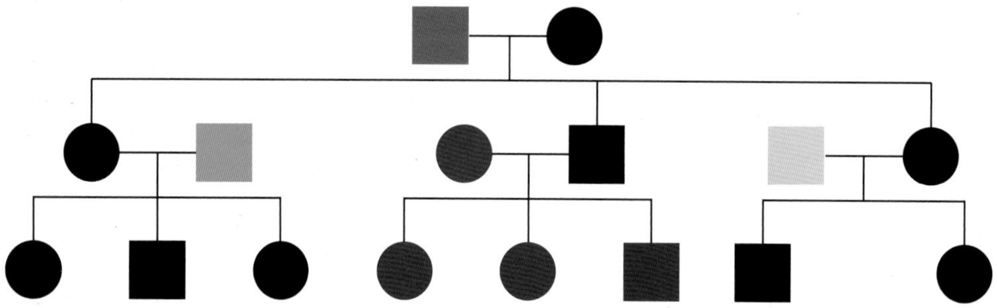

Figure IV.A.15.0: Pedigree ("Family tree"): Maternal inheritance pattern of mtDNA for 3 generations with the grandparents in the top row. As is the standard, circles represent females, squares represent males. Colors show the inheritance of the same mt genome (from mother to offspring, i.e. children).

GOLD STANDARD WARM-UP EXERCISES

CHAPTER 15: Genetics

1) Which of the following is the LEAST likely reason for the phenotype of PKU disease lacking phenylalanine hydroxylase?

A. An added nucleotide in the genetic code results in an altered sequence of nucleotides which gets translated into an altered sequence of amino acids.

B. A deletion in the genetic code results in an altered sequence of nucleotides which gets translated into an altered sequence of amino acids.

C. The stereochemistry of the chromosome becomes altered.

D. A deletion in the genetic code creates a stop codon in the nucleotide sequence.

2) In general terms, what is the primary genetic difference between a hepatocyte (a liver cell) and a muscle cell?

A. The amount of DNA

B. The number of chromosomes

C. The number of genes

D. The expression of genes

3) Over 10 million North Americans are treated for thyroid diseases and, overwhelmingly, women are much more likely than men to succumb to these conditions. Is it reasonable to conclude that thyroid disease is sex-linked?

A. No, because thyroid disease appears to be caused by a defect of the immune system and not a defective DNA sequence.

B. No, because if the disease was sex-linked, there would be a high incidence in the male, rather than the female, population.

C. Yes, because the high incidence of the disease in women suggests that a gene found on the X chromosome codes for the disease.

D. Yes, because the same factor increases the risk of women getting the disease, regardless of familial background.

4) Although the cloned sheep Dolly contains the exact DNA as her genetic mother, there are a few visible and behavioral differences in Dolly. This is most probably due to:

A. the sheep in which the embryo was implanted.

B. the induction of specific genes not expressed in the mother.

C. mutations caused by incubation in the nutrient-deficient solution.

D. environmental factors.

5) In fruit flies, males have XY sex chromosomes, females have XX, and white eye color is sex linked. If red-eyed (heterozygous) females are crossed with white-eyed males, what would be the expected eye colors and sexes of the progeny?

A. ¾ white-eyed female and ¼ red-eyed male.

B. ½ red-eyed female and ½ white-eyed male.

C. All red eyed, half male and half female.

D. ¼ red-eyed female, ¼ white-eyed female, ¼ red-eyed male and ¼ white-eyed male.

6) The members of a homologous pair of genes are separated during meiosis of reproductive cells so that each gamete contains one of the alleles. The preceding is an expression of which of the following laws?

A. The law of segregation
B. The law of sorting
C. The law of independent assortment
D. The law of gene isolation

7) Which of the following refers to a cross in which traits are considered simultaneously?

A. Filial cross
B. Double cross
C. Dihybrid cross
D. Punnett cross

8) Which of the following terms refers to the frequency with which a gene is expressed in a detectable way?

A. Penetrance
B. Polygenetics
C. Codominance
D. Allelism

9) Which of the following terms refers to the collection of all alleles of every gene present in the members of a population?

A. Genetic assortment
B. Population
C. Gene diversity
D. Gene pool

10) Although there is some evidence that pronounced differences in DNA content can interfere with chromosome pairing between species, the effect is surprisingly slight; hybrids between related species of grasses that differ by as much as 50 percent in DNA content have virtually normal chromosome pairing, chiasma formation and segregation. Which of the following processes likely occurs to allow the normal chromosome pairing observed in grass species?

A. The interstitial repetitive sequences in one homologous chromosome would loop so that pairing could occur.
B. The unpaired sequences in the homologous chromosome without the interstitial repetitive sequences would duplicate so that pairing could occur.
C. The homologous chromosome with the interstitial repetitive sequence would undergo a translocation so that pairing could occur.
D. The homologous chromosome with the interstitial repetitive sequence would undergo a deletion so that pairing could occur.

11) Von Willebrand's disease is an autosomal dominant bleeding disorder. A man who does not have the disease has two children with a woman who is heterozygous for the condition. If the first child expresses the bleeding disorder, what is the probability that the second child will have the disease?

A. 0.25
B. 0.50
C. 0.75
D. 1.00

12) A transfusion of red blood cells is being considered. Which of the following donors would NOT elicit and immune response in a recipient who is type B and Rh-negative?

A. One who was type A and Rh-negative.
B. One who was type AB and Rh-negative, but had been previously exposed to Rh-positive blood.
C. One who was type B and Rh-negative, but had been previously exposed to Rh-positive blood.
D. One who was type B and Rh-positive.

13) Given that the ABO system elicits a much stronger immune response (i.e. more immunogenic) than the Rh-factor, an Rh-negative type O mother carrying an Rh-positive child will most likely manufacture anti-Rh antibodies if fetal cells enter the maternal circulation if the child is:

A. type A.
B. type B.
C. type O.
D. type AB.

14) The risk of hemolytic disease of the newborn increases with each Rh-positive pregnancy that an Rh-negative woman has. The main reason for this is that:

A. the probability of the fetus being Rh-positive increases with every pregnancy.
B. Rh-negative antibodies in the maternal circulation can cross the placental barrier to attack and hemolyse the erythrocytes of the fetus.
C. anti-Rh antibodies in the maternal circulation can cross the placental barrier to attack and hemolyse the erythrocytes of the fetus.
D. anti-Rh agglutins are not strongly expressed in the fetal circulation.

15) Nonsense mutations and frame shift mutations would most likely originate during which of the following?

A. DNA replication
B. Transcription
C. Translation
D. Splicing

16) Consider the following crossover frequencies:

Crossover	*Genes Frequency*
B and *D*	2%
C and *A*	7%
A and *B*	15%
C and *B*	20%
C and *D*	25%

Which of the following represents the relative positions of the four genes A, B, C and D, on the chromosome?

A. *ADCB*
B. *CABD*
C. *DBCA*
D. *ABCD*

17) From which grandparent or grandparents did you inherit your mitochondria?

A. Paternal grandfather
B. Maternal grandmother
C. Mother's parents
D. Grandmothers

How can you distinguish the sex chromosomes? Pull down their genes! :)

GS ANSWER KEY

CHAPTER 15

		Cross-Reference			*Cross-Reference*
1.	C	BIO 15.1, 15.5	10.	A	BIO 15.5, 14.2, deduce
2.	D	BIO 15.1, 14.5.1	11.	B	BIO 15.3
3.	B	BIO 15.3	12.	C	BIO 15.2
4.	D	BIO 15.1	13.	C	BIO 15.2
5.	D	BIO 15.1, 15.3	14.	C	BIO 15.2, 15.3.1, 8.2
6.	A	BIO 15.3	15.	A	BIO 15.5, 1.2.2, 14.2
7.	C	BIO 15.3	16.	B	BIO 15.6
8.	A	BIO 15.6	17.	B	BIO 1.2.2
9.	D	BIO 15.4			

*** Explanations can be found at the back of the book.**

Go online to MCAT-prep.com/forum to join the discussion about our GS chapter review questions.

EVOLUTION

Chapter 16

Memorize	Understand	Clinical Correlation
efine: species, genetic drift	* Natural selection, speciation * Genetic drift * Basics: comparative anatomy * Basics: eukaryotic, prokaryotic evolution	Organisms like viruses, bacteria, and fungi, as well as gene-based processes like cancers, can evolve to become resistant to host immune defences and medications. Concepts developed in evolutionary biology have been applied to genetic engineering affecting many areas of research including antibiotics.

MCAT-Prep.com

Introduction

Evolution is, quite simply, the change in the inherited traits of a population of organisms from one generation to another. This change over time can be traced to 3 main processes: variation, reproduction and selection. The major mechanisms that drive evolution are natural selection and genetic drift. Chemical evolution led to cellular evolution and, ultimately, to the enormous diversity within 3 Domains and 6 Kingdoms.

Optional Gold Standard Resources

Free Online Q&A + Forum

Flashcards

Special Guest

16.1 Overview

Evolution is the change in frequency of one or more alleles in a population's gene pool from one generation to the next. The evidence for evolution lies in the fossil record, biogeography, embryology, comparative anatomy, and experiments from artificial selection. The most important mechanism of evolution is the **selection** of certain phenotypes provided by the **genetic variability** of a population.

16.2 Natural Selection

Natural selection is the non-random differential survival and reproduction from one generation to the next. Natural selection contains the following premises: i) genetic and phenotypic variability exist in populations: offspring show variations compared to parents; ii) more individuals are produced than live to grow up and reproduce; iii) the population competes to survive; iv) individuals with some genes are more likely to survive (greater fitness) than those with other genes; v) individuals that are more likely to survive transmit these favorable variations (genes) to their offspring so that these genes become more dominant in the gene pool.

It is not necessarily true that natural selection leads to the the Darwin-era expression "survival of the fittest"; rather it is the genes, and not necessarily the individual, which are likely to survive.

Evolution goes against the foundations of the Hardy-Weinberg Law. For example, natural selection leads to non-random mating due to phenotypic differences. Evolution occurs when those phenotypic changes depend on an underlying genotype; thus non-random mating can lead to changes in allelic frequencies. Consider an example: if female peacocks decide to only mate with a male with long feathers, then there will be a selection pressure against any male with a genotype which is expressed as short feathers. Because of this differential reproduction, the alleles which are expressed as short feathers will be eliminated from the population. Thus this population evolves.

The three forms of natural selection are: i) **stabilizing selection** in which genetic diversity decreases as the population stabilizes on an average phenotype (*phenotypes have a "bell curve" distribution*). This is the most common form of natural selection. It is basically the opposite of disruptive selection, instead of favoring individuals with extreme phenotypes, it favors the intermediate phenotype; ii) **directional selection** when an extreme phenotype has a selective advantage over the average phenotype causing the allele frequency continually shifting in one direction (*thus the curve can become skewed to the left or right*). It occurs most often when populations migrate to new areas with environmental pressures; iii) **disruptive selec-**

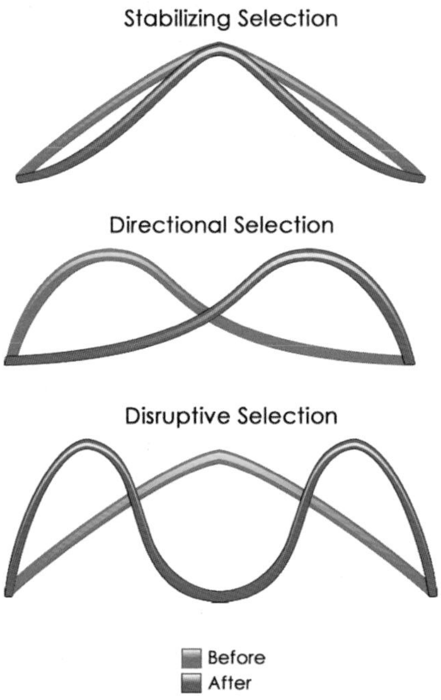

tion where both extremes are selected over the average phenotype; this would produce a split down the middle of the "bell curve" such that two new and separate "bell curves" would result. For example, if a bird only ate medium sized seeds and left the large and small ones alone, two new populations or groups of seeds would have a reproductive advantage. Thus by selecting against the group of medium sized seeds, two new groups of large and small seeds will result. This is an example of group selection causing *disruptive selection*.

16.3 Species and Speciation

Species can be defined as the members of populations that interbreed or can interbreed under natural conditions. There are great variations within species. A **cline** is a gradient of variation in a species across a geographical area. **Speciation** is the evolution of new species by the <u>isolation</u> of gene pools of related populations. The isolation of gene pools is typically geographic. An ocean, a glacier, a river or any other physical barrier can isolate a population and prevent it from mating with other populations of the same species. The two populations may begin to differ because their <u>mutations</u> may be different, or, there may be different <u>selection pressures</u> from the two different environments, or, *genetic drift* may play a role.

Genetic drift is the random change in frequencies of alleles or genotypes in a population (recall that this is antagonistic to the Hardy-Weinberg Law). Genetic drift normally occurs when a small population is isolated from a large population. Since the allelic frequencies in the small population may be different from the large population (*sampling error*), the two populations may evolve in different directions.

Populations or species can be <u>sympatric</u>, in which speciation occurs after ecological, genetic or behavioral barriers arise within the same geographical boundary of a single population, or <u>allopatric</u>, in which speciation occurs through geographical isolation of groups from the parent population {Sympatric = live together, Allopatric = live apart}. Mechanisms involved in allopatric speciation are represented in the two preceding paragraphs.

The following represents some isolating mechanisms that prevent sympatric populations of different species from breeding together: i) habitat differences; ii) different breeding times or seasons; iii) mechanical differences (i.e. different anatomy of the genitalia); iv) behavioral specificity (i.e. different courtship behavior); v) gametic isolation (= fertilization cannot occur); vi) hybrid inviability (i.e. the hybrid zygote dies before reaching the age of sexual maturity); vii) hybrid sterility; viii) hybrid breakdown: the hybrid offspring is fertile but produces a next generation (F_2) which is infertile or inviable.

16.4 Origin of Life

Evidence suggests that the primitive earth had a reducing atmosphere with gases such as H_2 and the reduced compounds H_2O (vapor), $NH_{3(g)}$ (ammonia) and $CH_{4(g)}$ (methane). Such an atmosphere has been shown (i.e. Miller, Fox) to be conducive to the formation and stabilization of organic compounds. Such compounds can sometimes polymerize (*possibly due to autocatalysis*) and evolve into living systems with metabolism, reproduction, digestion, excretion, etc.

Critical in the early history of the earth was the evolution of: (1) the reducing atmosphere powered with energy (e.g. lightening, UV radiation, outgassing volcanoes) converting reduced compounds (water, ammonia, methane) into simple organic molecules (the 'primordial soup'); (2) self-replicating molecules surrounded by membranes forming protocells (very primitive microspheres, coacervates assembling into the precursor of prokaryotic cells: protobionts); (3) chemosynthetic bacteria which are anaerobes that used chemicals in the environment to produce energy; (4) photosynthesis which releases O_2 and thus converted the atmosphere into an oxidizing one; (5) respiration, which could use the O_2 to efficiently produce ATP; and (6) the development of membrane bound organelles (*a subset of prokaryotes which evolved into eukaryotes,* BIO 16.6.3) which allowed eukaryotes to develop meiosis, sexual reproduction, and fertilization.

It is important to recognize that throughout the evolution of the earth, organisms and the environment have and will continue to shape each other.

16.5 Comparative Anatomy

Anatomical features of organisms can be compared in order to derive information about their evolutionary histories. Structures which originate from the same part of the embryo are called homologous. **Homologous** structures may have similar anatomical features shared by two different species as a result of a common ancestor but with a late divergent evolutionary pattern in response to different evolutionary forces. Such structures may or may not serve different functions. **Analogous** structures have similar functions in two different species but arise from different evolutionary origins and entirely different developmental patterns (see Figure IV.A.16.1).

Vestigial structures represent further evidence for evolution since they are organs which are useless in their present owners, but are homologous with organs which are important in other species. For example, the appendix in humans is a vestige of an organ that had digestive functions in ancestral species. However, it continues to assist in the digestion of cellulose in herbivores.

Taxonomy is the branch of biology which deals with the classification of organisms. Humans are classified as follows:

Kingdom	Animalia
Phylum (= Division)	Chordata
Subdivision	Vertebrata
Class	Mammalia
Order	Primates
Family	Hominidae
Genus	*Homo*
Species	*Homo sapiens*

{Mnemonic for remembering the taxonomic categories: King Philip came over for great soup}

The subphyla Vertebrata and Invertebrata are subdivisions of the phylum Chordata. Acorn worms, tunicates, sea squirts and amphioxus are invertebrates. Humans, birds, frogs, fish, and crocodiles are vertebrates. We will examine features of both the chordates and the vertebrates.

Chordates have the following characteristics at some stage of their development: i) a notochord; ii) pharyngeal gill slits which lead from the pharynx to the exterior; iii) a hollow dorsal nerve cord. Other features which are less defining but are nonetheless present in chordates are: i) a more or less segmented anatomy; ii) an internal skeleton (= *endoskeleton*); iii) a tail at some point in their development.

Vertebrates have all the characteristics of chordates. In addition, vertebrates have: i) a vertebral column; ii) well developed sensory and nervous systems; iii) a ventral heart with a closed vascular system; iv) some sort of a liver, endocrine organs, and kidneys; and v) cephalization which is the concentration of sense organs and nerves to the front end of the body producing an obvious head.

16.6 Patterns of Evolution

The evolution of a species can be divided into four main patterns:

1. Divergent evolution – Two or more species originate from a common ancestor.
2. Convergent evolution – Two unrelated species become more alike as they evolve due to similar ecological conditions. The traits that resemble one another are called analogous traits. Similarity in species of different ancestry as a result of convergent evolution is homoplasty. For example, flying insects, birds and bats have evolved wings independently.
3. Parallel evolution – This describes two related species that have evolved similarly after their divergence from a common ancestor. For example, the appearance of similarly shaped leaves in many genera of plant species.
4. Coevolution – This is the evolution of one species in response to adaptations gained by another species. This most often occurs in predator/prey relationships where an adaptation in the prey species that makes them less vulnerable leads to new adaptations in the predator species to help them catch their prey.

16.6.1 Macroevolution

Macroevolution describes patterns of evolution for groups of species rather than individual species. There are two main theories:

1. **Phyletic gradualism** – This theory argues that evolution occurs through gradual accumulation of small changes. They point to fossil evidence as proof that major changes in speciation occur over long periods of geological time and state that the incompleteness of the fossil record is the reason why some intermediate changes are not evidenced.
2. **Punctuated equilibrium** – This theory states that evolutionary history is marked

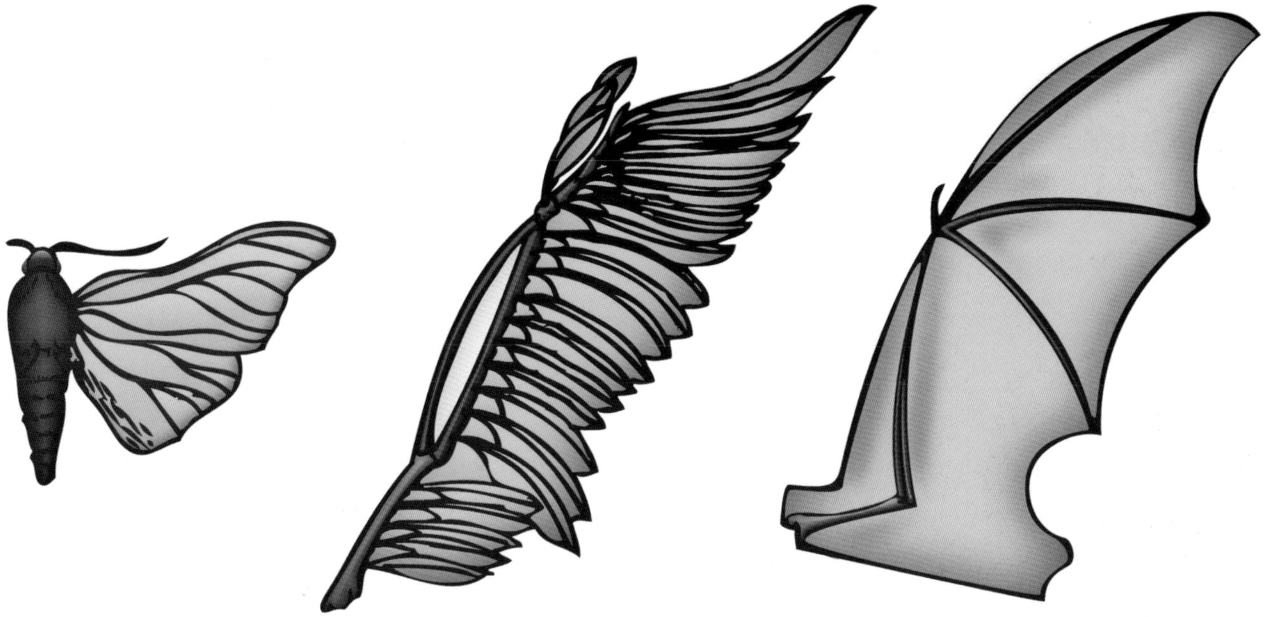

Figure IV.A.16.1: Analogous and homologous structures. The light blue wings represent analogous structures between different species: a flying insect, a bird and a bat, respectively. The bones are homologous structures. For example, green represents the humerus, purple represents the radius and ulna, red represents metacarpals and phalanges. Of course, insects have no bones. See the skeleton in BIO 11.3 to remind yourself of the meaning of some of these bony structures homologous in humans.

by sudden bursts of rapid evolution with long periods of inactivity in between. Punctuated equilibrium theorists point to the absence of fossils showing intermediate change as proof that evolution occurred in short time periods.

16.6.2 Basic Patterns for Changes in Macroevolution

1. Phyletic change (anagenesis): gradual change in an entire population that results in an eventual replacement of ancestral species by novel species and ancestral populations can be considered extinct.
2. Cladogenesis: one lineage gives rise to two or more lineages each forming a "clad". It leads to the development of a variety of sister species and often occurs when it is introduced to a new, distant environment.
3. Adaptive radiation: a formation of a number of lineages from a single ancestral species. A single species can diverge into a number of different species, which are able to exploit new environments.
4. Extinction: more than 99.9% of all species are no longer present.

16.6.3 Eukaryotic Evolution

Eukaryotes evolved from primitive heterotrophic prokaryotes in the following manner:

1. Heterotrophs first formed in the primordial soup (mixture of organic material) present in the early Earth (BIO 16.4). As the cells reproduced, competition increased and natural selection favored those heterotrophs who were best suited to obtain food.
2. Heterotrophs evolved into autotrophs (capable of making own food) via mutation. The first autotrophs were highly successful because they were able to manufacture their own food supply using light energy or energy from inorganic substrates (i.e. cyanobacteria).
3. As a by-product of the photosynthetic activity of autotrophs, oxygen was released into the atmosphere. This lead to formation of the ozone layer which prevented UV light from reaching the earth's surface. The interference of this major autotrophic resource was caused by the increased blockage of light rays.
4. Mitochondria, chloroplasts, and possibly other organelles of eukaryotic cells, originate through the symbiosis between multiple microorganisms. According to this theory, certain organelles originated as free-living bacteria that were taken inside another cell as endosymbionts. Thus mitochondria developed from proteobacteria and chloroplasts from cyanobacteria. This is the belief of the endosymbiotic theory which counts the following as evidence that it bodes true:
   A. Mitochondria and chloroplasts possess their own unique DNA which is very similar to the DNA of prokaryotes (circular). Their ribosomes also resemble one another with respect to size and sequence.
   B. Mitochondria and chloroplasts reproduce independently of their eukaryotic host cell.
   C. The thylakoid membranes of chloroplasts resemble the photosynthetic membranes of cyanobacteria.

16.6.4 The Six-Kingdom, Three-Domain System

Genetic sequencing led to the replacement of the 'old' Five-Kingdom system of taxonomy (BIO 15.5). Under the current system, there are six kingdoms: Archaebacteria (ancient bacteria), Eubacteria (true bacteria; BIO 2.2), Protista (a diverse group of eukaryotic microorganisms), Fungi (BIO 2.3), Plantae ('plants'), and Animalia ('animals'). The Archaea and Bacteria domains contain prokaryotic organisms. The Eukarya domain includes eukaryotes and is subdivided into the kingdoms Protista, Fungi, Plantae, and Animalia.

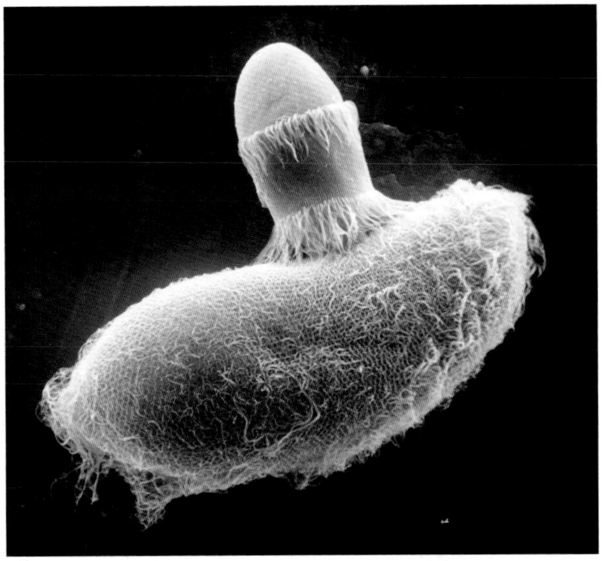

Figure IV.A.16.2: David and Golliath: Two animal-like unicellular, ciliated protists in an epic struggle. The larger of the two carnivores, Paramecium, is attacked from above by the smaller Didinium. In this case, the organisms were preserved for this SEM micrograph (BIO 1.5, 1.5.1) before the outcome could be determined. Like other ciliates (ciliaphora), they can reproduce asexually (binary fission) or sexually (conjugation); osmoregulation is via contractile vacuoles; and, they are also visible using a light microscope.

Six-Kingdom, Three-Domain System

- Archaea Domain
  - Kingdom Archaebacteria
- Bacteria Domain
  - Kingdom Eubacteria
- Eukarya Domain
  - Kingdom Protista
  - Kingdom Fungi
  - Kingdom Plantae
  - Kingdom Animalia

Don't forget to create your own Gold Notes and review them frequently. Try to spend most of your time completing/reviewing practice questions and tests (problem-based learning). Good luck with your studies!

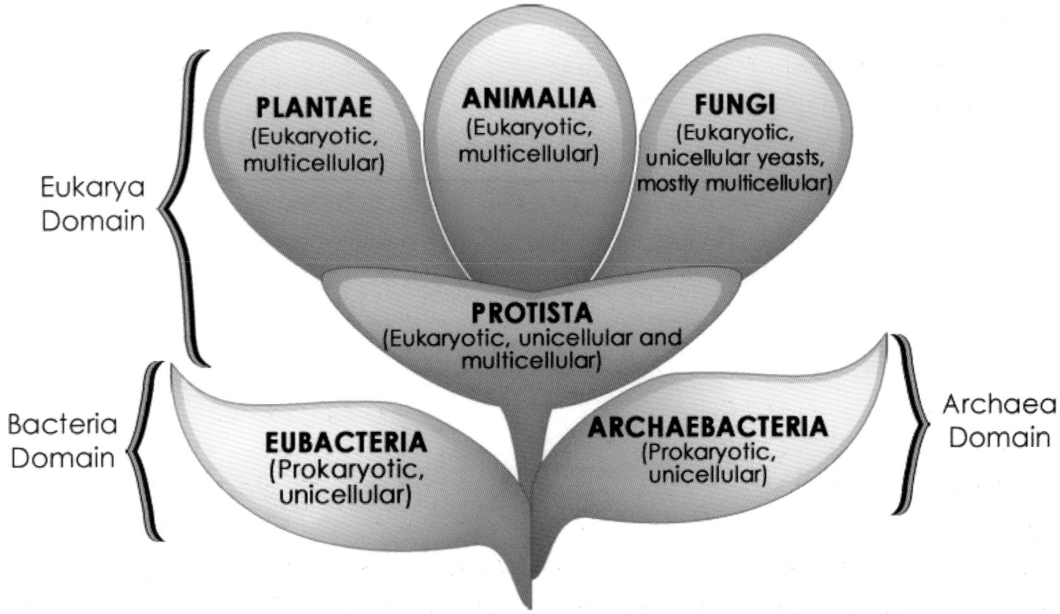

Figure IV.A.16.3: The Six-Kingdom, Three-Domain System.

GOLD STANDARD WARM-UP EXERCISES

CHAPTER 16: Evolution

1) All of the following can provide evidence for evolution EXCEPT one. Which is the EXCEPTION?

A. Fossil record
B. Embryology
C. Spontaneous generation
D. Comparative anatomy

2) Which one of the following would cause the Hardy-Weinberg principle to be inaccurate?

A. Individuals mate with each other at random.
B. There is no source of new copies of alleles from outside the population.
C. The size of the population is very large.
D. Natural selection is present.

3) Which statement most accurately reflects what geneticists refer to as "fitness"?

A. Fitness reflects the number of mates each individual of the population reproduces with.
B. Fitness is a measure of the contribution of a genotype to the gene pool of the next generation.
C. Fitness refers to the relative health of a population as a whole.
D. Fitness is the measure of the relative health of individuals within a population.

4) The increasing occurrence over time of very colorful male birds with a reduction in moderately colorful male birds is an example of:

A. directional selection.
B. stabilizing selection.
C. disruptive selection.
D. the bell curve.

5) Which one of the following populations would most quickly lead to two groups with few shared traits?

A. A population with stabilizing selection
B. A population with disruptive selection
C. A population with no selection
D. A population with directional selection

6) The random loss of alleles in a population is called:

A. natural selection.
B. mutation.
C. genetic drift.
D. nondisjunction.

7) Which of the following molecules is thought to have been absent from the primitive reducing atmosphere?

A. Ammonia (NH_3)
B. Water vapor (H_2O)
C. Oxygen (O_2)
D. Hydrogen (H_2)

8) All of the following is true about a protocell EXCEPT one. Which is the EXCEPTION?

A. It would have contained a biochemical pathway for energy metabolism and self-replicating molecules.
B. It would have been present before the development of a true cell.
C. It might have been like a coacervate droplet in which a semipermeable boundary allows some materials to be absorbed from the surrounding environment.
D. It did not contain a nucleus but had a cell wall and circular DNA.

9) The appearance of photosynthetic cyanobacteria and aerobic bacteria in the early history of the Earth:

A. eliminated the conditions that originally led to the first life on Earth.
B. resulted in the development of an oxidizing atmosphere on Earth.
C. led to the production of the ozone layer and thus reduced the amount of UV light reaching the Earth.
D. All of the above.

10) A taxon consisting of the most closely related species is called a(n):

A. genus.
B. family.
C. order.
D. class.

11) The structural similarities between the flippers of whales and the arms of humans are used to show that:

A. humans and whales have a common ancestry.
B. humans began life in water.
C. whales evolved from humans.
D. whales can swim but humans are not meant to swim.

12) All chordates possess a:

A. hollow dorsal nerve cord.
B. vertebral column.
C. closed vascular system.
D. tail in the adult form.

13) The theory that evolutionary change is slow and continuous is known as:

A. punctuated equilibrium.
B. geographic isolation.
C. gradualism.
D. speciation.

14) Unicellular eukaryotes could be found in:

A. Fungi and Eubacteria.
B. Fungi and Protista.
C. Fungi, Protista and Eubacteria.
D. only Protista.

GS ANSWER KEY

CHAPTER 16

		Cross-Reference			Cross-Reference
1.	C	BIO 16.1	8.	D	BIO 16.4
2.	D	BIO 15.4, 16.2	9.	D	BIO 16.4, 16.6.3, 16.6.4
3.	B	BIO 16.2	10.	A	BIO 16.5
4.	A	BIO 16.2	11.	A	BIO 16.5
5.	B	BIO 16.2	12.	A	BIO 16.5, 16.6.4
6.	C	BIO 16.3	13.	C	BIO 16.6.1
7.	C	BIO 16.4, 16.6.3	14.	B	BIO 16.6.4

*** Explanations can be found at the back of the book.**

Go online to MCAT-prep.com/forum to join the discussion about our GS chapter review questions.

CHAPTER REVIEW SOLUTIONS

Questions or Concerns? Go to www.mcat-prep.com/forum

Question 1 D

See: BIO 1.1, ORG 12.1.1

Proteins spanning the plasma membrane contain hydrophobic regions (mostly uncharged, neutral molecules), which tend to associate with the hydrophobic lipid bilayer, and hydrophilic regions (mostly charged or polar molecules), which tend to associate with the inside or outside hydrophilic environment of the cell. In order for a protein to rotate through the plane of the bilayer, hydrophilic regions would have to traverse the hydrophobic bilayer. As a rule, interactions of this nature (hydrophobic-hydrophilic) are energetically unfavorable.

Question 2 B

See: BIO 1.1, ORG 12.1-12.2.2, CHM 4.2

It is unlikely that weak forces, such as Van Der Waal's, would provide the stable protein-protein interaction needed to anchor a protein to the plasma membrane. On the other hand, covalent bonds occur intramolecularly as opposed to intermolecularly, eliminating answer choice *C*. We would not expect a peripheral protein or the portion of an integral protein facing the extracellular fluid to be hydrophobic, because of the hydrophilic nature of the fluid. This leaves us with answer choice *B*.; the interactions are likely to occur between a charged (hydrophilic) portion of the integral protein with the charged portion of the peripheral protein. The interaction in electrostatic charges is based on 'opposite charges attract'.

Question 3 D

See: BIO 1.1

The question gives a function of glycoproteins. The question asks which of the cellular components has characteristics that would suit the special functions of a glycoprotein. A phospholipid bilayer is a membrane, and one of the functions of the oligosaccharide attached to a protein is to anchor the protein to a membrane and facilitate recognition.

Question 4 B

See: BIO 1.2.1

To answer this question basic knowledge of the function of various cell components is necessary. The Golgi apparatus functions in protein modification like glycosylation (the addition of poly/oligosaccharides).

Question 5 B

See: BIO 1.1.1

The question states that sweat is less concentrated (with electrolytes) than blood plasma. The question asks how electrolytes would be transported *from* blood plasma (high concentration) *to* sweat (low concentration). Osmosis is the mechanism by which water, not electrolytes, is transported across membranes. Active transport is used to move molecules *against* their concentration gradient. Simple diffusion is the movement of molecules in the direction in which they naturally tend to move: from areas of high concentration to areas of low concentration, as in this case.

Question 6 D

See: BIO 1.2, 1.2.1, 7.5F

Microfilaments are important in phagocytosis and locomotion. All the choices provided are involved directly or indirectly in both processes. Flagella are used by sperm for locomotion; endocytotic vesicles are formed during phagocytosis at which point they can fuse with primary lysosomes to form secondary lysosomes; granulocytes are phagocytic cells of the immune system. Thus the only difference is that all are organelles except granulocytes which are cells. *Note:* an organelle is simply a cellular structure that has specialized functions. That includes flagella, cilia, vesicles, etc., and of course the ones that you are used to reading about (mitochondria, lysosomes, etc).

Ref: http://en.wikipedia.org/wiki/Organelle

Question 7 C

See: BIO 1.2

You must be familiar with cellular structures to answer this question.

Question 8 D

See: BIO 1.1, 1.2.1

Membrane receptors are proteins which are usually produced by rough endoplasmic reticulum (as opposed to free ribosomes).

Question 9 D

See: BIO 1.2.2

The question identifies the transporter (protein carrier) as ATP-dependent. Only active transport is a carrier-mediated transport system that requires energy in the form of ATP.

Question 10 B

See: BIO 1.2.2, ORG 12.2.2

You can solve this problem by knowing 2 basic facts: (1) thymine is a pyrimidine; and (2) sulfur is not a component of nitrogen bases. Note: sulfur is a component of the amino acid cysteine which can make disulfide bonds with itself creating cystine which stabilizes the tertiary structure of proteins.

Question 11 A

See: BIO 1.2.2

Option *D*. is an accurate description of how the nitrogenous bases bind together to form the helical structure. Option *C*. is also a feature of the molecule which aids in maintaining the shape. The hydrophobic bases are kept in the center of the helix while the hydrophillic backbone interacts with the outside environment. Option *B*. is similar to option *D*. in that it describes the bonds which give the helical molecule its strength. Option *A*. is a description of a negative consequence of DNA not holding its helical structure. It is not a process or interaction by which DNA maintains its shape.

Question 12 C

See: BIO 1.3

The order of events in the cell cycle is: G_1, S (*synthesis*), G_2,

Prophase, Metaphase, Anaphase, Telophase. If a drug prevents prophase from occurring, most cells will be arrested at the stage immediately prior to prophase, G_2.

Question 13 C

See: BIO 1.2.2, 3.0

Bidirectional replication suggests that replication will occur in two directions. The only option consistent with this is option *C.* which states that DNA replication will begin on both sides of the origin.

Question 14 D

See: BIO 1.2.2

Drawing a diagram would be helpful for you to visualize the circular replication of the chromosome. In the first replication a uniformly normal circular chromosome would replicate producing two molecules that are half normal and half labelled (one parent strand, one new ^{3}H-thymidine labelled daughter strand). The preceding is the essence of semi-conservative replication. When this molecule replicates (the second round of replication), the parent strand will be the template on one branch of the replication fork and the labelled strand will be the template on the other branch of the replication fork. The parent (normal) strand will produce another half normal, half labelled molecule. The labelled strand will produce a new molecule in which both strands are labelled (e.g. has twice as much labelled portion as the other daughter molecule).

Question 15 A

See: BIO 1.2, 1.3

The question indicates that colchicine inhibits segregation of the daughter cells during mitosis. Segregation is accomplished in anaphase, whereby the spindle microtubules guide the sister chromatids to opposing sides of the cell. Based on this information, we would expect colchicine to disrupt spindle formation. Note that answer choices *B.* and *C.* both refer to the same cell process (DNA replication), and therefore, can be eliminated on this basis alone.

Question 16 C

See: BIO 1.2.2, BCM 1.5

You must be familiar with the method by which DNA is linked together. You should know that the chain is made by additions to the hydroxyl group of the third carbon in the sugar. Thus if the nucleotide will not accept a bond (= *phosphodiester*; BCM 1.5), then the hydroxyl group at C3 must be missing.

Question 17 B

See: BIO 1.2.2

DNA polymerase is the only enzyme listed that functions to build the new chain of complementary DNA.

Question 18 C

See: BIO 1.2.2, BCM 1.5

Note the word *deoxy*nucleoside. This should alert you to the fact that you are dealing with DNA and not RNA. The only option listed that is used in RNA but not DNA is *C.*, dUTP (A = adenosine; G = guanosine; C = cytosine; U = uracil).

Question 19 C

See: BIO 1.2.2, BCM 1.5

The DNA double helix is composed of a sugar-*phosphate* backbone from which bases extend towards the center of the helix. Although amino acids in proteins do not contain phosphate, there are 2 amino acids whose side chains contain the sulfur atom. Therefore, if the bacteriophage enter the bacterial cell to replicate (= form progeny) in a medium containing labelled sulfur and phosphate molecules, we would expect the phosphate and sulfur atoms to be incorporated into DNA and protein components, respectively.

Question 20 B

See: BIO 1.2.2

Carrier-mediated transport is the only option listed that has a maximum rate at which molecules can be helped to cross the membrane. At this point all of the carrier molecules are operating at their maximum rate and increasing the concentration gradient will have no effect. If the method of transport was simple diffusion, more and more molecules would diffuse as the concentration gradient increased (see the classic curves: BIO 1.1.2F). Osmosis is the diffusion of water, and it would increase as the concentration gradient also increased.

Question 21 A

See: BIO 1.1.3

The receptor-mediated endocytosis of ligands (e.g. low density lipoprotein, transferrin, growth factors, antibodies, etc.) are mediated by clathrin-coated vesicles which are found in virtually all cells.

Question 22 A

See: BIO 1.4.1

Desmosomes include cell adhesion proteins like cadherins which can bind intermediate filaments and provide mechanical support and stability. Tight junctions anchor to the actin component of the cytoskeleton.

Question 23 B

See: BIO 1.4.1

A tight junction surrounds a cell like a belt, preventing substances from passing between cells (occlusion). Note that an adherens junctions, AKA "belt desmosome", are anchoring not occluding junctions.

Question 24 A

See: BIO 1.5

The total magnification is calculated by multiplying the ocular magnification by the objective magnification so 10 x 40 = 400 times magnification of the specimen size. An excellent light microscope can comfortably magnify up to 1000 times.

Question 25 D

See: BIO 1.5, 1.5.1

Electron microscopy (TEM and SEM) cannot observe live organisms as a vacuum is required and the specimen is flooded with electrons. The most specific answer is a confocal microscope which is a state-of-the-art fluorescent microscope that can visualize the fluorophore labeling on a molecule, using, for example, a technique like FRAP.

CHAPTER REVIEW SOLUTIONS — CHAPTER 2

Question 1 A

See: BIO 2.1

You should know the basic structure of a virus. HBsAg is described as a protein. A virus is very simple in structure and the protein outer coating is called the *capsid*. Viruses do not have 'slimy mucoid-like' capsules around them like some bacteria.

Question 2 D

See: BIO 2.2

Prokaryotes (bacteria) have no nuclei thus no nuclear membrane. The do have both plasma membranes and cell walls. If you chose answer choice B then you may have forgotten that some eukaryotes also have cell walls: fungi, plants.

Question 3 B

See: BIO 2.1

All viruses require cells to replicate: obligate intracellular parasites. However, some viruses use DNA as genetic material and viruses may infect numerous cell types including bacteria (phage). Specific knowledge of HIV is irrelevant.

Question 4 C

See: BIO 2.2, 4.5

To begin with, the issue of gram positive or gram negative is irrelevant and should not distract you. This question actually reduces to the following simple concepts: your mouth is sometimes open (*exposed to oxygen*) and sometimes closed (*little or no oxygen*). Thus in order to survive in your mouth, a bacterium would need to be able to produce energy in the presence or absence of oxygen (= *facultative anaerobe*).

Question 5 D

See: BIO 1.1, 2.2, 4.1

From the description in the question it is clear that glucan is formed outside of the bacteria. It adheres to the teeth and is present between bacteria. Therefore, the enzyme which catalyzes the formation of glucan must be located on an external surface of the bacteria.

Question 6 D

See: BIO 2.2-2.3

The question is asking for a difference between a bacterium and a fungus. Options *A.*, *B.* and *C.* may very well be correct attributes of the organism stated, but for it to be the correct answer it must be a characteristic that the other organism does not also possess. Bacteria are prokaryotes and therefore do not have a nucleus. Fungi, on the other hand, are eukaryotes and therefore contain a nucleus, so this is the difference between the two organisms. Note that both fungi and bacteria have cell walls, ribosomes and can undergo anaerobic metabolism.

Question 7 B

See: BIO 2.2

The suffix 'coccus' refers to the shape and means sphere. The suffix 'bacillus' also refers to the shape and means cylindrical. *{P.S.: never let the mere size of a word or molecule intimidate you!}*

Question 8 A

See: BIO 2.2, 15.5

Answer choices *B.*, *C.* and *D.* are processes by which bacteria multiply or by which they change their genetic makeup thereby enhancing their chances of survival (which contributes to their proliferation). Answer choice *A.* sounds very similar to these bacterial processes, but is not associated with an increase in viability or with multiplication.

Question 9 C

See: BIO 1.3, 2.2

In the span of two hours, the bacteria will have divided eight times (8 x 15 min = 120 min = 2 hours). You can think about it like this: in 15 min (#1 = 1st doubling time), the 10 bacteria will all have duplicated, making 20. After another 15 min (#2 = 2nd doubling time), all of those 20 bacteria will have duplicated, making 40. This doubling goes on and on a total of 8 times: #3 = 80, #4 = 160, #5 = 320, #6 = 640, #7 = 1280, #8 = 2560.

Alternatively, there are equations for doubling time and half-lives, and you should be familiar with how to use them. For doubling time, $X \times 2^n$, where X is the number originally present and n is the number of doubling times. Thus we get:

$$X \times 2^n = 10 \times 2^8 = 10 \times 256 = 2560.$$

For half-lives, $X \times (1/2)^n$, where X is the number originally present and n is the number of half-lives.

Question 10 C

See: BIO 2.3

An exponential curve describes the growth of an organism reproducing by budding or cell fission. In this graph, curve C is representative of exponential growth.

Question 11 B

See: BIO 2.3

You must understand the basic processes involved in the reproduction of fungi to answer this question. Budding is a common process in plants and fungi (includes unicellular yeast like Candida). It also occurs in certain animals, particularly the

Hydra (sponges). In fungi the bud stays for a while, and then detaches to grow fully as a new individual. Budding is a form of asexual reproduction since the process results in the formation of new individual but is a clone of the primary organism.

Question 12 C

See: BIO 2.2

Nitrogen fixation is the conversion by certain soil microorganisms of atmospheric nitrogen into compounds that plants and other organisms can assimilate. Some bacteria are photosynthetic and others are chemoautotrophic obtaining energy via chemical reactions including the oxidation of nitrogen, iron, sulfur and hydrogen gas.

Question 13 A

See: P2, S3

The passage clearly states that the protein dystrophin is located on the inner surface of the plasma membrane (P2, S3). All that is required for this question is that you recall that protein hormones (answer choice *A.*) do not diffuse across the plasma membrane (BIO 1.1, 6.3) and thus have their effect on the outer surface of the membrane (cf. steroid hormones). This recognition is then transduced into an intracellular message using intermediates like intrinsic proteins which span the membrane and cyclic AMP.

Question 14 C

See: P3, S3, S5; BIO 2.2, BIO 4

To clone a piece of DNA, large quantities of DNA must be produced (P3). The method by which this is done is through the use of bacterial plasmids. The foreign DNA is inserted into plasmid DNA (not capsid, as in option A.). The bacterial plasmid is replicated through the normal life cycle of bacteria, which is short enough to allow rapid replication of the foreign sequence. For cloning to take place sites must exist where foreign DNA can be inserted. However, inserting the DNA is of no use unless the bacteria can complete its usual life cycle after being altered in such a way.

Question 15 D

See: BIO 1.2.2, BCM 1.5, BIO 4

Let's translate the question into more basic language: if you have a DNA molecule (*plasmid*) and you want to add another DNA molecule (*foreign DNA*), how can this be done? The answer is that a DNA molecule is elongated via phosphodiester bonds (answer choice D.). DNA *replication* is a completely different mechanism as it refers to the duplication of DNA strands *within* a DNA molecule which is related to appropriate base pairing (cf. answer choice *C.*) and occurs in a semi-conservative manner (answer choice *A.*). Answer choice *B.* is irrelevant.

Question 16 C

See: deduce, BIO 4

Answer choice *A.* is false because we are looking for a functional gene for dystrophin! Answer choice *B.* is false since it does not refer to any cloning techniques as requested in the question. Answer choice *D.* is false since it is known that dystrophin (P2) and not troponin or tropomyosin is responsible for muscular dystrophy. Answer choice *C.* presents a possible method to treat the disease by: (a) using a cloning technique and (b) inserting the needed gene into diseased cells which would then make them capable of producing dystrophin. {Incidental: this type of research is currently being done on humans using special viruses to insert the missing gene into the cells of the patient}

Question 17 D

See: BIO 5.2

You must understand the structures and processes involved in muscle contraction to answer this question. If you do not remember, it's OK, we'll review the details in Chapter 5!

CHAPTER REVIEW SOLUTIONS — CHAPTER 3

Question 1 C

See: BIO 3.0

You should be familiar with the names of different enzymes involved in the replication, transcription and translation of DNA. Even if you don't know, it is easy to make a good guess just by looking at the names. You are asked for an enzyme that will help synthesize a chain of RNA. You can then narrow it down to a choice which includes the word RNA. The two choices are either replicase or polymerase. In producing a strand of RNA, nothing is being replicated. A chain (polymer) of RNA is being made which is complementary but not identical to the strand of DNA. It is easy to conclude that RNA polymerase must be involved (BIO 3.0).

Question 2 B

See: BIO 1.2.1, 3.0

Releasing factors need to be located near ribosomes engaging in protein synthesis. You should know that such ribosomes are located in the cytosol (answer choice *B.*) or associated with *rough* endoplasmic reticulum, not within the nucleus, nor *smooth* endoplasmic reticulum, nor mitochondria.

Question 3 C

See: BIO 3.0, 1.2.1

rRNA is synthesised from a DNA template in the nucleolus.

Question 4 A

See: BIO 3.0

The codon is on mRNA and the anti-codon is on tRNA.

Question 5 D

See: BIO 3.0

Also, a ribosome consists of a large and a small subunit. In eukaryotic cells, each subunit is assembled in the nucleolus where we find a relatively high density of rRNA.

Question 6 A

See: BIO 1.2.2, 3.0

CAT in DNA becomes GUA in mRNA because C pairs with G, A pairs with U and T pairs with A. Then GUA in mRNA is paired with CAU in tRNA. There is no thymine in RNA.

Question 7 D

See: BIO 1.2.2, 3.0

In BIO 3.0, see Table IV.A.3.2.

Question 8 B

See: BIO 3.0

Degeneracy is the redundancy of the genetic code. Degeneracy occurs because there are more codons than encodable amino acids. The consequence is that a single amino acid can have multiple codons.

Question 9 C

See: P1; E; BIO 4.1, ORG 9.4

The name of an enzyme is usually related to its function. In termination, cleavage of an ester bond is required (P1). Therefore, esterase is the most appropriate name.

Question 10 D

See: P3; E; BIO 3.0, 4.2

Peptidyl transferase is involved in making the peptide bonds in the forming amino acid (P3). In termination, the activity of peptidyl transferase is altered by releasing factors so that a molecule of water may be added (= hydrolysis) instead of another aminoacyl tRNA (P3; E). So, if peptidyl transferase activity is inhibited, both of these processes are inhibited.

Background: enzymes often let you know their activity by their name. Peptidyl transferase transfers one amino acid to another thus creating a peptide bond: the continuation of this process creates and elongates a protein.

Read P3 again.

Translation of all the above: peptidyl transferase is important for 2 things: (1) peptide bonds and (2) when modified, peptidyl transferase can permit water to attack. So both (1) and (2) will not occur if peptidyl transferase activity is inhibited.

Question 11 A

See: ORG 8.1, 9.4

Attack of the carbon shown in Figure 1 by water will cause the oxygen that is already attached to the sugar to leave the amino acid (see arrow in Figure 1). The oxygen of the water will become part of the amino acid as it loses its hydrogens.

CHAPTER REVIEW SOLUTIONS — CHAPTER 4

Question 1 C

See: BIO 1.2.2, 4.1.4

The polymerase chain reaction utilizes DNA primers that anneal to the DNA template. DNA polymerase then extends the DNA primers in an effort to replicate the DNA strand. These steps are identical to those of DNA replication in a cell (BIO 1.2). However, in a cell, the cycle occurs once per cellular division.

Question 2 A

See: BIO 1.2.2, BCM 2.9, deduce

Since mammalian cells function at 37 °C, this is also the optimal temperature for enzyme activity. The temperatures used in PCR, which are well above 70 °C, would easily denature human DNA polymerase which is why a heat resistant DNA polymerase is required. Using human DNA polymerase would require new enzyme after each cycle, and therefore would not be very efficient.

Question 3 B

See: BIO 15.3, BCM 4.1.4

According to the information provided in this chapter (which might be provided in an MCAT passage prior to the question), sex determination can be determined by amplifying intron 1 of the amelogenin gene which is found on the sex chromosomes. Due to a deletion, intron 1 on the Y sex homologue is shorter than intron 1 on the X sex homolog. This difference in size can be used to distinguish between males and females because males have one X and one Y chromosome while females have two X chromosomes. Therefore, females will have only one uniform size of intron 1 which does not bear the deletion. In contrast, males will have 2 different sizes of intron 1 following its amplification. Hence, B. is the correct answer choice.

Question 4 D

See: BIO 15.3, BCM 4.1.4

A male individual, which contains one X and one Y chromosome, should have 2 types of intron 1. The passage states that intron 1 on the Y chromosome has a deletion which renders it smaller in length than the corresponding allele on the X chromosome, thereby providing males with 2 different size fragments. Females which have 2 X chromosomes will then have only 1 type of intron 1 of uniform size.

Question 5 A

See: BIO 15.7, BCM 4.1.4

A Southern blot is routinely used in molecular biology for detection of a specific DNA sequence in DNA samples. Southern blotting combines techniques including the transfer of electrophoresis-separated DNA fragments to a filter membrane and subsequent fragment detection by probe hybridization.

Question 6 B

See: BIO 1.2.2, 2.2, 4.1.2, 4.2.1

If a circular plasmid is improperly digested, it will likely result in a mixture of nicked, supercoiled, and linear DNA. Although the different forms of the DNA are the same mass, they will travel through the gel at different speeds – nicked DNA (one strand is digested, but not the other) will travel the slowest, while supercoiled DNA will travel the fastest. For cloning purposes, researchers desire linearized plasmids, which allows them to insert a gene of insert in the cut site.

Question 7   C

See: BIO 2.2, 4.1.1, 4.1.3

The inclusion of an antibiotic resistance gene (e.g. common antibiotics include ampicillin, kanamycin, chloramphenicol) in a DNA plasmid gives the researcher much more control over the final product, especially in cloning. It allows for the positive selection of potentially viable clones (A) by allowing only E. coli with complete plasmids to survive on antibiotic agar plates, presumably the cut plasmid and the gene insert. It also serves as a good control in several steps in the cloning process – by plating E. coli transfected with cut plasmid + ligase (no gene insert) on antibiotic plates, researchers can test that the restriction digest was complete. A properly digested plasmid will not yield any colonies (D), assuming a double-digestion using two different restriction enzymes. Antibiotic resistance also helps prevent the growth of unwanted E. coli, whether it's E. coli that's missing the plasmid, or foreign E. coli (B). However, antibiotic resistance does not protect against bacteriophages, which are viruses. It's a good thing, too, as bacteriophages such as λ phage are often used in cloning to deliver genetic material to bacteria pre-transformed with antibiotic resistance genes! Thus, C is the right answer.

Question 8   A

See: BIO 1.2.2, 4.1.4

A polymerase chain reaction requires a DNA template that contains the target gene to be amplified, as well as forward and reverse primers, DNA polymerase, deoxynucleotide triphosphates, as well as a buffer solution that likely includes cations like $Mg2^{+}$. Ligase is not required, as there is no cut DNA to be fused together.

Question 9   D

See: BIO 4.1.3

Salmon sperm is frequently used as a "blocking" reagent to reduce non-specific binding between the DNA fragments to be screened and the hybridization probe. While it is not likely that a high quantity of the hybridization probe will bind non-specifically to the DNA, especially under high-stringency conditions, it may still occur, due simply to the electrostatic and hydrogen bonding interactions between complementary DNA pairs. However, an excess of foreign DNA (it is unlikely that there is much homology between salmon DNA and a researcher's gene of interest, unless they are studying fish!) will help reduce non-specific binding (and thus background noise) of the probe by binding weakly to the library DNA. During the hybridization process, the probe will bind to its target with a higher affinity, displacing the salmon DNA.

Question 10   A

See: BIO 4.2.3, BCM 1.1.2, BCM 1.2

The isoelectric point gives the pH at which a molecule carries a net zero charge. Thus if the isolectric point of a protein is pH=2, it will be negatively charged at pH=7. If a protein has an isoelectric point of pH=9, it will be positively charged at pH=7. In ion exchange chromatography, cation exchange chromatography binds positively-charged molecules, while anion exchange chromatrography binds negatively-charged molecules. The more negatively-charged a molecule, the stronger it binds to an anion exchange column. As an increasing salt gradient is applied, the negative ions in the salt compete with the negatively-charged proteins bound to the column, eluting the less-negative proteins first - in other words, those with a higher isoelectric point.

Question 11   B

See: BIO 4.2.2

Denaturation leads to the unfolding of the protein, disrupting its secondary and tertiary structures. Regardless of the natural oligomerization state of the protein, on a denaturing SDS-PAGE gel, the protein will likely run as a monomer, retaining only its primary structure.

Question 12   C

See: BIO 1.1.2, 4.3

The resting potential of excitable cells is approximately -60 to -70 mV. When the cells are depolarized, the resting potential becomes less negative. This occurs because of a sudden influx of cations, changing the resting potential to a value of between -40 and -50 mV.

CHAPTER REVIEW SOLUTIONS   CHAPTER 5

Question 1   A

See: BIO 5.1

The area or space between the terminal ending of a neuron and a successive cell is called a synapse.

Question 2   A

See: BIO 5.1, 1.1, 1.1.3

The presynaptic terminal contains vesicles and is enveloped by the plasma membrane of the nerve cell (= neurolemma). Proteins are the carriers or transporters in plasma membranes.

Question 3   B

See: BIO 5.1.1-5.1.3, deduce

In order to answer this question, you can go by memory or look at Table 1. The table indicates that the intracellular K^{+} concentration is much larger (30 times) than the extracellular concentration. Consequently, by simple diffusion the ions will move from inside the cell to the outside. In other words, K^{+} will move from the cytosol to the cell exterior.

Question 4 A

See: BIO 1.2.2, 5.1.1-5.1.3, deduce

Answer choice *A.* is a false statement making it the correct answer! Table 1 shows us that the inside of the membrane is negatively charged (V_m = -70 mV), yet there are 10 times the number of sodium cations *outside* the membrane as compared to inside. The question suggests that there should be a strong gradient for positively charged sodium to diffuse into the *intracellular* fluid (recall opposite *charges attract*). Also, since Table 1 shows that the ionic concentration of sodium outside the cell is so much greater than inside, then this would be another reason that sodium should diffuse into the cell. Thus the only way for sodium to be driven against its charge and concentration (= *electrochemical*) gradient is by *active transport* not diffusion.

Question 5 D

See: BIO 5.1.1-5.1.3, deduce

Let's begin by translating the question: *how do we make the membrane potential (V_m) more negative*? The easy way to answer is simply by looking at the equilibrium potentials of the ions in Table 1. Only chloride and potassium have equilibrium potentials more negative than V_m. If the permeability of either of the two ions could be increased then V_m would become more negative (i.e. the value would become closer to that of the ion whose permeability increased). Thus answer choice *D.* is the only possible answer. In reality the membrane is always very permeable to potassium and that is an important reason resting V_m is negative. Thus increasing the already very high potassium permeability is not an important factor in membrane hyperpolarization. Imagine what would happen if the permeability to sodium suddenly increased: Vm would tend towards the equilibrium potential of sodium which is positive (= *depolarization*).

Question 6 C

See: BIO 4.2, 5.1, 11.2

At the neuromuscular junction, a depolarization of the cell due to an action potential causes the opening of Ca^{2+} channels in the presynaptic terminal. An increase in intracellular calcium leads to the fusion of acetylcholine-filled vesicles to the membrane. Acetylcholine (Ach) diffuses into the synapse where it binds to receptors on the post-synaptic membrane, leading to the activation of muscle fibers. The enzyme acetylcholinesterase, also present in the junction, terminates the signal by deactivating Ach. The deactivation of the enzyme by DFP will lead to a relative increase in Ach in the synapse and consequently, the Ach signal will be amplified, leading to muscle tetany (= successive activation of a muscle fiber over a short period of time such that the muscle does not have time to recover from an action potential, and it is in a constant state of activation). Note that an action potential is referred to as an "all-or-none" phenomenon; once the minimal threshold has been reached for a particular cell, the action potential has a characteristic magnitude and duration, which cannot be altered by an increase in stimulus. Therefore, an increase in Ach binding as a result of DFP deactivation will lead to an increase in frequency of activation of the action potential in the post-synaptic membrane as opposed to an increase in the magnitude of the action potential (as stated by answer choice *D.*).

Question 7 D

See: BIO 5.1.1-5.1.3, deduce

The figure provided illustrates the membrane permeability of both Na^+ and K^+. The permeability is dependent upon how long the respective channels remain open. As can be seen in the graph, the permeability for Na^+ increases sharply and decreases within 1 ms, whereas the peak for K^+ is much lower and decreases within approximately 2 ms. As a result, the Na^+ channel opens and closes more quickly (turnover rate) because its permeability increases and decreases at a faster rate.

Question 8 A

See: BIO 4.2, 5.1.1-5.1.3, deduce

Maintenance of a negative membrane potential following depolarization is due in part to the ATPase. During an action potential, K^+ and Na^+ channels open to allow the ions to move down their concentration gradient. However, in order to keep the intracellular and extracellular levels of the ions, energy must be used to move the ions back against their concentration gradients. That is, in order to repolarize the cell, K^+ must be brought into the cell while Na+ is brought out. This is accomplished by the Na^+ /K^+ ATPase which uses ATP to move 3 Na^+ ions out of the cell in exchange for 2 K^+ ions into the cell. This net movement will provide a negative resting membrane potential. Consequently, inhibiting the ATPase will simply cause both the ions to reach equilibrium since they will only be able to move down their concentration gradient.

Question 9 C

See: BIO 5.1.1, 5.1.2

During an action potential, repolarization of the membrane is due in part to the increased permeability of the K+ channels which allows the ions to move out of the cell. If the K+ channels were only partly blocked, repolarization would occur at a much slower rate resulting in a longer action potential beyond 1ms as is shown in the previous diagram. This would have detrimental effects on an organism since the transmission of information via nerve impulses relies on rapid action potentials.

Question 10 B

See: BIO 4.4, 4.9, 5.1.1

The sodium-potassium pump uses energy to transport these molecules against their concentration gradients. Cyanide is an inhibitor of an essential enzyme of the electron transport chain (cytochrome oxidase), which is a major source of ATP (*energy*) for the cell. If cyanide is added to the cells, considerably less energy will be produced, and the sodium potassium pump will be unable to function.

Question 11 A

See: BIO 5.1.1-5.1.3

To answer this question you must know that acetylcholine is an excitatory neurotransmitter that is important in motor neurons. Acetylcholine must cause an action potential in the following cell to continue the signal to the appropriate muscle. Action potentials start with the membrane becoming temporarily more permeable to sodium ions, causing depolarization of the membrane. Therefore, the post-synaptic membrane (*motor end plate*; BIO 5.1F) will become more permeable to the positive ions immediately following acetylcholine being released from the pre-synaptic membrane and reaching receptors on the post-synaptic membrane by diffusion.

Question 12 B

See: BIO 4.4, 5.1.1; CHM 1.5

Since the exercise is "vigorous," mostly anaerobic conditions prevail. Therefore, one molecule of glucose produces 2 molecules of ATP. Since we have 2 ATP, now you can multiply the given equation (in this question) through by 2. Thus the coefficient for potassium becomes 4.

Question 13 D

See: BIO 5.1.2, deduce

We can see three graphs. The first (A) is the "control" which is actually a classic tracing of an action potential. The next curve (B) demonstrates that adding curare drastically *reduces the depolarization*. The final curve (C) demonstrates that the addition of eserine greatly *increases the depolarization* [*notice that the x and y-axis for (C) is several times greater than (A) or (B)*]. Thus curare (B), which reduces depolarization, may block (bind) acetylcholine (ACh) receptors on the muscle cell (= *postsynaptic membrane*) preventing ACh from engaging in depolarization. And eserine (C), which increases depolarization, may prevent the hydrolysis of acetylcholine thus prolonging and increasing its depolarization capability.

Question 14 B

See: BIO 5.1.2

You need to examine the figure carefully to determine that between four and five msec the membrane potential is in the process of returning to its resting potential [note that (A) and (B) are drawn to the same scale]. The lowest point in the curve has just been passed at four msec. The period between the highest point of the curve and the lowest point corresponds to the absolute refractory period in which another action potential cannot be generated. In the process of returning from the lowest point to the resting potential, action potentials may be generated but with difficulty. This corresponds to the relative refractory period.

Question 15 B

See: BIO 5.1.1-5.1.2

We are told that the muscle cell engages in an "all-or-none" action potential. In other words, either the action potential occurs (100%) or it does not occur (0%), but there is nothing in between. Another way of considering the concept "all-or-none" is graphically. The Figure in BIO 5.1.2 is a classic action potential curve which occurs under natural conditions. Thus in nature, either the curve occurs essentially as drawn or it does not (i.e. no action potential), but the action potential curve does not occur in a graded fashion (all-or-none). Thus answer choice *A.* is false.

Question 16 D

See: BIO 5.2

This is a classic MCAT and college/university-type question. The process of muscle contraction must be well understood to answer this question. Option *C.* contains a correct statement, however it does not answer the question as it is not related to muscle contraction.

Question 17 B

See: BIO 5.2

This answer should be committed to memory, as it is the subject of regular MCAT questions. The thin actin filaments in the myofibrils of muscle cells are attached to troponin and tropomyosin.

Question 18 D

See: BIO 5.2

You must understand the structures and processes involved in muscle contraction to answer this question.

Question 19 A

See: BIO 5.2

Tropomyosin is an actin-binding protein that regulates actin mechanics. In resting muscle, tropomyosin overlays the myosin binding sites on actin. Upon release of calcium from the sarcoplasmic reticulum calcium binds to troponin which "unlocks" tropomyosin from actin, allowing it to move away from the binding groove. Myosin heads can now access binding sites and thus bind to actin. Once one myosin head binds, this fully displaces tropomyosin and allows additional myosin heads to bind, initiating muscle shortening and contraction involving the hydrolysis of ATP. Once calcium is pumped out of the cytoplasm and calcium levels return to normal, tropomyosin again binds to actin, preventing myosin from binding which, along with the gain of ATP, assures that myosin releases actin.

Question 20 C

See: BIO 1.1, 5.2-5.3

The sarcolemma and the neurolemma are specialized plasma membranes located in muscle cells and neurons, respectively. Recall that the plasma membrane consists of a lipid bilayer, in accordance with the Fluid Mosaic Model. The basement membrane, formed from a homogenous noncellular material lies at the base of the epithelial cells of the body.

Question 21 B

See: BIO 1.1, 5.2 paragraph 4

The synaptic terminal faces the muscle and the acetylcholine released must reach receptors on the muscle. These receptors should logically be located on the surface of the muscle with which the neurotransmitter will first come into contact (*motor end plate*, BIO 5.1F). However, it should be known from the biology review that muscle fibers are covered by a plasma membrane, or sarcolemma (BIO 5.2). This will be the first surface the neurotransmitter comes into contact with, so it should contain receptors (BIO 1.1).

Question 22 B

See: BIO 5.4.1

From the question it is found that collagen involves a disaccharide linked to hydroxylysine. If all hydroxylysine residues are replaced by asparagine, the function of collagen is sure to be affected. It is necessary to know from the biology review that collagen is an important component of the loose connective tissue in order to correctly answer the question. It is possible, however, to narrow down the options. One function of the oligosaccharide part of the glycoprotein is to aid in recognition. Since only the protein part of the glycoprotein is changed, protein recognition should remain possible. This rules out option *D*.

Question 23 C

See: BIO 5.4

Adult connective tissue includes blood, bone and cartilage.

Question 24 D

See: BIO 5.4.1, 5.4.2

Fascia is considered to be the 'packaging material' of the body as it a sheet of fibrous connective tissue enveloping, separating, or binding together muscles or other soft structures of the body.

Question 25 A

See: BIO 5.4.1, 5.4.4

Collagen is the main structural protein (= organic) found in animals and thus it is an important constituent of bone, cartilage, tendon, and other connective tissue.

Question 26 B

See: E; T; CHM 6.5.1

If $[K^+]_o$ = 0.55 mol/L = 550 mmol/L then this is 100 times the value of $[K^+]_o$ in Table 1 which is only 5.5 mmol/L. Thus $60\log(100) = 60\log 10^2 = 120$ mV.

Note: the MCAT does not permit the use of calculators. So if you happen to get one of these questions requiring the use of logs, you must be quick and efficient. If you are aiming for a perfect score then you should review the sections cross-referenced.

Now let's pretend that you did not notice how the problem could be solved easily and you had 2 other things that you won't have for the MCAT: lots of time and a scientific calculator. If you did, then you would do the long calculation using the approximation of the Nernst equation given in the passage, using the data in Table 1 where $[K^+]_o$ = 0.55 mol/L and $[K^+]_i$ = 150 mol/L and your scientific calculator would estimate E_k to be -86 (not far from the real value of -90 in Table 1). If you then used $[K^+]_o$ = 0.55 mol/L = 550 mmol/L in the same equation, your calculator would suggest about +34. And so, the difference would be 34 – (-86) = 120 mV, success! But, there would not be enough time to do the other questions!

Question 27 A

See: E

The purpose of logarithms is to mathematically convert a curve that is increasing exponentially into a straight line. Logarithms are used frequently in Biology (Nernst, Goldman, exponential growth) and General Chemistry (pH, pK, kinetics/rate of reaction).

CHAPTER REVIEW SOLUTIONS CHAPTER 6

Question 1 D

See: BIO 6.1

12 pairs of cranial nerves leave the brain stem.

Question 2 C

See: BIO 6.1

The hypothalamus is crucial for homeostatic controls including heart rate, blood temperature, thirst, sex drive and hunger.

Question 3 A

See: BIO 6.1, 6.1.4

This question requires that you know the functions of the cranial nerves. The most important one to be familiar with, the vagus nerve, innervates smooth muscles of internal organs (i.e. the bladder). Micturition is urination.

Question 4 D

See: BIO 6.1.4

The sympathetic nervous system is involved in 'fight or flight' reactions. These reactions include many of the same effects that are caused by increasing physical activity.

Question 5 D

See: BIO 6.1

Only two of the answer choices should seem possible: the ganglion and the nucleus. A ganglion is a cluster of nerve cell bodies in the *peripheral* nervous system, while a nucleus is a cluster of nerve cell bodies in the *central* nervous system.

Question 6 A

See: BIO 6.1.5

The muscarinic type is a G-protein coupled receptor that mediates a slow metabolic response via second messenger cascades (involving cAMP), while the nicotinic type is a ligand-gated ionotropic channel that mediates a fast synaptic transmission of the neurotransmitter (no use of second messengers).

Question 7 C

See: BIO 6.2.4

The transparent cornea constitutes the anterior $1/6^{th}$ of the eye.

Question 8 A

See: BIO 6.2.4

The vitreous humor is a transparent jelly-like tissue filling the eyeball behind the lens.

Question 9 B

See: BIO 6.2.4

The iris helps to control the intensity of light impinging on the retina by alternating the diameter of the pupil; however, the iris does not stand between light and the retina as the other 3 tissues do.

Question 10 D

See: BIO 6.3

Endocrine secretes into the circulatory system; exocrine secretes through ducts to the epithelium ('outside' of the body); apocrine concentrates products at the free end of the secreting cell and are thrown off along with a portion of the cytoplasm (i.e. mammary gland); holocrine: the entire secreting cell, along with its accumulated secretion, forms the secreted matter of the gland (sebaceous glands, BIO 13.3). Apocrine and holocrine are subdivisions of exocrine.

Question 11 C

See: BIO 6.3.1, 6.3.3

Hypothyroidism causes a depression in metabolism, growth, and muscular activity.

Question 12 D

See: BIO 6.3.3

The parathyroid produces parathyroid hormone which increases blood calcium levels.

Question 13 A

See: BIO 6.3.1, 6.3.3

The anterior pituitary is induced by TRH to release TSH which stimulates the thyroid to release thyroid hormones.

Question 14 C

See: BIO 6.3.1, 6.3.2

Adrenal hormones such as glucocorticoids and catecholamines function to convert glycogen to glucose for energy use. The main hormones of the adrenal cortex: glucocorticoids (cortisol), aldosterone, androgens. Catecholamines like epinephrine and norepinephrine are made by the adrenal medulla. Aldosterone causes water to be retained to increase blood volume. Sodium is also retained (and ends up in the extracellular fluid, not in the nephron). Potassium is excreted into the urine. Glucocorticoids function to increase blood glucose. They do this by stimulation of gluconeogenesis (forming new glucose from amino acids/ lipids) and decreasing glucose storage, by preventing it from going into the muscle and fat cells. They do not cause glycogen metabolism. The breakdown of glycogen from stores in the muscle and liver for quick energy is stimulated by epinephrine (made by the adrenal medulla) and glucagon (from the pancreas).

Question 15 B

See: BIO 6.3.3

This question simply asks what is responsible for increasing calcium in the bones. Of the 4 possible choices, only calcitonin would have such an effect. Calcitonin, which is secreted by the thyroid gland, stimulates osteoblast activity while inhibiting osteoclasts activity, thereby increasing calcium levels in the bones. Parathyroid hormone and osteoclast activity both have opposite effects.

Question 16 A

See: BIO 6.3, 6.3.1

The hypothalamus is an important part of the brain involved in homeostatic control and important endocrine regulation. In terms of the endocrine function, the hypothalamus both secretes releasing factors which controls hormone secretion from the anterior pituitary AND produces/secretes hormones directly into the posterior pituitary. Gonadotropins (FSH, LH) are secreted by the anterior pituitary.

Question 17 B

See: CHM 9.9, BIO 6.3.3, 6.3.6

According to Figure 1, free thyroxine (thyroid hormone) is involved in an equilibrium reaction with both tissue protein-bound thyroxine and plasma protein-bound thyroxine. By Le Chatelier's principle, a change in the system (increasing free thyroxine) will cause the system to evolve in such a way as to minimize the change. So adding more free thyroid hormone will cause both equilibria to shift to the product side, producing more tissue and plasma protein-bound thyroxine.

Still not clear? OK, let's look at it this way: there are a couple of ways that you could have properly interpreted Figure 1: (a) a true equilibrium has double arrows (arrows in both directions between reactants/products); notice that the answers follow this rule; or (b) notice that the single direction arrow leading to the TSH is a broken arrow. The fact that the arrow is broken (not like the others) should have made you question the meaning of that arrow. Then, on reflection, you would remember that increases in thyroxine leads to decreased TSH due to a negative feedback loop.

Question 18 D

See: BIO 6.3.3

The prefix 'hypo' tends to refer to things that are low or slowed down in some way (lethargy). The prefix 'hyper' tends to refer to things that are elevated or overactive (i.e. your kid brother!).

Question 19 A

See: BIO 5.4.4, 6.3.3

Hyperparathyroidism refers to an overactive parathyroid gland. This condition leads to an increase in the level of calcium in plasma and tissues. This calcium comes from the breaking down of bone by *osteoclasts*, which are stimulated by parathyroid hormone.

Question 20 B

See: BIO 5.4.4, 6.3.3

If it is true that elevated levels of extracellular phosphate results in the calcification of bones and tissues (answer choice *B.*), then circulating calcium must be *lowered* in order to participate in the calcification process. However, parathormone *increases* circulating calcium. Thus in would be logical that parathormone finds ways to reduce extracellular phosphate in order to avoid the calcification process.

Question 21 C

See: BIO 1.1.1, 6.3.1 and F

On a hot day, the body would tend to conserve all the water it can. Thus the bladder would contain less urine than usual. Since the body is trying to resorb water not electrolytes (i.e. ADH, BIO 6.3.1, 6.3.1F) the urine the bladder contains would be more concentrated with solutes (less water present). This corresponds to a small amount of hypertonic urine. {*For the definitions of hypertonic and hypotonic, see* BIO 1.1.1}

Question 22 C

See: BIO 6.1, 6.1.4, 6.3.2, 6.3.3

By process of elimination: answer choice A suggests that the parasympathetic nervous system could stimulate adrenaline (= epinephrine) which is actually the hallmark product of the *sympathetic* nervous system; answer choice C). Answer choice B suggests that the body's response to cold is sweating which is incorrect. Answer choice D is wrong for suggesting that the parasympathetic system would be involved in a process like shivering AND that dilating blood vessels of the heart would be relevant to the body's response to a cold environment.

Question 23 D

See: BIO 6.3.1, 6.3.2

Aldosterone increases intravascular salt which leads to passive reabsorption of water from the renal tubules; thus more water in blood vessels means higher pressure.

Question 24 C

See: BIO 6.3.1

The thyroid gland incorporates iodine into two compounds, triiodothyronine or T_3 (contains 3 iodine atoms per molecule) and thyroxine or T_4 (contains 4 iodine atoms per molecule), which are responsible for the increase in basal metabolic rate seen upon thyroid stimulation by TSH.

Question 25 A

See: BIO 6.3, 6.3.1

You should know about the excretory system and the hormones which affect it, which would allow you to choose the correct answer immediately. As well, you should also know the functions of different hormones, which would allow you to eliminate those that do not affect the urine.

Question 26 A

See: BIO 6.3.6, 6.3.7

Many endocrine glands are linked to neural control centers by homeostatic feedback mechanisms. The two types of feedback mechanisms are negative feedback and positive feedback. Negative feedback decreases the deviation from an ideal normal value, and is important in maintaining homeostasis. Most endocrine glands are under the control of negative feedback mechanisms.

Negative feedback mechanisms act like a thermostat in the home. As the temperature rises (deviation from the ideal normal value), the thermostat detects the change and triggers the air-conditioning to turn on and cool the house. Once the temperature reaches its thermostat setting (ideal normal value), the air conditioning turns off.

Positive feedback mechanisms control self-perpetuating events that can be out of control and do not require continuous adjustment. In positive feedback mechanisms, the original stimulus is promoted rather than negated. Positive feedback increases the deviation from an ideal normal value. Unlike negative feedback that maintains hormone levels within narrow ranges, positive feedback is rarely used to maintain homeostatic functions.

If calcium decreases, the parathyroid glands sense the decrease and secrete more parathyroid hormone. The parathyroid hormone stimulates calcium release from the bones and increases the calcium uptake into the bloodstream from the collecting tubules in the kidneys. Conversely, if blood calcium increases too much, the parathyroid glands reduce parathyroid hormone production. Both responses are examples of negative feedback because in both cases the effects are negative (opposite) to the stimulus.

However, if the body temperature is elevated and that abnormality only makes the body temperature rise even more, then this is positive feedback.

CHAPTER REVIEW SOLUTIONS — CHAPTER 7

Question 1 A

See: BIO 7.2, 7.3

The answer to this question represents basic facts about the circulatory system.

Question 2 D

See: BIO 7.3

This is a classic MCAT/Sesame Street type of question: "one of these things is not like the other . . ." The vena cava, the pulmonary artery and the femoral *vein* all carry deoxygenated blood to the lungs. Among our choices, only the aorta carries blood away from the lungs. Thus the aorta would be a perfect place to have receptors which would indicate whether the carbon dioxide exchange in the lung required an increase or decrease in respiratory rate in order to improve the quality of the blood supply to the rest of the body's organs.

Question 3 A

See: BIO 7.3

Arteries are well know for having a relatively large number of collagen and elastin which gives them the ability to stretch in response to each pulse or heart beat (relatively high pressure). Veins do not have as many elastic fibers as arteries as the pressure in veins is relatively low.

Question 4 C

See: BIO 7.2, 7.3, 7.5.1

Deoxygenated blood coming from the systemic circulation is pumped through the right ventricle, to the pulmonary artery and finally, toward the lungs. From the lungs, the *oxygenated* blood, containing oxyhemoglobin (= hemoglobin bound to oxygen) travels through the pulmonary vein toward the left side of the heart. Note that the pulmonary *vein* consisting of *oxygenated* blood is the exception to the rule; in most cases, *oxygenated* blood is located in the *arteries* while *deoxygenated* blood is in the *veins* of the circulation.

Question 5 B

See: BIO 7.3

vein --> lung cap.

This question can be translated thus: if something enters a vein in your arm, where is the *first* capillary bed which will be encountered? The following is simply part of the basic cardiovascular anatomy you need to know: vein in arm (= *upper body*) --> larger veins --> *superior* vena cava --> right atrium of the heart --> right ventricle of the heart --> pulmonary artery --> smaller arteries in the lung --> arterioles in the lung --> *capillary beds in the lung* --> venules in the lung --> veins in the lung --> pulmonary veins --> left atrium of the heart --> left ventricle of the heart --> aorta --> many different arteries --> many different arterioles --> many different *capillary beds of the body system* including those that supply the heart muscle, the arms, the kidneys, the brain, the liver, etc. --> venules --> veins, and the story repeats itself.

Question 6 B

See: BIO 7.5.1

$Hb + O_2 <=> HbO_2$

Clearly if you increase oxygen in the equation provided (which you should be able to derive), the equation must shift to the right (Le Chatelier's Principle).

Question 7 C

See: BIO 3.0, 4.3, 7.5.1

$Hb + O_2 <=> HbO_2$

Answer choice *A* is impossible because oxygen must bind reversibly so that when it reaches relatively deoxygenated cells, it can exit the red blood cell to provide oxygen to the tissues. Answer choice *B* is incorrect because in order for oxygen to go from the interior of an alveolus in the lung to the interior of a red blood cell in a capillary, essentially all oxygen must dissolve in plasma. Answer choice *D* is a true statement which does not answer the question. Allosteric proteins have different configurations (BIO 3.0, 4.3). Hemoglobin has cooperative binding which means that each oxygen facilitates the binding of the next oxygen (BIO 7.5.1) which occurs as a result of changes in the molecule's configuration.

Question 8 D

See: BIO 7.5.1

When you consider the human body, think about what would most urgently require oxygen to be off loaded from hemoglobin: a very active muscle. And what are the features of an active muscle? It is hot, acidic (lactic acid), hypercarbic (high carbon dioxide), high in phosphates (like 2,3-DPG which is high in glycolysis), etc. Thus all the preceding features of an active muscle, including increased temperature, would lead to oxygen leaving Hb (ie. low % Hb oxygen saturation) and going to the oxygen starved overworked tissue.

Question 9 D

See: BIO 7.1

The circulatory system is involved in thermoregulation via constriction/relaxation of the arterioles that allow changes in blood flow to the surface of the skin, where radiation occurs. In addition, the blood contains components of the immune (e.g. white blood cells) and endocrine systems (e.g. hormones) which are circulated throughout the body.

Question 10 B

See: BIO 7.5

In humans, mature red blood cells are flexible biconcave disks. They lack a cell nucleus and most organelles in order to accommodate maximum space for hemoglobin. RBCs develop in the bone marrow and circulate for about 120 days in the body before their components are recycled by macrophages.

Question 11 B

See: BIO 7.5.1

The question states that "the net effect of GBP is to shift the oxygen-binding curve . . .", thus the curve may move in one direction or the other but there is no suggestion that the shape of the curve is altered. Therefore, to answer this question, we only need to identify a curve with the same shape as the oxygen-binding curve (= oxygen dissociation curve) which is sigmoidal.

Question 12 C

See: BIO 7.5.1

The effect of GBP is to cause a greater release of oxygen at areas of lower oxygen tension, without affecting the ability of hemoglobin to pick up oxygen at high pressures (i.e. in the lungs). To release oxygen to the cells, the affinity of hemoglobin for oxygen must be low, but only at those points at which oxygen is needed (where oxygen concentration is low).

Question 13 B

See: BIO 4.2, 7.5.1, 11.2

Body tissues other than lung, in other words parts of the body with relatively low oxygen concentrations, both myoglobin and hemoglobin with GBP begin to release oxygen at a tremendous rate. The question can be translated thus: which of the following tissues can deplete its oxygen reserves quickest and thus would benefit most from a molecule which is used to delivering oxygen to oxygen-starved tissue? Oxygen debt can be most pronounced in skeletal muscle. Voluntary or *skeletal* muscle can deplete its oxygen stores so quickly that it switches to anaerobic respiration thus incurring an oxygen debt. The oxygen tension (= *partial pressure* = *concentration*) in this tissue is extremely low and will therefore benefit most from an influx of oxygen. {*Note that myoglobin like myosin implies muscle*}

Question 14 D

See: BIO 4.4-4.5, 7.5.1, 12.4.1

This question reveals an interesting physiology lesson. Here is a statement you can easily deduce or should be memorized (!): *an exercising muscle is acidic, hot and has a high partial pressure of carbon dioxide; an exercising muscle requires increased quantities of oxygen* (= answer choice *D*.).

For your interest, we will examine the details: an exercising muscle is acidic because of (i) the accumulation of lactic *acid* and (ii) the high partial pressure of carbon dioxide which results in an increase carbonic *acid*. An exercising muscle is hot because of the increased metabolic rate and blood flow. Carbon dioxide is in high concentration in an exercising muscle since it is a product of aerobic respiration. If you were to draw a sigmoidal shaped oxygen-binding curve to the right of answer choice *B*. in Q11, you will notice that for a given partial pressure of oxygen, the curve shows a greater tendency to unload oxygen (= *a lower oxygen saturation*). Thus the exercising muscle gets increasing oxygen delivery as the curve shifts to the right.

Question 15 B

See: BIO 7.5.1

This question boils down to the following: as described in the answer for the previous question, if the tissue is acidic then it needs increased oxygen delivery to those tissues. Only answer choice *B*. delivers oxygen to the tissues.

Question 16 C

See: BIO 7.2

Thicker walls in a particular part of the heart would indicate that it is more muscular, and therefore is more efficient or forceful during its contraction. This immediately rules out answer choices *B*. and *D*., as they suggest that the thicker walled chamber would be less efficient or forceful. It should be known from the biology review (BIO 7.2) that the ventricles are more muscular (thicker-walled), but in the event that this is not initially known, information regarding the function of both the atria and the ventricles can be derived. First, systole, the period of contraction, refers to the period of contraction of the ventricles not the atria. This would indicate that the contraction of the ventricles might be more relevant in some way. Second, during diastole, atrial contraction occurs after most of the ventricle is already filled and serves to push the small amount of blood necessary to complete the filling into the ventricles. Since the atrial contraction does not need to move a large amount of blood (the ventricle is already mostly full), it does not need to be as muscular.

Question 17 A

See: F, BIO 7.2-7.4

Following vertically down from position P in Figure 1, note that it occurs during a period of diastole. The last paragraph of the passage gives information concerning the actions of the heart during diastole which would lead to answer choice *A*. In P1, S2 diastole is described as a period of ventricular relaxation, ruling out answer choice *B*. Position P in Figure 1 occurs during a period of diastole and it occurs at a point about halfway through that period, ruling out answer choices *C*. and *D*. Alternatively, the answer can be deduced through information in the passage and figure.

Question 18 A

See: F, BIO 7.2-7.4

This question indicates that we should be looking at the graph representing "Heart sounds" in Figure 1. The graph for heart sounds can be described thus: a horizontal line is followed by a narrow burst of spikes or activity; prior to the spikes is the label "1st" implying that the spikes represent the 1st heart sound. The first heart sound begins immediately after the first long vertical line. By following this vertical line downwards, we can note any other events which may initiate or occur at the time as the first heart sound: beginning near the bottom of Figure 1, note that the first heart sound occurs (i) in phase 2 of the cardiac cycle; (ii) at the beginning of ventricular SYSTOLE; (iii) during a period that the aortic and pulmonary valves are not opened (i.e. closed); and (iv) the first heart sound begins exactly when the position of the AV valves *just become closed*. Therefore, strictly according to the figure, during ventricular systole the AV valves suddenly close just as the first heart sound is created. Thus answer choice *A*. is the only plausible answer.

Question 19 C

See: F, BIO 6.1.4, 7.2-7.5

This question is easily answered by reading the graph and remembering the direct relation between ejection fraction and stroke volume. Compared to the curve labeled 'control', the curve labeled 'sympathetic stimulation' is always at a higher stroke volume for a given end-diastolic volume. However, by looking at stroke volume values for both curves at any end-diastolic volume value (i.e. 200), it is clear that the stroke volume for sympathetic stimulation is always less than twice the control (i.e. 160 vs. 100), thus eliminating answer choice *A*. Thus we are left with answer choice *C*.

Question 20 C

See: F, BIO 7.2-7.4

Close analysis of Figure 1 (*compare to* previous questions) reveals that during the period that the aortic and pulmonary valves are OPEN, the curve for left ventricular volume drops (= *decreases*) but does not rise (= *increase*).

Question 21 B

See: Appendix Ch 12

Ejection Fraction (EF) = stroke volume / end diastolic volume

It is usually given as a percentage but can be given as a fraction. The importance is to know the relationship between the variables.

Question 22 D

See: Appendix Ch 12

Recall that the volume of blood ejected from a ventricle during systole is termed stroke volume. So the amount of blood that remained in the ventricle (was not ejected) would be the end systolic volume. As described in the passage, the ventricle would be 'full' at the end of diastole. So the maximum volume (end diastolic) minus the blood remaining (end systolic) would equal the blood ejected (stroke volume).

Memorize: SV = end diastolic volume - end systolic volume

Questions or Concerns? Go to www.mcat-prep.com

Chapter Review Solutions — Chapter 8

Question 1 C

See: BIO 8.2

Helper T-cells belong to the group of T lymphocytes and are required for the activation of other T lymphocytes (such as cytotoxic T cells) as well as B lymphocytes. Activation of B lymphocytes will lead to the production of specific antibodies which will recognize invading foreign organisms, whereas the activation of cytotoxic T cells will cause the direct elimination of these microbes.

Question 2 B

See: BIO 2.1, 2.1.1, 8.2

In order for any virus to infect a cell, the first step must be to specifically recognize the host cell. This is accomplished when the viral capsid makes contact with specific receptors on the target cell. Since different cell types will have different cell surface receptors, depending on the virus' protein envelope each virus will be very selective as to the cells it infects. Hence, in order for the HIV to infect the cell the viral envelope must first make contact and be recognized by helper T cell receptors.

Question 3 D

See: BIO 2.1, 8.2

In order to be effective, the vaccine must elicit an immune response without giving the person the full-blown disease. Before injecting the virus it must be cloned, but it cannot simply be injected in its natural harmful form. Also, the protein coat is how the immune system will initially identify the virus in order to produce antibodies against it. For this reason, the protein coat should not be destroyed. The most important thing is to ensure that the virus will be unable to cause harm (inactivated), yet will still elicit the appropriate immune response.

Question 4 C

See: BIO 8.1, 8.2

Basic knowledge of the immune response would be helpful here; nonetheless, certain options can be ruled out. The question has asked for an explanation of why the first immune response differs from the second. An appropriate answer should include some information about both responses to show the difference. Options *A.* and *B.* contain one statement concerning only one of the two immune responses. This is not useful in explaining why the two are different. You should also know that macrophages do not produce memory cells, and this rules out option *D.* By carefully examining the graph it is clear that the antibody concentration in serum is higher (*more intense*) and faster in the secondary response. This is consistent with option *C.* and information from the biology review.

Question 5 D

See: BIO 8.1, 8.2

By injecting a person with an inactivated form of an antigen, an immune response is elicited in which antibodies are produced and memory cells are made that will react quickly in the event of a subsequent infection. This is the process by which vaccines work (= "active" immunity). The antigen is inactivated so as to activate the immune system *without* risking the development of the disease or infection. Injecting the person with the antibody itself may help the person if they have been infected by something displaying the corresponding antigen (= "passive" immunity), but it will not induce the body to produce its own antibodies nor memory cells, so it offers no future protection against a subsequent infection.

Question 6 D

See: BIO 8.3

You should be familiar with the function of the spleen from the biology review. The spleen does not produce blood cells in the adult.

Question 7 A

See: BIO 8.2, deduce

Rejection will occur when the recipient produces antibodies against foreign antigens present in the tissue of the donor. Tissue matching, which would ensure that the antigens present in the tissue match those of the recipient would decrease the likelihood of an immune response (this is analogous to matching blood types for donation). A second method would consist of decreasing the immune response by suppression of the system. This is accomplished with medications or by X-irradiation of the B-cells, which produce the antibodies, located mainly in the bone marrow and lymph tissues. Answer choice A. would damage the tissues to be transplanted, which would not decrease the chances of rejection.

Question 8 B

See: BIO 8.2

An antibody is composed of a pair of heavy and a pair of light polypeptide chains, and the generic term 'immunoglobulin' is used for all such proteins.

Question 9 D

See: BIO 8.1, 8.2

The immune system attacks antigens which are usually proteins on a foreign agent ("non-self") that activate an immune response. One's immune system does not normally attack one's own cells ("self").

Question 10 A

See: BIO 8.3

The spleen has many functions, among which, it is considered to be a blood storage organ because of the activity of its red pulp.

Question 1 C

See: BIO 9.5; ORG 12.3.3; deduce

Cellulose is passed through the mouth, stomach and small intestine unchanged. It is only because of bacteria in the large intestine that cellulose gets broken down at all. This would indicate that humans do not possess enzymes to break down this particular polysaccharide. Because of the preceding, cellulose is often referred to as "dietary fiber".

Question 2 C

See:BIO 9.3

The components of gastric juice in the stomach should be known from the biology review. One of these, pepsinogen, converts to its active form in low pH to become pepsin. Pepsin acts to break down proteins in the stomach. However, the great majority of digestion is completed in the small intestine.

Question 3 D

See: BIO 1.1.2

Membranes are usually semipermeable. Small neutral molecules can pass relatively freely by diffusion. Monosaccharides, however, are large polar molecules thus require some assistance in crossing the hydrophobic interior of plasma membranes. Exocytosis and endocytosis are found most commonly in the context of releasing proteins or ingesting large particles (i.e. viruses, bacteria). Therefore, carrier mediated transport is most likely.

Question 4 D

See: BIO 9.5

From the biology review it should be clear that bile salts do not *absorb* fat, they *emulsify* fat. This immediately rules out options *A.* and *B.* Most products of digestion are absorbed and processed in the liver, but fat products are an exception. Fats are absorbed into the lymphatic system via lacteals, giving answer *D.*

Question 5 D

See: BIO 9.3, 9.4

The question is asking why an enzyme exists in the stomach which is present in an inactive form until conditions exist in which it is converted into its active form (e.g. a zymogen). You should be able to recognize that the question is referring to pepsinogen and should be familiar with its function. Nothing exists in the stomach which would break down pepsin should it remain in its active form. As well, pepsinogen converts to its active form, pepsin, in the presence of low pH. It would not make sense that the active enzyme would neutralize the acid, as this would cause the enzyme to be converted back to its inactive form. The inactive form offers no enhancement of activity, but suggests some form of protection, either for the enzyme itself or for surrounding cells. Option *D.* makes sense because if the enzyme remained active even when not needed, perhaps it could continue to function on molecules it was not meant to break down.

Question 6 D

See: BIO 9.4.1; BCM 1.4

Bile helps to emulsify fats (i.e. lipids including triacyl glycerol) for digestion as well as the absorption of fat soluble vitamins A, D, E and K.

Question 7 C

See: BIO 9.3, 9.4.2

This question is asking: which of the following enzymes are present in the gastro-intestinal tract? Among the answer choices, carboxypeptidase, trypsin and pepsin are correct.

{Note: in order for a parasite to have gained access to the intestines, it must have passed through the stomach.}

{Aiming for a perfect exam score? Do you remember the name of the antibody that attacks intestinal (parasitic) worms? See the table in BIO 8.2}

Question 1 D

See: BIO 10.3

The nephron is the functional unit of the kidney and contains Bowman's capsule and the renal corpuscle.

Question 2 A

See: BIO 10.1

You should be familiar with the structures involved in the excretory system from the biology review.

Question 3 B

See: BIO 10.3

The kidney is a filtration-reabsorption-secretion (excretion) organ thus the first step is filtration which occurs at the level of the glomerulus.

Question 4 B

See: BIO 10.3

The countercurrent multiplier system uses electrolyte pumps so that the loop of Henle can create an area of high urine concentration in the medulla. Water present in the filtrate in the DCT and collecting duct flows passively down its concentration gradient. This process reabsorbs water and creates a concentrated urine for excretion. Some desert animals have disproportionately extensive loops of Henle because of their vital need to preserve water.

Question 5 A

See: BIO 10.4

When the detrusor muscles contract, the internal sphincter opens, or conversely, the internal sphincter is closed when the detrusor muscles relax.

Question 6 C

See: BIO 10.3

The loop of Henle of juxtamedullary (= "at the edge" of the medulla) nephrons form the countercurrent multiplier in the kidney.

Question 7 C

See: BIO 10.3

The fluid in the descending limb is relatively hypertonic (see the illustrations regarding the countercurrent principle, BIO 10.3) while the ascending limb is becomes relatively hypotonic.

Question 8 B

See: BIO 10.3, 1.1.1, 7.5.2

Over 75% of the water and dissolved substances lost through the Bowman's capsule is reabsorbed (obligate) back into the blood at the proximal convoluted tubule level.

Question 9 C

See: BIO 10.4, 11.2

You should be familiar with the different types of muscles and where they are likely to be found. Smooth muscles often form the lining of organs such as the stomach which can be filled with some substance and contracts in an involuntary manner. Skeletal muscles are involved in voluntary movements. We know that the detrusor muscles (and thus the internal urethral sphincter) are controlled in part by parasympathetic neurons, which would indicate a degree of involuntary action (BIO 10.4). The external urethral sphincter can be contracted even when the detrusor muscle is strongly contracting, indicating some sort of voluntary control. These descriptions fit the functions of the smooth and skeletal muscles for internal and external urethral sphincters, respectively.

CHAPTER REVIEW SOLUTIONS CHAPTER 11

Question 1 A

See: BIO 11.2, 5.2, BCM 3.1, 3.2

When aerobic respiration, increased use of energy (ATP) requires more oxygen, more glucose, more hydrolysis of ATP and more CO_2 is produced.

Question 2 D

See: BIO 11.2, 5.2, BCM 3.1, 3.2

Conversion to anaerobic respiration means less efficiency, less ATP, increased lactic acid (fermentation), more need for glucose which means more breakdown of glycogen and reduced production of the waste products of aerobic respiration; $CO_2 + H_2O$.

Question 3 C

See: BIO 11.2, 5.2, BCM 3.1, 3.2

Glycolysis is much faster (though less efficient) than aerobic respiration. Note that fermentation in vertebrates produces lactate not alcohol.

Question 4 D

See: BIO 5.4.3, 11.3.1

Cartilage can exist in all of the listed tissues. However, the question asks about cartilage in adult tissues. In children who are still growing, a disc of cartilage exists between the epiphysis and diaphysis of long bones, but in adults, this cartilage has been replaced by bone. The other tissues listed will remain as cartilage even in adults.

Question 5 B

See: BIO 11.2

The difference between tetanus and tonus is that the former is a sustained contraction, lacking any relaxation, while the latter describes the state of partial contraction of all muscles.

Question 6 C

See: BIO 11.3.3

Tendons are composed of dense connective tissue and they connect muscle to bones.

Question 7 C

See: BIO 11.3.2

Motion of a joint in one plane gets its name from a hinged door which has a similar limitation in motion.

Question 8 A

See: BIO 11.3.2, 11.3.3

See the diagram of the skeleton in section 11.3.

Question 9 A

See: BIO 11.3.3

The axial skeleton includes the skull, thoracic cage (sternum + ribs), vertebral column, sacrum and coccyx.

Question 10 C

See: BIO 11.3.3

Phalanges are the bones of the fingers and toes.

Question 1 A

See: BIO 12.2, 12.3

You must be familiar with the structures of the upper and lower respiratory tracts to answer this question. The larynx comes before the trachea.

Question 2 B

See: BIO 12.3

The vocal cords are twin infoldings stretched horizontally across the larynx.

Question 3 D

See: BIO 12.3

The terminal bronchiole forms part of the conducting portion of the respiratory system.

Question 4 B

See: BIO 12.3

Surfactant is secreted into alveoli by pneumocytes type II. The surfactant reduces surface tension and prevents the fragile alveoli from collapsing.

Question 5 A

See: BIO 12.4.1

The factors that stimulate breathing are high carbon dioxide, low pH, high acidity, and low oxygen levels in the blood.

Question 6 D

See: BIO 12.3

The lung is covered by a membrane (= the pleura). Lungs reside in the thoracic cage which includes the ribs, sternum and the muscles between the ribs (intercostal muscles). If blood accumulates in the space outside the lungs (the pleural space or cavity), since the thoracic cage is firm, the blood will apply pressure on the pliant lung thus reducing the size of the lung (reducing the surface area for the exchange of oxygen and carbon dioxide). Thus blood oxygen levels can become dangerously low.

Question 7 C

See: BIO 7.2-7.3, 9.1-9.3, 9.5, 12.3-12.4

You should know enough about each of the systems listed so that this question should seem easy. The circulatory system has vessels which are elastic and muscular, indicating that stretching may occur. The respiratory system also involves muscles and stretching. The digestive system includes the stomach, and anyone who has ever eaten too much knows that there is some stretching going on (BIO 9.1/2/3/5)! The endocrine system, however, includes glands which secrete different substances into the circulatory system. Its function does not seem to rely on stretch receptors.

Question 8 B

See: BIO 1.1.2, 12.3

Active transport moves molecules against a gradient and requires energy. Blood returning to the lungs from the rest of the body is deoxygenated and comes into contact with a high concentration of O_2 in the lungs. Clearly O_2 does not need to be actively transported and, rather, will readily diffuse. The alveoli of the lungs require such fast and efficient transport of O_2 into the body and CO_2 out of the body that only the rapid process of diffusion will do.

Question 9 C

See: Chap. 12 App.; P1, S3; dimensional analysis

Minute ventilation = tidal volume x respiratory rate

Minute ventilation = 500 ml/breath x 12 breaths/minute x (1 L)/(1000 ml) = 6.0 L/minute

Incidentally, the average total lung capacity of an adult human male is about 6 L of air.

Question 10 D

See: Chap. 12 App.

The following are the definitions of the answer choices in order from A to D: Tidal volume is the amount of air inhaled and exhaled normally at rest. The functional residual capacity is the sum of the residual volume and the expiratory reserve volume. The vital capacity is the maximum volume that can be exhaled following a maximal inhalation. Total lung capacity is the maximum volume of air present in the lungs.

Incidentally (in case you did not read this in the previous solution!), the average total lung capacity of an adult human male is about 6 L of air.

Question 11 A

See: BIO 12.4, Chap. 12 App. P2; P3, S2

By various mechanisms (BIO 12.4), inspiration increases the size of your chest, or more precisely, your thoracic cavity. The increased amount of air in the chest in combination with the chest's desire to return to its initial position (= recoil) leads to an increased pressure in the lungs (= transpulmonary). Airway radius is inversely proportional to airway resistance (P2).

Question 12 C

See: Chap. 12 App.; BIO 12.4

The passage explains that there exists fibers which *pull* on the airways and become *stretched* during inspiration. The preceding implies that the radius of the airway is increased by the stretching of the fibers. Thus both transpulmonary pressure (compare with the previous question) and lateral traction result in an increase in airway radius.

Question 13 B

See: BIO 12.4; deduce

Clearly if food is stuck, for example, in the trachea then inspiration may pull the food into the lung (= *not good!*), but expiration could expel the food from the body (= *much better!*). The events in expiration normally include decreasing the size of the thoracic cavity and relaxation or raising of the diaphragm (BIO 12.4). The fact that the Heimlich Maneuver includes an upward abdominal *thrust* means that it is a *forcible* maneuver which suddenly increases the size and pressure in the thoracic cavity thus dislodging the food.

If you were to try applying upward pressure to your abdominal cavity (not too much pressure!). You will notice that your chest (thoracic) size increases. Of course, your thoracic volume is decreasing due to the abdominal contents entering the chest cavity.

CHAPTER REVIEW SOLUTIONS — CHAPTER 13

Question 1 A

See: BIO 13.3

Sweat glands are exocrine glands which secrete their products to the outside of the human body.

Question 2 C

See: BIO 13.1

The answer is a basic fact about the skin as an organ system.

Question 3 D

See: BIO 13.1, 7.3

Body heat and water loss are increased by increasing blood flow in the dermis of the skin which occurs by relaxation of the smooth muscle (= media, BIO 7.3) of blood vessels in the skin (vasodilation). The result is cooling by radiation, the production of sweat, and evaporation of sweat due to heat at the surface of the skin causing cooling.

Question 4 B

See: BIO 7.1, 13.1

The effect of two changes to the temperature of the body on sweating is being questioned here. One change, exposing the skin to heat, affects the outer parts of the body. The other, drinking iced water, affects the inner core of the body. The question clearly states that sweating only occurs as a result of a rise in core body temperature. Therefore, heating the skin will not affect sweating. Since we now know that it is the iced water which will affect sweating it is a question of exactly what effect the iced water will have. A rise in core body temperature causes an increase in sweating, so it stands to reason that a decrease in core body temperature (caused by the iced water) will cause a decrease in sweating.

Question 5 D

See: BIO 13.3

Holocrine (= wholly secretory) is a type of glandular secretion in which the entire secreting cell, along with its accumulated secretion, forms the secreted matter of the gland; for example, the sebaceous glands which secrete oils. Apocrine concentrates products at the free end of the secreting cell and are thrown off along with a portion of the cytoplasm (i.e. mammary gland). Apocrine and holocrine are subdivisions of exocrine.

CHAPTER REVIEW SOLUTIONS — CHAPTER 14

Question 1 C

See: BIO 14.1, 14.5

Fertilization normally occurs in the Fallopian tubes (oviduct).

Question 2 A

See: BIO 14.1, 10.1, 10.2

The ureter connects the kidney with the bladder (BIO 10.1, 10.2) and is not directly related to the male gonads.

Question 3 A

See: BIO 14.1

The structures and processes of the male reproductive system should be understood from the biology review.

Question 4 D

See: BIO 14.2

You must understand the process of gametogenesis in females to answer this question.

Question 5 C

See: BIO 14.3

The corpus luteum in the ovary secretes estrogen and progesterone in the luteal phase.

Question 6 B

See: BIO 14.3

Estrogen causes proliferation of the uterine lining (endometrium).

Question 7 A

See: BIO 6.3.1F, 14.3

You must be familiar with the menstrual cycle to answer this question. If you know which hormones the pituitary gland secretes (FSH, LH), you can narrow down the choices since the question asks which hormone the ovary secretes. One of the hallmarks of the follicular phase is that estrogen causes thickening (*proliferation*) of the uterine lining (*endometrium*).

Question 8 A

See: BIO 14.3

The expulsion of the egg from the ovaries is referred to as ovulation. Ovulation, which occurs at approximately day 14 of the menstrual cycle, is induced by an LH surge. Thus, LH is responsible for ovulation.

Question 9 C

See: BIO 14.3

The hormonal cycle of women is relatively complex and involves all four sex hormones (LH, FSH, estrogen and progesterone), at one point or another. Following the menses, caused by a low concentration of estrogen in the blood, the cycle continues in the follicular or proliferative phase in which FSH (= follicle stimulating hormone) stimulates the production of estrogen and the maturation of the follicles in the ovary. At midcycle, a surge of concentration stimulates ovulation (i.e. eg production).

Question 10 D

See: BIO 14.2, 14.8

The nucleus of sperm carries either an X or Y sex chromosom which determines the sex of the offspring.

Question 11 B

See: BIO 14.5

The ectoderm will develop into the epidermis and the nervou system.

Question 12 C

See: BIO 14.5

The 3 primary germ layers (ectoderm, mesoderm, endoderm) ar first seen in the gastrula after the invagination of the blastula.

Question 13 D

See: BIO 7.2, 7.3, 14.7

You can only understand fetal circulation if you understan normal adult circulation. The *ductus arteriosus* connects th pulmonary artery to the aorta. If the ductus arteriosus remain open or patent after birth, some of the deoxygenated blood fron the pulmonary artery will flow through the ductus into the aort which contains fresh oxygenated blood from the newborn' lungs. Thus the mixing causes a decrease in oxygen and a increase in carbon dioxide partial pressures in the aorta. Th aorta leads the blood into systemic arteries and circulation.

Question 14 C

See: BIO 14.6

The placenta is derived from the maternal endometrium and th embryonic chorion.

Question 15 C

See: BIO 14.2

Crossing over occurs with synapsing homologous pairs o chromosomes (tetrads or bivalents) appear in prophase I. Ther are no tetrads in prophase II (there are only sister chromatids).

CHAPTER REVIEW SOLUTIONS — CHAPTER 1

Question 1 C

See: BIO 15.1, 15.5

An inability to produce phenylalanine hydroxylase would least likely be accounted for by the altering of the stereochemistry of the chromosome because such an alteration is too general of a cause for specific mutation.

Question 2 D

See: BIO 15.1, 14.5.1

It is important to understand that all cells in the body have th same genetic information, that is, they all have the same DNA content. What differentiates between one cell type and anothe is the induction of the various genes within the cell's genome For instance, only the genes in a hepatocyte that are relevant to its function will be turned on. Although these same genes are also found in a muscle cell, they will not be expressed in the muscle cell (BIO 14.5.1). Hence, answer choice *D.* is the correct answer.

Question 3 B

See: BIO 15.3

You should be familiar with the reasoning behind sex-linked diseases. The disease in question cannot be sex-linked because it occurs more often in women. If the gene for this disease were located on sex chromosomes, the male would get the disease more often.

Question 4 D

See: BIO 15.1

The process of morphogenesis (alteration of physical and behavioral characteristics) from one generation to the next relies on both genetic and environmental factors). Although 2 organisms may have the same DNA, certain external factors including peers and family, and location of upbringing will affect the disposition of an individual. It is for this same reason that although 2 identical twins may look the same, their attitudes and character may be completely different.

Question 5 D

See: BIO 15.1, 15.3

Sex linked means that the gene in question is present on the X chromosome. Let E = red eye which is dominant and e = white eyed which is recessive. We are crossing heterozygous females X^EX^e with white eyed males X^eY.

	X^E	X^e
X^e	X^EX^e	X^eX^e
Y	X^EY	X^eY

Question 6 A

See:BIO 15.3

By definition.

Question 7 C

See: BIO 15.3

To consider the law of independent assortment, one should consider a case with 2 traits (usually on different chromosomes) which is called a dihybrid cross (as opposed to a monohybrid cross such as Aa x Aa).

Question 8 A

See: BIO 15.6

By definition.

Question 9 D

See: BIO 15.4

A gene pool is the sum of all the genes in a population.

Question 10 A

See: BIO 15.5, 14.2, deduce

Option *B.* suggests that sequences in the chromosome will duplicate themselves and then pairing could occur with the repetitive sequences in the homologous chromosome, which is not possible since duplication is a random mutation {*note that the suggestion that "unpaired sequences . . . duplicate" (i.e. mutation) is not the same as replication/duplication using the repetitive sequences as templates*}. Option *C.* suggests a translocation of the unmatched genetic material to allow pairing. However, translocation occurs randomly and could not guarantee that the correct sequence is moved each time. Option *D.* suggests that the chromosome with the unmatched sequence will undergo a deletion. Like translocation and duplication, deletion would occur randomly. Secondarily, a deletion would rarely be so large as to delete an entire repetitive sequence. The only reasonable option is answer choice *A.* in which the unmatched sequence can be temporarily moved out of the way (looped).

Question 11 B

See: BIO 15.3

We are told that Von Willebrand's is an autosomal dominant disease. Let V be the allele for the disease while v is the absence of the allele for the disease. Thus the father is vv and the mother who is heterozygous is Vv. The Punnett square reveals the following:

	V	**v**
v	Vv	vv
v	Vv	vv

Thus the frequency of Vv is 0.50 (= 2/4) and that of vv is also 0.50 (= 2/4). Since the gene is dominant all heterozygotes (Vv) will have the disease. The chance that the next child expresses the disease is not dependent on what happened to the parent's previous children.

Question 12 C

See: BIO 15.2

Type B blood cells contain B antigens and anti-A antibodies; consequently, any blood type with A antigens (i.e. type A and/or type AB) would trigger an immune response (antibody-antigen response). Type O can be donated to any blood type without triggering an immune response (this is why Type O is referred to as the universal donor) but it is not an option. We now know that type B must be in our answer.

The presence of the Rh antigen would elicit an immune response in a person who is Rh-negative. Thus answer choice D. is incorrect. Note that if a person has had previous exposure to Rh-positive blood, their serum would contain antibodies but their blood cells remain Rh-negative.

Question 13 C

See: BIO 15.2

According to the question, antigens of the ABO system are more inclined to elicit an immune response than those of the Rh system. Therefore, to unmask the presence of the less immunogenic Rh factor, the immune response would be maximal if antigens of the ABO system did not interfere (i.e. same blood type).

Question 14 C

See: BIO 15.2, 15.3.1, 8.2

An Rh-negative woman carrying an Rh-positive fetus will produce antibodies (called anti-Rh antibodies) against the Rh antigen of the fetal cells usually at delivery, when the fetal erythrocytes cross the placental barrier. Therefore, anti-Rh antibodies should not affect the first Rh-positive newborn; however, their presence in maternal circulation will substantially increase the risk of hemolytic disease for the next Rh-positive fetus, in accordance with answer choice C. Since the presence of the Rh factor is determined by the parents' genes, the probability of the fetus being Rh-positive will be the same for every pregnancy of any two given parents (eliminating answer choice A.). Answer choice B. is incorrect because antibodies are not characterized as Rh-positive or Rh-negative, but are simply referred to as anti-Rh antibodies.

Question 15 A

See: BIO 15.5, 1.2.2, 14.2

By definition, mutations are rare, inheritable, random changes in the genetic material of the cell. Consequently, in order to alter the genetic material one must alter the DNA sequence of a cell. Whether it is a nonsense mutation or a frame shift mutation, in order to alter the DNA base pairing requires an error in a process that involves DNA. This mode of thought leaves either answer choices A. or B.. During DNA replication the double helical strand becomes separated as DNA polymerase uses each strand as a template to form a new strand. During transcription, the DNA strand acts as a template to produce an mRNA strand. Comparing both processes, it is most likely that genetic mutations occur during DNA replication, since in this process an error can occur as the polymerase adds an incorrect base pair to DNA. Such an error will be amplified in the following generations as the cell divides. An error by RNA polymerase during transcription will only alter the mRNA sequence and leave the DNA sequence intact. Hence, answer choice A. is the best answer.

Question 16 B

See: BIO 15.6

The further away the two genes are on the chromosome the higher probability there is that they will crossover during synapsis. Thus *C* and *D* are furthest apart, *C* and *B* are next furthest apart (*B* and *D* are very close) and *C* is least far from *A*. Thus there is only one choice.

Question 17 B

See: BIO 15.6

In most species, including humans, mitochondrial DNA is inherited solely from the mother; and so, the mother of your mother is your maternal grandmother.

Chapter Review Solutions — Chapter 16

Question 1 C

See: BIO 16.1

The other 3 answer choices are enumerated as evidence for evolution (BIO 16.1). Spontaneous generation is an obsolete concept regarding the ordinary formation of living organisms without descent from similar organisms. For example, the idea was that certain organisms such as fleas could arise from inanimate matter such as dust, or that maggots could arise from dead flesh.

Question 2 D

See: BIO 15.4, 16.2

Evolution goes against the foundations of the Hardy-Weinberg Law. For example, natural selection leads to non-random mating due to phenotypic differences.

Question 3 B

See: BIO 16.2

One way to define fitness, is to describe it as the probability that the line of descent from an individual with a specific trait will not die out. Notice the focus is the gene. Note that is not necessarily true that natural selection leads to the "survival of the fittest"; rather it is the genes, and not necessarily the individual, which are likely to survive.

Question 4 A

See: BIO 16.2

Directional selection is when extreme phenotypes have a selective advantage.

Question 5 B

See: BIO 16.2

In disruptive selection, selection pressures act against individuals in the middle of the trait distribution. The result is a bimodal, or two-peaked, curve in which the two extremes of the curve create their own smaller curves. Such a population, in which multiple distinct forms or morphs exist (= polymorphic) would share fewer traits than other forms of selection.

Question 6 C

See: BIO 16.3

Genetic drift is the random change in frequencies of alleles or genotypes in a population (= antagonistic to the Hardy-Weinberg Law).

Question 7 C

See: BIO 16.4, 16.6.3

Photosynthesis, which releases oxygen, converted the primitive atmosphere from a reducing one into an oxidizing one. Note that the most abundant gases in our current atmosphere is nitrogen (78%), followed by oxygen (21%; CHM 1.1).

Question 8 D

See: BIO 16.4

All the answer choices seem reasonable except D. which describes prokaryotes whereas protocells are the precursors of true cells, and specifically, prokaryotes.

A coacervate is a tiny spherical droplet of assorted organic molecules (i.e. lipid molecules) which is held together by hydrophobic forces from a surrounding liquid.

Question 9 D

See: BIO 16.4, 16.6.3, 16.6.4

As a by-product of the photosynthetic activity of autotrophs, oxygen was released into the atmosphere. This lead to the formation of the ozone layer which prevented UV light from reaching the earth's surface. The termination of the major autotrophic source resulted from the blockage of light rays.

Question 10 A

See: BIO 16.5

Singular taxon, plural taxa, the study is taxonomy; species are grouped into genera (a genus).

Question 11 A

See: BIO 16.5

The study of homologous structures in mature organisms provides evidence for the evolutionary relationships among certain groups of organisms. This field of study, comparing structural similarities, is called comparative anatomy. The more similar the structures of 2 different species, the closer the evolutionary link, and the more recently they would have shared a common ancestor.

Question 12 A

See: BIO 16.5, 16.6.4

You must be familiar with characteristics of the phylum Chordate and the subphylum Vertebrate. While vertebrates share many characteristics of chordates, they are somewhat more complex in that they have vertebral columns and closed vascular systems. Chordates have a tail at some point in development, but not necessarily in the adult form. The only option that applies only to chordates is the hollow dorsal nerve cord.certain groups of organisms. This field of study, comparing structural similarities, is called comparative anatomy. The more similar the structures of 2 different species, the closer the evolutionary link, and the more recently they would have shared a common ancestor.

Question 13 C

See: BIO 16.6.1

Phyletic gradualism is a model of evolution in which species evolve gradually, slowly and uniformly. Punctuated equilibrium is where species remain stable for long periods of time and then, due to a large environmental change, change rapidly in response. Both theories are supported by the fossil record.

Question 14 B

See: BIO 16.6.4

Eubacteria are prokaryotes. Yeast are unicellular fungi which are eukaryotes. Protista are eukaryotes that can be algae-like, animal-like, fungus-like, unicellular or multicellular.

Questions or Concerns? Go to www.mcat-prep.com/forum

INDEX

A

B

C

D

E

F

G

H

I

J

K

L

O

P

R

S

Gold Standard MCAT has more that 20 years of experience constructing simulated MCAT practice tests. When you are ready to practice with full-length exams, we'll be ready for you. Gold Standard MCAT: Learn from our experience.

Good luck with your studies.